J. S. BACH

Peter Williams approaches afresh the life and music of arguably the most studied of all composers, interpreting both Bach's life by deconstructing his original Obituary in the light of more recent information, and his music by evaluating his priorities and irrepressible creative energy. How, even though belonging to musical families on both his parents' sides, did he come to possess so bewitching a sense of rhythm and melody, and a mastery of harmony that established nothing less than a norm in western culture? In considering that the works of a composer are his biography, the book's title *A Life in Music* means both a life spent making music and one revealed in the music as we know it. A distinguished scholar and performer, Williams reexamines Bach's life as an orphan and a family man, as an extraordinarily gifted composer and player, and as an energetic and ambitious artist who never suffered fools gladly.

PETER WILLIAMS held the first Chair in Performance Practice in a British university (Edinburgh) and the first Arts and Sciences Distinguished Chair at Duke University, North Carolina. His books include *The European Organ* (1966), *Bach: The Goldberg Variations* (Cambridge, 2001), *Figured Bass Accompaniment* (1970), *The Organ in Western Culture 750–1250* (Cambridge, 1993), *The Chromatic Fourth During Four Centuries of Music* (1998) and *The Organ Music of J. S. Bach* (Cambridge, second edition 2003).

J. S. BACH

A Life in Music

PETER WILLIAMS

Bio
Bach
Johann Sebasti
398-B/75

CAMBRIDGE UNIVERSITY PRESS
Cambridge, New York, Melbourne, Madrid, Cape Town, Singapore, São Paulo

Cambridge University Press
The Edinburgh Building, Cambridge CB2 2RU, UK

Published in the United States of America by Cambridge University Press, New York

www.cambridge.org
Information on this title: www.cambridge.org/9780521870740

© Peter Williams 2007

First published 2007

Printed in the United Kingdom at the University Press, Cambridge

A catalogue record for this publication is available from the British Library

ISBN-13 978-0-521-87074-0 hardback
ISBN-10 0-521-87074-7   hardback

SE

Contents

Preface

This approach to the imperfectly known work and life of Johann Sebastian Bach makes particular use of the Obituary (*Nekrolog*) in newly translated excerpts, as a thread leading through the maze of fact and conjecture about him. Presumed to have been drafted in the months following the composer's death and not published until some four years later, it joined two other obituaries in a periodical edited by one of his former Leipzig pupils (see *List of references*). A delay of four years was not uncommon at the time and need not imply faint public interest in its subject, although there does remain a question whether there had been difficulty in getting it published.

Apart from some closing memorial verses in the form of a cantata-text, the Obituary has two main sections, now attributed to two other former pupils: a factual-biographical part by the composer's second surviving son Carl Philipp Emanuel (here 'Emanuel')[1] and a shorter critical-evaluatory part by another former pupil, Johann Friedrich Agricola (here 'Agricola'). I have followed this plan, first expanding the biographical part in Chapters 1 to 7, then the evaluatory part in Chapter 8, and finally adding a brief epilogue and a glossary. In the course of this, questions are raised to which the present book often provides no clear answer, partly because so often one simply does not know, partly because the way a question is framed can imply a possible answer.

Much of what Emanuel reports here and in his later letters must have come from his father either by word of mouth or indirectly from written-down and even published documentation, and suggestions about these different sources are made from time to time. Like any biography the Obituary had an agenda of its own, conveying not only some touching incidents told presumably by the hero-subject himself (while ignoring others less touching) but also the kinds of thing its younger, university-educated

---

[1] 'Emanuel', as in Burney's *History*. Some more recent English-language authors refer to 'Carl' (probably his name within the family), many German authors to 'Ph. Em.' or 'Carl Ph. Em.', 'K. P. E.', etc.

authors would find important to say about a man whom they understood only in part. In doing this the authors laid a path trodden by his admirers ever since, so that what they say and – often much more important – do not say is a crucial part of the Bach picture.

Since this book can not match or even absorb all the work of the research institutes in Leipzig and Göttingen, it aims to treat his life and music as revealing certain priorities, partly by making comparisons with other music and musicians of the time. On its treatment of the keyboard music, see some remarks in the Epilogue. Bach's life seems so integrated that it becomes difficult to disentangle the creative composer, the career professional, the virtuoso player, the conscientious teacher and the ambitious artist. Accordingly, despite its roughly chronological arrangement the book discusses many a detail of the music in more than one place, with cross reference, each relevant to more than one aspect of the life and work. Book 1 of the Well-tempered Clavier, for example, occurs in the narrative apropos biography (when and why it could have originated), teaching (vis-à-vis other books), the exploration of forms (types of composition), 'pure' musical interests (e.g. in the hexachord), and other topics (organization, tuning, instruments, fingering, etc.). The intention is less to give thumbnail sketches of a vast output than to consider what much of it suggests of the composer's preoccupations, in the belief that in this respect, works are biography. The title 'A life in music' therefore indicates not so much 'a life spent in music' as 'a life glimpsed through the music'.

In the text to follow, abbreviations and bracketed references (with name, date and page number) are expanded in the *List of references*, while qv indicates an entry in the *Glossary*.

Acknowledgments

Such a book as this is made possible only by publications of the Bach-Archiv, Leipzig and the Bach-Institut, Göttingen, and in particular I would like to acknowledge the fundamental work of the *Bach-Dokumente* prepared by †Prof Dr Werner Neumann and Prof Dr Hans-Joachim Schulze (four volumes at time of writing), and of the many authoritative contributors over the years to the *Bach-Jahrbuch* and the *Neue Bach-Ausgabe*. A list of references at the end of the book makes clear my indebtedness to many secondary sources and certain previous biographies, from Spitta 1873 to Wolff 2000. The book grew from a short volume in the Cambridge University Press series *Musical Lives* (originally suggested by Penny Souster), and has since been patiently supported by Dr Victoria Cooper and Rebecca Jones. For various kindnesses I would like to thank Mr Michael Black (Cambridge), Dr Brian Cookson (Gloucester), Prof Dr Martin Geck (Dortmund), Dr David Wyn Jones (Cardiff), Dr Michael Kube (Tübingen), Dr Raymond Monelle (Edinburgh), Dr David Ponsford (Cirencester), Dr Tushaar Power (Duke University) and Dr Peter Wollny (Leipzig). My former colleague Dr David Humphreys (Cardiff) was unstintingly helpful over the final draft and became the source of many improvements to it.

For setting the music examples I thank most warmly Dr Gerald Hendrie, the first Professor of Music in the Open University, scholar of Handel and Gibbons, composer, organist, and a friend of decades.

The excerpt in Example 1, from the MS LM 4708, appears by kind permission of the Irving S. Gilmore Music Library, Yale University.

1 Map of Northern Germany in the time of J. S. Bach

2 Map of Thuringia and Saxony in the time of J. S. Bach

CHAPTER I

Early years, 1685–1703

The Obituary begins

Johann Sebastian Bach belongs to a family in all of whose members equally a love for and skill in music seem, as a common gift, to have been imparted by nature.

Emanuel Bach was familiar with the outlines of his family's musical history, since quite apart from any anecdotes about it that circulated amongst its members, his father spent time around the age of fifty compiling a selective genealogy. This is the 'Origin of the musical-Bach family', *Ursprung der musicalisch-Bachischen Familie* (Dok I, 255–61), a document known to Emanuel in whose household it was later copied. Though contributing little to published biographies of the day, Bach carefully compiled this genealogical list (sometimes referred to as a 'table') either from scratch after many enquiries or, more likely, revising and enlarging an older document begun by a previous member of this large family. Still an indispensable source of information, it numbers fifty-three Bachs in the course of two hundred years or more, many of them professional musicians well-known in Central Germany, though only a few became so in a larger Europe – Sebastian himself and, as perhaps he anticipated in part by then, one or two of his sons.

Emanuel added to the genealogy in which he and five brothers figured, and made use of it to begin the Obituary more tellingly, even proudly, than John Mainwaring was able to begin his biography of Handel ('George Frederic Handel was born in Hall[e] . . .'). Since the Obituary opens in the present tense, the question immediately arises whether it was prepared during the composer's lifetime, in the form perhaps of a CV or biography for one of the several lexicons being published in Leipzig. The two other obituaries printed in the journal in which it appeared begin by referring less ambiguously to their deceased subjects. And as Emanuel's narrative continues, a further point might strike the reader: now and then one has the impression that he was citing from press cuttings at his disposal, leading one to wonder further whether such had been assembled by his father and kept with the genealogical table. Possible instances of press cuttings are identified below as they occur.

It is easy to imagine personal reasons why a composer would compile such a genealogy at or near his own half century, especially one who had lost so many close relations as Sebastian had from early childhood on: his parents (mother at her own half century, father two days short of it), gradually all seven of his siblings (one before he was born, two while he was a small infant), his first wife (she too had been an orphan), ten of his twenty children (an eleventh aged 24 died in 1739), plus a particularly beloved employer.[1] This catalogue of bereavements may have been larger than was usual with professional people (by his late fifties, for example, Telemann had lost only two of his surviving seven children), but the wider the extended Bach family, the more constantly news of deaths within it must have circulated amongst relatives or, just as bad, been taken for granted. For example, ten of eleven children of Johann Günther, great-great-grandson of Sebastian's great-grandfather, died before their mother. Sebastian's first conscious bereavement was when he was six years old (brother Balthasar), his last nine months before his own death (grandson Sebastian Altnickol), so that when his own entry in the genealogy says he is still living 'by God's will', this is no empty formula.

In working on his genealogy in about 1735, the composer might also have been as much open to the day's fashion for studying family tables as to any more profoundly personal urges of his own. For family tables were well known in the book-centre of Leipzig, where throughout the 1720s and 1730s Johann Hübner was publishing aristocratic and other tables for what was evidently a ready market. One such book had some 333 tables, doubtless meant to be an evocative number, and it could well be that Hübner's publications encouraged Bach to work on a list of 'musical Bachs', perhaps even to think of having it published. There are several implications in the careful collection of its materials, such as that he was a born collector and portfolio-organizer, as so much of his music also suggests, and in particular that he was more of a letter-writer than is now known or was said by Emanuel to have been (Dok III, 290). Both the various blanks he left in the table (e.g. when a date was unknown) and certain musical specifics (e.g. that Johann Günther was singer and schoolmaster at a certain church in

---

[1] Perhaps fifty was an important age in Thuringian/Saxon tradition. At fifty, Handel apparently planned a visit to his native Halle (HHB, 254), and later in Weimar, at about that age, Goethe drafted *Der Mann von fünfzig Jahren*, concerning a man and a much younger woman.

Erfurt) suggest he had a variety of sources: existing information, correspondence, conversation, visits to and from, hearsay.

In listing the musicians of the large, well-distributed clan to which he, an early orphan, belonged, Bach does several things: establishes the story of an exceptional family, omits mere family-lore anecdotes, and salutes an art practised to the greater glory of God. The story is not a fairy tale but sets out an (as it were) apostolic succession, one not entirely unlike the genealogical tables in two of the Gospels and parts of the Pentateuch, consciously or otherwise. So well-read in both Old Testament and New Testament were genealogists including J. S. Bach that there was little difference between conscious and unconscious allusion of this kind. The first name, Veit Bach, was of a man said there and in the Obituary to have fled Hungary for his Lutheran *Religion* (Dok I, 255), meaning perhaps not Lutheranism as such – Hungary (today's Southern Slovakia?) was predominantly Protestant early on – but Christianity: these lands were under threat from Turkish Muslims. From Veit a Tree of Jesse springs, branches of a Protestant tree active over generations. Chiefly as a result of this geneaology, the Bachs have become the best-known of all musical dynasties, though positions of higher prestige were occupied by some of the Couperins in Paris.

It seems that a few years later, the genealogy was joined by another family document of sorts, the Old-Bach Archive (*Alt-Bachisches Archiv*), a collection of choral works by older family members. Now constituting some two dozen pieces, perhaps more formerly, they include music by Johann Christoph (organist in Eisenach admired by Sebastian, cousin of his father), Georg Christoph (Sebastian's uncle) and many by Johann Michael (first father-in-law of Sebastian, also praised by him in the table). Some of the copying work was done by Johann Christoph and by his father, the text and parts of another by Sebastian's father, but the biggest contributor-copyist has been identified as not a Bach but Ernst Dietrich Heindorff, cantor in Arnstadt, who died in 1724. This suggests that the archive was first assembled as a 'repertory for use in Arnstadt, during Heindorff's cantorate' rather than a Bach family document as such (BJ 1998, 138, 147), and that much of it passed to J. S. Bach when the organist there, his first cousin Johann Ernst, died in 1739. In the following years he then added to the Archive himself, perhaps contributing such early autographs as the score or parts of cantata BWV 71 and other early works such as BWV 4, 106 and 131 now incompletely preserved. He also wrote much of the text underlay for Johann Christoph Bach's 22-part motet 'Es erhub sich ein Streit' and parts for his 'Lieber Herr Gott, wecke uns auf'. This last, in which he was helped by a student, dates from his final months and could have been for his own funeral (see p. 268). So it seems that the Archive continued to be made up piecemeal over the years, even after Emanuel – who spoke of Christoph's latter motet being performed in Leipzig (Dok III, 292) – took charge of it under the name *Alt-Bachisches Archiv* (Dok III, 502).

As well as how, quite why Bach should carefully preserve such an Archive, providing some titlepages, completing some texts, making corrections and even some performance materials from it, is an interesting question. Likely, of course, is 'family loyalty': preserving work by other Bachs, a natural furtherance of his work on the family tree. And just as his own name featured in the genealogy, so representative manuscripts of his own music could have been added to the Archive, or planned to be. Was this one of the reasons for making certain fair copies in his maturity, such as the late collection of organ chorales or even the Mass? Also likely is that the Archive was still supplying him with service-music from time to time despite its out-of-date idioms. For it is often forgotten that as well as modern cantatas, there was a good deal of much earlier music sung in the main Sunday services – motets, chorales, chant. Presumably by the time the Archive passed to Emanuel along with the main copy of the genealogy, its value was chiefly family-antiquarian. But this was something not insignificant for the wider Bach family, judging from a letter of 1728 written by another Bach, Johann Nicolaus, who too was aware of the family's tradition of coming originally from 'Hungary' (BJ 1989, 213), as was Walther in his *Lexicon* of 1732.

To imply in the 1730s that music was an honourable family-trade was a reflection of the growing respect for art and the artist, *Kunst und der Künstler*, words conspicuous in the Obituary itself and becoming deeply respected over the German Enlightenment and Romantic periods. This was not a dynasty of shoe-makers or bakers but, as the genealogy's title said, 'musical Bachs', which for the Obituary also included those who were active in devising new musical instruments. Walther (*Lexicon*, 64) suggested that it was perhaps because those called Bach were devoted to music that their very name was melodic (B A C H, qv). A surgeon and a shop-keeper who qualified for inclusion in the list of 'musical Bachs' were, one assumes, gifted amateurs, different from the early Bach who had been a court jester/fiddler but is not listed, despite Sebastian's likely knowledge of him, his very portrait having been engraved and published (see Geiringer 1954, plate iv).

Unlike true family-trees, the genealogical table lists no mothers, wives or daughters any more than the Leipzig Communicant Lists do when they name Bach and with him, fairly regularly, one or more of his sons. The current professional position of three sons is described in a letter of 1730, when Bach notes that his wife sings well, and also says of his first child, Catharina Dorothea, that she is unmarried and plays 'not badly' (*nicht schlimm*: Dok I, 68). It was through the boys that the list of 'musical Bachs' would grow – hence, in a letter of 1748, Sebastian informs a cousin about Emanuel's 'two male heirs' without mentioning their sister. Yet his own mother, a Lämmerhirt, was undoubtedly musical, being a member of a family closely involved with music in Erfurt, the area's largest town and a Hanseatic city with allegiances far afield. Elisabeth Lämmerhirt was also related to two other significant musicians, composers to whose music her gifted son was to respond one way or another: J. G. Walther (she was Walther's great-aunt's step-sister) and J. H. Buttstedt (she was his wife's second cousin). Something surely came to Johann Sebastian Bach from his mother, as it came to his sons from their gifted mothers, both of whom like-wise belonged to professional musical families.

'HONOURABLE THURINGIANS'

It would be something to wonder at that such fine men should be so little known outside their fatherland if one did not bear in mind that these honourable Thuringians were so content with their fatherland and their standing that they would not venture far from it at all, even to go after their fortune. (*Obituary*)

Emanuel is speaking here of earlier Bachs, 'worthy men' the memory of whom deserves to be kept fresh, musicians he had learnt about from the genealogy. Whether he is fairly representing his father's views at any but particular moments of discontent in Leipzig, can not be established. But for readers, the relevance of what he says to the biography that follows can not have been missed. Especially the musicians amongst them would assume that normally the highest status could only be measured by success abroad, first by leaving home to study and then by occupying a position of prestige in an important city or a royal court of renown such as Prussian Berlin, where Emanuel and Agricola were both working by the time the Obituary was published.

One sees this same interest in a student's studies or a master's successes in Johann Mattheson's collection of biographies published in Hamburg a few years previously, the *Ehrenpforte* 1740, which generally made a point of reporting a composer's broad learning-experiences. Telemann, an upper middle-class boy, had travelled, come into contact with Polish music, written operas for the free city of Hamburg, visited Paris, and actually declined the Leipzig cantorate: altogether, a varied and productive musical life of fame and obvious success. Sebastian's successor in Leipzig, Gottlob Harrer, had 'spent some time in Italy' and learnt composition and the job of a cantor there (Dok II, 480), something which Emanuel, who had also applied for the job on his father's death, later admitted he had not (Dok III, 255). The 'Jena Bach', Johann Nicolaus, had spent some time in Italy, as Emanuel would know from Walther's *Lexicon*. At about the time the Obituary was published, Emanuel's younger brother Johann Christian was leaving to study in Italy, and was soon to find success in Milan and London, freelancing in the modern way. But the biggest *eminence grise* behind this and other statements in the Obituary, more than is often now recognized, is surely Handel. For some decades the garrulous Mattheson had been lionizing Handel and reporting on his successes, and no doubt news of his great if fluctuating wealth in England had reached his native city of Halle and nearby Leipzig. Handel, moreover, was not a Thuringian.

To what extent Emanuel is reporting his father's views on 'not venturing far' can only be guessed: the various grumbles he expressed over pay and conditions, particularly in Leipzig in his forties and fifties and presumably aloud *en famille*, may have led him or the Obituary authors to feel a need to justify his remaining there until he died. When in his genealogy Sebastian refers to a certain other Johann Christoph Bach as one who

never took a job [*function*] but sought most of his pleasure [*Plaisir*] in travelling (Dok I, 260)

he is surely expressing disapproval, even sarcasm. In any case, for it to be true that J. S. Bach had the chance to achieve fame abroad but chose not to, he would have had to remove himself more permanently from his native province in his late teens or early twenties than he did. Handel and Christoph Graupner had done so, one from Halle, one from Leipzig, both of them going to Hamburg and then beyond. Or he would have had to treat the Leipzig cantorate as a stepping-stone to Dresden or elsewhere, and perhaps had tried to do this but without success. It would be dreadful to imagine him towards the end of his life regretting how he had spent it, wondering what he had missed in the musical centres of Europe, and having to find consolation by willing himself to be content with what he had done in his home country 'for God and his neighbour'. To put it no more strongly: there is little evidence that Bach wanted to stay in Leipzig or was happy as cantor of St Thomas.

The theme of contentment with one's home country was not unknown in biographies of German heroes familiar to Bach and his sons, such as

Camerarius's life of Melanchthon, the early reformer and revered colleague of Luther. Melanchthon too was orphaned (aged eleven), expressed fidelity to his fatherland and place of origin, was headstrong, and educated himself by assiduously studying what others had written: all motifs to occur in the Bach Obituary. By 1700, several editions of Melanchthon's *Life* had been published in Leipzig, and in a general way at least, he was still widely influential through his directives on preaching and the scriptures. (Melanchthon's portrait had been drawn by Albrecht Dürer, who, though well travelled, similarly let it be known that he preferred remaining in Nuremberg to seeking fame and riches elsewhere. His family was also said to have originated in Hungary.) To listeners for whom a cantata's musical rhetoric was equivalent to a sermon's verbal rhetoric as outlined by Melanchthon, parallels between Luther's colleague and J. S. Bach would have appeared close. They both strove 'for God and their neighbour'.

Though it could be true that Thuringia was culturally less confined than either Hamburg in the North or Munich in the South, it may be rather wishful thinking to see it as an important cultural crossroads. Travel overland being as difficult as it was, really lively contact between cities on major water-routes such as Amsterdam-London or Dresden-Hamburg would have been a easier than, say, Dresden-Eisenach. Yet a province's very narrowness is not a disadvantage when its traditions are healthy and lively. Self-contained Thuringia was a province of marked character and traditions, culturally lively, competitive from city to city, and vigorous in a range of artistic endeavours. Here, in such a province, an exceptionally gifted and voracious boy could well be stimulated both to learn what he could from elsewhere and to rely on his own achievements. Of course, local or national pride can mean underrating the foreign, as is clear later in Emanuel's sarcastic reference to the celebrated French organist Louis Marchand. Nevertheless, for a Protestant boy in 1700 to be receptive to foreign achievement or to seek personal development abroad, taking in what other musical cultures have to offer and making use of it in his profession, was far more common than for a young musician from Roman Catholic countries.

The Obituary's word 'fortune' indicates both financial and artistic success. Certainly the various Bachs including Sebastian did progress financially over their career, doing so without the kind of risks Handel, never a family man, took. In terms of annual income in guilders, J. S. Bach earned 28 as a young court musician, as a minor parish organist 50 then 85, as court organist 150 then 200, as concertmaster 250 to 300, as court capellmeister to 450, as cantor about 800, plus not insignificant payment in kind at each stage, as was customary with organist positions in Protestant Germany (lodging, fuel, cereals etc.). Whether, like some organists in northern cities, Bach was able himself to hire out seats in the organ-galleries of the churches he served is not recorded; nor is his income from teaching known in detail, although it is not unlikely to have been larger at each stage than his successive salaries (see also p. 110). But clearly, his fame and fortune did not match Handel's. How well situated financially the family was in *c.* 1730, with six children at home including one at university, is a question the composer himself may not have known quite how to answer: as is clear with Telemann in Hamburg, there was nothing unusual in a composer-cantor supporting a large household and at the same time devoting vast energies to composing and directing musical events, all without either the large reward or the occasional disaster known to many an opera-composer.

When it praises those 'honourable Thuringians' staying at home and aiming to please loyal countrymen instead of a few and 'perhaps even envious foreigners', a provincial-nationalistic element creeps in to the Obituary. (Something similar but much more insidious is still there when Richard Wagner, another Leipziger, complained bitterly of those fond of fame and wealth abroad while having no fatherland themselves. II, 35.) But it is not at all certain whether the young J. S. Bach would have agreed with the Obituary authors when, for all anyone knows, he too had the broadest of horizons.

BIRTH, FAMILY

Johann Sebastian Bach was born in 1685, on March 21, in Eisenach. His parents were Johann Ambrosius Bach, Court and Town Musician there, and Elisabeth *née* Lemmerhirt, daughter of a town official in Erfurt. (*Obituary*)

Only after setting the composer's context in general terms does the Obituary turn to its main subject, but from those two brief sentences (composed from records in a family bible?) its readers would have learnt much about his background. Although some idea of the cultural significance of Eisenach, a city of about 7,000 inhabitants, may be gained now by recalling its associations – with Tannhäuser, with a medieval 'combat' between minstrels, a saint (Elizabeth of Thuringia), Martin Luther (a native, translating the New Testament imprisoned in its castle) and J. S. Bach – only the last two would have been in the forefront of Obituary readers' minds. Probably more familiar to them was a well-known book, Walther's *Lexicon*, where they could also learn that 21 March was barely four weeks after the birth of *Georg Friedrich Hendel* in Halle, a bigger town and by the time of the *Lexicon* also the seat of a university.

Johann Sebastian was the youngest of eight children in the family and the last known infant born to his mother, then aged forty-one. While Johann was a common family name, 'Sebastian' came from the main godparent, as was customary: Sebastian Nagel was *Stadtpfeifer* or municipal musician in Gotha and a colleague of Ambrosius, both members of musical ensembles active in a local court, its town and the churches. By the time of Sebastian's birth, his father had been director of the municipal music in Eisenach for fourteen years, a violinist who had earlier served the city of Erfurt. There in Erfurt, on 8 April 1668, he had married Maria Elisabeth Lämmerhirt, a young step-sister of Ambrosius's uncle's wife, daughter of a town councillor and thus bourgeois by class. Had Ambrosius succeeded a few months before March 1685 in obtaining the release he sought from the duke and council at Eisenach in order to return to Erfurt, Sebastian would have been born there, as his brother Christoph had been, the brother who was to take him in at the age of nine. It was also to Erfurt relatives that his sister Marie Salome was to return when their mother died.

At least indirectly, Erfurt played a big part in Johann Sebastian's musical background, and it is rather surprising that he is not known ever to have sought a job there. Its musicians over the years included Pachelbel (who taught the elder brother Christoph in Erfurt, from 1686), Nicolaus Vetter and Buttstedt (Pachelbel pupils), Effler (Sebastian's predecessor in Weimar), Walther (a Buttstedt pupil) and Adlung (organist and influential writer on organs) – all well-known names in the world of German organ music for the best part of a hundred years. For Johann Michael Bach, who posthumously became Sebastian's first father-in-law, Erfurt would have been the local capital city, and there too various Bachs remained prominent town musicians right until Napoleonic times. In 1716 Sebastian returned to the city to test a new organ in the Augustinerkirche (Augustinian Church, Erfurt's 'Austin Friars'), where Luther himself was ordained priest in 1507. This organ was the work of the privileged Erfurt builder J. G. Schröter, with whose family Sebastian remained in contact, and whose pupils included Franciscus Volckland, builder of several instruments in and around Erfurt still today in recognizably historical condition. It is quite possible that an abiding sense of pride in Erfurt's and Eisenach's associations with Martin Luther was still with the composer in 1739, when for the first time he published some organ music, Clavierübung III, which drew on Luther's hymns.

His municipal position in Eisenach suggests that Bach's father was a gifted musician, officially praised as a versatile and effective music director (BJ 1927, 141), better paid than his predecessor, himself an employer of four musical assistants (two journeymen, two apprentices) and presumably a good violinist. His musical handwriting as well suggests an accomplished musician. His duties in the town included playing in the wind band twice a day from a balcony or tower of the town hall, participating on Sundays and Feast Days (main service and vespers) in the music in the Georgenkirche (St George's Church, where Sebastian was baptised), and in various ceremonial events civic or private, for which he had the *privilegium*. Whether such musicians as Ambrosius considered themselves primarily wind or string players is not clear or very significant, but judging from the support shown to his eventual widow by the cantor of the Georgenkirche, his senior colleague, he was much respected (Dok II, 4). So, consequently, was his family.

Although Cantor A. C. Dedekind would have been known to the boy, both as a composer of music for various occasions and as his class-teacher in 1694–95, a more certain influence on him was the church's organist at the time, Ambrosius's cousin and colleague, Johann Christoph Bach. This is the Bach uniquely and conspicuously called in the genealogy 'a profound composer' (*ein profonder Componist*), one of whose fine, expansive motets Sebastian probably planned for his own funeral. If so, one might see in it a further sign of Bach's sense of family and tradition, wishing to acknowledge in death his having belonged to a dynasty of church musicians.

It is often now conjectured that as an active organist and composer – neither of which Ambrosius is known for certain to have been – Johann Christoph, described a few years after his death as 'a real wonder of an organist' (BJ 2004, p. 158), allowed the boy Sebastian to learn as many basics of organ-playing and organ-construction as he could, although had he been a formal teacher, the genealogy would probably have said so. Johann Christoph laboured many years to improve the large organ in the town's major church, and perhaps the boy was as much interested in this as he was in accompanying his father to *his* various duties. Also, because Christoph lived eight years longer than Ambrosius he is likely to have been a bigger musical influence on the boy than his father was, especially over the early teenage years: see also below, p. 14. Such influence on his childhood would be a further reason for Sebastian drawing on Johann Christoph's work for his own funeral.

Presumably, Ambrosius's sons sang in the *Schülerchor*, the choir of schoolboys providing music in the three churches of the town, including the Georgenkirche, whose recorded repertory of choral music included some by Josquin, a composer known to have been admired by Luther himself and thus especially appropriate to Eisenach. The choir also sang twice a week in the streets of the town, at music for special events, and even perhaps in some years a sung Passion on Good Friday (BJ 1985, 53). The kinds of contact between the town's musicians or within musical families are not difficult to imagine, although where Forkel, for his book of 1802, got his information about convivial family gatherings of the musical Bachs over this period – siblings and cousins meeting annually and singing chorales, quodlibets and popular songs – is unknown. The picture is plausible, however, and it is likely that Forkel had seen the token of one Bach-family gathering: a vocal work for birthday celebrations between Bach's father and uncles in 1689, preserved in the Old Bach Archive (see Leisinger 2002, 378).

Sebastian's schooling is not documented before 1693 when he entered the Latin School in Eisenach in which Luther had been a pupil almost exactly two hundred years earlier, a boys-only school which taught German and Latin literacy, confessional study such as the Catechism and psalms, and no doubt some degree of numeracy. For children from five to (finally) twelve years old, attendance at the mixed primary 'German School' was compulsory in the dukedom (BJ 1994, 180), either providing them with the first part of the more senior Latin School's curriculum, except for the Latin, or instead, eventually releasing them into the world of pre-apprenticeships. One of the German Schools of Eisenach was to be found in the street in which the Bach family lived, its schoolmaster a professional connection of Ambrosius. That Sebastian was younger at entry than his brothers had been, went straight into the fifth class not sixth (lower), by 1695 was placed higher than his elder brother Jacob, and later moved to a senior school, suggests him to have been a brighter than average child and one already well-taught by somebody. Also, living far longer than any of his siblings, who died at six months, 6, 10, 18, 40 (Jacob), 49 and 51 years respectively, he seems to have been the fittest physically, as indefatigable in body as in mind.

LOSS OF PARENTS

Johann Sebastian was still not ten years old when he saw himself deprived of his parents by death. He made his way to Ohrdruf to his eldest brother, Johann Christoph (organist there), and under his guidance laid the foundations for his keyboard playing. (*Obituary*)

One cannot tell for sure whether Emanuel intended any pathos with his words 'still not yet ten years old' or 'made his way' (*begab sich*), and if he did whether it came from the composer himself. But considering how common such things must have been – Sebastian would have known only four of his siblings – to have 'seen himself deprived of his parents by death' does seem a more evocative way of saying 'his parents had both died'. There was no such shade of meaning in Walther's *Lexicon*, which merely recorded that his eldest brother instructed him in 'the first principles' (*Principia*) of keyboard-playing. Nor was there when J. J. Quantz, in his own autobiogaphy, reported that his mother died when he was five, his father five years later aged 48, having (like Bach's father) married a second time.

Perhaps Emanuel did not know that his father's elder brother Jacob, likewise orphaned, went with him to Ohrdruf, and that his grandfather's nephew Johann Ernst was in the same school at the time. (Or if he did know, he omitted to say so, as endangering the wished-for pathos?) The two brothers must have taken part in the funeral processions of their parents to the Eisenach cemetery, either as family mourners or as boys in the choir, and certainly neither's prospects can have been good at that moment. Their Ohrdruf brother was only modestly situated himself, though content enough there to decline a job at Gotha a year later (BJ 1985, 60). Even if, as is possible, the father left him money to take in the younger boys as family-member apprentices, the costs of a regular apprenticeship under an established master were surely now out of their reach. Whether in Sebastian's case the loss affected him in such a way as to lead to the single-mindedness, defiance and even irascibility that people have read into the pitifully small number of later documents concerning him is another big unknown, except perhaps to Freudians. Handel lost his father around his twelfth birthday, but his biographer notes only that it 'produced a considerable change for the worse in the income of his mother' (Mainwaring 1760, 29), a remark probably by Handel himself. Again, it is not personal feelings but practical circumstances that, so far, are the business of biography.

Bach's mother had died before his father, about 1 May 1694, so at that point, there was less of a financial problem than nine or ten months later. Until then, Sebastian and Jacob had remained with their father who remarried some seven months later (27 November 1694), only to die not long after that (20 February 1695), leaving a widow who already had four children of her own. Ambrosius's last known signature of 21 January 1695 has been interpreted as showing an unsteadiness of the kind discerned in his son Sebastian's handwriting half a century later (BJ 1995, 181), raising the question whether they both suffered from diabetes.

At the age of nine to lose both parents within a year could have been mitigated only by warm relations within the remaining step-family, but nothing of this kind is recorded, or is likely to have been the case. It is over Sebastian's stepmother's name that a curious request was made on 4 March 1695 to the town council, in which, having quoted the local ruler of

Arnstadt as saying 'he should and must have again a Bach' for a position once held there by one Johann Christoph (Ambrosius's twin, †1693), she went on to say that this was not possible because 'in the last few years the musical species of Bachs has withered' (Dok II, 5). Perhaps this was to strengthen her case for a pension, for by 1695 her elder stepson Johann Christoph was already a professional organist. If by then Sebastian was showing great musical aptitude – something that cannot be taken for granted, however – was she following convention in ignoring a child of 9–10 years old? Or was there little love lost between herself and her three younger stepchildren? All three soon moved on to other relations, and the step-family fades from history.

So common was bereavement and so normal was it for relations to take in family orphans – Sebastian's parents had while he was a child (at least two cousins), and both he and his own children Emanuel and Elisabeth were to do so – that one can only guess how the death of parents was taken, how anxious financially Christoph became when responsible for two younger brothers, and how hard life was in any respect for any of them. Christoph himself was only twenty-three at the time, married a year before. His brothers received charity income (free board) as poor scholars, Sebastian for a longer period as a chorister, a position which may also have brought in other moneys from municipal events. Whether his foundations as a keyboardist were laid by his brother Christoph in regular lessons or as circumstances allowed is not recorded, though it may be wrong to assume that young musicians merely picked up what they could within an active musical family. There would have been music copying to do (and to have checked), spinets to tune, services to deputise in, perhaps odd jobs in connection with the continous work on the organ of Christoph's church.

At the early apprentice age of fourteen or so, and presumably at some cost to their father, Christoph had studied for three years with Pachelbel in Erfurt and – to judge by his impressive later MSS of organ-music – become a player of wide interests, indeed 'a very artistic man', *optimus artifex* acording to his church's registers. Perhaps it was from Pachelbel, or from an inherited alertness to the new and the challenging, that Christoph acquired an interest in French organ music and passed it on to his younger brother. His marriage of October 1694 had been the occasion for some music in which their father had participated along with Pachelbel, whom presumably the boy Sebastian heard (and was heard by?) on that occasion. Ohrdruf was a minor town in comparison with Eisenach, but the Michaeliskirche church library was better than many, and its organ was meant to be up-to-date and adequate for the repertory of the time. According to the contract of 1690 (BJ 1926, 145ff), the instrument was to have had two manuals and twenty-one stops, including chair organ and a pedal solo stop for bringing out the hymn-melody in the chorales (i.e. settings with cantus firmus, qv). Work on it in the later 1690s could well have interested a young teenager.

Emanuel says again later that his father learnt the 'first principles' in keyboard-playing from his brother, going farther and adding that his instruction in Ohrdruf was as an organist 'and nothing more than that' (Dok III, 288). So the boy taught himself composition. In broad terms all this might be true, but the additional remark was also part of a picture of self-reliance consistently drawn by Emanuel, who was underlining for his correspondent what the *Lexicon* said. (So little did Emanuel know of his father's Ohrdruf period that he thought Christoph died in 1700 and left his brother to make his own way: see below). The two brothers shared an interest in both local and foreign keyboard music, and presumably, had his father still been alive, the boy would have worked more on string instruments. As it was, Sebastian was to produce early imitations of the various kinds of keyboard music composed by the two acknowledged masters of that region of Germany, Pachelbel and Kuhnau, though when and in what order are too uncertain for his rate of development or precise indebtedness either to them or his brother to be traced.

For the arts of composition in a broader sense, the praise given in the genealogical table and Obituary, and indeed elsewhere during the eighteenth century, to the other Johann Christoph Bach, organist in Eisenach, could be an indication of his powerful influence on the young Sebastian. Emanuel singles out more qualities in Johann Christoph's music than he does for any other composer in the Obituary (Dok III, 80–81):

he is strong in the invention of beautiful ideas

also in the expression (*im Ausdrucke*) of the words

composes as elegantly and melodiously (*galant und singend*) as taste at the time allowed

also composes some uncommonly full-voiced music

played on organ and Clavier in never less than five real parts

While some of these are vague, and none is related directly to his father, Emanuel's last point is surely repeating what he had heard him say. Also, Emanuel must have studied some of Johann Christoph's scores, for as an instance of his inventiveness, he reports him having the courage to use the augmented 6th, a chord much favoured by Emanuel's generation. It also remarks on the motet in 22 parts, composed 'without any detriment (*Eintrag*) to the purest harmony'.

1 Organ chorale, BWV 1092, opening
  b. 8, *sic.* The single flat was added by the copyist, unsure
  of the early original harmony, which needed no flats?

Some extant organ chorales, if correctly attributed to J. S. Bach, must date from about the time of his mid teens, including many of the so-called Neumeister Collection, BWV 1090–1120, chorales not always distinguishable from work of Pachelbel's pupils and thus not quite securely attributed. (Early choral works that are similarly known only from much later copies, such as Cantatas 150, 106 and 196, are less doubtful, because they are less early and have more recognizable hallmarks.) In some of the modest Neumeister chorales, however, there is both a sureness of harmonic touch and an imagination, even waywardness, in the treatment – interesting repetitions, changes of direction, brief cadenzas, effective closes – that are exceptional amongst Thuringian composers of *c.* 1700 and such as one would dearly like to be proved authentic. Sometimes, a setting might give the impression of being a written-down improvisation of the kind an adventurous teenager could produce. Example 1 already shows three ways of treating a melody: bb. 1–4 a simple harmonization is broken up with an 'echo' at the octave below, bb. 5–7 line 1 of the hymn-tune is accompanied by note-patterns, bb. 8–9 line 2 is four-part harmonization with passing notes. All three suggest, on a miniature scale, a well-taught grasp of what can be done, not necessarily in such quick succession nor with such an imaginative little 'echo', but with complete understanding of music's grammar.

At other moments in the collection there are ideas much more likely to have been worked out on paper, particularly moments of purer counterpoint and of original hymn-tune paraphrases. Generally, the scale is inexpansive, and the idiom does not go beyond the low ambitions of an organist-functionary; but with suitably optimistic hindsight, one can glimpse what was to come.

It may seem strange that there is still so much uncertainty as to who composed what amongst these and other keyboard pieces often attributed to Bach, but 1700 was too early for conspicuously gifted boys to be such a wonder that their work would be systematically preserved. As a recognised and written-about phenomenon, the child prodigy barely existed yet in music, especially the composer-prodigy. When early pieces do survive, as also with Handel at much the same age, they do so by chance or in a form as revised and copied out later, and even some of the more assured works of Bach such as Cantata 4 can be challenged on the dual grounds that (i) the source is inconclusive, (ii) the musical style and form belong to a common fund. Fortunately, the registers of the Ohrdruf Lyceum, a school of some distinction that was going through troubled times when Sebastian was first there,[2] at least show him to have been successful in schoolwork, being fourth in the *prima* class (largely for eighteen-year-olds, and with a wide curriculum) when he left aged almost fifteen, in March 1700. Another sign that he was smarter than most?

THE 'MOONLIGHT EPISODE'

During his time with his elder brother, a memorable incident had occurred:

The delight our little Johann Sebastian took in music already at this tender age, was uncommon. In a short time, he had mastered completely ['brought under his fist'] all the pieces which his brother had voluntarily given over to him to learn. A book full of keyboard pieces by the then most famous masters Froberger, Kerll and Pachelbel, which his brother owned, was however denied him, in disregard of all entreaty, and who knows for what reason. [Nevertheless,] at night when everyone was in bed, he copied it out by moonlight, never being allowed a light. After six months this musical booty was happily in his own hands, and with exceptional eagerness he was secretly attempting to put it to use when, to his greatest dismay, his brother became aware of it and without mercy took from him the copy he had prepared with such trouble. (*Obituary*)

Considering how rarely any intimate detail appears in the Obituary, this story, doubtless told by Bach himself and looming large in family tradition,

---

[2] Terry 1928, 26–7 reports on the removal in 1697 of the *gottlos* cantor and Latin teacher, J. H. Arnold, after various problems that may well have affected the boy's class (the *tertia* or Third).

is particularly useful in touching on motifs familiar in many a musician's life, in particular the glimpse it unwittingly gives of how important music-copying was for a young musician's training.

Several things can be learnt from it, therefore, such as that it must have been a large book, to take six months to copy (even in secret) and to provoke such a reaction. Apparently, the MS was of keyboard music and contained work by 'southern' composers (Froberger and Kerll were Roman Catholic, Pachelbel was by now working in Nuremberg). The repertory is unlikely to have been an organist's service-music, rather a miscellany of suites, preludes, toccatas of various kinds, etc., of interest to a professional musician and of use in his teaching. (So is another MS from this period and region, now lost but associated with the young Handel and once containing work of comparable composers.)[3] If the music by Froberger derived from either of his new publications of suites, in Mainz 1696 and Amsterdam 1698, then Johann Christoph was well up-to-date – and therefore all the more justifiably proprietorial about his hand-made copies.

The repertory as a whole might just support the idea that when Sebastian eventually moved on from Ohrdruf north to Lüneburg rather than south to Nuremberg (see below), one reason was to learn other kinds of keyboard music, something more expansive than could be found in an album of 'Froberger, Kerll and Pachelbel'. Perhaps he had an inkling of Buxtehude's abilities from a copy made by his brother or someone else of the fine G minor Praeludium BuxWV 148, an outstanding work that seems to have been known in Central Germany for a decade or two. Another verisimilar but rather emotive detail Emanuel gives is that the MS was not only considered valuable enough to put under lock and key but was unbound and could be rolled up and pulled through the grill-doors of the cupboard by 'little hands', though quite how this was done is not easy to envisage. This and the 'six months' could be Nestorian embellishment for the sake of more pathos.

Most importantly for the Obituary's agenda, the story gives a picture of how industrious and single-minded the young orphan was, how deep his feelings were, how much he deserves our sympathy despite his deceit. The story must have come from Bach himself, and is thus revealing on several fronts, but how far he had meant to malign the elder brother is uncertain. Emanuel could be to blame for the Obituary's account conveying no sense

---

[3] Reported as containing music by Zachow, Alberti, Froberger, Krieger, Kerll, Strungk and others (HHB 5, 17). These names likewise imply a keyboard miscellany rather than an album of music for organists to play in services.

of loyalty to his own uncle or even consideration for his first cousins, at least four of whom were still living. As for Christoph himself, according to his CV (where he mentions only his late parents and godparent: BJ 1985, 60), he seems to have been content to remain an organist, and one could read in the confiscation of his younger brother's work several things: personal envy, genuine solicitude, or sheer annoyance. Unauthorized copying of valuable and hard-won professional materials was improper, especially if they were then put to use, as Emanuel, not sensitive to the issue, says they were. Was the boy presuming to play them, at home or even in his brother's church?

Hinting at having been similarly deceitful, Telemann had already described voraciously copying whatever his teacher left lying around (1740, 355). Bach's own practice after childhood also reveals a little about the copying of a teacher's music, though whether he charged them to see materials, as J. G. Walther said his teacher Buttstedt had charged him in 1702 (Beckmann 1987, 68), is not recorded. Pupils copied sections from manuscript collections (or drafts) of keyboard works such as the suites, the Orgelbüchlein or organ sonatas, but few if any of these are complete single copies in the order of Bach's own manuscripts. It rather looks as if he 'controlled' pupils copying his music for their own use. A single concerto here, a selected group of chorales there? Copies of keyboard works made in the 1720s by J. P. Kellner, for instance, seem to have been made singly, and grouped together only later. More substantial copies made by them, as when J. Schneider apparently copied out the English and French Suites in Leipzig, could have been commissioned for sale to a client or for some other special purpose. It is not difficult to imagine how sharp Bach's own reaction would have been to find a pupil copying a valuable manuscript of his without permission. This is so even if accredited pupils did have access to his music, as one later confirmed (P. D. Kräuter: see p. 112). If Sebastian was in effect apprenticed to Christoph, permission to copy was granted only in certain connections.

Clearly, there was also something improper in a young ward's defiance and deception of a guardian *in loco parentis*, one solicitous, amongst other things, for the boy's eyesight. (On whether excessive copying as a young musician had any effect on his later eye-problems, see p. 263.) And perhaps there was a further, more musical reason for Christoph's action. The brothers' father had been a violinist active in various spheres, Jacob became an oboist, and Sebastian, if brought up to devote as much time to the violin as the keyboard, could look ahead to being more than a church organist. The education and the later production of his more eminent

German Protestant contemporaries (Handel, Telemann, Mattheson, Fasch, Graupner) were all far less dominated by keyboard music than his were, though they too were exceptionally able keyboard-players. If Bach developed as a string-player, as might have been his father's wish, he could become capellmeister to a great king or, better still, opera and music director of an important city. If he pursued keyboard-music too single-mindedly he could expect only organistships, at best the cantorate of a major church . . .

In what year the young Bach dedicated his Capriccio in E major, BWV 993 and harpsichord Toccata in D minor, BWV 913 to his brother (both of which refer to him in some extant copies) is not known, though the Capriccio's turgid formlessness (when compared to the Chromatic Fugue's, for example) and harmonic poverty (when compared to the Passacaglia's) are early signs. The piece, if genuine in all respects, suggests at least two things, one musical, one personal: that already the young composer was interested in creating length, in sustaining a movement without the aid of a text or programme; and that despite the Moonlight episode there had been and remained a positive contact between the brothers. This last is also suggested by Christoph possessing copies of his brother's harpsichord toccatas (written in part for him?) and by two extant, rich MS collections of music (the Andreas Bach Book and the Möller MS) for which Sebastian might have contributed other composers' music, directly or indirectly, after he had left the Ohrdruf home. See Postscript for possible examples.

According to these MS collections, other composers with music known to the brothers include Albinoni, Buxtehude, Böhm, Buttstedt, Flor, Kuhnau, Lebègue, Lully, Marais, Marchand, Pachelbel and Reinken – a wider survey than is ever found in collections of keyboard music across Europe except, oddly, in England, where a significant amount of foreign music is found at the time. Other Bachs from Thuringia, including Johann Christoph (b. 1676) and the Johann Ernst who had been at school in Ohrdruf, had wide contacts and could also have supplied a route by which some pieces got into the MS collections. Consequently, there is a tantalizing uncertainty about what the brothers Sebastian and Christoph could have learnt from each other and indeed from other Bachs, but considering the special use made of Albinoni's Op. 1 sonatas *à 3* by both the brothers, a 'lively interchange' of ideas between them seems very likely. Two sonatas of Albinoni appear in the Möller MS, and three of his subjects are used by Sebastian in well-paced fugues, including the B minor, BWV 951/951a, whose fugue-theme is surely the most beautiful either brother had yet come across.

Although the Andreas Bach Book and the Möller MS date from after Sebastian had left Ohrdruf, they suggest that the brothers, whatever their contact, shared wide interests: German, French and Italian music, suites, fugues, chaconnes, toccatas, overtures etc. As for contact: in 1708 Christoph's wife was godmother to Sebastian's first child, as in 1713 Sebastian was god-father to one of Christoph's twin sons. Another of Christoph's sons, Bernhard, came to Weimar in 1715 to study with (or serve as apprentice to) his uncle, going on to an appointment at Cöthen in 1719, no doubt also on his recom-mendation (Dok II, 47, 202–3); and in 1724 another, Heinrich, came to him in Leipzig for some years. The Obituary says that Bach had his 'Moonlight' copy returned to him only on his brother's death, and if this did happen, it could have been *via* Bernhard, perhaps as a fraternal bequest. Either way, the original anecdote underlines the importance of these manuscript albums for both learners and professionals. At least one other student of Pachelbel's, J. V. Eckelt, had made a comparable collection a few years earlier (in 1692: see Wolff 1986), and noted which music he copied had been purchased from Pachelbel, implying the charge for lessons covered other copies.

The motif of adult resistance to a child's musical gifts is found again in Mainwaring's biography of Handel who, when his father

forbad him to meddle with any musical instrument . . . found means to get a little clavichord privately convey'd to a room at the top of the house. To this room he constantly stole when the family was asleep. (Mainwaring 1760, 5)

And presumably he played it by moonlight. So an exceptionally gifted and strong-willed child conquers family resistance, and for his biographer this persistence becomes important. In connection with Handel, Mainwaring also refers to the mathematician Pascal, who as a child prodigy pursued studies 'against the consent of [his] parents, and in spite of all the opposition'. Parental resistance, or at least preference for a son to be other than a musi-cian, is a motif in not a few autobiographies of the time, such as Telemann's, Quantz's and Kellner's (qv). Studying by moonlight was itself a desirable motif for an orphan's biography: it appears again in Melanchthon's, and again suggests a young spirit, ardent, self-reliant, serious, never afraid of hard work and of self-improving study.

THE MOVE TO LÜNEBURG

[In 1700] Johann Sebastian made his way, in company with one of his schoolfel-lows called Erdmann . . . to Lüneburg and to the St Michael Gymnasium there . . . our Bach, because of his unusually fine treble voice [*Sopranstimme*], was well received. (*Obituary*)

It is likely that the phrases 'in company with', 'unusually fine treble' and 'well received' reflect the subject's recounting of this period in his life. Emanuel gives no date but claims that the move occurred after Christoph died. Yet this did not happen for another twenty-one years: he must have misunderstood, for his father certainly knew Christoph had not died in 1700, having later taken in two of his sons, one after he did die, in 1721. Emanuel was still at home then, presumably knew that Johann Heinrich's father was dead, and later misremembered. Or he was guessing, relying on his father's genealogical table which also left blank Christoph's dates of birth and death (Dok I, 259) and unable to imagine any other reason why he would leave for Lüneburg. Or – and this could be so in any case – perhaps Emanuel was suing for sympathy in demonstrating his father's initiative, for in itself there was nothing unusual in a fifteen-year-old going away as an apprentice, often at some remove from the family home. Normally supported by parents, an apprenticeship – or any next stage of life – must have been problematic for an orphan.

Considering how few names of people there are throughout the Obituary compared with other biographies appearing around 1750, it is surprising that it would name Erdmann, who though in the same class in 1700 was three years older and had died nearly twenty years before the Obituary was published. But Bach remained in contact with him for many years, still in 1726 addressing him as 'most worthy brother' (BJ 1985, 85). Companionship at a key juncture of anybody's life might well remain something never forgotten, but there are several significant things in the Obituary's sentence. It suggests that he had formed a close friendship with an older and eventually rather distinguished person and had talked of it, for unusually, the Obituary records for posterity this friend's title, 'baron and Imperial Russian resident in Danzig' (as elsewhere, Emanuel is not averse to a little name-dropping). It also shows a degree of drive and courage in its subject. In short, here was a coming together of talented teenagers, one of them something of a mentor to the other, perhaps, but both of them adventurous and ambitious.

The school register reports Bach leaving Ohrdruf on 15 March 1700, before the end of the school year and still before his fifteenth birthday, *ob defectum hospitiorum* (Dok II, 7–8) – probably meaning that his free place at table, or subsistence as a charity boy, had expired, as it would at age fifteen unless he were kept on as some kind of assistant. The same phrase had been used for Erdmann two months earlier and need not imply that Christoph was refusing the boy board and lodging in his own home, though it might, for Bach was noticeably younger than Erdmann when his support was withdrawn. The register said that Bach 'took himself off' to Lüneburg (*se contulit*), but only that Erdmann had left (*abiit*), which looks like a significant distinction: Erdmann left school in the usual way, Bach took responsibility for himself before his fifteenth birthday, at Erdmann's invitation? Whether or not some kind of known epidemic in Ohrdruf early in 1700 prompted their departures, and whether they actually went together, as implied by Bach's not unambiguous reference later to Erdmann as 'travel companion' (*Reisegefährte*: BJ 1985, 85), some important friendship between them can be supposed.

Fifteen, or even fourteen, was an age when generally boys did become more independent, and the move looks very much as if it were pre-planned, perhaps as a fifteenth birthday 'gift'. At about that age Christoph Bach had gone to Pachelbel, and at fourteen Jacob Bach had returned to Eisenach as apprentice to his father's successor. Quantz's curriculum was somewhat different: he reports that when eleven years old he became a *Lehrbursche* (junior apprentice?) for five and a quarter years, then *Geselle in Condition* (indentured journeyman?) for two and a quarter; this was to the town musician of Merseburg, successor to his uncle to whom he had gone as soon as his father had died (1755, 199). Sebastian seems to have taken the opportunity of his good treble voice to leave Thuringia before it was too late, and enter an important establishment farther to the north, a decision both personal (friendship with Erdmann) and musical (better composers in a bigger northern city). To the south, Nuremberg was not only much nearer but Pachelbel was there, since 1695 writing more imaginative music than he seems to have done while still in Thuringia. But Pachelbel himself had recently looked north for a good teacher for his son (see below, p. 46), and judging by J. V. Eckelt's album of pieces already mentioned, studies in Nuremberg did not include much music by the great northerners.

It could be that there was something of a south/north divide in a boy's training: either to Nuremberg or to Lüneburg. The latter was much farther and harder to get to than the former, making it at least desirable to be accompanied by an older friend. Amongst the places en route interesting to anyone well-acquainted with the professional literature was Halberstadt, not only with a cathedral whose late-gothic organ had been famously and uniquely described by Michael Praetorius, but with the Martinikirche (St Martin's Church), whose organist was Andreas Werckmeister, author of several important books, including the *Orgelprobe* (see p. 60), about organs, organ-building and studies relating music to theology and arithmetic. Many seeds of curiosity and even of a lifelong interest would be sown by a visit to Werckmeister, who at the time had no rival in his published work on organs, in his studies of temperament and number symbolism, and even (so he claimed in a published description of the Gröningen organ 1705) in his possession of manuscripts by Praetorius.

Other cities en route included Brunswick, where a distant relative mentioned in the genealogical table (Dok I, 256) was cantor. But if the boys were in Lüneburg in time for its Easter rehearsals in late March (see Wolff 2000, 477), there cannot have been time for much visiting en route, either professional or private. For the boy, just fifteen years old, to be 'well received' in his new position as Emanuel reported, if it did happen, meant that his gifts were recognized – from an audition perhaps, or a testimonial from Ohrdruf, or on-the-spot participation in the choir. Even if this claim was made only much later, it was an important one to make in view of Lüneburg's prestige, a remark comparable to the later praise given to the mature Bach by the doyen of northern musicians, Adam Reinken – another event reported in the Obituary.

It has been supposed that the new and effective cantor in Ohrdruf, Elias Herda, a trained theologian, had encouraged or arranged for the two friends to try Lüneburg, having lived there himself for some years. This is more than likely, especially as Bach went on to sing treble in the special 'matins choir' (*Mettenchor*) of the Michaeliskirche, where he was given free board, a small monthly honorarium, and instruction in the school (Dok I, 69), all of which suggests there had been an audition of some rigour for what we would now call a 'chorister's music scholarship'. He joined in time for the Holy Week and Easter services of 1700, a point at which the Lüneburg school year began – something he (or Herda) had planned? But soon, his 'unusually fine treble voice' broke, and for eight days he could only sing and speak in octaves. Emanuel, who is surely quoting his father's account here, says this occurred 'some time after' the move to Lüneburg, a detail which could be read as anticipating the suspicion that he had gone there on false pretences. But the chronology is uncertain, and since voices often broke later than nowadays, it was not unknown for boys fifteen or older to expect to remain in a choir and choir-school for some time.

Despite their respective ages, both Bach and Erdmann were listed amongst the trebles in April and May 1700 (*Diskantisten*: Dok II, 9), and it is unlikely that Sebastian's voice settled so quickly that he soon sang bass. The question arises whether the Obituary's term *Sopranstimme* actually meant adult male soprano, and thus whether the seventeen-year old was still singing falsetto with the trebles after his voice broke. Unfortunately, the terms are not reliable enough to form a view on how regularly, if at all, adult males sang treble in church choirs. 'Soprano' is the usual label for treble parts in the cantatas – an Italian term for an Italian genre – and when in 1740 Bach praises a former boy of St Thomas's school, Leipzig for his contribution as a *Sopranist* (C. F. Schemelli, then twenty-six years old: Dok I, 145), he could be referring to him either as former boy-treble or a more recent adult falsetto-soprano.

At Lüneburg, Bach remained a scholar in the top class (the *prima*) until 1702, in a school known to have had a distinguished humanist curriculum, including rhetoric, Greek, and German verse. The good repute of both the Ohrdruf Lyceum and St Michael's School, Lüneburg, also raises the question whether Bach desired or had been encouraged to go to a city with a good school, something appropriate for a boy too intelligent and advanced for his age to have gone the common route of apprentice to a church organist. At the same time, neither Bach nor Herda can have been ignorant of the presence across town, in the Johanniskirche (St John's Church), of the gifted and doubtless inspiring composer Georg Böhm, who was in a position to further a boy's career. The church-library at the Michaeliskirche was also exceptionally well-stocked, one of the best in Protestant Germany. The 'matins choir' consisted of fifteen of the more gifted musicians, probably SATB or SSATB, part of the bigger instrumental-vocal ensemble of a well-appointed church, and given the special duty of singing daily matins (corresponding to daily evensong in an Anglican cathedral or collegiate chapel today). This was in addition to the Saturday vespers and the Sunday services in which the whole choir took part. Such were heavy new duties for a boy whose voice was about to change, especially as from the particular reference to an 'unusually fine treble voice' one supposes that once there, he was singing solos.

That the young Bach had a conscious desire to study church music, organs and organ-playing in North Germany cannot be assumed, not even that he particularly admired 'northern' music. Nor is enough known about his cantor in the Michaeliskirche (St Michael's Church), August Braun, to know whether he exerted a strong musical influence on the teenager, though the silence itself may be indicative. As for Georg Böhm: many of his pieces contained in the (later) Andreas Bach Book and Möller MS are harpsichord works written with something of a French *manière* (qv), and there may have been comparable volumes of organ-music, now lost but once circulating. It is not known at what point Bach got to know Werckmeister's *Orgelprobe*, but familiarity with it at some point seems very likely (see p. 61). It is a book Thuringers would regard as 'local', whetting many a musician's appetite for hearing big instruments with colourful effects, such as were known farther north, including those built by the peerless Arp Schnitger, author of a dedicatory poem in Werckmeister's book.

Or perhaps Bach had an inkling that his voice was about to break, and took steps to belong to a distinguished church choir in a cosmopolitan city when it happened, a city offering suitable work. It was an interesting choice, for after all, closer to Ohrdruf than Lüneburg were the cities of Halle, where a year or two earlier the famed Zachow had taught the young Handel (HHB 4, 17), and Leipzig, where Kuhnau was admired and an influential figure in Saxony. Was the Lutheranism of Halle too Low Church in important respects? The published work of Kuhnau was not imaginative enough in its melody or harmony? Georg Böhm's keyboard music made a stronger impression than Pachelbel's, Zachow's, Kuhnau's or Reinken's? Also important, perhaps, was that Böhm had connections in Ohrdruf, his birthplace, and it is not hard to imagine J. S. Bach both exploring family connections and also following where a discriminating taste led him.

Yet questions remain. If, at the age other boys entered regular, even humble apprenticeships, and young Bach went to a fine school far away with a potentially distinguished friend, was it to train for a profession other than church musician? If so, did he return to Thuringia two years later because of some failure (financial or otherwise) to advance as desired? On this, see further in the Postscript. Or, as some would prefer to think, because of an irresistible pull towards church music?

VISITS TO HAMBURG

From Lüneburg he travelled from time to time to Hamburg, to hear the then famous organist of St Catherine's, Johann Adam Reinken. (*Obituary*)

If one reason for the move to Lüneburg had been to study under a northern master, it is difficult to see how this would materialize for a teenager without apprenticeship money. The reference to Reinken suggests ambition on the part of the boy, and such visits serve the biographer as a substitute for the apprenticeships he would normally be able to report at this point. Why Bach should visit Reinken in Hamburg rather than the more gifted Buxtehude in Lübeck is not obvious: because Hamburg was nearer (he could not have visited Lübeck so easily 'from time to time'), because more of Reinken's music was known, being published, even because Reinken's string-music was of particular interest to him – though Emanuel might not have known this.

It is also the case, however, that for musicians and organists of Emanuel's generation, Reinken's longevity made him better known than Buxtehude, and his fame therefore bestowed special credit on any young learning musician. (On knowledge of his organ-music, see below pp. 147ff.) Moreover, without doubt, Bach's eventual fame as a virtuoso organist, and the two Obituary authors' personal experience of his virtuosity, led them often to make a point of his involvement with organs or organists, doing so to the neglect of his overall musical development and interests.

The Obituary says he went to Hamburg several times. Not only does it show no awareness that schooling in Lüneburg could have opened up other careers outside church but it also says nothing about what must have been a major attraction in Hamburg – its opera, by now in the hands of Reinhard Keiser, whose directorship was soon to draw the young Handel to Hamburg. The city was after all the second largest in the Empire after Vienna, and a very flourishing period for its opera is well documented for the years around 1702. Often published biographies show a composer making a point of hearing opera, whether in Berlin (Telemann), Florence (Stölzel) or several Italian cities (Quantz). Bach's first job as a court musician, a little later than this and probably just before his eighteenth brthday, might mean that he was or had been looking in the direction of courts and theatres rather than churches, and any opera of Keiser would have given him insights into setting words rhetorically, planning a sequence of movements, writing appropriately with instrumental colour, and so on. But Emanuel does not (care to) say so.

So there are many possible questions which, were one to know the answer, would give some idea of the kind of boy the young Bach was – whether he planned his career carefully, whether he made decisions for professional or personal reasons, whether he was at the time, or indeed ever, as interested exclusively in keyboard and church music as the Obituary authors wished to suggest. It could be that he did come to recognize Buxtehude as the more important master for church and keyboard music, even seeing him as a 'mentor successor' to his respected but deceased Eisenach relative, Johann Christoph. Hence he took leave from his church job in 1705 for the express purpose of visiting Buxtehude (see below). But simply 'to hear Reinken' in Hamburg cannot be the whole story, with respect either to his professional ambitions or to his wider musical interests. Did he have no interest in opera in Hamburg, and is there no question that like Handel and Telemann (as many readers of the Obituary knew) he went there for that very purpose? And then chose to turn his back on it?

Nowhere does Emanuel imply any of this, but nor, curiously, does he mention the presence in Lüneburg of Georg Böhm, a composer to at least rival Reinken. Böhm's Johanniskirche was the biggest in the city, and he may have recommended to young musicians in the town that they take themselves off to Hamburg, as he had himself. Though having no clear direct connections with the choir of the Michaeliskirche, Böhm was never-theless the most gifted composer Sebastian could have come across so far, with an unusual melodic flare for setting chorales and a sense of drama in other works. Whether from observation or actual instruction, many of Bach's earlier organ-works such as the Praeludia in C major and D minor, BWV 531 and 549a, are closer to Böhm's style than anyone else's, unaware of this though Emanuel very likely was. Assuming that his extant suites were already composed by *c.* 1700–02, they would have opened up to Bach a fund of instinctive ideas – indeed, as the best available current models of French style by a German composer. The two men were still in contact in 1727, as is clear from Böhm having copies of two of Bach's partitas for sale, confirming their common interest in keyboard suites.

In a later letter about his father, Emanuel actually crossed out the phrase 'his Lüneburg teacher Böhm' to replace it by 'the Lüneburg organist Böhm' (Dok III, 290), but this conforms all too well to the image of his father as the self-taught composer learning *sine duce*, as it was said of Melanchthon, 'without a guide'. Shortly after the Obituary's publication, Quantz too was claiming in print to have taught himself not only in composition but in playing a whole range of string and wind instruments, mostly not to any great extent but such as is 'necessary, even indispensable' to a composer of church music (1755, 199–201). In his case, however, teaching himself was something he did despite being a formally instituted apprentice. His clear description of how useless apprenticeship could be – especially for an unusually talented teenager? – goes some way to suggesting why neither Handel nor Bach travelled this route to professional qualification.

Whether any strong influence of Reinken on the young Bach was entirely beneficial is another matter. He is a thoughtful composer, thorough in going through the motions and conventions of the prevailing genres (free prelude, fugue, suite-dances), and he probably inspired a few details in Bach's earlier keyboard works. In particular, one of Reinken's few extant toccatas (in G minor) anticipates the sectional shape and many note-patterns found in Bach's early harpsichord toccatas, always assuming these came second. But Reinken's very thoroughness could send a young com-poser in the wrong direction, and neither his melodic gifts nor harmonic inventiveness are always conspicuous. Emanuel, knowing his father's early toccatas, may himself have realized how Reinken's motoric and rather prosaic keyboard style had fundamentally influenced such early works, or his father had acknowledged in later years how important had been Reinken's fluent note-spinning. And not only the fluency but sometimes the themes, for in more than half a dozen early fugues of Bach, one hears

Reinken's rather long, rattling theme-types. Copies of keyboard transcriptions of two of Reinken's chamber sonatas (BWV 965, 966) were being
made by J. G. Walther a decade or more later but from what originals is
not known, nor whether Bach kept up an interest in such music in his later
twenties. Significantly, he seems to have re-composed the fugues in these
Reinken sonatas, whose unprepossessing gigues could well have influenced
those in English Suites Nos. 5 and 6 (see pp. 130f).

It might have been Walther, in his *Lexicon* of 1732, that influenced
Emanuel's emphasis on Reinken in the Obituary, for to him it gives much
more space than to Böhm. Though not as old as was later thought, Reinken
was also famous for presiding at the great organ of the Catharinenkirche
(St Catharine's Church), Hamburg, and was known to look after it exceptionally well. The instrument had some sixty stops including 32′ reed, distributed over four manuals in the Schnitger manner. The Obituary's
co-author Agricola said in another of his books that Bach admired not only
this great Hamburg organ but the fine condition in which Reinken kept it
(Dok III, 191). In other words, Reinken was a master such as the Obituary
authors apparently admired: both an artistic and a practical man, both a
creative musician of string and keyboard music and a skilled player *au fait*
with an organ's technicalities. But Böhm also had an unusually fine organ
in the Johanniskirche, Lüneburg, and it would have been strange if he were
not a similarly careful curator of it.

Also familiar to Böhm was Hamburg's flourishing and brilliant musical
life in theatre and church, for earlier he had participated in both. When
Walther's *Lexicon* speaks of another significant German organist visiting
Reinken for instruction, Georg Leyding, are we to believe that such young
musicians had no interest in Hamburg's theatre music? That is hard to
believe, and certainly, in more ways than one, the city's composers did leave
their mark on Bach. In addition to arranging or re-composing chamber
sonatas by Reinken for keyboard, he copied/arranged an anonymous
St Mark Passion of 1707 (attributed to Keiser by Bach but to F. N. Brauns
by some recent authors) and, more importantly, came to compose ABA
arias of a kind popular in Hamburg operas. Fortunately, the young Bach
continued to learn from many sources: his work as a teenager with several
Italian and French repertories and in his late twenties with Vivaldi concertos helped free him from limited northern horizons. Only wide experience
could have stimulated the kind of development that every player feels must
have come between, say, the early Capriccio in E major, BWV 993 and the
Chromatic Fantasia, or that every listener feels between Cantatas No. 106
and 208.

Like so many organs with which Bach came into contact, in Eisenach, Ohrdruf, Weimar and Leipzig, the instrument in the Lüneburg Michaeliskirche was regularly being worked on. Its mishmash of historical periods – a big Gothic main organ with pedal pulldowns, baroque chair organ and a *Brustwerk* – made it desirable for its players to keep to old genres such as stereophonic toccatas, simple chorale-settings and variations based on common-property formulas. These would have contrasted with any of the more modern string music that made its way into certain services at certain times, chamber sonatas imported from Venice and Rome, or Italianate sonatas of the kind being published in Hamburg. Whenever it was that Bach made the arrangements BWV 965 and 966, the busy counterpoint, limited harmonic and rhythmic invention, and the purely conventional rhetoric in Reinken's music, cannot have stirred a dormant genius as powerfully as would any of the string music of Corelli or Legrenzi he came across, although the Obituary authors might not have known it.

FRENCH TASTES

And from here too [Lüneburg] he had the chance, through frequent listening to a then famous band kept by the Duke of Celle, and consisting largely of Frenchmen, to give himself a good grounding in French taste [*Geschmacke*], which at the time was something totally new [*ganz Neues*] in those parts. (*Obituary*)

Again, rather than having regular teachers, Bach is learning through listening to various kinds of music, and must have relayed Emanuel's two important points: that the visits were 'frequent' and that the players were Frenchmen. So, having as a boy sung the standard repertory in one important Lutheran church, heard a famous organist play and direct in another, then (probably) heard Italian arias and recitative sung in Hamburg theatres, now he was experiencing French music as performed by the French instrumentalists employed in a duke's *cappella*. That this taste or style was 'something totally new [*ganz Neues*] in those parts' could well be something Emanuel heard his father say, and is not in itself very likely, though the 'French taste' in manner of performance might have been new to him. Here in short is another example of Bach learning (a) by personal experience with (b) diverse musical activity, and (c) in different parts of his home country. But French overture-suites, with all their many idiomatic characteristics, even perhaps the manner of playing them, were already circulating in much of Germany, sixteen of them through J. K. F. Fischer's *Journal du printems* (1695) and Georg Muffat's *Florilegium* (1698). Handel's biography, at a similar point in his life, also finds it important to testify to his grasp not

only of local German church music but also of French styles and in his
case various Italian as well, claiming that he instructed Corelli himself 'in
the manner of executing these spirited passages' in French *ouvertures*
(Mainwaring 1760, 56). Interestingly, in Telemann's case it was in Eisenach
that he heard players excelling in French music, or so he said later in speaking of the period around 1708 (1740, 361). His godson Emanuel surely knew
this remark.

The Duke of Lüneburg-Celle's band played in the ducal residence in
Lüneburg,[4] and since, as the Obituary unusually makes a point of saying,
the players themselves were mostly Frenchmen (thanks to the duke's
Huguenot wife?), the composer could well have spoken of the experience
as a revelation. So he learnt about French styles from the horse's mouth.
This important detail contrasts with a remark made in print by an earlier
Thuringian composer – P. H. Erlebach, preface to *Harmonische Freude*,
1693 – that he had learnt the art of French *ouvertures* from examining the
written music. But hearing Frenchmen play was important, for notation
gives only a pale impression of how vivid and tuneful the apparently
convention-choked music of France can be in sympathetic hands. A French
string-group introduced rhetorical gesture and expressive articulation such
as no-one is likely to have heard from local musicians, especially in church
cantatas. A French windband showed what a minuet or bourrée or gavotte
was better than would any local keyboard suite. The full Celle ensemble, if
as good as its reputation suggests, produced harmony of a sensuousness out
of place in church, and the manner of playing it – the rhythms, rubato,
articulation, ornaments – would, one imagines, have made a strong impression on any imaginative young musician.

A clear grasp of certain elements of French style is evident throughout
Bach's creative life, from the early keyboard overture in F major, BWV 820
right through to a movement in the Art of Fugue, BWV 1080.vi. Others
such as Telemann must have learnt from comparable experiences. Certainly
Handel had done so before his first operas in Hamburg (1705), even prefacing his first opera in Italy (*Rodrigo*, 1707) with a fine, idiomatic and very
extensive French suite. One can assume that here and there Bach had
already heard *ouvertures* or ballet-suites, something entirely different from
any Parisian organ music he had got to know by then. Perhaps again, Böhm
had recommended these visits to the duke's band, having himself previously shown an intimate grasp of many details of French style. The Duke

---

[4] The Obituary's phrase 'from here' (*von Lüneburg aus*) implies that Emanuel thought Bach had to go
to Celle to hear the band.

of Celle's theatre also had Italian opera for a time, but it was the French court ensemble founded in 1666 that became famous.

Unfortunately, too little is certain about such 'early works of J. S. Bach' as the F major Overture, BWV 820 for anyone to be confident that it is totally authentic and thus an index of how well he had assimilated style-details. Its very fidelity to the harmony, rhythms and melody typical of a Parisian composer of *c.* 1690 leaves one to wonder whether it was an arrangement of an imported work or a very clever and musical imitation. Perhaps the difference is not as important as it might seem. There are certainly hints of its authenticity in tiny details, as for example in the way the stately dotted-note introduction ends with a big chord the first time but not on its repeat, for exactly the same can be found in Bach's later overtures, in *Clavierübung* II and IV. (This reproduces Parisian practice, when the first violin shoots off with a lively fugue at this point, a subtle detail that takes the word *fuga*, 'flight', literally.) To what extent visits to the Celle band first introduced Bach to other French mannerisms, in harmony, string-bowing, leaning grace-notes and lilting rhythms, is hard to know, since his earliest organ and vocal music would not have been the place for such details. But he certainly kept an interest in the true *manière*, and it is probably fair to say that the mature overtures for orchestra (BWV 1066–1069) and for harpsichord (in Clavierübung I, II and IV) enrich elegant French styles with a harmonic sophistication, varied melody and well-wrought counterpoint – the results of his characteristic 'thoroughness' – that are seldom if ever found in France itself.

It was not only Parisian idioms that were being assimilated and imitated but Italian as well, as is clear in other early work for keyboard that employed classical vocal counterpoint (Canzona in D minor, BWV 588) or violinistic fugue-themes drawn from Corelli and Legrenzi (BWV 579 and 574). So many of the genres Bach came into contact with, whether through his brother or the master musicians of Hamburg and Lüneburg, seem to have been thoroughly explored by him, as if in each case he was stretching its definition to take in his own ideas while leaving the genre recognisable. Not only imported music gave him genres to explore. Three early works called 'Fantasia' (B minor BWV 563, C major BWV 570, C minor BWV 1121) explore the old idea, found in keyboard music of a much earlier period, of developing a single, simple musical idea very thoroughly and freely, indeed fantasy-like. But the end-result in these three pieces is totally different, each with a distinct character deriving from the original theme. Such pieces from his teenage years are for keyboard and not yet particularly extensive, but undeniably they lay the foundation for the tireless reworking of convention so familiar in the mature work.

CHAPTER 2

First appointments, 1703–8

In [January] 1703 he went to Weimar, and became a musician of the Court there.
(*Obituary*)

What the series of events was during 1702 can be only partly recon-
structed, but it seems that Bach completed two years at senior school,
visited Hamburg either during or shortly after them or both, heard the
French players of Celle, at some point returned to Thuringia, by July 1702
was applying to become organist at the Jacobikirche (St James's Church),
Sangerhausen, and instead went into service at the court in Weimar six
months later. When exactly in 1702 he left Lüneburg is unrecorded but
probably as the school year ended at Easter, when he was just seventeen.
Nor is it recorded whether he was moved to return to Thuringia through
penury, professional disappointment (no job in Lüneburg or Hamburg)
or love of homeland, as the Obituary said. (On this, see also Postscript.)
Perhaps he went temporarily to his brother in Ohrdruf again, or sister
Marie Salome in Erfurt, both of whom were by now better circum-
stanced.

The order of events would be rather the reverse of the flute-virtuoso
J. J. Quantz's, who records that at much the same age, he set his sights on
Dresden or Berlin, metropolitan capitals in which he could hear better
things than he could at home (1755, 202). Similarly, Handel, having briefly
became organist at home in 1702 and been introduced to many styles of
music by his teacher, went off to Hamburg, launched on his many-sided
career. But when Handel's biographer says that not wishing to add to his
mother's expenses, 'the first thing which he did . . . was to procure scholars, and obtain some employment in the orchestra' (Mainwaring 1760, 29),
he is describing a situation very likely known to the seventeen-year-old
Bach. How far either they or Quantz did procure 'scholars', as well as
playing in an orchestra, is an interesting question: Handel surely had more
opportunity in a big city than Bach had in Sangerhausen or Weimar, or

wherever he was in the second half of 1702, although in most places there must have been aristocratic children to teach.

Forkel seems also to have been puzzled why Bach left the wider promise of Lüneburg, asking Emanuel for the reason and only being told 'I don't know' (Dok III, 288). Doubtless the boy needed income and could already have learnt that he preferred the world of church and court music to that of opera and city theatres, in which case the return says much about him. But one cannot know this for certain and 'Was a career in church really the one he wanted?' is a fair question to ask at several points in Bach's life. If he had merely heard of the Sangerhausen job en route from Lüneburg to Thuringia (Sangerhausen was not obviously or inevitably on his way home), there was an element of serendipity here. But if he had kept up homeland contacts with a view to hearing of such jobs, his preferences are a little clearer, leading one to wonder if he had had it in mind to succeed in the foreseeable future the admired and possibly ailing Johann Christoph Bach (son of his grandfather's brother) in Eisenach.

In such a society, a seventeen-year-old is not likely to have returned to an elder brother's house, although if it was to Ohrdruf that Bach did first return – or re-visited from nearby Weimar or Arnstadt – one could more easily understand how his own elder brother's keyboard MSS came to include certain music: eleven works of Georg Böhm, some others by Böhm's predecessor in Lüneburg, Christian Flor, and a group of pieces by the French composers listed above, p. 19. It would be strange if manuscripts brought back from Lüneburg did not include chorale-settings by the northern organists, though at the time contacts between organists and musicians were so many and so effective that rarely can one say for certain how any of them got to know the music they copied.

The Sangerhausen job fell through, for against the church authorities who favoured Bach, the reigning Duke of Weissenfels – successor to the duke who had been impressed by the child Handel (see Mainwaring 1760, 9) – let it be known, with the force of a decree, that he preferred another, better-experienced candidate. Some thirty-five years later, history worked one of its ironies: in this fine church, Sebastian's third son Johann Gottfried Bernhard Bach, not yet twenty-two, became organist on his father's recommendation, though alas not with long-lasting success (see below, p. 247). In the intervening years, other connections with the House of Weissenfels were maintained, including the conferring of a title of 'Saxon-Weissenfels Capellmeister' on Bach, probably in 1729 (a titular or 'visiting' position) and the likelihood that he was involved somehow in the new Sangerhausen organ in 1728. Its builder was Zacharias Hildebrandt, a colleague in Leipzig, whose title of 'Saxon-Weissenfels Court Organ-maker' was conferred on him soon after Bach's, in 1730.

Probably from Christmas 1702, and certainly for the first half of 1703, Bach took a job at Weimar as 'court musician' (*HoffMusikus*: Dok I, 259) to the junior duke, Johann Ernst von Sachsen-Weimar. How or when he applied is not recorded – presumably he had waited in or near Sangerhausen until the appointment fell through in November 1702 – nor what instruments he was appointed to play, nor whether he was able to use his knowledge of French styles. A likely guess is that he played in both secular entertainments and chapel music, both violin and keyboard. His duties may have been such as to justify his next employers referring to him as the 'Saxon Prince's Court Organist' (*Fürstlich Sächsischer HoffOrganiste*: Dok II, 10), but in the court accounts he is listed as 'Laquey'. This word does not have quite the associations of English 'lackey', being used to mean an instrumentalist who is not yet a 'master' or *Meister* as formally defined (see Mattheson 1728, 58), and many a young musician at court was first appointed as a general servant. Bach may well have had lowly duties in addition to playing violin and keyboard, copying music, organizing the scores and parts, carrying music stands, tuning keyboards, substituting as organist and so forth. Quite possibly he did apply at Eisenach when Johann Christoph died in the following April, but the Georgenkirche was surely too important for an eighteen-year-old.

To be a court musician for a period was not a useless career move for a teenager, although as before it leaves open the question whether Bach was attracted more to this world or to the Church. Much depends on how far he inclined towards the violin and string music. The versatility required of keyboardists generally meant that in a court establishment they could be called upon to play the organ, while as an organist in church they would also expect to participate in town music. Although Bach soon left Weimar to take the organist's position in Arnstadt, he had been for six months part of an interesting musical establishment, participating in the junior duke Johann Ernst's private *cappella*, presumably with experienced musicians in the main ensemble. These included the violinist Johann Paul von Westhoff, who had published a set of solo violin suites in 1696: charming fiddle music of very likely influence on Bach's later works for solo violin, lacking the dense, abstract quality of Bach's but with a sure sense of violin-sound (see Example 16). Also in Weimar was the organist Johann Effler, to replace whom Bach returned as *Hoforganist* five years later, and who in his earlier positions had been succeeded by other Bachs.

Even if, in light of the versatility already mentioned, Sebastian did sub-stitute for Effler as organist during this period at the Weimar court, there is probably something a little *arriviste* in calling himself 'Saxon Prince's Court Organist' when he went to Arnstadt to test the new organ in July 1703. Presumably he did so for the sake of a church committee who would not then be happy appointing a *Laquey*-fiddler as their new organist.

The following year [in August 1703] he took on the duty of organist at the New Church in Arnstadt. Here he really showed the first fruits of his industry in the art of organ playing and in composition, the latter of which he had largely learnt only by observing the works of the most famous and thorough [*gründlichen*] composers of the time, and by applying his own contemplation to them. (*Obituary*)

Irrespective of any personal preference for court or church, there were good professional reasons to leave the former for the latter, even when the church ranked only third in an average town: for greater independence, for a regular contract, twice as much pay, rights to further fees, a less demand-ing schedule, less demeaning status, more work with the organ, proximity to other family members, young people to work with, and potential paying students.

At least seven Bachs had been town musicians or organists in Arnstadt before 1703, including Sebastian's father (a *Stadtpfeifer* qv), brother (briefly), and father's uncle (Heinrich, organist in the main town church for over half a century) – so the New Church, not having been well served by its organist recently, may well have seized upon this young man from Weimar, a musician both talented and knowledgable in organs. He was himself succeeded five years later by his cousin Johann Ernst, and the bur-gomaster in charge of the new organ project (no doubt an extra attraction in Arnstadt) was a brother-in-law of the admired and recently deceased Johann Christoph Bach of Eisenach. Perhaps Sebastian was recommended by the Court organist in Weimar, Johannes Effler (BJ 2005, 89f.), both as an examiner of the new organ and, presumably as a consequence of impressing the authorities, the new organist. If so, the appointment is an impressive sign of recognition and endorsement for an exceptional eighteen-year old.

The Obituary implies that having been an orchestral player he was now for the first time able to develop as an organist and composer, for which purposes he had qualified himself by careful study. This may be how he had spoken later, but it suits too well the picture of an ideal church musician to be totally reliable, and a further likely attraction in Arnstadt was its minor court and the chance of paid work there or in the town, even in an occasional rowdy operetta there (cf. Böhme 1931, 35). If the Obituary was drawing on some kind of chronicle – a particular family Bible, perhaps, with events recorded in the flyleaves – and if church music had been paramount in the years Emanuel knew his father best, he could have had no idea what the young Bach's professional desires had been at this point. In having already remarked four times on his learning processes – instruction from brother, visiting Hamburg, hearing Celle court-music, and now 'contemplating' other music – the Obituary is justifying something not obvious half a century later: how an eighteen-year old could come to be so qualified and authoritative. Emanuel's brother Christoph Friedrich was also to set out in the profession aged seventeen or eighteen, but as part of a court ensemble, not an independent organist.

In the summer of 1703 Bach, working in the court at Weimar, was brought across – the accounts specify hire of horses – to test J. F. Wender's new organ in the town's New Church (the Bonifatiuskirche or Church of St. Boniface), perhaps having been recommended as examiner to replace Johann Christoph of Eisenach. Evidently, as musician in Weimar and known amongst his many relations to be more familiar than other local organists with the great instruments of Lüneburg and Hamburg, he was thought able to judge the work of a builder thirty years his senior. It may not have been as extraordinary as it now seems for an eighteen-year old to give an authoritative report on an organ: his brother Christoph had done so at Ohrdruf when he was nineteen and apparently felt no qualms in accusing the organ-builder of little care and too high a cost (BJ 1985, 69). At Arnstadt, Sebastian seems to have inspected the new organ, reported on it (Dok II, 11), and then inaugurated it with the usual hymns and improvised solos, all probably in late June or early July 1703.

It can be assumed that a *Laquey* broke no binding conditions of employment at court when he left to become titular organist of a parish church elsewhere. The Arnstadt contract of 9 August 1703 gave Bach a salary of fifty guilders, plus thirty thalers for board and lodging (*Kost und Wohnung*, Dok II, 12). Probably the living costs were added because for such a church there was no house or apartment tied to the job, as was otherwise common. Or Bach, as a bachelor, did not qualify for one, lodging perhaps in one of the two houses owned by the burgomaster, to whose wife the mother of his bride-to-be Maria Barbara was sister (Dok II, 27). The salary compared very well with the thirty guilders for ten weekly services paid to the interim (and evidently unsatisfactory) organist whom he replaced, Andreas Börner, and with the forty guilders for his own successor four years later. (Börner's wife was also one of Bach's distant cousins. Did Bach knowingly oust him, a local organist boasting no court title?) Though entitled to other fees, the superintendent himself had a salary only twice as much as his young organist's, implying that Bach was expected to take on duties of a cantor too, as both his predecessor and successor were also to do – hence one of the complaints that were to arise later.

From these various events and their timetable one receives clear impressions of an eighteen-year-old with initiative: known through local family connections, he was invited as a supposed organist in a court of major prestige to approve a new organ, did so with authority, played the inaugural recital, solicited (or was solicited) to become its organist, negotiated a good contract, and by 14 August 1703 was installed in his new position. One hopes this process had the formal approval of the Weimar court chamberlain, for Bach had been paid there for the quarter that should have taken him up to September 13th (Dok II, 10). Duties were to play chorales and preludes at four services per week, probably plus some duties in the almshouse (*Hospital*) that contributed to his salary, and the contract laid down other conditions of so standard a kind as to be re-used for the next organist. According to this contract, the organist was to remain reliable and competent, fulfil his duties, appear promptly for services, play fittingly (*gebührend tractiren*), take care of the organ (giving notice if repairs were needed), allow no-one access to it without superintendent's knowledge; and

in your life and conduct to nurture fear of God, sobriety and a conciliatory spirit [*Verträglichkeit*], keeping yourself from evil company and hindrances to your calling, and in all things (as appropriate for a servant and organist who loves honour) to conduct yourself faithfully to God, the High Authorities and your superiors. (Dok II, 11–12)

High Authorities meant the local lord, the Count of Schwarzburg, the superintendent and consistory court, and any of their officers. Taken literally, the contract gave some dozen grounds on which an organist could be dismissed, hence the several charges levelled against the young organist some two years later (see below).

The new and colourful Arnstadt organ had twenty-three stops, pedal and two manuals, and was displayed against the back wall of a light, galleried church, high up in the special third gallery, its tone completed with a bigger bass sound than comparable instruments in north Germany, and tuned so as to allow more keys than older instruments. Its builder was highly respected in the province, and an organ of this kind, new and one hopes in faultless condition, was indeed something to encourage a young composer. One can guess that here he wrote organ-chorales of a kind famil- iar from some of the so-called 'Neumeister Collection' (see p. 15) but also some longer pieces: sectional chorale-fantasias that required two manuals, sets of variations on chorales (music also suiting the harpsichord), and pre- ludes or toccatas in various sections. Some works suggest an intimate grasp of music by other modern composers, for example Georg Böhm's toccata- like preludes and Pachelbel's fluent counterpoint, each of which seems to have informed many a Bach work of a similar kind. Another composer of up-to-date influence is likely to have been Johann Kuhnau, cantor in Leipzig: early works such as the Capriccio in B flat, BWV 992, which describes in six movements the events around someone departing on a journey – perhaps his friend Georg Erdmann (Wolff 2000, 75) – show him to have known and assimilated Kuhnau's programmatic sonatas published in Leipzig in 1700, the so-called 'Biblical Stories'.

Emanuel's mention of 'composition' implies more than organ music, much of which must in any case have been improvised, and since it is clear from the complaints made about him in February 1706 that he was expected to participate in the church services' ensemble music, one can suppose he was already trying his hand at composing such music himself. There are moments in Cantata 150 and 196 that look contemporary with some of the early organ music, with harmony, counterpoint or melody drawing on what was conventional but with unexpected details of ori- ginality. This really is choral music, in No. 196 with varying textures and melody, from melismatic to syllabic, that are already responding to voices and their expressive range. The short phrases, unadventurous harmony and ready formulas of melody and counterpoint found in Cantata 150, often described as the earliest extant cantata, have in the past raised many doubts about its authenticity, but it took a gifted musician to apply so confidently the old techniques of block chords and rhetorical rests to produce a line rising three-and-a-half octaves from basses to Violin I in order to allude to the words '*Direct me* in your truth' (see Example 2).

Particularly interesting in both Examples 1 and 2 is the straightforward harmony, breaking with no conventions but both applied in a decidedly rhetorical way, to which alert performers can respond. Any similarity between them is less striking than what is different between choral and key- board music, as already grasped by a young composer.

By 'the then most famous and thorough composers' from whom Sebastian learnt by observation, Emanuel was probably implying those he lists in a later letter to Forkel (see p. 44): worthy composers the opposite of frivolous,

2 Cantata 150.iv, opening (*tutti*)

trained to handle harmony expertly. Whether, as Telemann later reported of himself (Mattheson 1740), Bach took the widely circulating and nationally admired works of Agostino Steffani or Johann Rosenmüller as models – i.e. for italianate vocal and instrumental music respectively – one cannot say, unfortunately, though Steffani appears in one of his brother's albums. But known to Emanuel or not, a prime influence was also the more local Thuringian composers, including his father-in-law-to-be Johann Michael Bach, whose chorale-settings, though almost totally free of harmonic tension or inspired melody, are literate and at times hard to distinguish from pre-sumed work of the young Sebastian. There are too many uncertainties about the 'Neumeister Collection' of organ chorales for one to be quite sure whether or how their composer is reacting to Pachelbel's idioms, but typical of J. S. Bach would be the originality of some of their cadences, i.e. the one point in any piece of music that is traditionally the least original.

Generally, there are signs throughout his life that Bach was responding to, or striving to do better than, local composers or minor talents who at successive periods might have appeared to be competitors: Buttstedt and Hurlebusch for fugues, Daniel Vetter for chorales, Westhoff and J. G. Graun for violin music, Kauffmann and Walther for chorale-collections, Telemann or Graupner for cantatas, his elder sons for certain *galant* chamber music. Although a major study in itself, a few hints about such responses will be found here and there in the present book. For the moment, however, one must assume as well that a range of traditional Lutheran choral and vocal writing had also been observed, imitated and mastered over several years, from Lüneburg on, before it was possible for a composer in his early twenties to create such assured and at times touching works as the early Cantatas 106 and 131.

Whatever gifts Bach developed at Arnstadt, he did so beyond the requirements of his position in a relatively minor church, where he had to play only the chorales, presumably with their preludes, plus a voluntary before the service. How far he participated in other music at Arnstadt is undocumented in any detail, but he surely was not reticent or idle or unwilling. It could well be that Emanuel remarked on 'the first fruits' of organ-playing because his father did make a point of composing such music at this time, taking efforts to rise above the conventional, and speaking of it in later years with some pride. A young, single-minded, energetic, self-improving organist would not necessarily please the authorities, of course, and in 1705 and 1706 he was formally questioned by them about his work, amongst other things why he would not perform ensemble music with the student singers and players (Dok II, 20). His answer, in stating a desire for a competent music director, implied that he would not play with an incompetent – such as J. A. Rambach, one of the students. He also added that he would give an answer in writing to the particular question why he would not participate (Dok II, 21), but how truculent these replies were, or merely discreet in avoiding publicly naming names, is impossible to know, since the clerk was reporting only the gist.

Bach was certainly within his rights not to play in ensemble music if it was not spelt out in his contract, and this incident sets a pattern for protecting those rights throughout his career. A music director, not the organist, would be responsible for ensemble music and appropriately paid – perhaps by his actions Bach was looking for promotion now he was nearly 21. That from the beginning he bargained for a good salary seems clear, whether his Weimar title as cited in the record ('organist at a prince's court') was proper or the result of misunderstanding, as it might have been (see BJ 2003, 90). At the same time, that the church had justifiable expectations of its gifted young organist is suggested by its new organ and its respectable library, which contained not only older *a cappella* music for the choir (much as at Lüneburg, if on a smaller scale) but more recent cantatas with instruments. If any of this music plus the usual chorales was there to be heard in the service, it would have been the cantatas, with their necessary rehearsals and need for a good director, that the young organist was objecting to.

The consistory court, including Superintendent J. G. Olearius (one of a family of distinguished clergy), had other problems with Bach, as courts often do with young people. Whether an older organist would have been formally examined in this way is not yet clear: archival work on the life of German organists and cantors is still sparse and has yet to produce other examples. But it surely will, for in the nature of things, it seems unlikely that J. S. Bach was alone amongst organists young or old in being asked to explain himself in connection with matters that were all within his contract. At Arnstadt, in April 1706, the town council complained to the consistory court about the behaviour of the town's students (Spitta I, 312), including the wearing of rapiers at school, so perhaps there was a 'culture of complaint' in the town. And the same consistory, with its authority as a moral supervisor, had had trouble with an earlier Bach: Sebastian's father's twin brother Christoph, who in 1673 was (in modern terms) sued for breach of promise and went to a higher court, in Weimar, for judgment (Spitta I, 156–160).

In Sebastian's case, the problems centred on the way he fulfilled his duties and on his relations with the student players with whom, younger than many of them, he declined to play in ensemble and appears not to have got on well. On 4 August 1705 there was a brawl in the marketplace, as a consequence of which the very next day he was interrogated by the court, and over the next few weeks accused further of speaking or behaving 'like a dog's *etc*', insulting the bassoon (*sic*) of one J. H. Geyersbach, a student, and drawing his rapier when accosted about it.

At a court appearance he is accused of calling Geyersbach a *Zippel Fagottist* (Dok II, 16), but quite what was reprehensible about this is not entirely certain. *Zippel* could be a dialect version of *discipulus*, a common word for schoolboy, as in documents at Ohrdruf (Dok II, 7), and by extension could mean a callow or clumsy or stupid person (*Deutsches Wörterbuch*, 'Zippel', 'Tölpel'). So Geyersbach, who was three years older, was being called a schoolboy bassoonist or an oafish learner. But *Zippel* might also mean the male member (Marshall 2000, 501), and if, across the centuries from Bosch's painting of a woodwind instrument protruding *ex ano* in the *Garden of Delights, c.* 1500, to today's American slang, *Fagott* circulated *sub rosa* to mean homosexual, then there would have been a doubly offensive pun. For his part, Bach had first accused Geyersbach of attacking him and had asked the court for protection, despite admitting that he was wearing a rapier – which, by the way, might imply that he was in uniform for some court music that evening (Wolff 2000, 87), although those earlier complaints against students wearing swords suggest that it was not unusual.

There were four other chief complaints. First, in February 1706, the court wanted to know why Bach had absented himself too long on a study-trip to Lübeck (discussed further below) and whether he was prepared to play in ensemble music with the students – with whom, so it seemed to the court, he had no wish to get along (*sich nicht comportiren wollen*). Then in

November 1706 he was asked again about performing with the students and, furthermore, what he meant by allowing a girl into the choir gallery and letting her take part in the music.

This last, the third complaint, is the well-known incident of *die fremde Jungfer*, often translated in the past as 'the strange' or 'unfamiliar maiden'. *Jungfer* means she was unmarried, though it is unknown if this was Maria Barbara (whom Bach married a year later) or her elder sister Barbara Catharina (who was his witness during the market-place brawl) or someone else. *Fremd* means not 'strange' but 'unauthorized': the girl, whoever she was, had not been authorized to enter the gallery or sing with the choir, as she should have been first. (Was she there as soloist to replace a boy-treble? That too was subject to the authorities' permission.) Like other organists, Bach had signed a contract with a clause to admit no-one to the organ and presumably its gallery without higher permission. So had Johann Pachelbel at Erfurt in 1678, where 'no unauthorized person' was to touch the organ (*kein Frembder:* in DTÖ 17, viii).

While, therefore, there is less of a frisson about this famous incident than has often been thought, all the complaints – non-cooperation, aggressive behaviour, unauthorized admittance – were nonetheless serious, being matters covered in an organist's contract. So were the criticisms made after the Lübeck visit about the way he played chorales: a fourth complaint. The Obituary does not mention such things, either not knowing them or, more likely, doing as Emanuel later asked his correspondent Forkel to do: pass over stories of 'his youthful pranks' (*Fechterstreiche:* Dok III, 286). But as with the stories told at various times by or about Telemann or Handel, anecdotes are not useless. They can point a moral, as when the young, indigent Bach on his way to Lübeck is supposed to have found ducats in some thrown-away fish-heads, a story first told in 1786 (Dok III, 424) and not unlike other widely scattered legends about treasure and fish: providentially, he finds some money but puts it to use in furthering his studies. Another incident, first told in 1775, of the elderly Bach jumping out of bed to resolve a six-four chord left in the air by young Johann Christian and boxing his ears (Dok III, 291), says much about either the hero or the nature of the posthumous hero-worship. But which? Both anecdotes would have worked against the image Emanuel Bach was presenting.

FURTHER INFLUENCES

In the art of the organ [*in der Orgelkunst*] he took to himself the works of Bruhns, Reinken, Buxtehude and some good French organists as models. (*Obituary*)

As is also suggested by his brother's albums, these names are likely to have featured in Sebastian's studies, from MSS he brought back to Thuringia or those that regularly circulated amongst musicians, and a question is why there are not more names, corresponding to the very full contents of those albums. Emanuel did not know them, his father had not spoken of them, they were largely forgotten by 1750? The names he does give were all, as is appropriate for the Obituary's hero-composer, strong fugue composers, as Emanuel noted later (Dok III, 288), and furthermore, appeared prominently in other writings of the time. Certainly by the time the Obituary authors heard Bach speak of composers he admired, these names had a higher reputation than such local composers as Kuhnau, whom also he had once certainly imitated. Even Bruhns, whose music was the least well known of the three listed by Emanuel and of which there seems never to have been very much, had become familiar, indeed notorious, after stories told about him by Mattheson in his book of 1740. In short, the Obituary's names were selective and non-local, and therefore convey little of the range of the young Bach's studies. Neither here nor elsewhere does it do more than hint at what he was learning about non-keyboard music, string music in Lüneburg, choral in Lübeck.

A question not yet fully answered about such early works as Cantatas 150, 71 and 106, in which old genres are treated with an already well-developed gift for melody, is how much more influential were great composers like Buxtehude than local musicians. Both the forms (such as chaconne) and the techniques (such as the chromatic fourth, qv) being explored in Cantata 150, perhaps an Arnstadt work, show him to be perfectly in control of current conventions, although there were other Thuringian composers also capable of exploring them. In the case of Cantata 71, its layout in block choruses of woodwind, brass, strings and choir, could have been prompted by the polychoral performances of Buxtehude, whose Marienkirche (St Mary's Church) still has its separate minstrel galleries high above the nave, encouraging a musical stereophony. But it is just as likely to have been inspired by more local and modest practices going back a century or more. One could view the visit to hear Buxtehude, discussed below, as resulting from a desire to see and hear a grander version of the kind of music and even stereophonic sound-effects already familiar in Thuringia, including perhaps even in Arnstadt. Cantata 71 shows other signs that he was alert to musical developments: its fourth movement is the composer's first known essay in ABA form (qv), its sixth is imaginatively scored (cello above bassoon), the vocal writing is very practical, and throughout there is a freshness of sound more pronounced (in my view) than in the keyboard music.

From various sources it seems that French organists with whose work J. S. Bach became partly familiar before his late twenties include Raison, d'Anglebert, Boyvin, Dieupart, Du Mage, de Grigny and Marchand, but exactly when in each case is less certain. Did he know Raison's *Premier Livre* of 1688 while still at Arnstadt, a book whose two unusual and differing ostinato movements (qv) surely gave him the fugue-subject and probably the whole ground-bass theme of the organ Passacaglia? The point of the Obituary's remark could be to emphasize that the dominant repertory for Bach, the professional organist, was German Protestant and that the French (and Italian) styles familiar from keyboard albums copied at the time were more appropriate outside church and church music. By saying 'French organists' rather than 'French composers' Emanuel is distancing himself and his father from the influence of the other music of France – secular or liturgical, chamber or theatre – especially of recent decades, hence his reference to 'old, good Frenchmen' in a letter to Forkel (Dok III, 288).

Whether Emanuel realised it or not, elements of the harpsichord styles of d'Anglebert, Dieupart and Marchand, in particular the subtle broken textures, are behind various pieces buried in the 'miscellaneous early or doubtful works' of the young Bach, such as both the Sonata and the Toccata in D major (BWV 963, 912a). And yet in exploiting traditional note-patterns, these works, like the Aria variata, BWV 989, achieve little that German predecessors did not, even if now and then a newer harmonic tension is beginning to provide them with more interest. There are also slightly awkward moments for the player that cannot always be the result of unreliable copyists. In the case of non-keyboard music, an intimate understanding of French *manière* can be traced only in later music, such as the *ouverture* of the Advent cantata, No. 61 (1714). This may appear not to have much to do with Parisian organ music, and yet its paraphrases of the chorale-melody are as much French as German: Grigny too paraphrased in this way in his hymn-settings. Thus would a cantata – here from 1714, but also before and after – gather together all and any kinds of musical idiom, not only for the Greater Glory but for the musical challenge it offered. Applying modern French rhythms in the accompaniment to an old German chorale melody is exactly the mixing of styles to which Bach was attracted throughout his life and which took many different forms.

In the letter of 1775 to Forkel, Emanuel names not a single one of the French composers he said had been 'loved and studied' by his father, despite citing in one sentence nine Germans: Froberger, Kerll, Pachelbel, J. K. F. Fischer, N. A. Strunck, Buxtehude, Reinken, Bruhns and Böhm (Dok III, 288), only two of whom were prominent as choral composers. The German focus is rather of a piece with the Obituary's patriotic agenda and with other writings of the time. For true though it could well be that Emanuel's father and uncle admired those particular German composers, a somewhat similar list of 'famous men' had already been published by Emanuel's colleague Joachim Quantz in 1752, composers who it seems had benefited from assimilating Italian and French tastes. These men, according to Quantz, had developed the art of organ-playing beyond the old Netherlanders – Reinken originated in Deventer – and this was an art to culminate in the work of J. S. Bach. Another and similar message is re-conveyed in Emanuel's own treatise, the *Versuch,* either as a simple response to Quantz's book or in order to re-affirm it. What Emanuel has to say about the influences on his father has to be seen against this background of such writings of the time.

Emanuel does mention one non-German organist by name, the long-dead Frescobaldi, some of whose music had probably penetrated to Thuringia before Bach acquired a copy of *Fiori musicali* (dating it 1714) and who had long been a big influence on other German composers, including Froberger and Buxtehude. There is no direct evidence that through Buxtehude the young Bach became acquainted with any of the books of Frescobaldi, but certain repetitive note-patterns in the Passacaglia suggest that he might have done. If Emanuel was acquainted with his father's copy of *Fiori musicali* there would have been good reason to mention him in the Obituary. Or perhaps he had heard him speak of Frescobaldi over the years, even recently. But what then about other influential Italians? Perhaps Legrenzi, Corelli and Albinoni are not mentioned because they were forgotten in Germany by *c.* 1750, or because Emanuel knew few if any early works of his father that had made use of their music, transmitted in MSS that may not always have cited their names in the title.[1] Emanuel does not mention Vivaldi either, although sudden acquaintance with various Vivaldi concertos some years later must have changed his father's ideas for ever.

Just as likely is that working on themes by other composers was something Emanuel's generation no longer admired, however much it had been a habit in Central Germany and one which Handel had no reason to abandon when he wrote for English audiences. Was it as a careful, objective historian 'putting the record straight' that in his book of 1802, Forkel made so much of Vivaldi's influence on Bach's evolving ideas on musical form (see pp. 89f)?

---

[1] If Bach drew on Corelli for the Allabreve BWV 589 or Frescobaldi for the Canzona BWV 588, the extant sources do not say so; but nor does every extant version of the Fugue BWV 574 acknowledge Lengrenzi.

FROM ARNSTADT TO LÜBECK

At a certain moment here in Arnstadt he had so strong an urge to hear as many good organists as he could that [in the autumn of 1705] he set out for Lübeck, actually on foot, in order to hear the famous organist of St Mary's, Dietrich Buxtehude. He stayed there not without benefit for almost a quarter of a year, and then turned back to Arnstadt. (*Obituary*)

Here, as further testimony to the self-taught master and self-aware artist, the words 'so strong an urge' convey the composer's own sentiments, even perhaps his words. 'At a certain moment' also raises the vision of a young, impatient man of great energy who found his first appointment a little too constricting: he was twenty years old and apparently as keen to enlarge his musical experience, as thirty years later he was to record his musical genealogy. Curiously, although the Obituary says 'many good organists', as would fit in well with a plan for self-improvement, only Buxtehude and (previously) Reinken are mentioned by it, and the reader is left to wonder whether there had been others. (On this, see also the Postscript.) And 'good organists' would include those also experienced and successful as choral composers, though again the Obituary does not say so.

Emanuel probably knew little of the trouble Bach found himself in with the authorities when he returned, and yet there is already a sense here of the artist disregarding whatever stood in the way of his art. Setting out to walk far in order to increase one's learning – the wandering scholar – was not something despised in mid-eighteenth century Germany. Moreover, the very phrase 'on foot' for a journey of some 400 km contrasted sharply (and deliberately?) with the picture of the reception given to Handel and Mattheson at Lübeck in 1703 (Mattheson 1740, 94): another touch of pathos in the story of self-improvement, and probably owed to the composer himself. Both he and his biographers knew that by *c.* 1705 the cities of Hamburg and Lübeck were familiar to other musicians from Bach's and Handel's homelands, including Telemann (Leipzig), Graupner (Leipzig), J. C. Schieferdecker (Weissenfels) and the Christoph Bach described in the genealogy as fond of travelling.

Some readers, however, might have wondered why Bach had not gone some years earlier to study with Buxtehude or even with Pachelbel, his brother's teacher and sister's godfather. But Pachelbel, in the preface to his recent harpsichord variations *Hexachordum Apollinis* (1699), had mentioned Buxtehude as a teacher for his own son Wilhelm, aged thirteen, and the reverence attaching to Buxtehude seems to have been proverbial and persistent. As for Bach, although it was not unknown for the young, salaried organist of a modest town to acquaint himself with the best in his profession, nor was it totally commonplace either, and his prolonged absence from Arnstadt raises the question whether he was taking the initiative to look for an important job, including Buxtehude's own (see below, p. 55). Lübeck, though half the size of Hamburg, was strong in church music and organ playing, and it is particularly unfortunate that the nature of the contact Bach had with Buxtehude is undocumented. Whether it was anything out of the ordinary – some formal instruction, perhaps as a paying guest in the master's house, some temporary assistance in the running of a major church's music, etc. – the Obituary does not say. Emanuel might not have known exactly how his father stood to Buxtehude and had no wish to give the impression that he was still a mere pupil or apprentice, or that he had unsuccessfully tried for other jobs at this period.

Justifiably, the Arnstadt consistory court summoned Bach in February 1706 to explain an absence four times longer than the month the superintendent had originally allowed him, for a study-trip 'to understand one thing or another in his art' (Dok II, 19). If, in October or November 1705, he really had set out on foot from Arnstadt, he could not possibly have journeyed to Lübeck, undertaken serious or formal studies and journeyed back within a month; nor would he have been able to hear all of Buxtehude's mixed sacred concerts during Advent, the *Abendmusik*, which were surely part of the point. In finding a substitute to play in his absence, as he did, had he not already supposed (or soon learnt) that a month was not enough? Furthermore, special music performed in Lübeck during December 1705 to mark the death of Emperor Leopold I and succession of Joseph I was worth waiting for. Bach's reply to the court, that he had made provision for a substitute and could not be criticized on these grounds, reads defensively, for he must have known such absence was against his contract.

Not the least interesting word in his explanation was the wish to improve his 'art' (*Kunst*), the new shibboleth justifying the breaking of rules, such as absence without leave. But the court must have wished that his *Kunst* had been improved as they wanted it to be, for it went on to reprimand him further, complaining that

until now [about 2 February 1706] he had been making many odd variations [*wunderliche variationes*] in the hymns, mixing up in them many strange keys [*Thone*] so that the congregation has become confused by it. In future, if he wants to bring in a wandering key [*tonum peregrinum*], he has to stay with it and not turn conspicuously to something else too quickly or, as he as so far been used to doing, even playing in some opposing key [*Tonum contrarium*: Dok II, 20].

Obviously the clerk and/or the non-musicians present were using technical terms loosely. *Tonus peregrinus* cannot mean the mode of this name to which the Magnificat was often sung, rather that the music 'wanders' through keys with gratuitous modulations or unexpected chromaticisms. *Tonum contrarium* is not a regular musical term, implying much the same kind of harmony: to the parishioners, 'a wrong key'. Even *variationes* is not quite clear: does it mean he was interfering with the melody or with the harmony or even form of the chorales? Despite the uncertainties, however, the main lines of the complaint are clear enough: a young organist was wilfully or otherwise annoying the clergy and people with over-adventurous harmonies of a kind unsuitable for a regular parish church, and they knew enough to be able to say what they did not like.

The adverbs 'until now' or 'so far' (*bißher*), appearing twice, suggest that Bach had been offending in this way before he ever went to Lübeck. It is quite possible that certain extant chorale-settings attributed to him, even if in the literature they have often been too confidently labelled 'Arnstadt Chorales', do represent the kind of gratuitous chromaticism liked by some of the more adventurous organists of Thuringia in the period around 1700. After all, these hymns were very familiar to the congregation, frequently sung and memorized, and often with many more verses than is acceptable today. So some variety introduced by the organist (especially a young, irrepressible organist) was not unreasonable, up to a point. Even nowadays, many organists find interfering with a hymn's basic harmonies, particularly in the final verse of what are now much shorter hymns, irresistible.

There is a further point. In principle, to use wandering keys and/or unexpected harmonies was at the time a standard means of responding to a text, part of the expressive vocabulary of the time, found in any church music, even the very chorales in the St John and St Matthew Passions, 'coloured' to fit the story. Words of penitence, for example, drew from the organist or composer a descending chromatic line (something easy to introduce against almost any melody), words of hope an ascending chromatic line (not quite so easy but still practical). A large number of Bach's much later chorale-settings for organ also explore these same 'affective' devices and were open to the same kind of criticism. Even certain Orgelbüchlein chorales, in the very unusualness of their harmony, would have startled an ordinary parish-church congregation or, if used as introductions to the singing, left it uncertain what the tune was. At least the first note of the hymn-tune is usually clear enough.

And there was another complaint:

so far Bach had played somewhat too long, but after an indication of this was given him by the Superintendent, he had immediately fallen into the other extreme and had made it too short. (Dok II, 20)

Since the complaint was apparently made by the prefect Rambach, a student some years older and whose conducting Bach had apparently criticized, obviously there were bad relations between them and they were unable to sort it out in private. Had Rambach politely remonstrated and met with aggression and territorial self-defence from the organist? Or was this a diversionary ploy of the choir-prefect, since on the same occasion he was punished with detention for going off during a sermon to visit the wine-cellar?

'Too long' and 'too short' must apply to the preludes Bach was playing, but preludes to what exactly is not specified: to the service as a whole (the opening voluntary), to the ensemble music (during which the performers tuned) or (most likely) to the congregation's hymns? Rambach is not merely referring to the interludes played between the lines of a hymn, and conceivably, the fault lay in all of these? A long-standing quarrel thirty years later in Leipzig also concerned Bach's bad relations with a choir-prefect, though in neither case is it clear whether the reason was personal (some incompatability), professional (the prefects were not good enough), or territorial (prefects were not of his choosing, as they should be, but the clergy's). Whichever it was, it would have been exacerbated by any natural contrariness in Bach's nature, such as is all too evident in the present incident: first he played too long, then too short.

BUXTEHUDE

Since there is no record of what Bach heard or played or learnt in Lübeck, what exactly the visit of 1705–6 contributed to the composer's maturing grasp of musical language and form has to be conjectured. It is not certain that in the sacred evening concerts (*Abendmusiken*) Buxtehude was still playing such long chorale-fantasias as his 'Nun freut euch' BuxWV 210, whose 229 bars may have been suitable for such concerts but had been composed decades earlier. Nor were such fantasias ever imitated to their full extent by Bach, except apparently when he was playing in Hamburg much later (pp. 149f).

There is also no record that Bach heard any of the quasi-operas on New Testament stories fashionable both in Lübeck and Hamburg, made (as one of them, *Himmlische Seelenlust* 1684, described itself) 'in the operatic manner with many arias and ritornelli', but he surely made a point of it. That such works had five sections or acts spread over the five Sundays of the *Abendmusiken* is significant in two particular respects, whether or not Bach took part: here could lie the explanation for his extended stay in Lübeck (thus an example of his priorities, now with choral music) and a precedent, thirty years later, for his six-act Christmas Oratorio spread over the six days of Christmas and Epiphany. And in addition to any experience he had of such unique concerts, no young man with musical gifts could have been indifferent to Buxtehude's pleasing harmony, charming melody and clever counterpoint, familiar from so much of his music for voices or instruments, and keyboard music both for church and for the home.

Such qualities must have been in particular evidence in the Lübeck church concerts, whose scope, planning and standards of performance were renowned. Of the two pieces by Buxtehude known to have been performed in December 1705 (cantatas BuxWV 134 and 135), the latter had a violin or string ensemble of twenty-five, probably the biggest group that Bach would have ever heard so far. Had the music, now lost, conformed to Buxtehude's usual style, it was offering examples of how to construct cantatas from many sections, each in a marked style (a prelude for strings, a short solo or duet, choral interjections, etc.), sensitive to the conventions of the day (certain keys for certain effects, etc.) and sustained by a characteristic sense of melody. Bach seems to have responded to Buxtehude's big organ works, the multi-section *praeludia*, much as younger Italian violin composers responded to their predecessors' work: by developing the short sections characteristic of seventeenth-century instrumental music towards the longer, self-contained, full-fledged movements of the standard sonata as it was established by 1700 and beyond.

For a young composer, Buxtehude's melodic gifts in his cantatas were inspiring, as they were in his organ-settings. No home-grown Thuringian composer often if ever went beyond conventional formulas to create, as Buxtehude did in both choral and organ music, such winsome and new melodies out of the old hymn-tunes, weaving them around with ornamental gestures typical of sophisticated paraphrasing techniques (qv). Perhaps Bach was particularly taken with Buxtehude's ostinati (qv) from hearing them in performance – including any there were in lost choral works? – and brought four of them back for his brother to copy and himself to play, then at some point responded to them with his own Passacaglia in C minor for Organ, BWV 582, by taking the idea so much further, i.e. searching for greater length and development. These steps of development are not documented, alas. But even if the Passacaglia's theme is owed (in both its phrases) to André Raison, and in this way conforms to the neophyte composer's working with a master's material, the piece turns out to be more sustained, organized and thorough than any possible models, German, French or Italian. It absorbs the usual language of variations of the time and gathers them together in a continuous, rounded work, one in which tension rises and falls in waves before working towards a climax worthy of many a Romantic symphony.

Were organ music after 1750 to have retained the prestige it had when Bach was young, the Passacaglia's striking achievement as a structure conceived by a composer in his early twenties, drawing on precedents but at a stroke far exceeding them, would be more widely recognized by later music historians (and concert-audiences) than it generally is. Mastering the various ways to write for a choir in the early cantatas did not lead Bach, it seems, to a unified and sustained structure anywhere to match the Passacaglia's.

Not only that but in demonstrating its composer's grasp of ordered time, the Passacaglia is a work of particular significance in his musical biography. Its second section, the fugue, is part of the overall concept,[2] exploring at unheard-of length venerable permutation techniques for its three themes (qv), doing so with a new sense of working logically to the climax, and using the lingua franca of the day to give free rein to his ability to organize. Nowhere could Bach have learnt much of this except in his own imagination. Length itself seems to have interested both the young Handel and the young Bach, even in stylized suite-dances that had usually been compact, and should not be underestimated as a spur to creative thinking. The thoroughness with which so many compositional challenges are undertaken is, at a naive level, already demonstrated in works earlier than the Passacaglia – in a shorter piece that consciously runs through a long series of changing time-signatures (the prelude-fantasia BWV 921) or through many changing textures (the organ chorale BWV 739) or spins prolifically out of one melodic motif into another (nearly twenty of them arise in the fifty-four bars of the Fantasia, BWV 1121).

With such pieces of the early period, there is a most striking range of idiom and shape, not only in these smaller works but in others such as the Praeludium in G minor, BWV 535a and the Capriccio in B flat, BWV 992. Versatility itself, as demonstrated in person by Buxtehude, must have been

---

[2] The oldest extant copy (Andreas Bach Book) passes to the fugue without a break, and no source authoritatively suggests otherwise. Also, the Passacaglia proper ends on a weak beat and rises to the mediant, implying *attacca senza pausa*.

3 a Organ chorale, BWV 736, opening
   b Capriccio, BWV 992.vi, b. 27
   c Passacaglia, BWV 582, b. 104

something the young composer admired, studied and emulated. A certain rhythmic stiffness in the contrapuntal imitation one feels in Bach's early counterpoint raises several technical questions such as, Did he learn to write tonal answers (qv) in fugues, as in Example 3 (a), purely from observing what older composers did, and should authenticity then be doubted when in a so-called early work the answer is real? And, are the collisions and avoidable awkwardnesses in certain earlier music, requiring agility in Examples 3 (b) and 3 (c), a result of composing at a desk and writing in tablature, in which such things are less obvious on paper than in staff notation? Both 3 (b) and 3 (c) are trickier to play than three parts need to be.

Despite the sectionality of those early pieces, there is also a sense of continuity and phrasing, and the approach is fertile, even alarmingly obsessive, a combination that can be glimpsed throughout the composer's life. Perhaps most important of all is the grasp of harmonic tension and the way harmonies can be made to move. This is clear not least in those early keyboard works that are taking up ideas current amongst composers generally, such as repetitive note-patterns or chromatics. As is the case in other connections, to trace such ideas as they matured is made difficult, impossible even, by the many uncertainties surrounding the 'early works', but some outlines can still be glimpsed. Thus the two early works, Praeludium, BWV 921 and Fantasia, BWV 922 make use of repetitive note-patterns and

4 Praeludium, BWV 921, final bars

chromatics still rather dogmatically and prosaically, but already with a sense of drive and rhetorically timed cadences, as is suggested by Example 4.

Conventional handling of a chromatic theme as in BWV 922 would eventually lead to the originality found in much later work as, for example, in the opening bars of Cantata No. 3 (1725), where the chromatic fourth is used as no-one else ever used it. Many a cantata movement appears to take up a detail from keyboard music but now realized with more colourful *Affekt* for a more public effect.

Apropos the Lübeck visit, Bach certainly had a lot to explain at Arnstadt, even if it cannot be known from the consistory minutes how acerbic his manner actually was. The criticisms themselves ring true for a young composer with big ambitions, a restless talent, and now probably with his confidence strengthened by contact with Buxtehude. (Performers often return from a great teacher with heightened self-confidence.) His deeply creative interest in types and techniques of counterpoint went beyond what was required by Thuringian parishioners, and one would like to know how much and what examples of such counterpoint he came across, and whether this happened by chance or design. Various contrapuntal techniques had already been explored in the music he knew and worked on – those works by Albinoni, Corelli and Legrenzi (the art of combining different themes) or Antonio Biffi (the art of writing stretto, or a theme overlapping itself) – and he kept up such interests. Hence, perhaps, his work some years later on carefully transcribing Vivaldi's D minor Concerto (BWV 596), one attraction of which was surely its example of quadruple invertible counterpoint, very unusual in such music.

In Lübeck at the time of his visit, any hymns Bach heard were probably not accompanied by the organ, though an interesting and extensive prelude may have introduced them, played by Buxtehude or an assistant, either composed or improvised. A young man would want to try his hand at the same kind of thing, but what the good people of Arnstadt New Church wanted was for their organist to play the hymn-tune in a straight-forward manner – 'melodically' (*thematicè*), as Pachelbel's contract in Erfurt had it – so that they all, congregation and choir, knew what and when to sing.

THE MÜHLHAUSEN APPOINTMENT

In 1707 he was called as organist to St Blasius, Mühlhausen. However, this town could not have the pleasure of keeping him long. (*Obituary*)

On Advent Sunday, 1706, two or three weeks after the most recent com-plaints against him at Arnstadt, Bach was in the small town of Langewiesen, testing and (probably) inaugurating a new organ, along with a senior col-league, Johann Kister of Gehren nearby. If Bach were not to be absent from his own church in Arnstadt on such an important Sunday, he must have left immediately after the 8 a.m. service, covering the twenty-five miles to Langewiesen as best he could. The church 'inspector' present in Langewiesen was also from nearby Gehren (Dok II, 22), as originally was the family of Maria Barbara Bach to whose father Kister was a successor, and to whom Bach was to be married barely a year later. Nothing exact is known of how these various people and places were connected and how Bach came to be appointed as organ-expert, but connections there must have been.

Since the occasion was only five months before Bach was arranging his audition in Mühlhausen, the Obituary's emphasis at this point on organ music and organ playing appears to be justified. In 1705 Buxtehude's age was nearly seventy, so Bach might have originally gone to Lübeck to solicit his job in the Marienkirche, with its outstanding organs (one of them with over fifty stops) and the famous musical life it contributed to in a distinguished city. One is bound to wonder whether any such idea came to nothing for the same scurrilous reason Johann Mattheson gave as to why neither he nor Handel had wished to replace Buxtehude: none of them could accept the 'marriage condition' (1740, 94), which was – to marry Buxtehude's eldest daughter, ten years older than they. (Buxtehude's eventual successor did marry her, as he had married his predecessor Tunder's daughter and, in Hamburg, Reinken had married Scheidemann's.) There is no clear evidence whether the marriage condition was implicit or explicit, but apprentices or successors often did marry their master's daughter or widow, becoming a 'partner' to 'take joint control of the family business', one with assured income and legally entitled fees, and not unlikely to produce in turn a musical child as the next successor. (There is no evidence that Bach's son-in-law Altnickol sought to succeed him in Leipzig, perhaps because he had been cantor not organist, with undesired duties to the school.) Any such marriage condition also freed the church and council from having to provide for a deceased organist's family, a pressing concern in Lübeck and no doubt elsewhere at a time of commercial depression (see Edler 1982, 73, 80). Nevertheless, why Mattheson, Handel and Bach all declined, if they did, one can only guess.

In December 1706 in the historic town of Mühlhausen, the organist of St Blasius ('Divi Blasii') died, and by the following April Bach was auditioning for the position, probably having been informed or encouraged again by local contacts. Mühlhausen had many connections with Hamburg, personal, commercial and probably musical, and its potential must have seemed superior to Arnstadt's. A major city, it had a proud position in local Reformation history and boasted over a dozen churches, including the two big gothic structures of the Marienkirche and the Blasiikirche. By Bach's time it was marked by communal strife of various kinds and by a factiousness between the churches, orthodox *versus* Pietist, the latter of which was likely to prefer simpler music. Although Forkel, guessing or passing on something Emanuel had told him, said that about this time Bach received several offers – a hidden reference to the Lübeck situation? (1802, 6) – the only certain event is the organ-testing at Langewiesen. Perhaps for some time he had been searching for broader prospects than Arnstadt gave him but without startling success; either this or Forkel had some inkling of the Problem of Buxtehude's Daughter.

'To be called as organist' is the usual formula found at the period, less pretentious than the modern professional's claim to be 'head-hunted'. In some sense not now clear, Bach competed with others for the post in Mühlhausen, a more important church than the Bonifatiuskirche, Arnstadt. Probably, the chief burgomaster Conrad Meckbach was very much on his side, through local connections of a kind already suggested. J. G. Walther too applied, encouraged by the organ-builder Wender, and took the trouble to prepare a pair of cantatas; but then he withdrew, for some reason finding Mühlhausen 'hateful' (*verhasst*: see Beckmann 1987, 70, 219f). He was still speaking of 'hatefulness' over twenty years later, despite soon finding a good position at Weimar instead. Did Bach have anything to do with any of this?

At Mühlhausen, it seems certain that music for the audition included one or two cantatas. Bach's, sung on Easter Sunday 1707, was therefore quite possibly Cantata 4. Assuming it to be authentic, Cantata 4 must be a work from this period and particularly appropriate not only to the day but, as a set of particularly intelligible tuneful variations on the hymn, to a church committee. The hymn-tune must have been running in their heads afterwards, for the cantata's charming use of current ideas – a string prelude, brilliant violin solos, melodious solos and duets, a running bass, a recognisable hymn-melody in various guises, a fine tune to start with, and all handled with a secure harmonic sense – would surely have been found as pleasing as it is today. (More so than Pachelbel's arrangement of the same chorale?) As minuted, the parish council's decision after the Easter audition was quickly taken, and Bach was asked three weeks later what he would require as salary and payment in kind (Dok II, 22–5). He asked for the same salary as at Arnstadt, the same goods as his predecessor (approximately a bushel of grain per week and brushwood for each day of the year), and removal expenses, but nothing is clearly stated about lodging.

The Mühlhausen agreement of 15 June 1707 specified that Bach be loyal to the town *Magistrat*; do his best for the community; perform his duties 'willingly' and be available at all times, specifically for the Sunday, Feast Day and Holy Day services; keep the organ in good condition and report its faults, take care for its repairs and its music (i.e. control what was played with it); live respectably and avoid dubious *compagnie* (Dok II, pp. 24–5). By *music*, the council may have expected the organ and organist to work in cantatas with choir and instruments. Bach shook hands, obtained release from Arnstadt on 29 June (a week after his first cousin Johann Ernst had applied to replace him), returned the organ keys there, and apparently began at Mühlhausen on 1st July. He made over his Arnstadt salary for the third quarter (from 15 June) to this cousin who, however, seems to have been confirmed only eleven months later. Perhaps it had been of no advantage to Johann Ernst Bach to have his cousin's support.

The previous organists at Mühlhausen, J. G. Ahle and his father, were distinguished citizens of the town as well as significant musicians in their own right,[3] and since Bach's new salary was higher by more than thirty

---

[3] In his *Geistliche Arien* (Mühlhausen, 1662), J. R. Ahle had published the well-known melody (complete with rising augmented 4th) to the chorale 'Es ist genug', re-harmonized at the end of the cantata BWV 60 (see Example 24).

per cent – usually, his predecessors had other employment too – what he could offer the church and town must have been recognized. The Ahles, both of whom published as much if not more than Bach was ever to do, had helped create an active and musically engaged community, to which their young organist-successor was surely attracted. J. R. Ahle's devotional arias were still being sung and admired in nineteenth-century Mühlhausen, strophic chorale-like songs with instrumental ritornelli, which, though simple, do bridge the gap between hymns and secular songs. In this way, they served a 'social' purpose quite as much as did, in a different way, the singing method for children that Ahle also published.

Although Bach's contract did not specify that he was to compose can-tatas, the organist of his church customarily supplied at least one great cele-bratory piece each year: a cantata, complete with trumpets and drums, for a service at the Marienkirche on the election of the town council, music for which Bach was paid some four and a half guilders in 1708. (In 1709, when he returned from Weimar to present the following year's, he was paid over six, plus half as much again for travelling costs.) In addition, he was to have further paid duties at several other and smaller churches in the city, alter-natively with the organist of the other main church. Altogether, there were some six regular weekly services, plus feastdays, weddings and funerals, at all of which the organist played chorales and preludes based on them, and regularly accompanied concerted music. A later organist in Mühlhausen (1730) agreed to similar conditions and was expected to be industrious and willing in his duties, in ensemble music as well as the chorales, and very likely to keep the five organ reeds in tune (BJ 1987, 77). This last was not the lightest of duties.

In February 1708, Cantata 71 for the council election was performed twice on consecutive days in the two main churches, and, at some expense, was printed and published – not only the text but, in movable type, the music's nineteen vocal and instrumental parts. Perhaps this was done at Bach's urging, although the Ahles had already established Mühlhausen, unusually, as a place for musical publications. (So was Leipzig, but no Bach cantatas were published there, or indeed anywhere else.) In idiom Cantata 71 is at times rather like Buxtehude's, with short-breathed melody, triadic harmonies and contrasting blocks of sound, though without quite the same lightness of touch. Some similarities have also been found between it and a festive Mühlhausen cantata by P. H. Erlebach, performed with success there three years earlier, which suggests that Bach was saluting local trad-ition, just as he was later to do in Leipzig with his Magnificat. Though not a set of variations like BWV 4, Cantata 71 runs through quite as many different styles, but on grander and more continuous scale, with instrumental groups of brass, strings and woodwind, and with solo contributions from the organ as well as the usual continuo accompaniment. The effect is rather restless and episodic in its naive stereophony, but with some sweet melody and unexpected tone-colours. Equally following the book are its standard formulas for setting a text, as in using a crown-shaped motif c-e-g-e-c for 'God is my King', or an *affettuoso* oboe solo to allude to the turtledove.[4] This exploring of music's common-property vocabulary, though effortlessly competent, gives an impression more of playfulness than deep thinking.

The autograph score of Cantata 131 carries a note that it was composed 'at the desire of G. C. Eilmar', archdeacon at the Marienkirche, Mühlhausen, a known antagonist of the superintendent of Bach's church, and one with whom, through personal contact, Bach could well have agreed on the importance of well-wrought church music. A municipal thanksgiving was the moment for some music of bigger scope and for bigger forces than usual. Both it and Cantata 71 show an increasing grasp of how cantatas of several movements can be built, with a virtually *ad hoc* sequence of introductions, choral songs, arias, chorales, interludes and so on, now contrapuntal, now homophonic, the whole informed by particular images in the words and music. Such a way of setting a text is still that of the late, or even early, seventeenth century, in which the music changes character in response to the words and in accordance with conventional associations between sounds and meanings – bright triadic music for a celebratory text, for instance, quickly changing to something else. The distinction between recitative (syllabic prose) and arias (melismatic, poetic) in which a few stylized words are repeated, is not yet developed, and might never have become so without impetus from outside the world of Lutheran cantatas.

Although it may be around this time, 1707–8, that Bach made his copy of an Italian cantata by Antonio Biffi that contained recitative, neither Cantata 131 nor 71 yet includes any. Was it not yet felt appropriate for vernacular Lutheran settings? But these cantatas do contain antiphonal choruses, constantly changing textures, brief instrumental solos, polychoral instrumentation (brass+drums against strings, etc.), SATB solos, fugue, permutation fugue, aria, and duet aria, all producing a freshness missing from the more run-of-the-mill Italian imitations of the day. The very range

---

[4] Some formulas of this kind were long-established: the cantata's words 'Day and night' use the same *figura* or motif as 'he hath put down' in the Magnificat of William Byrd's Great Service.

of Italian tempo words in the scores of Cantatas 71 and 131 and in the Capriccio, BWV 992 shows Bach wishing to air his increasing knowledge. These early works are generally short-phrased or even short-breathed, recalling earlier German choral music such as Schütz's, in which at any given movement there is likely to be many a tonic and dominant on a strong beat. Such early works of Bach have their touching moments but little of the dazzling expanse of form and melody achieved by Handel in Italy at about the same period, with 'Dixit Dominus' or 'Laudate puerum'.

As far as one can judge from the works of Handel and Bach dating from around 1707–8, there is no doubt which of the two composers was producing music of greater or more immediate impact. Bach has nothing yet to equal the moments of splendour in Handel's early Latin and Italian music, although the care with which the themes are worked in Cantatas 106 and 71, and the beautiful qualities of Cantata 106 in a good performance, hint at what he was to achieve. One could argue that the bar-by-bar sounds are more original than in any keyboard music. These various early works survey many more forms and genres than Handel does in his psalm-settings, a point one could take further if so many 'early Bach works' such as the old-style Wedding Quodlibet, BWV 524, the Cantata No. 4, and the Frenchified motet BWV Anh. III 159 were finally proved authentic. Working the hard way without the sparkling facility of Handel, Bach seems to have sustained a greater inventiveness across a broader spectrum and over a longer period, indeed throughout most of his life. In later years, he fell back on what he had accomplished in his youth much less often than did Handel, if at all.

THE MÜHLHAUSEN ORGAN

Two other records of Bach's musical life in Mühlhausen throw some light on his activities and interests. The first is his taking on pupils: various reports speak of J. M. Schubart studying with him from 1707 to 1717, and of J. C. Vogler from the Arnstadt period onwards – significant, since both seem to have followed him to Weimar, at some point in his years there. Schubart was described in Walther's *Lexicon* as studying keyboard-playing 'continuously' with Bach over these years (*Clavierspielen... beständig*), meaning he moved to Weimar with him in 1708. Doubtless there were other pupils, and these two are known only because they were apprentice-assistants succeeding their teacher. Vogler's copy many years later of a C major Prelude (BWV 870a, a version of that eventually opening Book 2 of the Well-tempered Clavier), plus the fingering he wrote into it, might – just – represent his earlier work with his teacher, both on learning how to create keyboard preludes and on how to play them. On doubts about such fingerings, however, see below p. 306.

The second activity is organ-advising, something likely to be much more frequent than records show, particularly in the little Thuringian village churches then having an organ built for the first time. In February 1708, Bach's plans for something altogether grander were presented: a newly rebuilt organ for his church in Mühlhausen. This was less than twenty years since the last major work had been done on the organ, and the builder J. F. Wender again undertook the job, one of several organs he built in the neighbourhood. Perhaps Wender had been active in getting Bach the Mühlhausen appointment originally, knowing him from Arnstadt and apparently collaborating with him on some other organ examinations in the region. But successfully proposing an important organ-project only half a year after taking up his position suggests no ordinary, twenty-two-year-old musician content to accept current conditions. The project may say something about all three protagonists: the composer (energetically pressing for improvements?), the council-members (supportive and imaginative?) and the builder (more persuadable than some of his colleagues?).

Like Kuhnau and others drawing up organ-schemes, Bach, when he came to put pen on paper, seems to have described the Mühlhausen organ's faults and remedies mainly on the basis of the advice and procedures given in Andreas Werckmeister's book of 1698, the *Orgelprobe*, a guide for people involved in the costly exercises of commissioning and approving new organs. The book had authority for Bach not least because of the dedicatory poem by the Hamburg masterbuilder Arp Schnitger, with whose work he was by now acquainted. At least within the triangle Eisenach-Wolfenbütttel-Leipzig, Werckmeister was the local authority, of great influence through his writings, which also have some connection with those produced in Mühlhausen by J. G. Ahle. Consequently, a big question remains as to how expert in organ-building Bach actually was, whatever his later admirers said. Kuhnau, a university-educated cantor, would hardly have considered a craftsman's technicalities to be in his purview, and would automatically consult a book as recent, 'local' and full of good sense as Werckmeister's, as he seems to have done for a report at Halle in 1716, co-signed by J. S. Bach.

More is said below on Bach's supposed intimate knowledge of organs (pp. 307f), but in the Mühlhausen report one searches for signs of this without very much success. A good case that he 'missed hardly any minutiae' in it, mentioning even pipe-materials, has been made in Wolff 2000,

143–4, but against this one could equally claim that the details he stipulated – '14-ounce tin' for the case-pipes, some 'good wood' for an accompanying stop, presumably meaning oak – needed no more than basic knowledge. Nor, ten years later, did his specifying a lighter touch and shallower keyfall in the report at the Leipzig Paulinerkirche (St Paul's Church, Dok I, 164) suggest much more: these wished-for improvements may not even have been practical at that stage, though certainly desirable. It also seems to be the case that when in 1746 the organist at the Wenzelskirche (St Wenceslas's Church), Naumburg reported on all the faults in the new organ recently approved by Bach along with the privileged organ builder of Saxony, Gottfried Silbermann, he was implying, for whatever reason, that the two examiners had done their job only superficially (Dok II, 429–31). The report of 1724 on an organ in Buttstädt, near Erfurt, by Bach's colleague J. G. Walther, is far more detailed, careful and patently expert, reporting on the bellows, wind-pressure, chest, action, tuners' ill-treatment of pipes, even which pipes are overblowing (Mannheim 2004). Nothing comparable is known from J. S. Bach.

Nevertheless, by drawing on varied and undoubted experience – knowing Christoph Bach's organ-rebuild in Eisenach (completed 1707), visiting organs as far north as Lübeck, noting Werckmeister's model stoplist and following his advice – Bach's scheme at Mühlhausen is well-conceived and succinctly presented, with the salient points grasped and made clear. The musical potential of what he recommended was very promising, thanks probably again to good use being made of Werckmeister's advice: bellows and chests must be remade, for both a bigger capacity and an evenness of wind; a good sub-suboctave bass must be introduced in the pedal to give a good foundation; the reed stops need to be improved (meaning their timbre brought up to date and made 'rounder'?); the Tremulant needs improvement (i.e. made more even and less extreme?); a 26-bell Glockenspiel is desirable (for the 26 note-pedal?) plus some new colour stops including a Fagott 16[1] (for ensemble music); there needs to be a thorough tuning (temperament not specified); and finally, the organ needs a complete new third manual or *Brustwerk*. It could be at Bach's request that a higher number of reed stops was included than was usual for the region, a result of his experiences in North Germany or even of reading Werckmeister's very recent monograph on the colourful Renaissance instrument at Gröningen.

On the puzzling question of why Bach wanted a row of Glockenspiel bells, see a remark below, p. 81. Bells were not uncommon at that time and place, and it is possible that at Gera in 1725 two revolving-stars-with-bells were added after Bach's examination there and at his request – for hymns 'on high feast-days' (BJ 2004, 102). Similarly, any particular taste that J. S. Bach had for strong bass tone complete with ample bellows-wind to supply it was quite typical of Thuringian organists, though less so of those in Hamburg or Dresden. One could say something similar about Bach's other apparent preferences in organ-building: only with the reeds did the Mühlhausen organ differ much from provincial Thuringian tastes in 1700 or so. Like the Fagott 16', the third manual or department was desired not only for continuo work and occasional solos but to satisfy the growing need for certain music in such churches, i.e. newer types of cantata with a greater variety of texture (solos, duets, choruses, instrumental sections) than before. The third manual's pipes would be located just above the heads of the players in the spacious west-end gallery, a direct support for their music and a help in their tuning-up beforehand. It seems that in the years since the organ had last been radically worked on, either its rôle had broadened or its new organist had new ambitions. Strangely, Bach says nothing about the action of the keys, though a new manual or chest ideally meant remade key-boards and playing-mechanism. Can he really have taken it for granted that the keyboard touch and action would be good, or was he not fastidious about such things?

There is a possibility that the sectional chorale 'Ein feste Burg', BWV 720 was written for this organ and shows Bach's practices. But the extant copy's details are typical of its scribe (J. G. Walther) and of the organs he knew, and have no certain authority.

FIRST MARRIAGE

Twice our Bach was married. The first time [on Monday 17 October 1707] was with Miss Maria Barbara Bach, the youngest daughter of the above-mentioned Johann Michael Bach, a good [*brafen*] composer. By her he had seven children, namely five sons and two daughters, amongst whom a pair of twins. (*Obituary*)

After the banns were recorded twice in Arnstadt, the bride's home town (Dok II, 28), the marriage took place in Dornheim, a village church nearby whose pastor was a family friend. This was four months after the move to Mühlhausen, when Dornheim would also have served as convenient 'neutral ground'. Emanuel gives no date for his father's first marriage, and only the year for the second. But since in both cases he briefly lists the children, it seems precise dates were of less interest, for if a family Bible recorded the children, it would have recorded the dates of marriage. No doubt he liked to have it on record there, however, that his maternal grandfather was a good musician, as his mother is also likely to have been. Again, perhaps, he had an eye to his father's genealogy, where Johann Michael is called a 'handy' (*habiler*) composer: an interestingly circumspect word, more discriminating than Emanuel's (*brafen*) and clearly meant to distinguish between Johann Michael and his brother Johann Christoph, the one called 'profound'.

With her sisters, Maria Barbara Bach had been living in Arnstadt since her mother had died in 1704, probably with the family of the burgomaster, whose wife was her aunt. Some five months older than Sebastian and likewise an orphan, she was related to him, sharing a great-grandfather, Johannes (†1626). Her father Johann Michael was younger brother of the Johann Christoph of Eisenach admired by Sebastian, and is represented by some chorales in the 'Neumeister Collection' and probably influencing Sebastian's early work in the local ways of writing chorales. Johann Michael's are simple settings, harmonizing and playing with the melodies in such a way as to leave them clear and unconfusing for the congregations. Some may have been circulating soon after he died in 1694; or perhaps early in his Arnstadt years Sebastian was shown some by his daughter Maria Barbara. (Either way, chorales atributed to Sebastian in the Neumeister Collection could still be teenage compositions, and some of them could have confused the Arnstadt congregation.) The truth about the situation here – dates, attributions, personal contacts – is, as usual, elusive, but a distinct possibility is that Sebastian and Maria Barbara were well acquainted some years before the marriage.

The ceremony took place two months after Bach received a bequest of fifty guilders from his Erfurt uncle Tobias Lämmerhirt, in memory of whom perhaps the exquisite Cantata 106 was written. This is another sectional work sustained by a keen sense of melody, not least when a typical scoring of the day, like the opening recorders and gambas, is rethought in a style that is becoming increasingly distinctive and way ahead of the Neumeister chorales. The style's hallmarks include consistently short phrases and a marked pulse whatever the metre, with few but telling syncopations. From his alert experience as an organist of chorale-melodies and of ways to treat them, Bach produced the final chorus's charming instrumental paraphrase of the chorale's melody. Much has been made of Cantata 106's well-informed assemblage of texts dealing with time and death, but rather than assume these had some special intensity for the young Bach one might see him striving to do a professional composer's job: to create sweet harmonies and fresh timbres and thereby draw in the listener to attend to the text.

For the wedding to Maria Barbara nothing about the music or any celebrations around it is known, although many members of the greater Bach
family lived within convenient distance. Both the Wedding Cantata 196
and the suggestive Quodlibet, BWV 524 might have been heard at the day's
events, the cantata in the service (or at the Dornheim pastor's own marriage
with another of Maria Barbara's aunts some months later), the quodlibet in
the kind of rowdy family gathering implied in some later reports, when
they wished to draw a picture of a 'human Bach'. But neither is documented. Cantata 196's opening string Sinfonia makes a telling contrast with
those of Cantatas 4 and 106. Its *Affekt* is as marked as theirs had been, with
a bright C major, wide texture, snappy rhythms, close imitation and a
moving bass, as distinct from slow, broken-up chords in the minor (BWV
4) or a gently throbbing, richly textured support for a pair of recorders
(BWV 106). The clear differences between the three cantatas appear to be
calculated by an already experienced speaker of musical language seeking
to apply different dialects for different purposes. Whether each was as isolated (a 'one-off') as it now appears is a tantalizing question, for if they
were, they suggest a composer already unwilling to repeat himself and in
this way too standing out from the norm.

In the years to follow, the children of Sebastian and Maria Barbara Bach
were:

*Catharina Dorothea, Weimar 29 December 1708
*Wilhelm Friedemann, Weimar 22 November (St Cecilia's Day) 1710
Maria Sophia and Johann Christoph, twins, 23 February 1713; did not
    survive
*Carl Philipp Emanuel, Weimar 8 March 1714
Johann Gottfried Bernhard, Weimar 11 May 1715
Leopold Augustus, Cöthen 15 November 1718, died within a year

The Obituary listed the children still living (*) and gave the two sons'
current positions, but no further details. With his first-born child, Bach
seems to have wanted to keep up his original family connections, presumably taking some trouble to contact members: the two godmothers were
the sisters-in-law respectively of his own mother and of himself. If in July
1713 he prepared the motet Anh. III 159 for the funeral at Arnstadt of Maria
Barbara's aunt, as seems possible (BJ 1998, 147), he was keeping up connections there too.

Only a formal document or two casts any light at all on personal matters
within the family. Thus a census reveals that Maria Barbara's elder step-
sister Friedelena Margaretha Bach lived with them, it is thought from about
the time the first child was born in Weimar (Dok II, 39). Like many an

unmarried sister, she was probably housekeeper, remaining so until she died in 1729, well after Bach's second marriage, to be replaced then as housekeeper by Maria Barbara's unmarried daughter Catharina Dorothea. (There was also at least one housemaid, known of by 1721.) How distressing Leopold's and the twins' deaths were, or how comforting Friedelena's presence was, no-one now knows. If, as is possible, on the very day the twins were born and one died, their father was away either in Weissenfels for a performance of Cantata 208 or on his way home from there (Dok II, 45), it would not be surprising if it were still being spoken of during Emanuel's childhood. He knew that his grandfather had a twin brother and in both the Obituary and the genealogy he still reports on how very alike they were – family lore from his father?

LETTERS AND WRITING

Twelve months after he was appointed at Mühlhausen and without waiting for the rebuilt organ to be finished, Bach moved to Weimar, where Maria Barbara gave birth to her first child. He had visited Weimar in June, perhaps by invitation, perhaps not, but in any case at a time when the Weimar court chapel organ was being worked on; and by the 25th of the month, he was writing a formal request for release from Mühlhausen (Dok I, 19–20). A week later his older cousin Johann Friedrich was appointed successor, and the parishioners apparently hoped to pay him less.

Bach's request for release is the document of an astute man, one keen to score more points than was necessary, and perhaps aware that his departure was earlier than decorum required. Thirty-five years later, another organist was still speaking of the 'great chagrin' felt by the Mühlhausen Council at Bach moving on to Weimar (Dok II, 405), and the Obituary itself remarked on the short time he held the post. The council recognized that it could not keep him if he wanted to go but requested he help see through the organ project, which he presumably did at least when returning to present election cantatas in 1709 and again perhaps in 1710. Documentation is missing for any actual organ-dedication, but Bach's request for release ended by expressing willingness to 'contribute further to the service of the church'.

The request, then, speaks first of his gratitude for the Mühlhausen appointment, then of his wish to have been able to create a well-regulated church music (*wohlzufassenden kirchenmusic*) such as he says was then becoming known in every town – though not, he implies, to his satisfaction at Mühlhausen. This must refer to a wish to put on cantatas, for which he needed the larger organ described in a previous section, and which would have been a commitment for the church. His letter expressed an aim of the kind he was to return to in Leipzig many years later, i.e. for a 'well-regulated church music'. The document then goes on to relate ways in which he had performed above the obligations of duty, namely by building a library of the 'choicest cantatas' (*auserleßensten kirchen Stücken*) collected from far and near, and by drawing up the new organ-project.

However, neither was very much above the calls of duty. Organists did draw up organ-projects (who else would?), and at least for musicians in important posts, to build up a collection of 'new pieces of church and other music' was expected. (This was so for the capellmeister of Arnstadt too: see the report in Schiffner 1998, 89). Then Bach twice speaks of meeting 'hindrance' and 'vexation' (*wiedrigkeit, verdriessligkeit*) in his job, despite support from many people in his church, and implies that in any case he needs a position with better pay, such as he has now found elsewhere. These are points of a kind he was to make again later in Leipzig, and imply, in the present case, that his Mühlhausen allowance for rent was inadequate. How crucial the money was, and how far tensions between the town's orthodox and Pietist factions were behind his quick departure, are open to conjecture, but Walther too, one recalls, had found Mühlhausen 'hateful'. By way of further comparison, it is striking that Telemann's request for dismissal from Hamburg, when he was offered the Leipzig job in 1722, is entirely taken up with money: what he now receives, what his costs are, what he needs for a household of eleven or twelve persons, what a suitable payment in salary and kind might be, what provision he needs against any incapacity, etc. (Kremer 1995, 422–3).

Meanwhile, God has brought it about that Bach has an offer at Weimar to be court and chamber musician – he does not say organist, significantly – where he has hopes for a church music of the kind he described. This sounds as if he was expecting to have the opportunity at Weimar for composing cantatas and other ensemble music, though he had to wait another six years for this to be formalized. Was he exaggerating the importance of the position he was going to, as at Arnstadt he had exaggerated the importance of the one he was coming from? If so, for reasons of self-aggrandisement or to reconcile his present employers, either (as he did earlier at Arnstadt) to an unusually high salary or (now at Mühlhausen) to an unexpectedly early departure? 'Chamber musician' at Weimar would be a grander appointment than 'court musician' and indicate membership of a select group producing regular and private music for the duke(s), rather than merely the town of Weimar's ceremonial and public music.

Similarly difficult to measure is the tone of the remark that the 'hindrance' he felt in Mühlhausen shows little sign of lessening, 'although it would delight the souls of this very church' if it did. Is there a desire here to speak on behalf of the congregation he served or to score a point against one or other of the clergy? If he thought that instigating the organ-project was to his credit, perhaps it had not been strictly necessary, resisted even, though for him desirable in the interests of the new kind of music he wanted. This too may have been more than some people wanted, but unfortunately, nothing is known of the music-scores he collected. 'Far and near' could indicate choral music originating in the northern cities, as well as the more local or provincial repertories of Thuringia and the dukedoms of Greater Saxony.

The request for release from Mühlhausen is the earliest autograph document now extant and raises what could be a significant question about the young Bach and his education: was the macaronic style of his formal letters typical more of the time or of himself? The sprinkling of French or Latin words, even in personal letters to his friend Erdmann (see below, p. 274), is more than one finds in letters of Handel or Telemann or Walther, for example. It may well reflect an old-fashioned and relatively limited experience in writing. Future research into Thuringian practices might suggest whether for their more formal writing, organists, particularly those thrust early into the profession, called upon letter-manuals of the kind that are well documented for English-speaking countries of the time. In the Mühlhausen request, it is noticeable that he uses German for negative terms (hindrance, vexation) but French or quasi-French when speaking of what he is trying to achieve (*fasonierten harmonie, apparence*, his *entree* at Weimar). Into his last decade, Latin or latinate headings will regularly accompany certain kinds of music, especially fugues and canons: as *sonata* is Italian (hence the consistent use in his sonatas of the terms *allegro, vivace*, etc.), so *canon* is Latin (hence the rubrics to match).

The partial use of Latin for anything formal or remotely legal was conventional, as in Kuhnau's contemporary letters to the Leipzig city fathers, and constant contact with clergy encouraged this. But in Bach's letters to people in authority, at Halle on 14 January 1714 (about a job for himself) or at Sangerhausen on 18 November 1736 (about a job for one of his sons), it is difficult to see exactly why he uses foreign terms other than as a gesture of wished-for status. Two of many examples taken from them are:

meine *excuse* machen dass anitzo die zeit es ohnmöglich hätte leiden wollen, einige *cathegorische resolution* von mir zu geben . . . (Dok I, 22)
[please] make my excuses that at present, time does not allow [lit. the time had wished to permit no possibility] for me to give any categorical decision

Eu: HochEdlen mit Dero vielgültigen *recommendation* u. *intercession* vor das *in mente* habende *subject* . . . (Dok I, 93)
your Honour, with so invaluable a recommendation and intercession on behalf of the person [I am] having in mind . . .

Various inferences about the care Bach gave his writing can be drawn from the extant letters and testimonials. A testimonial only signed by him includes macaronic touches that were, one assumes, actually dictated (Dok I, 127). The huge number of royal titles he appends (or in two cases, has his copyist append) in letters to the Elector of Saxony, three times in 1725 and again in 1737, leaves one to suppose he preserved a careful note of them for such purposes. His own well-known and beautiful monogram JSB, known first from a letter-seal of March 1722 (Dok IV, 168), shows a similar degree of careful deliberation. Like paper-makers with their watermarks, Leipzig engraver-publishers were fond of the contrived symmetry of such elegant designs, as with the initials FMF and JTB on documents illustrated in Neumann 1974 (pp. 318 and 350). The JTB monogram is strikingly close to the JSB, which indeed is a good deal more legible than some other monograms in early eighteenth-century Saxony, such as one of about 1710 in the wrought-iron screen in Schwarzenberg Town Church. Perhaps for Bach the idea originated through court personnel in Cöthen – hence the 'capellmeistership' crown? – although many years previously Johann Christoph had had an octagonal design incorporating J C B (Spitta I, 38). A special way of writing 'J S Bach' that appears on the Calov Bible titlepage (see p. 317), arose presumably because the JSB seal-monogram is impossible to write freehand?

Of course, the various foreign terms convey some wished-for *politesse*, but sometimes there is also a touch of foggy euphemism about them, such as one might employ around sensitive personal issues. Thus at Halle, he needed to explain why he had not signed the offer already sent in duplicate (*vocation in duplo*); at Sangerhausen, he was writing on behalf of a less than totally reliable son when he asks for a special *Faveur*. In 1730, he asks his friend Erdmann, who was not a musician, if he knows of a 'suitable job' (*convenable station*) for him in Danzig. In a letter of 1729 to a former pupil, French terms appear to give an ironic touch: he would be *reellement* grateful to be paid, and he hopes to be *capable* of being of service, which he would prove with all *dexterité* (Dok I, 57). In a nineteen-word receipt of 1747, three Latinate terms give it the wished-for formality (see Dok I, 204), like the 'p. t.' by his name on receipts he signed at Arnstadt as a young professional (? *per titulum*, 'by title').

Most of Handel's few extant letters are completely in French, including those to Mattheson and Telemann, to whom a letter of 1754 presumably had to be dictated (HHB, 483). Whether certain exceptional writings of Bach are his own unaided work – the French dedication of 1721 to the Brandenburg Concertos, the German verse for the young Prince of Cöthen in 1726 – is unknown, but they are presumed not to be. Yet the final reference to himself in the Brandenburg dedication as *moi qui suis avec un zele sans pareil* (Dok, I p. 217) is certainly telling the truth, and conforms to his other salutations. The following generation was taught a less self-conscious German, poets were consciously creating a literary language, and it is so that by 1747, when Bach writes the formal dedication of the Musical Offering to Frederick the Great, the only foreign term he uses is *Thema*, which has no obvious vernacular

CHAPTER 3

Weimar, 1708–17

In the following year, 1708, a visit he made to Weimar, and the opportunity he had there to be heard before the then Duke, led to the position of Chamber- and Court-Organist being offered him, of which he took possession straightway. (*Obituary*)

Does this mean that according to family lore it was by chance that Bach was heard by the duke? This would excuse him for taking another job so soon – or, for the readers of Walther's *Lexicon* biography, explain the date it gives for one job (1707) being so close to that of another (1708). By convention, the court-position he was offered would necessarily be as 'organist', but duties would not be exclusively in chapel or on the organ, rather those of a 'general keyboard-player': the Obituary's sentence need not even imply that it was (only) on the organ that he played for the duke.

There was nothing unusual in musicians visiting ducal and other courts hoping to be heard, and a gifted young organist from an important church in the Free Imperial City of Mühlhausen had much in his favour. Yet while a duke would appoint without the need to invite applications, hold auditions in public or have candidates vetted by committees, a post could not have been offered unless it was vacant or about to become so. This suggests one of two things: either that the 'visit he made to Weimar' was undertaken in the knowledge that the court organist Johann Effler was near to retiring; or that in visiting Weimar in the summer of 1708, perhaps officially or unofficially to inspect work on the organ (work completed 16 June), he learnt of Effler's intentions, put himself forward as succcessor and was auditioned there and then by the senior or junior duke. Emanuel would not know the full story.

The recent marriage and impending fatherhood must have made better pay desirable, and it is quite possible that Maria Barbara's condition had prompted him to look to Weimar. Or there were disagreements with his pastor in Mülhausen, J. A. Frohne, a defender of Pietism, on what constituted a 'well-regulated' ensemble music in an important church. Or there were personal tensions between the two main churches' clergy themselves, even perhaps a particular falling out that year over a cantata for June 24, St John's day (Petzoldt 2000, 187). Or Bach did not get on well with the town's instrumentalists and preferred a court's music-making to that of a parish church. Certainly the musical potential in Weimar was higher, and for Bach, promotion never led to less work or freed him from that inner drive to compose and perform. 'Chamber and court organist' meant participating in a wide repertory, even in the theatre if the occasion ever arose, and participating included composing as well as playing. Neverthless, it is the case that he, like clergymen, was called by God only to higher positions, and the request for dismissal from Mühlhausen has touches of self-excuse and disingenuousness, or at least of a barb or two thrown by one who was departing.

THE WEIMAR APPOINTMENT

Though much smaller than Mühlhausen, Weimar was a notable German 'residence city', seat of an absolute ruler, a domain subject less to powerful clergy and elected officials and more to the will of the reigning dukes. It was a city in whose cultural life music featured high, judging by a succession of well-known musicians who had worked there: M. Vulpius, J. H. Schein, Schütz (for a short time) and J. G. Walther, as well as Bach himself some years previously. (Much later in Weimar, Bach seems to have been largely forgotten. George Eliot, who stayed there in the 1850s and wrote a long essay on Weimar, mentions neither Bach nor the then-reigning duke's musician, Franz Liszt.) But whatever the reasons for leaving Mühlhausen, personal and professional contacts there did not cease. The Marienkirche's archdeacon and his daughter were each a godparent to Bach's first two children, and his election cantata of 1709 again had its text and music printed (no extant copy). Also, years later he was welcomed when accompanying his son Johann Gottfried Bernhard on the boy's successful application at the Marienkirche in 1735. It looks very much as if he had always had better relations in Mühlhausen with people at the Marienkirche than at his own church.

Having 'the opportunity to be heard by the duke' in Weimar, presumably in the court chapel rather than town church, sounds like suing for patronage, and he must have made a good impression as he played (or was invited as a colleague by the organist Effler to try) the organ then being worked on. As already noted, young Handel too had been 'heard' by a duke as he played, and this also was on the organ in a palace chapel. Moreover, as with Bach in Weimar, the story was one presumably told by Handel himself in later years. Clearly, it was a standard way of obtaining a ruler's attention, in Handel's case not yet for a job but for patronage or sponsorship. Louis Marchand had 'the honour to be heard' by Louis XIV and dedicated his *Premier Livre* to him in 1702, but still had six years to wait for royal appointment. (This foreshadows the more than three years Bach waited for royal appointment in Dresden in the 1730s.) J. P. Kellner, an important copyist of Bach manuscripts in the mid-1720s, reports in his autobiography of being heard while still at student age by several princes 'on command', presumably having sought their interest first.

At Weimar, the duke must have acted fast, as he was entitled to do, for by 20 June Bach's salary was approved and he was paid as for the second quarter of 1708, at a rate nearly double that at Mühlhausen. On 14 July, perhaps at his request, he also received an *ex gratia* payment of ten guilders on entering service – the phrase used in connection with the payment, *zum Anzugs-Gelde* ('for clothing money': Dok II, 35), probably refers to court dress expenses: Bach wore uniform. As at any court, hiring and firing of employees was not an open process, and the duke's appointment specifies little more than terms of salary, including payment in kind (corn, barley and beer allowances: Küster 1996, 186–7). The accounts also list allowances for firewood and coal, but as for good behaviour and obedience – a duke had no need to specify.

The payment of 14 July 1708 implies that by then the Bachs (Maria Barbara pregnant with Catharina Dorothea) were resident in Weimar, and also that his successor in Mühlhausen was already in place. The new 'chamber and court organist' was much better paid than most parish church organists and indeed his predecessors at the Weimar court, with a substantial salary-rise in 1711, and again on promotion in March 1714. There were also miscellaneous fees for extra events, for keeping the harpsichords in order, teaching *Clavier* to the duke's page, and for engagements beyond Weimar (organ-testing in Taubach, visit to Weissenfels, etc.). The Bachs seem to have lived in a fellow court-musician's house, at least until 1713; and by March 1709, perhaps from July 1708, Friedelena was living with them (see above, p. 64). In the professional sphere, one particularly kindred spirit at court, so one may guess, was the volinist J. G. Pisendel, composer of some solo violin music, the detail of whose personal influence on Bach, if any, one would very much like to know. There may also have been good contact with Telemann, then working in Eisenach but with feelers in many places. Emanuel said that in his youth his father was often with Telemann, (Dok III, 289), and whether or not this implies they became personally estranged later, it was probably in Telemann's music that Bach continued to learn what was fashionable, such as (in Leipzig) new types of music in 2/4 time or even words such as *scherzo*.

Also resident in Weimar from the year before was Bach's relative J. G. Walther, teacher of one of the scions of the ducal house, Prince Johann Ernst, and organist of the Town Church, the church to whose parish the young Bach family probably belonged and in which their Weimar children were baptised. Why Walther rather than Bach taught the young prince is unknown but may be the result of tensions in the ducal family: Johann Ernst was a member of the junior family, not Bach's employer, the reigning duke's. The range of godparents for Maria Barbara's children, three each, implies a wide circle of acquaintance in the town and the province. Bach too stood as godfather, to a son each of Walther (1712), of his own brother Christoph (1713), of the court organ-builder (H. N. Trebs, 1713), and a musical colleague in Weissenfels (A. I. Weldig, master of the pages, and Emanuel's godfather), while Maria Barbara stood for the daughters of a Weimar court trumpeter and of Sebastian's pupil Ziegler.

Although by 1708 Maria Barbara had her own (box-)pew in the court chapel, behind the capellmeister's wife, it is possible that the family also had its own pew in the town church for services at other times. A connection between the two organists Bach and Walther can be guessed by their evident and shared interest in particular methods of composition, especially the creating of chorales around little note-patterns, the *figurae* (qv) in much use by German organists at the time. Doubtless less self-reliant than his cousin, Walther seems to have been a much more prolific copyist of other people's organ-music, and possessed a great deal in manuscript. To judge by French, Italian and German works which they each owned or copied at the time, they also shared an interest in Palestrina and the old Latin contrapuntal styles (see BJ 2002, 17. How unusual this was is difficult to know, since so often it was Bach's name appearing in MS albums that led to some of them surviving into the age of antiquarian collectors and then public libraries.) Other acquaintances of theirs in Weimar, such as J. C. Vogler, also copied French music as they did, and in the same spirit of external inspiration the young prince himself was to compose concertos imitating Vivaldi with a musical competence rare for a teenage nobleman, if not totally unique.

The title of 'chamber musician', in addition to 'court organist', indicated duties in the general music-making at court, as member of a *cappella* of fourteen musicians, to whom were added a pool of seven trumpeters and timpanist as occasion required. Whether Bach's duties included playing harpsichord solos in court concerts is not documented, nor exactly what the works were in which he presumably did participate: solo sonatas (playing *continuo* with violin, gamba, recorder or oboe soloists), string and mixed trios, broken consort music for wind, strings and keyboard (works Italians called *concerti*). Another question is whether the set of parts Bach himself seems to have copied for the Anonymous St Mark Passion a few years into his Weimar job (the 'Keiser/Brauns' oratorio) records a performance he put on, in the chapel or somewhere else. If so, this was probably his largest performance to date – or if not performed, was meant to be so – and had been completed with some added new movements, in a chamber setting for a small group of performers: SATB, two violins, two violas, oboe and harpsichord. The added movements (two *bicinium* arias qv, recitative, instrumental prelude and fugue) are those of a still young composer using and adding to music from elsewhere, interested in ways to write for voices and instruments and making a new whole piece for local performance – a procedure more generally, and for much longer, familiar to Handel.

On other occasions, the six male singers and a handful of string and wind players made various chamber-like groups in various combinations possible, especially if or when other soloists joined them. The potential must have enthralled a young musician with such latent creative powers, one by no means monopolized by keyboard music, whether for pupils or for the duke's chapel. There seems every reason to suppose that the Weimar musicians built on the tradition for mixed consorts to create newer works in a wide variety of instrumental combinations. Various of these mixed consorts are glimpsed in several Weimar cantatas, fresh springs from which the mighty stream of Brandenburg Concertos issued later. Cantata 18 uses four solo violas for a sound and texture essentially old-fashioned, yet it also includes an example of the new recitativo secco with little sign of experimentation or novelty, except perhaps in the shortness of phrase. Example 5 already includes both a characteristic change of pace and *en passant* underlining of important words ('falls', 'fructify', modulation at 'Word').

One cannot be sure that such colourful cantatas were performed only in chapel or as part of chapel services. The cantatas that Bach was to write at Weimar seem to respond to the consort tradition, not only in their varied instrumental groups and a chamber-like choir (soloists?) but with a lightness of touch in melody and timbre that remained distinct from the later cantatas for Leipzig. At the same time, writing recitative in a cantata was

5 Cantata 18.ii
'Just as the rain and snow fall from heaven, and do not
persist but fructify the earth, making it fertile and increasing
so that it gives seeds to sow and bread to eat, so should the Word . . .'

itself a way of linking or reconciling 'church sounds' with 'chamber sounds',
as it had been for several generations of German composers.

The works being produced respond to a conception developing for the
Protestant cantata at the end of the seventeenth century as a result of newer
kinds of poetry, celebrated in Erdmann Neumeister's librettos published
separately in 1700 and gathered as a yearly cycle in 1704. His title of 1700,
Geistliche Cantaten statt einer Kirchenmusik (approximately 'spiritual cantatas in the place of a church anthem'), uses the word *cantata* in order to
allude directly to Italian chamber cantatas and their short sequence of arias
(poetry) and recitatives (prose). Any additional movements, such as instrumental overture, big choral movement and final chorale, were quite alien to
the Italian conception of cantatas, as of course were any chorale-melodies
introduced at any point within them. But the cantata-texts themselves, often
published and treated as self-contained poetry, could be musically realized
as recitatives, arias and choruses with biblical sentences; an appropriate

chorale could be added at the end if one was not included in the poetic text; and in general, the newly written texts would naturally encourage a 'theatrical' style of music at a certain moment in services otherwise filled with music of older kinds.

The court chapels of Meiningen and Weissenfels soon worked with such texts – at Weissenfels, the composer J. P. Krieger may have set them complete – but they were already criticized in 1709–10 as *theatralische Music* by the influential Leipzig cantor Kuhnau (DDT 58–59, xlii), a criticism reflecting the differences recognized at the time between court chapels and parish churches. But while the idea of such so-called madrigalian texts was given impetus by the cosmopolitan practices of royal Dresden, Neumeister supplied ready examples for the composer of any court or, eventually, of any parish church, especially texts of his from 1710 onwards that mixed biblical words and chorales with the new poetry. It is possible that at Mühlhausen Bach already had such settings in mind, but in any case from now on he seems often to have deliberately chosen Neumeister texts or those that had a similar way of poetically paraphrasing and incorporating biblical words.

The nearly ten years Bach spent at Weimar saw a huge development of deep, creative originality. In particular, the part played in church and especially chamber music by his growing experience in writing for instruments had long-lasting results. Although the sources do not show it, some instrumental music known in arrangements for Leipzig church cantatas (Nos. 146, 156, 188, 35) or as Leipzig harpsichord concertos (the D minor Solo BWV 1052, the C major Triple BWV 1064) may have originated in other guises and for other forces in Weimar concerts during Bach's later years there. Doubts sometimes expressed about the authenticity of strikingly original works like the C major Triple Concerto may reflect only the uncertainties over its original form, and therefore its date in the composer's worklist: no other composer of either *c.* 1715 or *c.* 1735 springs to mind as likely to have created its first movement's originality and amalgam of subtle counterpoint, extrovert rhythms, purposeful harmony and pleasing melody.

Sources and versions do not exist to clarify the history of such works, which is a great pity since only with them could one trace the composer's maturing style in his late twenties. A little clearer is his evolving conception of slow movements with prominent solos. Those prefacing the Weimar cantatas Nos. 12, 21 and 182 do not seem to me to owe much to Italian concertos but rather result from an imaginative composer's building on earlier German consort music, such as the *Sonatina* that prefaces Cantata 106. Nor, more importantly perhaps, can one be certain what the expressive or emotional impact of such slow movements was expected to be. The likelier that the well-known and bewitching *Largo* of the F minor Harpsichord Concerto, BWV 1056 derives from imitating a Telemannesque woodwind concerto of the Weimar period (see p. 244), the likelier that its later scoring in Leipzig – pizzicato strings in A flat major, with a *cantabile* harpsichord solo – was the result of aiming at a newer and more striking *Affekt* than originally. What was originally charming, light and fresh becomes more solemnly beautiful, prompting reflection, touching listeners at a more public concert.

In such pieces as these Vivaldi's influence (discussed further below) is certainly to be heard, and yet the effect is quite distinct: the spirit and even some details of the F minor *Largo* come closer to those in one or two of the Weimar organ-chorales than they do to any Venetian concerto. In the various discussions of what it was that Bach learnt in Weimar from Italian concertos, in particular what it was their brilliant ritornello movements taught him (see pp. 89f), it is easy to forget how revelatory the seductive lyricism of the better Venetian *slow* movements must also have been to him. Those of two concerto-transcriptions attributed to Bach, BWV 973 (Vivaldi) and BWV 974 (Alessandro Marcello), have a simple but stunning melos that one can suppose to have been quite as admired by him as any other characteristic of the Venetian concertos. The latter especially has a few changes-of-direction (interrupted cadences) that would be so imaginatively applied by Bach in one or two of his own concertos.

Such slow movements are surely the progenitors not only of several slow movements in Bach's concertos but also of a mature aria like 'Aus Liebe' in the St Matthew Passion. Similarly, that hard-to-define yearning quality one can sometimes sense behind the Vivaldian *Allegro* of a concerto like BWV 975 (see Example 6) surfaces again in works like the double concertos in D minor and C minor, BWV 1043 and 1060.

At the same time, the 'extrovert' tonic repetitions opening BWV 980 – the opposite of intricate counterpoint – could easily have inspired the more complex, throbbing reiterations at the beginning of Brandenburg Concertos Nos. 3 and 6. And then there are Vivaldi's 'preparatory chromaticisms': the sudden switch to the minor, or the sudden appearance of a chromatic chord, just before a cadence. The momentary colour introduced in this way continued to be seized upon by Bach in all kinds music, including fugues and canons.

Something further implied by such transcriptions as BWV 980 and 975 is that opening movements require a stately tempo, whether in 4/4 or 2/4. Either Bach assumed from the first that an Italian *allegro* was slower, less *dashing* than the Italians did, or he required a steadier interpretation of

6 Concerto (after Vivaldi), BWV 975.i, b. 23
(NB an early instance of Italian 2/4 metre in works of Bach)

string music when played on keyboard. Such a steadier tempo would be of a kind traditional in Germany, the 'standard 4/4' found in organ music of the previous generation. Today, in looking for bright, fast tempi through-out Vivaldi, our 'historically informed performers' will transfer the same approach to the Brandenburgs and solo concertos, driving them at a speed quite out of sympathy with taste and practice of the time.

Differences between Italian and French idioms would have interested a lively young composer at a ducal court employing good musicians, as is clear not only from the Weimar cantatas but also the later solo works for violin. Whether or how well Bach played such solos himself is not known, though his violin-playing is unlikely to have been neglected at Weimar and could have developed very well at this time, something the Obituary authors are unlikely to have known. In 1713 his pupil P. D. Kräuter wrote about the French and Italian music being heard at court, following Prince Johann Ernst's recent return from Holland with a trunkload of music, and claimed to be working on these styles with his teacher, J. S. Bach (Dok III, 650), both of which are likely to have involved some style-conscious violin-study. The Obituary was not alone in establishing its subject's credentials in French styles, something much valued outside church if not always within it. Especially in Weimar by *c.* 1715, there was ample opportunity for a wide repertory, and it could well be that the reason so little is certain about it is something quite mundane: that the scores, both for the chamber and for the chapel music, were the duke's property, kept in his library and not allowed to be copied, were later neglected, discarded and finally burnt in the fire of 1774 that destroyed the castle and its library. The paper itself on which the finished court music was written and the parts copied certainly belonged to the duke (see Dok II, 56), and one of the unknowns is to what extent the composer had his own stock of paper or had a right to the duke's. A likely arrangement is that he kept full scores of his cantatas, for later use or revision; the same with chamber music, though some may have been 'blank' scores ready for adapting to requirements; and keyboard music remained in drafted and re-drafted form before being finalized, if it ever were, in a set of pieces or for a particular purpose.

WEIMAR ORGAN COMPOSITION

His gracious lord's delight in his playing fired him to attempt everything possible in the art of how to treat the organ. Here, he also wrote most of his organ works [*Orgelstücke*]. (*Obituary*)

There must be several reasons why the Obituary so emphasizes the organ: its music was still in wider circulation than other Bach works, chamber and vocal music of 1715 was largely superseded, the authors knew little else of what was produced at Weimar, and the very uniqueness of the bigger organ pieces impressed itself on such later writers.

It is not clear which of the two Weimar dukes Emanuel is referring to, Wilhelm Ernst the senior or Ernst August the junior (his nephew), and perhaps he was unsure. The former was the controlling authority of funds and personnel, as events were to prove, but in 1775 Emanuel cited the latter as having particularly supported his father (Dok III, 289). It was also Ernst August's own father who had employed Bach for a time in 1703, as part of re-building the musical establishment, and it was his own younger half-brother Prince Johann Ernst whose string works are found amongst Bach's transcriptions. But whichever duke it was that Bach impressed, Emanuel is silent on one intractable problem of life in Weimar: the two dukes lived in such mutual enmity and territorial rivalry as would inevitably involve the chapel musicians one way or another, leaving those favoured by one to be discriminated against by the other. The atmosphere does not sound easy, and may account for several events outlined in the present chapter.

The situation does give some idea of life in an absolutist ruler's court. Shortly before Bach's arrival, the senior duke had decreed that the *cappella* musicians were not to play in the junior duke's residence without his permission, on pain of a fine and incarceration (Glöckner 1988, 137). The decree was re-issued two years after Bach's departure, presumably because it had been defied – during Bach's tenure? – and the conditions were then even stricter: the musicians were not even allowed to discuss the matter. In

response, the junior duke tried to compel them to choose to be his retain-
ers as well, failing which they would forfeit any payments they (like Bach)
had had from him, a forfeit which he would pursue through their children
and children's children. Although by then Bach was not involved, the contentious situation at court has some bearing on his problematic release in
1717, throws some light on his incarceration and raises questions about two
particular visits he had made: to Weissenfels in 1713 and to Halle for the
vacant organist's post later the same year (see below).

Given that Bach had virtuoso ability as a keyboardist and explored
each kind of organ music farther than any predecessor, continuing to do so
even when cantor and no longer a regular organist, it is still puzzling that
neither part of the Obituary, Emanuel's or Agricola's, acknowledges the
strides he must also have taken in chamber and harpsichord music, certainly in the later Weimar years. At Leipzig, did he never speak of having
taken a leading part in the duke's concert-life? Was he learning 'how to treat
the organ', the composer's own phrase in later years, when describing his
priorities at that period? Does Emanuel have in mind his father's obvious
advances in certain playing and composing techniques, such as the sophisticated dialoguing in his trios or the concert-like, monumental preludes
and fugues? He would know the sheer range of effect achieved between a
succinct chorale of nine bars (BWV 602) and a big toccata of more than
400 (BWV 540). The very size of a work like the Passacaglia or the variations on chorales is demonstrating 'how to treat the organ'. Does the
Obituary say nothing about the achievement in cantatas, solo string works,
harpsichord music, because these came after 'attempting everything possible' with organ music – because the first music he developed beyond
precedents was indeed for organ?

With the duke's approval and at his cost, the chapel organ was being
improved and enlarged over several years, in and out of commission over
1707–9 and again from June 1712 to May 1714 (Schrammek 1988). It could
never become very grand, placed where it was, and its sound must always
have been somewhat indirect in the chapel, if not actually dull or indistinct.
For it was located high in a sort of attic chamber 20m above the chapel-
floor, occupying the space around a small balustraded opening in the
ceiling, 4m × 3m, through which it sounded down into the rectangular
chapel. This, some 30m long and 12m wide, was occupied on the ground
floor and two running galleries not by a parish congregation but by court
personnel, who looked towards a liturgical east-end structure that was itself
not unlike a stage-set. This consisted of (in a vertical line) step, altar
rail, altar table, baldacchino, pulpit, an obelisk pointing up to 'heaven's

opening', then the attic gallery balustrade, some way behind it the organ, and finally a fresco in the domed ceiling above. Although documentary reference to some seats in the attic gallery conveys a picture of the singers and instrumentalists stationed there during services or rehearsals, whether they always performed from on high in this way is open to doubt.

The organ, the peak of the east end's *scena* or 'path to heaven', was not at the gallery front but back against its east wall, with bass pipes and bellows-chamber at the very back. In 1658 it had one manual only, which probably was all that could be accomodated comfortably; but then a second was added, its chest placed to the side and played presumably with a complicated action that might never have worked very well. Shortly before Bach was appointed, improvement was made to the organ by relocating the side-chest under the main chest. How room was made for this is hard to guess, but it probably made further work of improvement inevitable; this was done during Bach's term of office and resulted in an enlarged chamber being made for the organ, with the bigger bass pipes at the back. A row of tuned bells was also made (positioned just behind the music-desk, to be played by the pedals?), and the whole organ now comprised about two dozen stops – not a great inspiration or even means of realizing the new ideas he brought to organ-music. If after being in Weimar for five or six years he worked more with cantatas and chamber music, was this a natural development or a turning away from the organ?

Quite why Bach thought – as it seems he did – that as at Mühlhausen, the Weimar organ needed a row of bells, which were acquired at some cost from Nuremberg, is never explained, and one can only assume that they sounded at certain jolly moments, during chorales at Christmas and other festive times. Did he pick out the melody of 'In dulci jubilo' or the bass of 'Christ is risen' with his feet working the hammers? When an organist writing in 1742 specifically mentions Bach having a Glockenspiel installed at Mühlhausen (Dok II, 405), he is recalling something that must have been common knowledge. The tangible result of all this organ-building was that the music produced by Bach surveys a range of styles wider and on a bigger scale than had ever been achieved before by any organist in any European tradition, offering every subsequent composer a model to emulate as best he can. The duke may have 'fired him up' (*feuerte ihn an*) but many a court organist strove to please, and in Bach's case there must also have been an extraordinary creative urge, immense practical ability matched by permanent curiosity and untiring industry.

The Obituary's remark on the duke may serve another purpose: it may be a gracious acknowledgment from the composer but it also bears on the poorer support given him later in Leipzig. What is unclear is exactly the purpose of organ-music – for voluntaries before and after the service, or as items for private ducal concerts, or even demonstrations of the duke's new instrument (and of his star employee) for his visitors? A ruler of such known piety as the Duke of Weimar might well take pleasure in special organ-music being played in his own chapel by a gifted and well-paid employee, although compared to other court-chapels in that part of the world (Weissenfels, Eisenberg, Saalfeld) the Weimar chapel and its organ were not strikingly grand or impressive. Whether the organist played after the services as the congregation retired is uncertain, but if he did, there was a choice of toccatas, fugues, improvisations, eventually the transcribed concertos, and exceptional mixed genres such as a Fantasia on the Whit hymn. By now, all of these have become 'genuine' organ-works, distinguished from earlier music that had suited any keyboard instrument more or less equally.

To what extent the works as we know them represent the composer's improvisations or are a distinct kind of deliberated, written-down music is not clear from the phrase 'everything possible in the art of how to treat the organ'. Certainly he was expanding the organists' repertory to take in genres (trios) and forms (ritornello) that were primarily associated with other kinds of music, i.e. sonatas and concertos; so he was in cantatas, and such music could result only after deliberation, at most merely initiated by improvisations. A supposedly early work such as the 'Toccata and Fugue in D minor', BWV 565 might give an idea of what some organists could improvise with a few rhetorical gestures, thin harmonies, simple shape, much repetition and virtually no counterpoint. But too little is demonstrably reliable or even authentic about this famous piece for it to have anything certain to do with, or to say anything certain about, the young organist J. S. Bach.

Although it is clear that Bach did develop organ toccatas into big, subtle, fully worked concerto-like movements, tracing the steps in this evolution remains guesswork, for the dates of the various versions these works went through are still often quite uncertain. That seems to have been true for much of what he produced: early works such as the Albinoni fugues are as likely to have been revised, rewritten, and circulated in various states as the later big preludes and fugues were. So many works were as living, mutating organisms. How unusual Bach's practice was in this respect in impossible to know, since no comparable fund of sources exists for any other composer, and nor are all versions now known likely to be authentic. A further problem complicating chronology arises from the very originality:

thus the G major Praeludium, BWV 541 begins like an improvisation but continues as a highly organized movement, and is hard to imagine being improvised as a whole even by J. S. Bach, unmatched in the work of any other composer and difficult to date because of its sheer panache. A Fantasia in the same key (BWV 572) is more likely to represent the kind of music that Bach improvised in his late twenties, indeed for the delight of his duke in Weimar, either on organ or on harpsichord.

One particular question about all the keyboard music is how often Bach paired a prelude with a particular fugue to make a complementary pair on paper or in performance. This is less certain than supposed by anyone relying on later editions that do pair them, or, with the Well-tempered Clavier in mind, forgetting that even here, the earliest known versions of many of its preludes did not accompany fugues. Nevertheless, once the idea of a pair became familiar, and was already emerging in publications by J. K. F. Fischer and others, pairing must have seemed natural, not least in vocal music when the prelude was short and preceded a substantial fugue, whether in an early work (Cantata 131) or a late (Kyrie, B minor Mass). Nor ought players today assume that a fugue has to be 'bigger' than its prelude: the opposite is the case with many pairs.

There also remains the big question why in connection with Weimar nothing is said in the Obituary about harpsichord music, solo or otherwise. Because more-or-less public organ music was the duke's prime concern, and it suited the Obituary's picture of the great organ virtuoso? Or if it was not the organist's duty (nor anyone else's) to play harpsichord music in public, so it was slower to develop? The simplest answer is again that harpsichord and chamber music had moved on more than organ music, and while the latter was being copied, re-copied and studied by all the pupils (including both Obituary authors), chamber music from Weimar is less likely to have been. Such early chamber works as survived did so because of being re-used in other forms, in a few instances even as organ music.

The curiosity one can confidently attribute to Bach is suggested by other music he knew during his earlier Weimar years. Concertos of Albinoni and Telemann (Concerto in G, Bach's copy of *c.* 1709), masses by Peranda and others (see p. 107), organ and harpsichord works of Grigny and Dieupart, and a full Passion from Hamburg (the Anonymous St Mark), all copied or mined for material and no doubt part of a once larger fund of works – and one that continued to be added to for the rest of his life. The musical quality of these items varies, suggesting that his self-teaching was serendipitous and eclectic. He came to own copies not only of contemporary Thuringian music but of at least three important organ publications originating far from Weimar: the volumes of Ammerbach's *Tabulaturbuch* (Leipzig, 1571), Frescobaldi's *Fiori musicali* (Venice, 1635), and the MS copy he made of Grigny's *Livre d'orgue* (Paris, 1699/1700). Three exemplars, possibly more, of the Ammerbach seem to have been in his possession, and who knows what other imported volumes of the Frescobaldi kind there once were? Exactly how he got to know the Frescobaldi and Grigny publications is a guess, but the channel by which they reached Weimar could have been J. G. Walther, who habitually corresponded with other musicians. He too began a copy of the Grigny *Livre*, independently of Bach, and probably a little later.

Traces of Frescobaldi or Grigny in Bach's own music are seldom obvious. The former may have influenced much of his mature counterpoint, but nowhere does he keep strictly to Grigny's manner of writing for the organ. Did copying not lead him to grasp the beauty of the French styles, especially solos for the left hand? Or did he think their peculiar lyricism too indulgent for Lutheran chorales, Lutheran organists, Lutheran congregations? At other times, the thoroughness of his explorations of style or layout comes close to the pedantic. As if 'tidying up' the loose counterpoint of French duos, the Four Duets in Clavierübung III systematically include, without overstepping the confines of the chosen genre, varieties of pulse, metre, time signature, mode, key, form, imitation, counterpoint, motif, chromaticism/diatonicism etc., as if each was a pre-planned item, ticked off on a list of 'things to do'. Conceivably, an upbringing far from obvious musical centres left Bach both exceptionally curious and exceptionally determined, sometimes sacrificing the expressivity most people expect from music for the sake of some theoretical concept.

It is easy to miss the subtle signs of other composers' influence. For example, the seven exquisite Advent and Christmas Fughettas are more likely to have been prompted by the perfect little fughettas in Frescobaldi's *Fiori musicali* than by duller work of later German organists. Similarly, *Fiori*'s final Bergamasca is quite likely to be lurking behind the last of the Goldberg Variations, No 30, more so than is any other composer's theme. If the composition of these Fughettas and the Goldberg Variations belongs to much the same period, *c.* 1740, they would imply that the quality of Frescobaldi's book remained impressed on Bach for decades after he acquired a copy at Weimar in 1714 – and justifiably so. That he was still voicing admiration for Frescobaldi during the 1740s might explain why Emanuel came to single him out when speaking of otherwise unnamed foreign influences on his father.

OTHER DEVELOPMENT IN WEIMAR

The Obituary emphasizes Bach the virtuoso organist, but musical life in Weimar was fuller, so varied in its creative output as to suggest not only a hugely active life as performer of his own and the court's music but also as a serious student of styles from further afield.

A fundamental part is played in all of Bach's maturing work, instrumental and vocal, by his mastery of invertible counterpoint (qv), which generates virtually any kind of music, from cantata movements to the last keyboard works, from organ-chorales to the later Inventions, from a Mühlhausen cantata to the B minor Mass. With this mastery, different themes can be combined with a bass line, which is itself melodious in its own way, to produce the lightest, brightest *Affekt* (see Example 7 (a), re-composed as Example 7 (b)); or a canon can be made to work by dint of strange lines convincing the ear that all is well (Example 7 (c)). Examples 7 (a) and 7 (c) belong to much the same period (1712–13) and are quite typical. The German organist's custom of making canons at the octave from the melodies of Advent or Christmas hymns is clearly going to be challenged more severely by some melodies than others, and Example 7 (c) ('Gottes Sohn ist kommen') required ingenuity if the canon was to work, i.e. to make us think that the lines occur naturally.

Some earlier techniques, such as creating a set of hymn-variations by basing each one on a conventional note-pattern, barely survived into the Weimar period, and one can understand why. In 1802, Forkel claimed that Bach found writing sets of variations a 'thankless task' (p. 52), because of their reiterated harmony. Perhaps Emanuel or Friedemann had told him so, or Forkel assumed it from their rarity in the Bach oeuvre in comparison with Handel's or Mozart's, with which by then he was familiar. The remark does not quite do justice, however, to the way a chorale might be re-harmonized several times in a Passion or cantata, as if in its way a set of variations: for harmony can be varied as well as melody. All the same, there could be some truth in what Forkel said, and one notes that the four big, outstanding and indeed unique variation-works composed over more than thirty years – Cantata 4 for voices, the Passacaglia for organ, the Chaconne for violin, the Goldberg for harpsichord – do everything but reiterate the harmony in some simplistic way.

For his picture of a serious composer, Emanuel described the Weimar job in terms of organ music and, after his father was promoted as *Concert-Meister* in 1714, 'mainly church pieces' or cantatas. And yet of huge importance to Bach, something even changing the direction much of his music

7 a Cantata 208 (1713?).xiii, b. 5
   b Cantata 68 (1725).ii, b. 5
   c Organ chorale, BWV 600, b. 9

was to take, was his acquaintance in 1713 with the new instrumental concertos from Venice. Whether or not this was as sudden as evidence now
suggests, the vivid and seductive effect of these spectacular pieces, perhaps
glimpsed already in isolated examples making their way north, can be
imagined: a voracious, energetic composer in his late twenties suddenly gets
to know Vivaldi's *L'Estro armonico*. A revelation! The closer he kept to tradition in his organ and harpsichord music, the more startling must have
been 'Vivaldian effect', even when first viewed on paper.

When the young Prince Johann Ernst returned from a stay in Holland
in July (?) 1713, with copies of music by Vivaldi and other Italians, probably including Corelli and even Frescobaldi, the string concertos he
brought most likely took the form of sets of playing parts. There is good

reason to suppose that the prince's teacher Walther and the court key-boardist Bach soon had them on their music desks ready to play, or on their writing desks ready to score up. How aware Bach was that at the same period in the Protestant Netherlands one could hear such Italian concertos being played on the organ in certain public recitals is unknown, as is any wish the young prince may have had to introduce such events to Weimar; but both are possible. Nor were transcriptions the only way to assimilate Italian styles. Later in 1713, an aria written probably for the duke's birthday, BWV 1127, combined old and new: the German organist's *bicinium* (qv) with the Italian cellist's *continuo*; strophic form (traditional German) but with instrumental ritornello (newer Italian). Was the young ducal organist out to show what he had learnt? And why he, not the capellmeister? No doubt the work was one of many offerings to the duke by his musicians and poets, a chance survivor of a once voluminous output at a ducal court (see BJ 2005, 9).

If anything of Vivaldi's music such as the trio sonatas Op. 1 and 2 (1705, 1709) had previously penetrated to Weimar, the prince would have been alerted to search for more of their kind amongst the Dutch publishers and booksellers. And following his return with such music, not only were various concertos arranged by Bach for organ or harpsichord but there were longer-term consequences: it is hard to imagine the existence of at least some of the Brandenburgs and the solo concertos without the revelations offered by Vivaldi's Op. 3, 4 or 7. All these have a dashing quality beyond even Corelli. Vivaldi's way of organizing long abstract instrumental pieces by means of judicious repetition, inventive note-spinning and simple harmony handled with great rhythmic vitality, was such as to excite any lis-tener in a new way. Bach's Weimar friend Walther, who had shared his interest both in recent French music and in Palestrina, also arranged many Venetian concertos, probably at a period when the young prince was com-posing his own works in this style. Telemann got to hear of the prince's efforts and published some of his works, while Bach arranged others and copied out one of Telemann's own; to him sources attribute two transcrip-tions of a Concerto in C major by the prince, one for organ (BWV 595) and another, quite different in detail and some substance, for harpsichord (BWV 984).

How to give a piece of music length, to sustain and allow a movement to develop and come to a well-paced conclusion without inappropriate repeti-tion or uneventful continuity, was clearly a question of importance. So was another: how to create the faultless miniature. The result at Weimar was on the one hand the succinct preludes of the Orgelbüchlein and on the other the expansive movements as they were developed in cantatas and concertos. In both small and larger-scale works of the Weimar period, melodic flair merges with harmonic tension, melodies create logical harmony and vice versa, and there is an uncanny grasp of how a simple common chord can be as striking as a complex discord. Seldom if ever does harmonic grasp fail him, though it comes near it at one moment in the Fugue in F major, BWV 540, in a precipitous modulation from C minor to D minor. When a movement of carefully organized length strikes one as not very inspired, as in some arias of Cantata 12, it could be that too much attention paid to conveying a text can lead to a prosaic quality in the music's melody and harmony, especially when a convention is automatically applied – for example, chromatic intervals for something anxious, sad, regretful or in some other way negative. Yet one might justifiably consider the use of standard effects like the Neapolitan sixths in an aria of Cantata 12 to be an ingredient picked off the shelf, so to speak, for the sake of its predictably affecting quality. Even then, however, the slow melody's *Affekt* is still more touching than anything one is likely to find elsewhere, outside certain moments in Handel's Italian cantatas, and after all, the word-setting conventions later transcended in the Passions and Mass had to be established first.

Chromatics were another example of the time-honoured art of composing with formulas or note-patterns that can more or less automatically embellish coherent harmonies, and one much practised by Walther and Bach. Walther actually outlined many of these patterns or *figurae* and gave them traditional Italian names in an unpublished treatise written for the same Prince Johann Ernst, the *Praecepta* of 1708, while Bach produced a wide range of works constructed on the same principle. One could view the Little Organ Book (*Orgelbüchlein*) as the peak of this tradition, for its melodies are harmonized in such a way and with such note-patterns, many of them newly created, as would establish a mood for the text, even depict it. At times, one has the impression that Bach is realizing, at a level of unheard-of sophistication, the very details outlined by his colleague Walther. The two men were surely aware of each other's activities. Did they discuss such techniques, vie with each other, compete in creating particular types of music such as the canons on Christmas melodies? All this looks possible, for Walther's music often uses the very patterns handled more inventively by Bach. Yet the Orgelbüchlein is rarely doctrinaire and single-minded in this, especially when compared with earlier compositions by Scheidt or Steigleder, or later by Walther and Vetter (see below, Example 10). Escaping the constricting legacy of tradition in treating chorales in cantatas and organ-preludes is not the least achievement of Bach's Weimar years.

For creating shape and length, the little note-patterns are as tactics that need a strategy. In a cantata movement or prelude based on a chorale, there is no problem of form, since the chorale-melody provides it. But what of substantial pieces of music without such props? How correct one is to see Vivaldi's concertos as helping Bach shape movements in his own concertos – which, like the big organ preludes and fugues, are lone works anticipated by no predecessor and matched by no successor – is not obvious, despite observations famously made by Forkel in 1802. Forkel doubtless knew that Emanuel's colleague Quantz had acknowledged in print the impression Vivaldi and his 'beautiful ritornelle' had made on him, and how he had for a time taken them as a 'good model' in his own music (Quantz 1755, 205). Forkel was well read, and if Quantz had been bowled over by Vivaldi, so must his hero have been. But Bach had long been writing fugues which tend by nature towards a kind of concerto form, in which the 'subject' returns regularly after 'episodes', both of them varying in key, length, texture and scoring before returning to the original section in the home key. The principle of such ritornello form, especially where the opening and returning section is short or very short, had been familiar to Kuhnau and Buxtehude before 1700, and Cantata 131 (1707?) includes a shape of this kind, as already noted.

Whether in his early days in Weimar Bach had come across works of Torelli and Albinoni, and therefore seen further examples of movements planned with a distinctive theme returning after distinctive episodes, is inconclusively documented but plausible. In Albinoni's Op. 2 (1700) he could have seen examples of fugues in a clear ritornello form, comparable to his own Fugue in G minor, BWV 535a (*c.* 1705–7). And from elsewhere in Albinoni he could have learnt the effect of bringing back at some point in a movement the whole of the opening statement, as well as marking off sections with strong cadences. In this way he would find how to design a substantial movement other than by imitating Vivaldi's breathless continuity. Nevertheless, although the sustained endeavour evident in so much music of Bach, its avoidance of easy or lazy ways of proceeding, might have metamorphosed through sheer creative contemplation into the great structures without his knowing any Italian concerto, in fact the Italian conception must have been an inspiration.

The kinds of theme, rhythm and reiterated chords heard in cantata or concerto movements of Bach can very often be recognised as Italian in inspiration, though they are often sustained longer than they might be in Vivaldi's Op. 3 and 7, or in any of the other concertos transcribed by the Weimar organists. The impression Italian ritornello forms made on Bach is hinted at in such a work as Cantata 31 (Easter Sunday, 1715), where the opening instrumental *Sonata* uses a full orchestra to imitate a Vivaldian opening theme in octaves: a powerful stirring of the spirit on the day of Resurrection! What follows, however – arias with recycled episodes and, at the same time, a fund of distinctive melody – would not be mistaken for Vivaldi or Albinoni or, for that matter, any contemporary German composer. 1715 was also the year Albinoni's Op. 7 Concertos were published in Amsterdam, giving yet other examples for structuring instrumental pieces, and even if none of them had circulated earlier in MS, they could then have easily sped on their way to Weimar or Brandenburg or Dresden. By then too, Bach had also developed ritornello shapes in organ-chorales, with or without having regard to Vivaldi's concertos.

In the movements of the so-called English Suites for harpsichord, parts of which probably date from the later Weimar years, one sees another, comparable stretching of convention, in this case of the French dance-characteristics picked up from suites by Dieupart or d'Anglebert, or even from Couperin's *Premier Livre* of 1713. The English Suites (see also below, pp. 130f) are a good instance of how distinctive styles were adopted, for although on one level they are impeccable – well-wrought preludes, fugal gigues, courantes with model syncopations, sarabandes with model harmonies etc. – they lack the caprice and 'thoughtless' panache of Parisian composers. A similar point could be made about other of Bach's imitations throughout his life, including his version of the standard French *ouverture*: after the stately, rhythmically marked first sections, his second sections are always fugues, long, thorough and careful to a degree quite un-Parisian. The English Suites in particular try so hard, working their counterpoint so thoroughly and giving each idea full room to expand, that a player can soon find them less pleasurable and certainly less intimately suited to the harpsichord than relatively brainless pieces by French composers.

Apparent contradictions in Bach's music, at Weimar and throughout his life, give some idea of his inner musical life. One such contradiction is that the very completeness of his coverage – his tendency to 'tick off a list' of parameters – was no barrier to achieving quality or even, one might say, fun. For example, he may have deliberately planned the organ Toccata in C, BWV 564 to show off different ways of how to play with two manuals, which he and his pupils had at Weimar. The first movement uses them for echoes and then antiphonally; the second for a solo melody singing above its continuo accompaniment; the third for the contrast between subject and episodes in a long fugue. The result could be a mere didactic demonstration but is not, easily rising above the didactic with such verve and sense

8 Cantata 115.ii, iv, openings
a 'Ah, sluggish soul, how can you rest?'
b 'Pray, pray, even there in the middle of the watch'

of fun that no copyists, and very few players today, seem even to be aware that it can be interpreted in this way.

Another contradiction one might sense in Bach, especially in his orchestral writing, is less easy to pin down or confidently describe: the sensuality of his music at moments of marked piety. This is something that one comes across in cantata arias or in organ chorales throughout his life, there already in some Weimar cantatas, such as No. 54, but reaching greater heights some time after Weimar, in the mid-1720s. The harmony is often so new and rich that one can only assume that his piety somehow embraced the intense pleasure given by the sense of hearing and understood it as a God-given privilege. In the two arias of Cantata 115 (to take a later Leipzig work from 1724 as an example), the *Affekt* of penitence is calculated and explicit, and yet the first aria's rich texture and the second aria's minor-9th chords are sensuously rich, beyond the call of mere word-matching. (See Example 8.) One might describe the latter's contrapuntal lines and very slow, hesitant

9 Cantata 54, opening (harmonies only)
'Resist sin above all, otherwise its poison grips you'

tempo as 'evoking shame' or 'picturing the ingratiatingly repentant', but the sheer sensuality of the ninths is undeniable. Other examples, but now free of pious words or associations, are the opening bars of the Third and Sixth Brandenburg Concertos, with their pulsating chords, or Cantata 182, where the opening melody is pure delight (see Example 12). Cantata 54, in beginning unexpectedly on a throbbing discord, might be alluding to the text's command to 'resist sins', but the power of the allusion depends on the chord being beautiful in itself. The slowly unfolding harmonies are not quite as conventional as may appear at first, nor is their implied *crescendo* (see Example 9).

The sheer beauty of sound raises a question about music's powers of allusion in such music as the opening of Cantata 54. What is the repeated discord at the beginning of Example 9 conveying? – the power of sin (it is a seductive discord), or the desired resistance to sin (the discord evokes effort), or a sinful resistance itself (it persists without resolution)? Why in any case is the 'resisting' chord made so pleasurable – because we are embracing the pleasure of sin, reluctant to turn from it? Or is it that music having no true referent can authentically picture resistance to sin with any chord, if required to do so, and a good composer finds a beautiful one in order to draw in the listener, consoling not berating, persuading not ranting? The sensual side of Bach's personality cannot have been exclusive to music, and one wonders how he dealt with it in daily life, whether it was a problem for him to achieve both the cerebral and the sensuous, whether in his personal life he always achieved equilibrium between the two.

THE HALLE AUDITION

[In 1713,] after Zachow, music director and organist at the Market Church in Halle, died [7 August 1712], Bach received a call to this same position. He did indeed journey to Halle and perform his trial work there. Only, he found reasons to reject this position, which [Gottfried] Kirchhoff then took. (*Obituary*)

An oddity of this reference to the Halle job and its audition is that the late organist Zachow is mentioned by name when, in the Obituary's account of the Leipzig appointment ten years later, Bach's predecessor there (Kuhnau) is not. Zachow was also a Leipziger, son of a *Stadtpfeifer* and another early orphan. Was he named because, though not on the Obituary's list of composers whom his father admired, he was widely known (e.g. from Walther's *Lexicon*) as the teacher of Handel who during the previous winter had visited Halle and presumably Zachow himself (HHB, 57)? Perhaps Handel, who was much on the minds of the Obituary authors, had even been the preferred if quite unlikely candidate to succeed him, and was known to have been so, either at the time or later? And did Emanuel mention the actual successor, as he did not in connection with any other of the jobs involving his father, because Kirchhoff's own eventual successor in 1746 was his brother Wilhelm Friedemann?

There was no hurry to replace Zachow, both because work on building a large organ in the Market Church (Liebfrauenkirche, Church of Our Lady) had barely begun and because his widow was being supported for the customary six months or so. As far as the Bach biography was concerned, turning down jobs was not a thing to keep quiet about, especially since appointments by big parish churches were such public events that one's candidature became generally known. Walther's *Lexicon* reported that Kirchhoff, who was only third choice at Halle, had declined invitations from two prince's courts to become their capellmeister, something Kirchhoff must have told him. Telemann made a point of listing important offers he had not taken up (1740, 366), and Emanuel himself claimed more than once that while working for the King of Prussia he had had several advantageous offers (1773, 200).

Two big questions are whether Bach did apply in the normal way at the Market Church, Halle, and why in any case he declined. Quite possibly, he was or had been invited as an adviser for the building of the handsome, new, large three-manual organ of sixty-five stops at the west end of this fine hall-church, contracted for a month or so after Zachow died. If so, this was an indicator of his growing prestige, since Halle was until now the most distant place from Arnstadt for his professional engagement as organ-adviser, and this was an instrument of uncommon size. He did indeed become one of the organ's eventual examiners in 1716, with Kuhnau and C. F. Rolle (a Halle native), invited by the same church president with whom he had been in correspondence over Zachow's job. Those musical details in which the Halle instrument was not unlike that in Mühlhausen need not be significant, since a region's organs are generally similar and vary mostly according to size.

But Bach's two- or three-week stay in Halle over late November-December 1713 seems rather long just to report on the organ project, so perhaps it was true that he was asked to apply for the vacancy: indeed a sign of growing prestige, given the importance of the Halle church. He then explored the job fully and formally by composing and performing, on the first or second Sunday in Advent, a cantata as requested by the chief pastor J. M. Heineccius (who had backed the organ project), and would otherwise have gone back to Weimar, Bach said. That the church paid for his travel expenses, his first-class inn and the unidentified cantata, does seem to confirm that he was treated as a particularly honoured guest, and he claimed later not to have actually applied for the job, only to have 'presented himself' (*um die Stelle angehalten . . . mich praesentiret*: Dok I, 23). A distinction was evidently intended between the two, again like those people today who speak of being 'head-hunted', though probably with more justification. Telemann too, on one occasion when asking to be released from one job to take another, claimed not to have applied for the new position he was being offered.

This claim of Bach, written in a letter of 19 March 1714, was part of what looks like a tetchy reply to an accusation made by the people at Halle that in presenting himself for the job he had 'given them such a runaround' (*solche **tour** gespielet*) in order to solicit more money at Weimar. However, considering the contentious situation between the two dukes in Weimar that was involving their musicians, it is more than likely that Bach was having thoughts about leaving and looking for suitable positions elsewhere. Perhaps there was a genuine ambivalence in his mind, and the new responsibilities he took on at Weimar (see below) were proposed by him partly to get above the fray there, should he remain and not go to Halle. What is clear is that Bach, whether or not after soliciting, was invited by the church *collegium*, came over from Weimar, performed a cantata, was offered the job and was thought to have accepted it there and then (Dok II, 49), returned to Weimar in mid-December and was sent a draft contract; that he delayed a month and then declined, saying he had not yet received 'total release' from Weimar (*völlige dimission*: Dok I, 21); then asked for changes to be made at Halle to the salary (an increase) and duties (a reduction); said he would reply further and in full when current work at Weimar allowed (surely this was stalling?); and then, probably in February 1714, withdrew completely.

This was a week or two before the confirmation that he had been promoted to concertmaster at Weimar, with salary increase, a promotion it seems that he had requested (see Dok II, 53). The Halle people must have learnt of this – how, is itself an interesting question – and accused him of playing tricks, but in reply he asks why he should relocate even at the same salary, let alone a lower one, and particularly before entitlement to other fees in Halle had been clarified. This last is an important point, and yet the story is surely not quite to his credit. There is tetchiness in saying that he had no need to travel to Halle for the duke to raise his salary in Weimar, pride in claiming not actually to have applied for the Halle job, astuteness in making no mention of having asked for the promotion in Weimar, and disingenuousness in saying that a learned lawyer like his Halle correspondent could judge whether he was right not to change jobs for the same salary. These themes are not so very different from those in the letter he wrote at Mühlhausen when he left sooner than he would have been expected to.

All the same, it is surely true that Bach was highly valued in Weimar, and it could be that the frequency with which money and pay crop up in connection with him is a misleading consequence of his being represented today chiefly by formal documents and business letters. The facts that apparently he was well received in Halle at the organ-test of 1716 and had by then set a text by the Halle minister in Cantata 63 (Christmas Day 1714, in Weimar) suggest that by no means did he become *non grata* there. As at Mühlhausen, his withdrawal also seems not to have caused total resentment: the professional men he was dealing with would respect his professional ambition, and it could be that the church board at Halle, though genuinely disappointed, knew their offer was not good enough and were avoiding blame. Besides, even creative musicians need to be practical.[1] Halle's second offer, to Melchior Hoffmann of Leipzig, also failed, no doubt for comparable reasons, and salary increases affected the thinking of job-applicants then as now. Sebastian's elder brother Christoph did not succeed Pachelbel at Gotha when his current pay was raised, nor, for a similar reason, did Sebastian's son Christoph Friedrich leave Bückeburg for Altona, Hamburg, in 1759.

---

[1] Handel, not a family man, was freer to risk his 1,000 thalers-a-year position in Hanover when overstaying leave in London in the same year, 1713.

Nevertheless, it is clear that Bach was not backward in establishing himself as well financially as possible, especially perhaps in March 1714 when Maria Barbara had just produced another child, her fifth: Carl Philipp Emanuel. One wonders whether, when earlier at Weimar the duke raised his salary because his late predecessor Effler no longer required a pension, Bach had actually solicited on these grounds, and if so, why there was no mention made at that point of any ducal obligation to Effler's widow (NBR, 60). Later, his own widow in Leipzig, Anna Magdalena, was to live on modest pensions from church, city and university, but by 1759 his son, Christoph Friedrich, had learnt enough to negotiate a half-salary pension for his wife were he to leave her a widow (BJ 1998, 159).

MUSIC FOR HALLE?

Events in Halle do raise a question about Bach's priorities. Its splendid new organ, then in the making, was apparently not attractive enough for him to give up his position at a ducal court, any more than the fine organ in Hamburg Jacobikirche was a few years later when he was capellmeister at another court, Cöthen. Perhaps he did not care for large towns, though his later interest in Leipzig, Danzig and Dresden suggests otherwise. His new and promising duties at Weimar, complete with a salary increase, were no doubt important, so that to be 'just an organist' even in a prominent town-church was no longer attractive. Perhaps his Weimar colleagues were also a positive factor, raising his musical horizons beyond those of a town-church organist. Later on, remaining at Cöthen instead of moving to Hamburg (if he really had the offer) rather confirms this, for by then his colleagues at court were particularly distinguished. While opportunities for church music at Cöthen were apparently limited, at active, well-run courts there was a wider scope for many other kinds of music – concertos, *ouvertures* (orchestral suites), chamber cantatas, serenatas, songs, sonatas à 2, sonatas à 3, all kinds of keyboard music, etc. Was this what he most liked?

The Halle incident may also reveal how Bach geared his boundless creativity to the demands of particular jobs. If the earliest entries in the little album of chorales later called *Orgelbüchlein* are correctly dated to Advent 1713, perhaps it was begun not for services or teaching at Weimar but as a chorale-book for Halle, responding to the kind of Pietism (qv) of which Halle became a well-known centre. Music in support of this form of Protestantism would not be vaingloriously complicated or impersonal but aid the individual believer's 'rebirth' by directly appealing to personal feelings. It could and should elicit emotional response rather than teach doctrine, and many a listener will feel that that is exactly what certain works do that may have been connected with the Halle application – the dramatic change of mood from minor to major, *adagio* to *allegro*, in the course of the long Cantata 21, for instance, and especially the book of varied chorales later called *Orgelbüchlein*.

What Halle wanted of its organist is particularly clear. Musical stipulations of the Halle contract were the following (here paraphrased), or would have been had Bach signed:

> to accompany the chorales chosen by the minister 'slowly' and 'without special decoration' (*langsam ohne sonderbahres coloriren*)
>
> to play them in four or five parts (i.e. so the organist's harmony is neither too thin nor too thick)
>
> to draw the organ's basic or foundation stops (Principal, Quintaden, Gedackt, reeds) and change them in each verse (i.e. avoid both glitter and tedium)
>
> to realize the harmony with syncopations and suspensions (only) in such a way that the congregation feels supported by the harmony.
>
> (Dok II, 50)

Although 'accompany' could mean playing along with the congregation while it sang the hymn, it need not necessarily do so but instead refer to introductions, playing over the hymn-tune, interspersing its verses with interludes, giving the people a music matching the sentiments of the text. Perhaps in some apprehension of the large new organ then being built, the authorities were being careful to insure against wilful organists playing too fast, too loud and too complicatedly. Although the Halle clerk was rather uncertain of the technical language, his meaning is clear and could help explain how it comes about that the Orgelbüchlein settings are so different from the usual collections of chorales – richer, shorter, distinctive, 'warmer', full of *Affekt*, the harmony in four or five parts and discreetly realized with syncopations and suspensions. Many could serve as accompaniments to the hymn while it was being sung: is this why, unusually, they begin with the first note of the hymn-tune and continue with it unbroken?

When in 1746 Bach's former pupil J. G. Ziegler applied at the same church for the job that went to Friedemann Bach, he specifically said that his teacher had instructed him to play the hymns not indifferently but according to the *Affekt* of the words (Dok II, 423). This was something that the Halle church's ministers would have desired, as Ziegler must have known from holding positions in Halle for many years. Moreover, appropriate hymn-playing 'with beautiful harmony' had been specified at Halle on a yet earlier occasion, in 1702 when the 17-year-old Handel was appointed organist in its modest castle-cathedral (HHB, 18).[2] Such care seems typical of a city known for its devotional approach to all forms of religious observance, and whatever trial piece Bach had performed there – an Advent cantata? – he must somehow have convinced the authorities that it conformed to the kind of 'pious songs of penance and thanks' they had also required of the late Zachow nearly twenty years earlier (Serauky 1939, 377ff). That is, cantatas too were to fulfil the requirements of Halle's Pietism.

The Orgelbüchlein is doubly indicative of Bach's thinking: he could respond not only to the desires of a potential employer but to his own awareness of what other composers were doing. If, judging by the extant autograph, he began assembling the 164 chorales in late 1713, he did so soon after Daniel Vetter, a Leipzig organist, had published the second part of his collection of nearly 200 chorale-settings (*Musicalische Kirch- und Hauss-Ergötzlichkeit*, Leipzig, 1709, 1713). Other collections too were being made in the early eighteenth century, such as the book of over 150 fugues and preludes attributed to Pachelbel (1704), as well as Walther's complete yearly cycle of chorales, announced in print some time later (Mattheson 1725, 175). The 'standard' chorale-treatment associated with Pachelbel contrasts with Vetter's plain but useful settings, for these consist of two movements: a simple four-part harmonization of the chorale, followed by a simple decorative variation suitable for the spinet or clavichord, as the titlepages say. The book must have been successful, for a second edition appeared in Dresden in 1716.

The more common such collections in Thuringia and Saxony were, the more reason to think Bach was prompted by them to make his own, keeping to the usual way of embellishing chorale harmony with note-patterns – but do it better. These little note-patterns were lingua franca at the time, and it could strike a player now that Bach was consciously rejecting some of them while working others to new ends. In Example 10 (a), Walther's little semiquaver patterns are, though literate, commonplace, while Vetter's setting in Example 10 (b), though aimed at spinet or clavichord, is much less close than Bach's opening bar to the apogee of harpsichord idioms, the unmeasured French *prélude*. (See Example 10 (c): the *prélude* as token of Advent opening the church year.) Its expressive tmesis or semiquaver break in the melody of bar 1, imitated in the following alto and tenor, was the result of second thoughts.

---

[2] By then, this cathedral was also used as the Huguenot church: is this how Handel became so adept at French?

10 Advent hymn, 'Nun komm der Heiden Heiland'
   a J. G. Walther, verse 1 of a 3-verse setting, b. 3
   b N. Vetter, chorale No. 1, 'Variatio'
   c BWV 599 (Orgelbüchlein, No. 1)

No known documentation links Bach to Vetter's publication, but its final chorale does appear at the close of Cantata 8 (1724), and in the book's date, scope and aim there is a *prima facie* case for it having stirred J. S. Bach to surpass it. Was it a case of Halle's potential organist *versus* Leipzig's current organist?

In the event, alas, Bach completed little more than a quarter of the volume. Perhaps new duties at Weimar in March 1714 (see below) meant than he no longer played the hymns in chapel himself. Or, having now no need for small-scale chorales, Bach turned to longer, more demanding settings evidently known to some of his students. Had he gone to Halle, one can speculate further on how the cantatas could have become more 'approachable', more immediately 'affecting', less 'doctrinal' than many of those for Leipzig. On the other hand, it could be that Halle's Protestantism was less than an attraction for Bach, even part of the reason he remained at Weimar.

Practice at Weimar was distinctive, not least in chapel. According to a report made some twenty years later, *Choralsingen* at Weimar was led by a group of eight choirboys located in a gallery behind the altar, much nearer to the court personnel on the chapel floor than the main organ was (Jauernig 1950, 71). *Choralsingen* could mean either Gregorian intonations or the Lutheran chorales, or both, although the payment made in March 1714 (the month of Bach's promotion) for five blackboards on which the hymn-numbers were to be written does suggest that chorales were an important element in the services. This would accord with the duke's recent decree, applying throughout the dukedom, that the revised Weimar hymn-book be used and the numbers announced on boards. (The level of literacy this implies was no problem in a court chapel.) But a practical question remains, concerning any chorale, short or long, played at Weimar by its organ high and distant in a ceiling-gallery: is one to imagine first a prelude wafting down from on high, then the choristers singing, then a court congregation joining in, with verses separated by organ interludes or followed at the end by postlude?

THE WEIMAR PROMOTION AND CANTATAS

In 1714 [2 March] he was named Concertmaster at the same Court. However, the functions connected with this position consisted at that time chiefly in this, that he had to compose church pieces and perform them. (*Obituary*)

Concertmeister was a new title and may not even have had the connotations of that term such as were beginning to appear elsewhere, i.e. the violinist leading the band from the first desk. The force of the 'however' is that *Concertmeister*, a term more common by the time of the Obituary than it had been forty years earlier, would not normally mean the composer and director of cantatas for a court's chapel, the overall responsibility for which, and the court's music as a whole, remained the capellmeister's. This Obituary's clarification of the term could be either the composer's or his biographer's.

The official minute of the promotion to concertmaster says it was made at Bach's 'most humble request' (*uf sein unterth[änig]stes Ansuchen*: Dok II, 53) – a conventional phrase but, given the court organist's ambition, making one suspect that before Halle he had been pressing for promotion, chafing at the bit to write cantatas. The minute also specified that the court musicians were to appear at Bach's request for rehearsals, which are to be in the chapel and not 'in the house or anyone's apartment' (*im Hause oder eigenem Logiament*). Whether the latter referred to Capellmeister Drese's usual practice or, on the contrary, was planned to hinder Bach's taking over the musicians in his own lodging (the month Carl Philipp Emanuel was born), is uncertain. But the usual assumptions are that Bach preferred moving to the 'neutral' chapel and, fearing his authority about rehearsals would be questioned by the (older) instrumentalists, requested both stipulations to be put in writing. A year later, by 20 March 1715, Drese father and son were officially informed that Bach was to receive a capellmeister's salary (in fact, it was a little higher), which sounds like a ducal directive that they were to accept his status: something else he had requested, and something else the Dreses were unlikely to have been pleased about? The Weimar promotion and the Halle offer are saying much about the composer's ambition and astuteness, as well as the genuinely high regard in which he was held by his employer.

Though concertmaster, Bach continued to be court organist at least by title (Dok II, 63) and probably harpsichordist in chamber music. How much he played himself in chapel is not known, but his position in the world of organs was high, even unrivalled locally, and attracted attention from both prospective students and organ committees. When engaged as organ-examiner – Mühlhausen 1709 (?), Taubach 1710, Halle 1716, Erfurt Augustinerkirche 1716, Leipzig University Church 1717, the last three being major organs – he may customarily have played a public concert of his grander works, such as the various versions of the Preludes and Fugues in G major and C major, and indeed chorale settings. (At Halle, it is not known which organist played before or after the inaugurating sermon: the three examiners including Bach or the newly appointed organist Kirchhoff, perhaps all four. Dok II, 60.) A likely reason why the dating and purpose of Bach's bigger organ works are such guesswork is that they were portfolio works selected and revised as occasion required – in the case of the so-called 'Eighteen Chorales', thirty or so years later. 'Occasion' would include inaugurations and demonstrations.

The monthly presentation of a cantata as specified in the court document was previously the duty of the vice-capellmeister (whose response to this new arrangement is unrecorded), as it had been of his predecessor. Music in the other weeks was under the capellmeister, including arrangements that would have to be made to bring in extra instrumentalists for festive occasions. The Obituary's phrase 'and perform them' seems to be there to make it clear (as it might not otherwise have been) that it was to be Bach who directed as well as composed these cantatas, not the capellmeister – something perhaps specially negotiated and recalled in later years with pride. Not only does the court secretary's minute make clear that Bach was in charge for this monthly cantata but so does the Obituary, making one suspect that for the latter Emanuel had some original document to hand, such as a contractual letter of appointment or a copy of the court minute. In that case, however, not to include the further details contained in the minute – i.e. that his father's rank was next below the vice-capellmeister, and it had been at his own 'most humble request' that the title had been conferred on him – means that Emanuel omitted them.

The cantatas or 'new pieces to be performed monthly' were ensemble works of several movements sung after the Creed and before the seasonal hymn and sermon. Whether Bach specifically planned to form a complete monthly cycle of cantatas for the church year is not clear, and there are still doubts about when exactly some were composed. Half or so of the three years' output is probably lost. In many cases, cantatas were revised later, with their instrumentation updated for the different conditions in Leipzig, and in both places they were performed to congregation-members who had the text in front of them. How far the promotion itself to concertmaster was a reason to decline the Halle position is questionable, since there Bach would have had similar or better opportunities for church cantatas; but perhaps performance standards and the aristocratic context at Weimar were an attraction. In principle, the new church cantata-form, borrowing its kinds of music and text from chamber cantatas and operas, must always have been more at home in court chapels than parish churches, even if a hymn familiar to the congregation was added at the end, and one can not be far wrong to hear in the Weimar cantatas a wish to delight. For the duke's chapel Bach brought subtle, chamber-like works of refined forces (four singers, a five-part instrumental consort in cantatas), with newly created effects and colourful timbres, varying and unpredictable sequences of instrumental and vocal movements, with texts drawn from the newest devotional libretti. These last included some by Salomo Franck, Weimar court secretary and librarian, and Erdmann Neumeister, who was soon to become chief pastor of the Jacobikirche, Hamburg, the scene of another important job opportunity, in 1720.

The cantatas that were produced at Weimar and (still with Franck and Neumeister texts) at Leipzig, were far from the usual 'parish church music', and imply the spending of a lot of time and effort in seeking an expressive word-setting that reached the listener through pleasing and novel sound. In cantatas as these were emerging, fully fledged movements rather than mere sections would contrast with each other as they set, in a sequence, various texts drawn from Old or New Testament, from newly written poetry, and from the corpus of chorale-texts familiar to Lutheran congregations.

11 Cantata 196.i, b. 18
'He blesses the House of Israel, the House of Aaron'

Cantatas dating from after the 1714 promotion, composed for the period from Palm Sunday to Christmas 1714, have opening choruses mostly after an instrumental introduction, in which it certainly looks as if the concertmaster was aiming to please with a variety of concerto-like sounds.

Typical of cantata texts over the next twenty years is a mixture of biblical excerpts, new poetry and prose, extracting clauses or sentences from biblical or devotional passages, the whole often (normally?) rounded off both verbally and musically with a stanza from a familiar chorale. This final chorale would alone distinguish the church cantata from the secular, and where an extant cantata does not have one, there must often be the suspicion that it is lost or was simply not cued in to the extant score. In Leipzig especially, the chorale became a focal point: just as Neumeister texts, unlike those of Italian recitatives or arias, mix biblical words and chorale (Cantatas 18, 24, 28, 59, 61), so a final verse from an existing chorale-book rounds off Salomo Franck's texts (Cantatas 31, 72, 155, 161, 162, 163, 164, 165, 168, 185). Sources of old chorale variations for organ suggest, if they do not prove, that their last movement would 'summarize' the work with a final full statement of the original hymn, and cantatas since Cantata No. 4 seem to have followed suit. But this is something that had to evolve, and it is not always clear at what stage a pre-Leipzig cantata acquired its final chorale.

Typical of the choir's music is a counterpoint based on the permutation principle (qv), giving a concentrated and 'systematic' impression to the sound and very like the best achievements of previous composers (see Example 11). This is an old way of creating fugal counterpoint, and while in this instance the lines are still melodious despite the ingenuity, there often appear many short phrases and a certain repetitiousness in the service of the text. (In the permutation fugue of the Passacaglia, the two-bar phraseology has disappeared, and the counterpoint emerges new and unpredictable.) In Cantata 196, the young Bach had not gone much beyond imitating choral works by Weckmann and others he may well have heard in Hamburg or Lübeck. But its text, a formal Old Testament benediction from Ps 115, is not inappropriate for a learned display of solid, permuted themes, and not for the only time guessing which of two works came earlier (the Passacaglia or Cantata 196) can not be based on simple comparison: they are too different in genre and purpose.

Cantata recitatives and arias develop in idiom over the years but remain remarkably uniform, or enough so to make dating a cantata on such grounds most unreliable. A recitative as in Cantata 132 (1715) is distant from any simple Italian model: the text begins with a couplet, the phrases are variously punctuated (full stop, exclamation, comma, semicolon etc.), an arioso section includes melismas and repeated words, telling modulations mark the following sections, etc. Despite little melodic phrases character-istic of Italian recitative, there is a correspondence between particular words and their musical gesture that takes the listener into a Lutheran world. The result, since the words are of such significance and by no means a simple narrative, is distinct from and seldom mistakable for the pattering, secular recitative of Italy. At the same time, in a cantata such as No. 152 one also recognizes a wish to charm a court's congregation with chamber-like music of a kind they could have heard outside chapel services, melodious yet still full of contrapuntal devices such as imitation, and the whole now brought in *ad gloriam dei*. Choruses where they exist can be much like arias in shape and melody, as for a solo group. In the cantatas up to Easter 1715, scorings and types of setting are more varied than afterwards, and the earlier five-part orchestra (with two violas in the Parisian manner of J.-B. Lully) is reduced to four, as in chorales. The body of Weimar cantatas is the result of a constantly inventive creativity that draws on no standard formulas in setting each libretto, whether large-scale or small-scale.

A salary-increase in June 1713 implies, as do certain details in extant MSS, that Bach was sometimes providing cantatas irrespective of the 1714 promotion's requirements: Nos. 18, 199 and probably 54, chamber-like works without exclusive attachment to particular Sundays. In addition, there was No. 208 at Weissenfels in 1712/13, a unicum of a cantata whose position in the composer's development can hardly be overrated and is examined briefly below. Probably the first cantata to be performed under the new dispensation, No. 182 (25 March 1714, Annunciation and Palm Sunday) has an opening 'sonata' that leads off with a very charming melody between recorder and violin. See Example 12 (a). Was the violin played by the composer? The work is knowingly and elegantly setting the new tone, as the King of Heaven is welcomed in a bright cantata uniting chamber music, chamber choruses, recitative, a sequence of arias, a chorale and finally a choral dance rather like a passepied. The last movement of Cantata

12 a Cantata 182, opening Sonata for flute (recorder)
and strings. Text of following movement:
'Himmelskönig, sei willkommen'
('Welcome, King of Heaven!').

b Cantata 199.viii, 'Wie freudig ist mein Herz'
('How joyful is my heart'), final movement,
Introduction. C major version in *Kammerton*
(low pitch sounding about a tone lower),
viola part omitted.

199 has all the bright melody one supposes typical of a talented young man finding himself setting words like 'How my heart is full of joy' (Example 12 (b)) – a young man master of the bass line and incapable of resisting imitative counterpoint.

Two months into the new contract, No. 172 welcomes Whitsun with a dancing chorus and instrumental antiphony suitable for any birthday or celebratory cantata – so different from the intervening cantata, No. 21, that no-one, from capellmeister to page-boy, could have missed the musical range of which the new concertmaster was capable. Cantata 172 welcomes the Holy Ghost much as it might welcome the King of Saxony. Though in these works the vocal and, at times, instrumental parts were or could have been doubled, their essence is that of chamber music, written with specific instruments in mind, colourful and as self-generated or self-dependent as Haydn's early symphonies at Esterhaza.

Even when cantatas restricted the chorus to a final chorale, their chamber scoring would create a quite different effect from the chorales that closed the later Leipzig cantatas. In principle, they are not unlike finales in an Italian opera in which, after vicissitudes of plot and characterization, the soloists gather around to comment or participate, rather like a classical *chorus*. In Leipzig, however, bigger forces give a more 'congregational' feel to especially the final chorale, such as suits a large parish church whether or not the congregation actually joined in singing it. Athough the Weimar cantata texts by Salomo Franck are often described as ungrateful for any composer – too didactic and admonitory compared with the Leipzig texts of Picander, which have simple *Affekte* (qv) more convenient for a composer – No. 182 is sustained by a freshness of melody and apparently effortless invention that are by no means always the case in Leipzig. Composing once a month was less arduous, more a pleasure even, than composing every week.

Some eighteen cantatas for the period 1713–17 exist and another five are documented, leaving open some questions – not only where are the other twenty or so from three and a half years, but also how do the eighteen come to survive at all? Those two questions are related and imply that what survives of any ensemble works belonging to a composer's employer, depends on circumstances. The unusually sumptuous Christmas and Easter Cantatas 63 and 31, when the duke's *cappella* seems to have been strengthened, are good examples of works for which Bach must have preserved his own copies, for whatever reason. When a cantata of unusual shape is known from somebody else's copy, such as the short solo work No. 54, there must always be a question whether it is complete. The three months' period of mourning after the death of the young Prince Johann Ernst in August 1715 accounts for some of the 'unproductive' time, and strangely, no memorial cantata for him survives, from Bach, Walther or Telemann. The existence of the Hunt Cantata, BWV 208 in two versions for two dukes (Weissenfels and Weimar) is exceptionally well transmitted, because perhaps it was not secreted away in the choir library. It also raises another question about logistics: when two horn-players were brought in from Weissenfels for the later performance, someone must have arranged this, sent messages, negotiated payment, arranged rehearsals, got their parts copied, etc.

If in 1717 Bach did write no cantatas, as seems to be the case, was it pique at not automatically succeeding the deceased capellmeister Drese Snr in the previous December? Or that when Drese died, current arrangements simply ceased and needed to be re-negotiated? The cantatas for the later part of 1716 seem to be maturing in melody and harmony, hardly a moment to stop by choice. (Why the Advent cantatas for 1716 have no known recitatives is unclear and may be a result of unreliable sources.) Perhaps in 1717 Bach sometimes performed pieces by other composers, even by Drese Jnr, who had been in Venice and must have learnt something about recitative and ABA aria-form, and for all we know was a thorn in concertmaster Bach's flesh. (Nothing is known, however, of compositions by Drese Jnr.) In the later Weimar years Bach made copies of choral works, or had them made by copyists, including Latin works (chiefly Kyries) by other composers not now particularly well known, such as J. Baal, F. B. Conti, Peranda, J. C. Pez (from the *Missa San Lamberti*, Augsburg, 1706) and J. C. Schmidt, but to what extent such copies were for private study or for occasional performance in chapel is not made clear by documents. That in certain but possibly typical cases there are some separate performing parts makes it likely that the Kyries were intended for chapel. Perhaps in the case of the Pez Mass his pupil Kräuter had brought a copy from Augsburg, for purposes of re-copying, performing and possibly studying. However, most of these foreign works known from Weimar copies have little counterpoint of the strict kind (in *stile antico*), and for study purposes a repertory with no Lassus and chiefly Kyries from five Palestrina masses (BJ 2002, 14) was limited.

The variety of shape in the Weimar cantatas must be conscious, another example of attempting to survey what conceivable kinds of music there might be within a specific genre. One never knows quite what kind of melody or texture or scoring or shape or even type of movement is to come next, although each is likely to be colourful and fresh, as if Bach were always playing with the musical ideas. How touching or moving a court congregation would find the decorated chorale closing No. 161 or the picturesque door-knocking in No. 61 is hard to know, however. They look like the effects of a clever rather than a stirring composer. What becomes even clearer as time passes is his desire to be constantly expanding on the possibilities: having begun his Advent cantata No. 61 with a French *ouverture*-chorus, appropriate for the opening of the church year, ten years later he then began another Advent cantata (No. 62) with the same melody but now in the manner of an Italian concerto. These two opening movements are equally polished and confident in details of style, different in every respect except that they both start with the ancient hymn-melody and re-invent it to match the two styles of the day, French and Italian.

The Weimar court must also have conferred status and led to a variety of contacts. How Bach came to be involved in writing the big festive cantata BWV 208 for the birthday celebrations of the Duke of Saxe-Weissenfels in February 1712 or 1713 is not recorded, but it could have been from various kinds of connection he had: through the respective dukes, or the court secretary Salomo Franck (author of its text), or A. I. Weldig (former colleague in Weimar, now in Weissenfels, later Emanuel's godfather), or direct solicitation by himself, or perhaps through all four. Word of mouth must have been involved at some point. It is a pathbreaking work, the first of its kind for Bach, with elements both old (short-phrased melodies) and new (recitatives, horn solos), and it develops effortlessly, so it seems, the topics of hunting and pastorella according to conventions of the day. It is thoughtful but, characteristically, still full of tunes. Each of the seven arias explores its own particular *Affekt* or topic, and the obligatory hunting-horns in F major provide a strong tonal framework, to which a dramatic opening is given by the soprano's curtain-raising recitative. There is a pastoral which, though apparently just as conventional in its pair of recorders in thirds, throbbing bass and gentle *cantabile* for the voice, is developed towards something new and puzzlingly, if famously, memorable (see Example 13 (a)), the more so after the horns have introduced the bucolic in their own way (Example 13 (b)).

The plan of Cantata 208 resembles an opera-act with a series of arias in *da capo* (ABA) or concerto (ritornello) form, all freshly tuneful, with a grand total of fifteen movements. As a work not intended for a church service, its recitative is particularly significant, signalling the Italian theatrical style and showing the composer mastering the technique of recitative in the vernacular. (By coincidence, Handel's first English recitative in 'As pants the hart' HWV 251a, also belongs to 1712.) In Bach's Weimar works, Salomo Franck, court secretary-poet, naturally appears more often than Pastor Neumeister who, moving to Hamburg in 1715, plays such a big

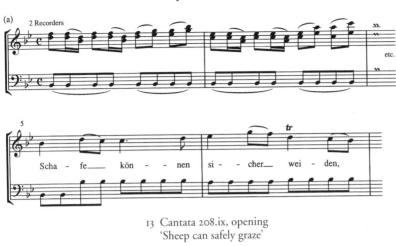

13 Cantata 208.ix, opening
'Sheep can safely graze'

part in Telemann's output. But for both poets, Bach shows early mastery in writing recitative, something that never leaves him: like Handel in his Italian cantatas, he produces a sense of melody and harmony where native Italian opera-composers are often formulaic and careless, even giving their recitatives over to pupil-assistants to compose. It is difficult to imagine Bach doing likewise.

In its very range of styles BWV 208 is a work that seems to lead naturally towards Brandenburg Concerto No. 1. This last may be either a compilation whose first movement originally prefaced Cantata 208, or a full concerto from the Weimar period later revised in order to open the Margrave of Brandenburg's set of six, fair copied in score in 1721 (see below, p. 134). No doubt the margrave was as much a hunter as the Duke of Weissenfels, and it was as appropriate to begin a set of concertos for him by alluding to hunting as it was a cantata for the duke. In going on to explore special instrumental combinations, the Brandenburgs build on much in the Weimar cantatas, although the leisurely paced harmonies of the third, fourth and sixth concerto are more mature, resulting in part from contemplating Vivaldi's string-idioms and, perhaps, from having moved away from text-bound cantatas for a few years by then.

Bach did not automatically become capellmeister on Drese Snr's death in December 1716, despite writing cantatas for that period (Advent) and hoping, one supposes, to be preferred above Drese Jnr, whose father had in turn succeeded his own father. When no appointment was made, interest in Weimar could well have waned, hence the blank months of 1717. Other possibilities are that the chapel music was deteriorating in the inter-regnum, and that Bach was more or less silenced for a year by the senior duke for his loyalty to the junior. The two dukes' constant quarrelling certainly exposed the distasteful side of a court run on absolutist lines, though in a major church, squabbling clergy were by no means unknown to organists. But whatever the situation, Bach's creativity would have had no trouble in turning more to chamber music were he to seek a different position elsewhere.

PUPILS IN WEIMAR

In addition, in Weimar he trained several fine organists. (*Obituary*)

Adding to the picture of Bach's activities at Weimar, in chapel and chamber, is the glimpse of a dozen or so pupils given by various sources. Adding also to his income: throughout his career, teaching fees could have amounted to at least his church salary at any one time and even as much as double. Emanuel would know of Weimar pupils probably both from his father and from later acquaintance with one or two of them, including his own relations.

Only miscellaneous chance references reveal an organist's teaching-income: thus for *Clavier* lessons that Bach gave Duke Ernst August's page in 1711–12, payment in kind was recorded in the court books (Dok II, p. 44); over the same period, lessons given by Vincent Lübeck have now been shown to be double or triple his church salary (Syré 2000, 109f); in 1729 J. G. Walther made it clear in a letter that without such fees, organists were in trouble. One can also assume two further 'supplements' to this kind of income: from payments for live-in pupils's board and lodging (as for P. D. Kräuter in Weimar, discussed below); and from higher fees for teaching well-to-do amateurs. Though no more than representative of what once existed, various extant MSS show Bach's keyboard works being copied, probably direct from his autographs, by pupils J. T. Krebs and J. C. Vogler, though for what purpose can only be surmised: models of composition or repertory for the present and future? J. G. Walther would make several copies of the same piece, perhaps to pass on or (like a contemporary of his, the London organist John Reading) to keep at different locations.

Although Bach's pupils are often now listed in such numbers as to imply that he had a brilliant reputation as a teacher, it is unclear how exceptional the numbers were or how unusual were the abilities of a few of them. Because of circumstances – an organist's responsibility for the organ in his church, the need for a trustworthy bellows-blower, etc. – boys could normally learn organ only by attaching themselves to such an organist. Hence the various written records of Bach pupils, fuller than they would be for the usual flute- or violin-teachers of the time?

Students' warm praise for their teacher when they applied for a job does not give a reliable picture of their studies, any more than it would today. Nevertheless, using a teacher's name to support one's bona fides is revealing on several counts. In 1728 and 1732, the fathers of two students, the latter remarking that his son's lessons with Bach in Leipzig had cost him 'not a little' (Dok II, 228), clearly saw them as a key qualification for their sons' career. So did another pupil, J. G. Voigt, who spoke of three years' study, also with Bach in Leipzig, also at great cost to his father (Dok III, 10). J. G. Ziegler's reference to being taught by Bach to play chorales according to their sentiment, something in itself plausible, was calculated to interest his prospective employers in Halle (see above, p. 97). Ziegler had already studied in Dresden and with Friedrich Zachow in Halle before he came to Weimar; so too another pupil, Lorenz Bach, had studied with Sebastian's elder brother in Ohrdruf before coming to him in about 1713. Thirty years later, the composer J. C. Simon of Nördlingen, who published some competent preludes and fugues, spoke of having been helped by three musicians: the first encouraged him, the second (this was Johann Nicolaus Bach in Jena) poured oil on the fire, but the third, the 'incomparable capellmeister Bach in Leipzig' (BJ 2000, 329), brought it into full flame. Nothing better could be said of any teacher.

Several useful pieces of information about the situation in Weimar emerge from a request by P. D. Kräuter in late 1711 to his school board at home, who were sponsoring his study with Bach, which lasted from March 1712 to September 1713 (Dok III, 649–50). It seems that he travelled all the way from Augsburg to Weimar for lessons with the court organist – clearly, there was nothing so very exceptional in the young Bach having gone all the way to Lübeck. As with Buxtehude, an organist's fame would not be as a composer but simply as 'the famous musician' (*dem berühmten musico Bach*), even if he were still only twenty-six. Whether by 1711 any of Bach's compositions had penetrated to Augsburg is not documented, nor whether Kräuter came because of his fame or through some connection (his own or his sponsors') with the court. In speaking of 'the famous musician', he could simply have been trying to satisfy his sponsors. His words are clearly less significant than the praise of 'Mr Handel, whom the World so justly celebrates', published in London even earlier in the librettist's dedication in *Rinaldo*, 1710. By 1717, however, Mattheson in Hamburg reports in print having seen both choral and keyboard works of 'the famous organist in Weimar' (Dok II, 65), and Kräuter doubtless took some music back with him to Augsburg when he returned home to take up a position in 1713. Transmission *via* students played a major part before the cheaper printed editions of the later eighteenth century.

For a year's lessons plus board and lodging, presumably in his own house, Bach asked 100 thalers which Kräuter got lowered to 80 or, for the sake of his sponsors, said he did. For the teacher to charge for lodging was normal; so did Buxtehude's predecessor Tunder in Lübeck (Edler 1982, 74). As to the musical instruction itself, the pupil received six hours a day of 'guidance' (*zur Information*), in composition, keyboard (*Clavier*) and other instruments. Perhaps 'six hours' was also to impress the Augsburg sponsors and included such things as copying parts for his teacher, though in his case none of them seems to have survived. He said he was free to look through his master's work, a detail which confirms the right of a fee-paying pupil to use and copy the teacher's work, and sheds some light on the Moonlight anecdote (p. 18). Students in Weimar are known to have contributed to preparing full scores of choral works with their teacher, in Kräuter's case the motet Anh.III 159, perhaps by Johann Christoph of Eisenach and later listed by Emanuel in the Old Bach Archive.

The picture given is one of serious sustained study, comparable to a professional college today if its curriculum were to be pared down to core studies. Lessons as we now know them but lasting six hours are unlikely. Rather, Kräuter's day-long contact was as an apprentice to a master, observing and being useful, accompanying him in his duties, hearing or participating in music that included newly imported works, learning how to compose Italian and French instrumental music, getting to know an organ's structure (and costs) from the work under way in the Weimar chapel, and altogether 'seeing, hearing and copying a great deal' (*vil sehen, hören und decopirt*). In formally requesting a longer leave of absence from his church, as Bach himself had not at Arnstadt, Kräuter mentions in particular Weimar's musical prince, Johann Ernst, his ability on the violin, and the chance the prince's anticipated return from Holland will give him, Kräuter, to learn the arts of Italian *concerti* and French *ouvertures* (i.e. suites). As the prince was still away when this request was made, somebody must have given Kräuter the information beforehand. Whoever this was – Bach, wishing to keep a good student? – it does give an idea of what was discussed and planned between musicians, and what their hopes were in a musically active ducal court.

At much the same period as Kräuter but in London, Maurice Greene was articled to the organist of St Paul's and eventually became his successor, as Bach's pupil J. M. Schubart succeeded him at Weimar, to be succeeded by yet another pupil (J. C. Vogler). As the Obituary makes clear, though whether with pride is not entirely clear, Bach himself had not been regularly articled as a pupil to a master in this way. His own children, with respect to their musical training, may have been treated similarly to live-in pupils, who could also have included a family cousin or two from time to time. As with the seventy-odd pupils documented from the Leipzig years, some of them would have been regular copyists for the performing parts of their master's cantatas and instrumental works, extracting them from his fair-copy score. Johann Lorenz, the cousin who had studied in Weimar for some years from 1713, felt himself qualified from what he had learnt there to be a cantor himself, which he subsequently became at Lahm in Itzgrund in 1718, and where the organ of 1732 remains in reasonably intact condition. His younger brother, Johann Elias, became tutor for younger Bach children in Leipzig 1737–42 and secretary to their father, as other pupils probably did for a certain period.

Johann Elias is notable for some surviving letters in which he gives a few details of life in the household twenty years or more after Weimar – pitifully few details, though from them we do learn that Anna Magdalena, Sebastian's second wife, was a keen gardener (several letters about this: BJ 2001, 173–7) and Sebastian himself had a sweet tooth, liking cider as well as (so other references say) beer, Moselle wine, brandy, tea, coffee and tobacco. The substantial bill for such things when Bach examined an organ at Gera in 1725 represents, one must hope, consumption over several days and by several people (BJ 2004, 114).

For a salaried musician, any live-in pupils and young relations who served as some kind of personal assistant were unlikely to have the elevated title 'treasurer' or 'secretary', as J. C. Schmidt Snr came to have with Handel in London. Nevertheless, some assistance was necessary, if less in Weimar than in Leipzig. Emanuel is speaking of the Leipzig years when he called the busy family house a dovecot (*Taubenhaus*: Dok III, 290), with people coming and going all the time, his father too busy to deal with necessary correspondence though happy to talk with visitors. But the Weimar situation cannot have been so very different, except that presumably there were fewer distinguished visitors. One of them, J. G. Pisendel, later to be concertmaster at the Dresden court, made a point of visiting Bach in Weimar in early 1709, or said much later that he did (Dok III, 189). Thirty years later, Johann Elias seemed to be speaking of the Bach house in Leipzig when he mentioned concerts taking place there (*bey uns*, 'chez nous': Dok II, 366), played by family and visiting musicians, and one can suppose the situation in Weimar to have been similar, with musical gatherings involving pupils, court colleagues and a precocious young Friedemann Bach. (On being too busy for correspondence, see a suggestion on p. 329.)

When Emanuel mentions organist-pupils specifically at Weimar, while there must have been many times more in Leipzig, he is establishing the authority Bach already had in his twenties. Only an occasional chance document from later years, such as a job application by one ex-pupil in 1726 (Dok II, 157), suggests that Bach had more students in Weimar than is now known. Equally uncertain is where and what exactly he taught them, especially but not only when the organ was out of commission. Perhaps in the Leipzig years, instruction for occasional pupils, university students and, as time passed, visiting admirers was less on the organ and more in music generally. And considering that church organs needed bellows-blowers, were 'organ lessons' mostly on practice instruments (blown by whoever was available) and covered all keyboard skills, including continuo-playing? J. P. Kirnberger, adopting the mantle of fugue-expert after Bach's death, wrote about studying fugues in such lessons, and found himself criticized by another mantle-wearer, F. W. Marpurg, while another pupil H. N. Gerber spoke of learning to play fugues, along with continuo-work. Instruction is discussed further below, but in Weimar it cannot have been very different from how it was in Leipzig.

If it was in Weimar that Bach conceived the idea of compiling a complete collection of fugues, the collection eventually to be called the Well-tempered Clavier, it could have been in response to two particular recent publications: J. K. F. Fischer's set of twenty more petite preludes and fugues (see below, p. 143), from which Bach appears to borrow a theme or two; and J. H. Buttstedt's would-be comprehensive treatise discussing fugal answers (Erfurt, 1716). The WTC, as assembled and copied complete in 1722 or 1723, surpasses other instructional collections by explicitly developing full-fledged preludes and fugues, varying them beyond anyone's previous imagination and displaying clearly the many ways a composer

14 Preludes Nos. 1 and 2, Well-tempered Clavier, Book 1

might proceed. Sometimes in the book, the didactic intent to survey the possibilities is quite patent, despite the quality of the music. Thus the first two preludes share a compositional technique in which each 4/4 bar is built up of a semiquaver pattern heard twice, but to totally different and identifiable ends:

one major and light, the other minor and dark

one of pure arpeggios, the other without arpeggios

in one the figure is divided between the hands, in the other they both play it

the first is predominantly higher in tessitura than the second

the first keeps its *figura* unchanged throughout, the second allows it to 'disintegrate' in the second half of the piece.

Here in effect are ten ideas, on combinations of which a composer could found his own prelude (Example 14).

Such playing with note-patterns typifies Bach's musical thinking in the Weimar period, to which a lot of keyboard music belongs, and at the same time was and is a useful approach for teaching and learning to compose music – cantatas as much as preludes for any instrument. For creating or improvising preludes to fugues, 'playing with note-patterns' is still the basis of the advice given by Telemann in *XX Kleine Fugen*, published in 1731. A interesting question for the performer of the preludes in Example 14, even today, is whether there is anything in the notation itself to suggest that they do not have the same tempi: it seems not.

By no means of minor interest are the transcriptions for harpsichord of Italian and other string concertos BWV 972–987, probably made in the later Weimar years and showing the taste not only for imported string music but for a new world of keyboard music. Whatever few Italian concertos had penetrated to Thuringia beforehand, now, at a stroke, there appeared groups of works showing in practical form how to shape sustained music when (i) it had no words to help provide it with a shape or organization, (ii) it could not rely on the usual formulas serving as a basis for most suites and variations of the day. In one conspicuous group of works, these and the concerto transcriptions for organ create a repertory of striking character, and present yet another peak of achievement in a genre quite widely known in their time and place. The transcriptions offer a range of new melodies and movement-shapes, new keyboard effects and layouts, comparing well with the more local produce and giving the player now, as they must have given Bach, a welcome breath of fresh air after the older German idioms. One can still find these transcribed concertos more effective in public performance than most suites and fugues, for unlike these, they were meant in origin to be precisely that: 'public music'.

As to Bach's art of transcribing: some of the transcriptions for keyboard suggest that he either did not understand the natural verve and rhetoric of Venetian string concertos or else wished to temper it with German 'seriousness'. It is otherwise difficult to understand why he sometimes filled in Vivaldi's rests with bits of busy counterpoint – gaps that are perfectly effective in string concertos – and at least in one case, cleverly derived these bits of counterpoint from one of Vivaldi's own themes (in the Concerto BWV 593). There are not a few such otiose moments, and one could make similar points about works based on other composers' themes. The two Fugues on a Theme of Albinoni, BWV 951/951a, generously shaped and inventively worked though they are, entirely miss or ignore (it is not clear which) the vividly violinistic nature of Albinoni's trio as he published it.

As already noted, it has been customary to attribute to the imported Italian concertos Bach's grasp of long-breathed structures, in which main themes return regularly enough to create a sense of organicism without tiresome repetition: so-called ritornello form. But a key difference is that Italian concerto forms are often loose and capricious, deliberately asymmetrical (half a theme here, a snatch of melody there), while many of Bach's are the opposite, long and thorough, each section going the distance and giving an impression of being exhaustive: the opposite of the loose and capricious. His harpsichord and violin concertos have long movements carefully planned around various keys, breaking off a returning theme in order to shoot off in another direction, resulting in a thoroughness or nimiety that becomes typical of many kinds of music in his hands.[3] Something of the kind can be seen in the Chromatic Fantasia and Fugue, a quite spectacular work that surely took time to evolve, with an overall harmonic and formal grasp in its two very different movements far beyond anything achieved in the free fantasias and the strict fugues of any predecessor. But the 'loose and capricious' have little part in it.

THE COMPETITION WITH MARCHAND

The year 1717 gave a new opportunity to our Bach, already so famous, to achieve still more honour: Marchand, a harpsichordist and organist famous in France, had come to Dresden and had himself heard with special approval before the king, and was so fortunate as to be offered a position in the king's service with considerable salary. The then concertmaster in Dresden, Volumier, wrote to Weimar to Bach, whose deserts were not unknown to him, and invited him to come to Dresden without delay, to challenge the arrogant Marchand to a musical competition [and test] who was the better. Bach accepted the invitation happily and journeyed to Dresden. Volumier received him with pleasure and obtained for him an opportunity to hear his opponent first, in secret. Bach then invited Marchand by a courteous hand-written note to a contest, in which he offered to play at sight anything musical that Marchand would give him, and promised himself ready and willing to do the same in turn. Certainly a great audacity! Marchand showed himself very willing. Time and place were arranged, not without the foreknowledge of the king. At the appointed time Bach found himself at the battle-scene in the house of a distinguished minister, where a large company of persons of high rank, and of both sexes, was gathered. Marchand kept them waiting a long time. Eventually . . . to the greatest astonishment, it was learnt that on the same day, and very early, Monsieur Marchand had departed Dresden by special coach. Consequently, Bach, now sole victor on the battleground, had enough opportunity to show how strongly he was armed against his opponent . . .

By the way, our Bach liked to give Marchand due credit for beautiful and very refined playing. (*Obituary*)

This story had been briefly told in print during Bach's lifetime, hence, perhaps, its now becoming the biggest single biographical item in the Obituary, twice as long as the Moonlight anecdote. But Emanuel does not take the opportunity to say more about his father, neither whether he was a fine interpreter of Marchand's suites, as was said later (Dok III, 125), nor even whether he was reluctant to talk about the competition, as was said later still (Dok III, 443). The latter is doubtful, for the differing details in

---

[3] Nimiety: Coleridge's word for the excessive regularity, the inappropriate thoroughness of Schiller's blank verse (*Table Talk*, 2 June 1834).

the story as variously reported look like the result of a middle-aged man's re-telling of an old anecdote about past triumphs – his very words, perhaps, in superfluous details like 'by special coach' (*mit Extrapost*). Like any good anecdote, this one implies a range of things, about contests such as were not uncommon at the time, and especially about published biographies and their sources.

Emanuel, probably knowing that the first reference in print to his father also belonged to 1717, surmised that he was indeed 'already so famous' by then, as he says. Or he could assume it from an account of the Dresden competition that had been published in 1739 by J. A. Birnbaum, university teacher of rhetoric, which mentions Marchand's importance, Bach's cour-teous letter to him and the Frenchman's flight. Birnbaum, who was also defending Bach against some recently published criticisms (see below, pp. 311f), had presumably learnt about it from the composer himself, who may have been goaded into publicizing a story that had taken place in Dresden, home of the newer musical styles preferred by the critic against whom Birnbaum was defending him. Birnbaum's account (Dok II, 348) appears in the second defence of Bach he published, not the first, as if the composer had meanwhile brought it to his attention: to have vanquished a French virtuoso in Dresden was a double feather in anybody's cap, espe-cially one criticized for too much artifice. Again, therefore, it looks as if Emanuel was taking up something already published, particularly as not long before Mattheson had told of another, earlier Dresden contest between the 'local' man Matthias Weckmann and another distinguished and admired visitor, J. J. Froberger (1740, 396).

From another and very different publication (Titon du Tillet's *Parnasse*, 1732), well-read musicians anywhere would know that Louis Marchand was considered by some to have been the best French keyboardist of his day, more naturally gifted than Couperin or Rameau. Pierre Du Mage already says in the preface to his *Premier Livre d'orgue* (1708) that his own music is modelled on *la savante école et dans le goût de l'Illustre Monsieur Marchand mon Maître*, and it is possible Bach knew Du Mage's book (it too was mentioned by Birnbaum), and therefore its praise of Marchand. Also, whether or not Emanuel knew it, Marchand was probably the composer of an anonymous piece in Anna Magdalena's album (see below, p. 158). Altogether, then, for the Obituary a story of Bach conquering Marchand was by no means point-less, in fact comparable to Handel instructing Corelli or surpassing Domenico Scarlatti, as recounted by Mainwaring just a few years later.

The salient points of a story probably not unique in the days of com-petitive meetings between professionals, seem to be these:

Marchand had been offered a well-paid position at the Court of Saxony

The Dresden violinist Volumier invited Bach over

Bach heard Marchand play (according not to Birnbaum but to the Obituary, which also reports his praise of Marchand's playing)

He wrote to him (in French?) suggesting an extemporization contest

Marchand agreed

The contest was to be in a minister's house, with the elector's knowledge

Many people (of both sexes) waited expectantly

But Marchand had left early that morning

The king rewarded Bach, but the 500 thalers were misappropriated by a servant.

Why the Obituary said the listeners were 'of both sexes' is unclear: because Bach had reported this himself, knowing that the queen (electress) was there as a potential employer, with a vested interest in Marchand's victory? What is pictured is a court appearance before people of fashion, not a church committee of the usual kind. No French sources give the story, but a Dresden document shows that Marchand received payment in the autumn of 1717 (BJ 1998, 14). Amongst the many embroideries given by much later versions are that modesty allowed Bach to speak of it only when pressed (unlikely), that the composers did meet (unlikely) and that Bach improvised on a theme given him by Marchand (possible – see FN 4).

Other conjectures are more plausible:

If (a big if) the story of the reward is true, the occasion cannot have been before October, i.e. shortly after the elector returned from Italy.

Since J. D. Heinichen was already court capellmeister, perhaps Marchand was to direct the Roman Catholic chapel, or the queen's music, and certain Dresden musicians were attempting to introduce J. S. Bach instead, as a Lutheran counterweight in a court of two factions.

The contest centred on harpsichord and chamber music. Although no extant sources suggest it, perhaps (parts of) the Fifth Brandenburg Concerto were first drafted for this occasion, with Dresden's musical 'specialities' in mind: harpsichord, virtuoso violin and transverse flute, this last for the first time in Bach's instrumental music. Its slow movement seems to use a theme by Marchand,[4] while the theme of the first resembles others by Vivaldi and Telemann (also in D major).

---

[4] See Pirro 1907, 429, also Louis Marchand, *Pièces d'orgue manuscrites*, Editions Fuzeau, facs. edn 90.400 (Fuzeau, 1990), f31'. The 'first version' of the Fifth Brandenburg Concerto is now dated to 1719 but there could well have been yet earlier versions.

As there was probably no fine organ available for a competition in Dresden until Gottfried Silbermann built his first organ there, in the Sophienkirche in 1718–20, some public virtuoso music for harpsichord, 'in a court minister's house', was more appropriate. Fine harpsichords were becoming of greater interest in Dresden, thanks to court patronage, and a possibility is that Bach offered this instrument – or that Marchand demanded it, since German organs were too different from what he was used to. By saying that Bach heard Marchand 'in secret', Emanuel or his source is implying that he did not make himself known, which seems out of character for J. S. Bach. Perhaps he tried, hence the idea that Marchand was too 'arrogant' (*hochmüthig*).

Three other conjectures concern possible job-searches:

Although Bach, anxious to leave Weimar, was committed to Cöthen (see below), the possibility of an incomparably better job in Dresden, where he could 'let himself be heard by the king', crossed his mind.

Two years later, Handel too was in Dresden, according to the same Count Flemming (HHB, 83) in whose house the Bach-Marchand contest was to have taken place, according to Forkel. Was Handel there too for a job – to succeed Lotti as royal opera-composer? Was Flemming contriving to get both Handel and Bach in Dresden, and did Emanuel know anything of this? (The grand occasion in 1719 was the marriage of the crown prince, when the new opera house was opened in the Zwinger Palace, an occasion when Quantz heard his first opera and when Telemann too was present, doubtless job-soliciting.)

If Marchand had already decided not to take the Dresden position and return to Paris, which is possible, perhaps he 'missed' the competition rather than shirked it.

The anecdote says nothing about any of this, but it seems entirely characteristic of something J. S. Bach told himself, that it should include a story about lost money. And who is speaking when the account adds this:

A Frenchman willingly turns down an offer made to him of a permanent salary of over a thousand thalers, and the German whose precedence he seems to concede by his flight was not even able take up the one *ex gratia* gift made to him by the king. (*Obituary*)

– Emanuel or his father? It could be either or both.

How or even whether Bach and the violinist Volumier were previously acquainted is not clearly documented, and there are many such questions about the circumstances of this abortive competition. By the time of the Obituary, every single significant personage who was or could have been involved had died, except the flute-virtuoso Buffardin who was no longer in Dresden. Consequently, it is not possible to know such things as whether any of Bach's works for solo violin, fair copied in 1720 as a set of six, had anything to do with Volumier, just as it is not whether the six later sonatas for violin and harpsichord had anything to do with Friedemann's violin-teacher Graun.

The reference to Bach made in print by Mattheson in 1717 includes a request for further biographical information, a request repeated in 1719, on each occasion apparently with no response (Dok II, 65, 75). Was the first request too close to the contretemps with the Duke of Weimar in November 1717 (see beginning of next chapter) for Bach to want to respond? Or he had read Telemann's autobiography of 1718 and was discouraged, repelled even, by its show of learning? Both could be the case, as again when the publicity Mattheson gave to Walther's library and his plan to publish some chorales (1725, pp. 175–6) evidently did not persuade Bach to ask for a similar notice in any of Mattheson's publications. A natural reserve, as well as its opposite, could be responsible for his silence, but neither makes it impossible that at least in later years, he kept a file of cuttings about himself, intended to join his genealogical table.

CHAPTER 4

Cöthen, 1717–23

THE CALL TO CÖTHEN

When our Bach had come back to Weimar [after the Dresden competition], and in the same year, the then Prince Leopold of Anhalt-Cöthen, a great connoisseur and lover of music, called him to be his Capellmeister. He took up the position without delay and held it for almost six years, to the greatest satisfaction of his gracious prince. (*Obituary*)

One reason Bach took up the position 'without delay' was that he was probably being paid some kind of retainer by Cöthen before the Dresden visit, whenever this took place in the autumn of 1717. The visit cannot have been later than early November – because from 6 November to 2 December 1717 Johann Sebastian Bach was in prison in Weimar, held in the 'district judge's chamber' or cell (*LandRichter-Stube*), on account of his 'show of obstinacy and for over-pressing his dismissal' (*halßstarrigen Bezeugung und erzwingenden dimission*: Dok II, 65), and was eventually released only on a dishonourable discharge. The Obituary says nothing about any of this, unless 'without delay' is an elliptical allusion to it: Bach so wanted to be free of Weimar he did not hesitate when the chance came, quickly removed himself, and later spoke about it in these terms.

Evidently, he had been accused and convicted by the duke on two charges, obstinacy and importunity, but neither is quite clear now. Several explanations are possible: 'obstinacy' means that Bach had resisted the decree against musicians playing for the junior duke; or had recently remonstrated against J. W. Drese Jnr succeeding as capellmeister, after Telemann had declined;[1] or had missed two important events at the end of October (the duke's birthday and the 200th anniversary of the Reformation) and made it known that

---

[1] As 'general capellmeister' to the main ducal or 'Ernestine line', so Telemann later said (Mattheson 1740, 364). It is likely that the Obituary authors knew this claim – it was in print, and Emanuel was in touch with Telemann – and also perhaps that whether they knew it or not, for some reason Bach chose not to compete with Telemann either at Weimar or (on other occasions) at Gotha or Leipzig.

he wanted to leave; or, as is quite possible, his demeanour was generally insubordinate. Other possibilities are that the senior duke was concerned about chapel standards, mortified to learn (if he did) that Bach was already accruing back pay at Cöthen, irritated by the junior duke's support for Bach, and jealous of his concertmaster's success in Dresden (if this had already happened). Whether Drese Jnr became capellmeister because Bach was agitating to leave, or vice-versa, is not clear from the known chronology. What is certain is that the junior duke had a personal association with the court of Cöthen, where the prince was his brother-in-law and about to employ his Concertmeister.

The duke's quasi-feudal treatment of Bach was nothing out of the ordinary. Both Weimar dukes were dictatorial, and during the junior duke's own reign later, a horn-player asking for dismissal was actually condemned to a hundred lashes and prison, and on escaping, was hanged in effigy.[2] If Bach's visit to Dresden took place before his incarceration, it could have been to get royal support for his request to leave Weimar – although the difficulties Quantz had in 1728 when trying to leave the Dresden court suggests there would have been no great sympathy from the Elector of Saxony. Besides, any approach to the king meant offending the Weimar duke by going above his head: note that Bach's offence in part lay, it seems, in exposing the matter elsewhere (*Bezeugung*, 'testimony'). At least the request for Bach's release was not denied on the formal grounds that he owed money, as his admired relation Johann Christoph's request had been at Eisenach some decades earlier.

Seventy and more years after the Weimar incident, E. L. Gerber, whose father was a Bach pupil during 1724–27, wrote what has sometimes been taken as referring to this imprisonment when he described the Well-tempered Clavier as being written – conceived? begun? compiled? – during a period in which the composer was depressed, bored and without an instrument (Dok III, 468). There are other periods to which this might apply, however: for example, Bach's second visit to Carlsbad with Prince Leopold in 1720 (see below), when he may have had nothing much to do. Either way, Gerber Snr must have heard something of the kind from the composer himself. For the Gerbers, the point of the remark was that their hero did not need a keyboard at hand for composing even complicated counterpoint, which in turn suggests that students did, but aspired not to.

---

[2] Glöckner 1988, 141. The University of Leipzig had a convicted but escaped student hanged in effigy on 8 March 1723 (Schneider 1995, 184), a few weeks before the Bach family arrived in Leipzig.

This particular point may be relevant to Bach's formal portrait made later at Leipzig, which shows him holding a piece of paper containing some difficult counterpoint (a canon), but not in the presence of an instrument. Portraits of Handel and Scarlatti, on the other hand, show them seated near a harpsichord,[3] though whether one is to understand this as their indispensable worktool or a mere emblem of their virtuosity is uncertain. Probably the latter.

THE MOVE TO CÖTHEN

The Weimar junior duke's marriage to the Prince of Cöthen's sister in January 1716 is the likely occasion on which the prince became aware of the court's concertmaster, either at the wedding itself or subsequently. Evidently, the prince's musicianship was impressive enough that word of it persisted into the Obituary over thirty years later.

So the opportunity to become the prince's capellmeister, whether or not actually solicited by Bach and/or encouraged by the junior duke, was too good to miss: the title signalled promotion, Weimar was becoming problematic, and the Cöthen prince was musical. The accounts do not make it as clear as usually supposed whether Bach was paid a retainer on 7 August 1717, and if so whether this was tantamount to deceiving Weimar, where he had not been released from his contract and was still being paid to the end of September. Or, when he signed for them on 29 December, payments could have been backdated by request and by some pre-arrangement (Dok I, 190; II, 67). But since the prince later referred to Bach as having been in his service since 5 August 1717 (Dok II, 93), it is difficult to quell the suspicion that he had been double-paid for a time and was deceiving the Duke of Weimar: not a sensible move, considering the duke's known authoritarianism.

Whatever the case, it looks from this and other circumstances that the young Prince Leopold was anxious to have Bach as 'capellmeister and director of our chamber music' at Cöthen (*ibid.*), and his enthusiasm became part of the picture Emanuel drew later when he remarked that along with the Dukes of Weissenfels and Weimar, the Cöthen prince particularly valued and rewarded his father (Dok III, 289). To these ducal admirers one may add the Kings of Saxony and of Prussia in later years, offering a glimpse

---

[3] Another portrait of Handel in the University Library, Hamburg (1749), shows him holding a score, with a copy of *Messiah* on a table, but no instrument. The well-known engraved portrait of Couperin (1735) is comparable.

of what Emanuel's father may have missed by his long service to the churches and burghers of Leipzig. Does the phrase 'particularly valued and rewarded' have any bearing on why Bach's predecessor at Cöthen, Augustin Reinhard Stricker, vacated the post? Stricker felt less valued, despite dedicating a published set of Italian cantatas to Leopold in 1715?

Precisely when the Bach family moved to Cöthen is unknown, but a guess is that it was in time for the prince's twenty-third birthday celebrations on 10 December 1717, with special music prepared for a prince who, according to the composer in a formula he used elsewhere, was 'as much a lover as connoisseur' of music (Dok I, 67). Prince Leopold also stood as godfather to the Bachs' first child born after moving there, Leopold Augustus. For a brief period Leopold Bach was a member of a family of seven, living in part of a house that appears to have been something of a centre for the Lutheran citizens of the Reformed city of Cöthen (see below).

Whatever being detained in the Weimar 'district judge's chamber' meant for a quite senior court-employee – something more like a room in a debtor's prison than a prison cell of popular imagination? – Bach is not likely to have been *incommunicando* there. Only two weeks after release from detention he was in Leipzig to test the newly rebuilt organ of the university church, the Paulinerkirche, and this must have been previously arranged somehow. So much travel within a short period – Weimar-Dresden-Weimar-Cöthen-Leipzig-Cöthen – seems excessive. Perhaps it could be that the visit to Dresden for the 'Marchand competition' was not a separate trip but an excursion Bach made during his stay in Leipzig, having met up with the violinist Volumier there, and not, as Emanuel said, hearing from him only by letter. (It was important for Emanuel to say that his father had been invited to Dresden, moreover by a court instrumentalist, since this would mean he had not offered himself to compete for a job.) Since Marchand's stay in Dresden is not precisely dated, it will never be clear how far the anecdote concerning him is a colourful re-interpretation of events by Bach himself. If it is, it reveals a great deal.

But in any case, the effect on Bach of a hectic schedule in four different places – prison, abortive competition, relocation, organ-examination – can only be guessed. For on 17 December, already as capellmeister to his highness the prince of Anhalt-Cöthen (*Hochfürstlich Anhalt-Cöthenscher Capellmeister etc.*), he signed a report on the Leipzig organ that shows no sign of skimping, indeed was prepared 'with diligence' according to a chronicler (Dok I, 166). He was surely invited for such a significant instrument on the recommendation of Kuhnau, at that time Leipzig cantor and a colleague at the recent examination in Halle, and he directed the examination in the presence of the current university rector, a former rector, two senate members, another organ-builder and another Leipzig organist. His unusually high fee of twenty thalers from the university was for taking formal delivery of the organ, testing it and listing its defects. The report – dictated or drafted and only signed by him (Dok I, 189) – comments in good detail on the organ's overall structure, its inner working, stoplist, voicing, tuning and key-action, recommends that a window behind the organ be covered up and a one-year guarantee signed with the organ-builder, and goes on to ask that consideration be given the builder for his work extra to contract (Dok I, 165). Much of this again resembles very closely points made in Werckmeister's *Orgelprobe* and is, one might think, a little too trusting of the builder. Three important church musicians, Kuhnau of the Thomaskirche (St Thomas, Leipzig), Kauffmann of Merseburg and Lindner of Freiberg, had already been considered as examiners (Dok II, 69): did they decline, and if so in protest that a previous bid by the young master-builder Gottfried Silbermann to rebuild the university's organ from top to bottom had come to nothing?

THE CÖTHEN APPOINTMENT

At 2,000, Cöthen's population was tiny, less than half Weimar's, its whole principality amounting only to some 10,000 inhabitants, and dominated by its court and palace.[4] In most respects it was like so many of the smaller German residence towns and not limitlessly stimulating, but its prince's musical interests have left it with a significant place in history. In other respects too the town and court were very different from Weimar. Not orthodox Lutheran but Reformed, the court is thought to have required no church cantatas and no organ music, despite half of its musicians being Lutherans. The attraction of the job, other than a rise in pay, must therefore have been its opportunities for non-church music and music-making, moreover with especially fine colleagues. Another and important factor is that its young prince seems to have become something of a personal friend to the composer, which alone must have given the job rather a different tone from Weimar's.

As a teenager, Prince Leopold of Anhalt-Cöthen had toured, heard opera in The Hague, brought back French and Italian music, studied in Italy with a competent musician (J. D. Heinichen, later capellmeister in Dresden),

---

[4] It is seldom clear from recorded population counts, however, whether the numbers are adults only, communicants only, householders only, etc.

played string and other instruments, returned to his inheritance with enthusiasm, and by 1717 had some fifteen musicians on his payroll. Unfortunately, it is not possible to compare the music he brought back from his travels with that imported in a similar way by Prince Johann Ernst of Weimar, but Bach certainly had the benefit of both. Because Leopold was a strong player himself, reliably said later to have played the violin 'not badly' and sung 'a good bass' (Dok III, 188), there is a temptation to surmise that concertos including the Third Brandenburg had the prince as a participant. There being no need to employ a chapel choir, resources could be directed to instrumentalists (strings, woodwind and brass), and while the number participating in the ensemble at any one point is not certain, the establishment generally matched that of many a much larger court's *cappella*. Leopold's was bigger and better paid than that at neighbouring Zerbst, for example. In addition, the town of Cöthen had a band of twelve *Stadtpfeifer* it could call upon, no doubt sharing at least some of its players with the court.

As the court was Reformed (Calvinist), the Bach family remained regular members of the town's Lutheran church, renting a pew in the Agnuskirche (St Agnus's Church), to the daughter of whose cantor Sebastian stood as godfather. For the prince, to be 'capellmeister and director of chamber music' (as the titlepage to Well-tempered Clavier puts it) meant director of some fifteen or sixteen first-rate musicians in chamber music and special-event cantatas, often with extra players. It is conjectured that some dozen cantatas were composed for birthdays, New Year, the prince's wedding in December 1721, etc., and now known only in part. (That *occasional* cantatas have left such a scrappy fund of copies, unless rewritten for other purposes, was normal: the many wedding cantatas composed, compiled or re-arranged by Bach's predecessors in Leipzig have also not survived.) The level of musical achievement at Cöthen must have been higher than at Weimar, with such musicians as C. F. Abel, viol player, whose son worked later in London with Bach's son Johann Christian; C. B. Lienicke, cellist, member of a scattered musical family;[5] and several other virtuosi on violin and woodwind. Before Bach's appointment Leopold had attracted several court musicians from Berlin, who had been dismissed on the succession of the philistine King of Prussia, Friedrich Wilhelm.

---

[5] Probably related to the viola-player D. Linike (Leneker, Lunecan), one of Handel's first copyists in London (a score of *Rinaldo*, 1711) and J. G. Linike, concertmaster at Weissenfels, who contributed to Handel's opera *Giulio Cesare* in Hamburg in 1725 (HHB, 52, 137).

While cantatas composed for various occasions at Cöthen, so far as known from surviving excerpts, have a common musical style overall – a chamber-like quality, dance-like, melodious in a kind of generalized italianate idiom – No. 194a pairs distinct styles such as Bach (and his prince?) liked: a French *ouverture* complete with fugue is followed by a series of Italian recitatives and arias. Comparable pairing but now in complete pieces is found in the solo violin works compiled in Cöthen, the *Sei solo* of 1720. Telemann constantly adopted styles, and Handel's first set of suites, published in the same year 1720, significantly begins with a French *ordre* followed by an Italian *sonata*, neither of them so-called but each with four movements and obviously contrasted. Adopting national styles must have been a natural extension of learning to work in the more modern genres and to apply characteristic details of each musical style. The very words, *suite* (French), *sonata* (Italian), *praeludium* and *fuga* (Latinate), earmark particular genres with distinctive characteristics that were observed by composers with surprising consistency. One can recognize in two arias of the Birthday Serenata for Leopold, BWV 173a, a pair of dances (bourrées) that are typical of *alternativement* movements in an orchestral suite.

Because of such identifiable distinctions, rather than the Brandenburg Concertos having a part-writing and motif-development that 'definitely predate the standards set by The Well-tempered Clavier' (Wolff 2000, 232), what they are doing is something quite different and for a quite different purpose. As music for group performance, more public than keyboard fugues, they are testing the limits of a distict genre, one for mixed or unmixed consort, i.e. the solo concerto or the concerto grosso whose solo group can vary from two to four instruments. The movement-shapes come from a variety of sources, suites (binary dances), sonatas (intricate ABA) and concertos (ritornello). To this unmatched array of forms and concepts, the rigorous keyboard counterpoint of the WTCi's fugues is more or less irrelevant, although by now, Bach's mastery of invertible counterpoint (qv) is evident everywhere, including instrumental music for concerts. It is not easy to establish the chronology of compositions from such comparisons, at this or any period in Bach's life, for his grasp of different genres and their characteristics means that, in effect, each is compartmentalized.

Other than his sons Friedemann and Emanuel and his nephew Bernhard (who did some work at court as a copyist), what pupils Bach had in Cöthen is not known for sure, although Bernhard's work suggests again the picture of a teacher soliciting on behalf of his students. Nor is it known whether he regularly played any organ in the town or visited organs in the neighbourhood for pleasure. Since his salary was twice and soon more than twice his predecessor's, with further payment for maintaining the harpsichord and lending his house for rehearsals, clearly he was highly valued. Chamber music must have been energetically developed under his direction – hence the copying done by Bernhard? – and he was enabled to hire performers from elsewhere for special occasions. Interestingly, in view of the directive in Weimar about locating rehearsals, at Cöthen Bach was able use his own house for rehearsing and got paid extra for it. Was this for the sake of privacy, status, convenience, greater geniality, a better-maintained harpsichord at home, bigger income, or stronger control over the preparation of performances?

Rehearsal activity (*exercitium musicum* each week is documented) suggests at least a weekly concert, played in the throne-room of the castle, but there could have been many other contexts or occasions for which incidental music was required. Various expenses for the music library are recorded. Unfortunately, since Cöthen's terms of employment are not known and may never have been written down, and since copies of music again belonged to the court and disappeared over time unless re-used by the composer, one can only guess that Bach produced many chamber works there. Losses from Cöthen are equalled by those elsewhere. Considering how much he produced in the first two years at Leipzig, both for the church and elsewhere, and how out of character it would have been for him to neglect composition, a great deal must be missing – perhaps the bulk of some 350 compositions all told (Wolff 2000, 200). That there was a great deal of musical activity is not doubted. The keyboard counterpoint of WTCI and the Inventions would cost even J. S. Bach a great deal of time and trouble, and from the point of view of effort the various sets of suites for keyboard or violin or cello would be the equivalent, if quicker to score, of many a cantata or concerto.

Cöthen music re-used in various guises later has often had its tracks covered over, and the strange fact remains that largely because the individual kinds of music are always so fully explored on each occasion, some of the best-known chamber and ensemble music of Bach has such an uncertain origin. What can be plausibly suggested as music suitable for Leopold's Cöthen ensemble can often be as plausibly suggested for the Leipzig chamber concerts, and extant sources need not be the last word on what existed, when it originated, and what form(s) it had taken. It is difficult to specify what in a violin concerto shows it to be 'maturer' or 'later' than a solo violin sonata when each has its own idiom and style, relating only superficially to any other. Dating much of this music is still problematic.

Evidently the capellmeister and five or six musicians complete with a harpsichord travelled with the sickly prince to Carlsbad, Bohemia, on 9 May 1718, where he took the spa waters and apparently had his musicians perform, perhaps holding semi-private concerts of a kind becoming popular in towns across Europe. It seems that the keyboard instrument taken to Carlsbad was no longer good enough for (solo?) concert work, for in March the next year, Bach was in Berlin to pick up a new two-manual harpsichord by Michael Mietke, the Berlin court instrument-maker whose extant instruments have served in recent decades for reconstructions of 'the Bach harpsichord'. Such an exceptional new instrument,[6] made not locally but by a builder probably recommended by those of the prince's musicians who had come from Berlin, would feature prominently in the chamber group, along with the virtuoso capellmeister himself. A two-manual harpsichord need be no louder than a single-manual, nor is it necessary for ordinary continuo work. Rather, it encourages variety of effect for solo sonatas and transcriptions, or trio-sonatas with flute or violin or gamba, or even concertos such as the Fifth Brandenburg.

In 1722, Cöthen acquired another striking instrument, a harpsichord with pedals, useful (so one may guess) for private practice, teaching the organ, concerts, composing, and not least for satisfying the acquisitive curiosity of princes and arousing the envy of their guests. Both instruments were surely asked for by Capellmeister Bach, and like other exceptional instruments, such as the lute-harpsichord made for the junior duke in Weimar, would have been something to make a public show to which a prince was not indifferent. How far the new Berlin harpsichord led Bach towards music idiomatic to the instrument in the way of his French and Italian contemporaries, is difficult to say. So often for him, an instrument is a tool for putting various versatile musical ideas into practice, not a source suggesting certain ideas suiting one instrument rather than another. Hence the near-indifference as to which instrument plays some of his music. In this connection, the keyboard transcriptions of Italian concertos are interesting, for two manuals are certainly possible if not specified in most movements, as if the option were left there. Perhaps it was. The layout of an Italian concerto, with its solos and tuttis, encourages such 'scoring', as of course it does in the later *Italian Concerto*.

The English Suites, probably in the making over several years from late Weimar to early Leipzig, tend towards the kind of true harpsichord writing

---

[6] A Cöthen inventory of 1784 still lists the harpsichord's maker as *Michael Mietke in Berlin 1719* (Dok II, 74), i.e. this is probably what its nameboard said.

one finds here and there in Handel: sustained harmonies and a sensitive legato that are still some way from the subtle and varied textures of a Rameau but closer than the writing shown in Example 3 (b) above. In much the same period, the French Suites are also moving towards 'sensitive articulation', and by the time of the Partitas in B flat, G major and especially B minor, *c.* 1730, Bach is scanning textures as varied as Rameau's. But the Inventions, in including so many galant details (pretty melody, certain sighing figures, a song-like line, delicate cadences), are already responding to good harpsichord tone and sensitive touch. How much any of this music was composed (or gathered in the sets as we know them) for playing on the new Berlin harpsichord is unknown, but the instrument may well have been an inspiration. For example, the big preludes of the English Suites are so written as to make two manuals plausible, really for the first time on this scale, even if in the absence of autograph MSS it cannot be known whether the composer ever indicated two manuals in any way.

In including so many of the standard details of suite-dances, the English Suites are the most French of Bach's sets, especially as copied and ornamented by his pupil H. N. Gerber. Why and when they became so called is no better known than it is in the case of the French Suites: the labels are surely meant to be distinctive, especially if later students ever called Six Partitas 'German Suites', as they might have done. Forkel said that the English Suites were composed for an English nobleman (1802, 56) and presumably sent over, which would explain why no autograph is known. But there is another possibility: since other German composers had recently published suites in London (Mattheson 1714 and Handel 1720), Bach sent his set to an English publisher, who would have been quite unused to such complexities as are found in its final gigue. A copy of the English Suites owned by Johann Christian Bach, the 'London Bach', was marked 'fait pour les Anglois' (NBA V/7 KB, 26), but this could indicate a publisher as well as a patron, even someone who had become known to Prince Leopold on his visit to London in 1711.

There are certain similarities between Bach's and Handel's set of suites: the first one in both sets is in A major; their two E minor suites open with a fugue; unusually, Bach's A major Allemande has distinctly (and unusually) Handelian moments; and both sets require longer keyboard compass than had been customary in Germany. If such similarities are reliable indicators, here then is another of Bach's sets of pieces inspired by a recent publication elsewhere and, in response, compiled from new and older material.

THE 'BRANDENBURG CONCERTOS'

It seems from the dedication of the *Six Concerts Avec plusieurs Instruments. Dediées [sic] à . . . Cretien Louis, Marggraf de Brandenbourg*, dated 24 March 1721, that when Bach had been in Berlin collecting the new harpsichord for his prince 'a couple of years ago', he had 'the good fortune to be heard' by the margrave, half-brother of Frederick the Great's grandfather (*il y a une couple d'années, le bonheur de me faire entendre*: Dok I, 216). Twenty-three years earlier, Werckmeister's *Orgelprobe*, a book almost certainly known to Bach, had been dedicated to the same patron, the *Marggraffen zu Brandenburg*, and probably neither Werckmeister nor Bach knew that this was less the title of a marquisate than a reference to the place of family origin.

Here again, this time written by the composer, is the phrase 'good fortune to be heard' by a prince. If 'a couple of years' means literally two, as seems to be the case, a question is, Why the delay? Was the set another of those compiled over time from older and newer material? No documents suggest that there was a vacant position at the margrave's court or about to be, nor that Bach was thinking of leaving Cöthen for any reason, such as tensions between Lutherans and Reformed factions. Nevertheless, nothing was ever lost by impressing royalty, and to prepare a fair-copy autograph score itself suggests a desire to be looked on favourably. Evidently, not only was Bach 'heard' by nobility, or in this instance royalty, but had been so by virtue of the nobleman's commands (*en vertu de ses ordres*) – though whether these were a response to solicitation or a freely given invitation is not to be discerned from the words. The dedication also says that the margrave commanded Bach to send him some compositions (*commander de Lui envoyer quelques pieces*), from the sending of which the still young composer might have expected some kind of future patronage. What he sent from Cöthen was some music for court chamber players, not for church or for solo performance, rather as he later offered the king in Dresden music for his theatre (see p. 221).

By accident or otherwise, the dedication in the fair-copy MS of the Brandenburgs, in French, is reminiscent of other French prefaces, especially the one to Louis Marchand's *Livre premier. Pièces de clavecin* of 1702, dedicated to the king, Louis XIV. Whether Bach had help with his dedication is unknown. Its final verbal flourishes recall those in yet another French publication, Jean-Henri d'Anglebert's *Pièces de clavecin* of 1689, whose ornament table Bach had copied a decade or so earlier (after changing the clef), in the manuscript now containing the copy he made of Grigny's *Livre d'orgue.* Furthermore, it is not obvious where Bach learnt the French word *concerts*, which was not a fully regular term before the 1720s, when it tends to mean pieces for mixed consort or ensemble rather than 'concerto' in the familiar Italian sense. Perhaps he had heard it from the handful of French musicians he knew in Celle, Weimar, Cöthen and Berlin, or from a now unidentified volume of music. Couperin's formative *Concerts royaux* may have been circulating in MS several years before being published in 1722, conceivably reaching Berlin-Brandenburg, but their scoring and scope are much more limited than Bach's. Generally, whatever the significance of this word *concerts*, with the Brandenburgs and the margrave a composer might well feel he was entering upon – participating in – a Europe-wide world, grander than anywhere he was coming from. If so, any disappointment that it led nowhere would be unsurprising.

For any Berlin court-members present in the 'hearing' of 1719, whether in the Berlin Stadtschloss (royal palace) or at the margrave's estate at Berlin-Malchow nearby, Bach had presumably improvised some harpsichord solos. Two conjectures are that he took along with him a version of the Fifth Brandenburg, and that its harpsichord solos were still fresh from the triumph over Marchand in Dresden: public music going from one court to another. The margrave's musical library as recorded on his death in 1734 lists many Italian concertos that would not have been much like French *concerts* in style or format, although the catalogue's terms *Concerte und Sinfonien* might include French pieces of some kind, and Lully's name does appear in the list (see Besseler 1956, 33ff). How the Brandenburg Concertos autograph came to survive when the library as such did not is also uncertain but may have something to do with Bach's pupil J. P. Kirnberger, who worked in Berlin from 1751.

On his return to Cöthen, and gradually compiling his pieces as a conventional set of six, Bach's procedure seems to have been much like that of most of his other compilations: that is, some movements composed earlier for various occasions were collected, arranged or rewritten and then joined by new movements or whole works, so as to complete a set of six variegated pieces planned for a particular purpose, and brought together to explore what can be done with the kind of music in hand, whether concertos, suites, fugues or anything else. A reasonable assumption would be that Bach also made another score of the finalized set of Brandenburgs for himself, though this may not have been necessary for any later use he was to make of some of their twenty-two movements. A much later copy of the separate instrumental parts of No. 5 made mostly by J. C. Altnickol seems to draw on a version earlier than the margrave's, which suggests that at least some fund of copies (instrumental parts) existed, as do several different kinds of later Leipzig works that re-use certain Brandenburg movements.

As with the other compilations, what the 'original' form of certain works or parts of works was is not always clear, other versions having been lost or superseded or left ambiguous. Sources themselves may have deliberately left open various options for instrumentation. Thus, based on the patchy extant documentation, it has been argued that No. 2 had two other authentic versions, one allowing horn as an alternative to trumpet, the other making a consort of the four soloists and continuo only, without the strings. This is not an implausible idea and rather confirms the nature of the work as a kind of broken consort, qv. No. 5 too may have had different versions depending on the size of the available harpsichord. In the case of No. 1, one version with fewer movements and headed 'Sinfonia' by a copyist (BWV 1046a) has been described in various ways: as an earlier work (even partly or wholly a prelude to Cantata 208), or a later (i.e. showing details of Bach's maturer part-writing), or as neither (i.e. both it and the Brandenburg version are based on a missing 'original').

The colourful scorings, though different from one another to a degree unusual in such a compendium, may reflect current practices more than is now sometimes assumed. Even No. 6's pairs of violas and gambas without violins were not unfamiliar in older German cantatas, either in texture or timbre. The scoring itself, therefore, is not a sign that this concerto was composed earlier than the others, or is 'archaic' in intention, or once had a different scoring. On the contrary, No. 6 in particular conforms to the composer's wording of the titlepage: *concerts*, consort pieces in several movements to be played one to a part by various combinations of instruments, either uniform or mixed ('broken consort'), either amateur or, more and more often, professional. No Brandenburgs require an 'orchestra' in any modern sense. From the terms employed in the various sources, including autograph, firm conclusions cannot be drawn on whether the composer expected (required) the bass to be doubled an octave below, nor is it always obvious (as it is with modern instruments) which octave-level tone a violone is producing.

No. 3 expands the notion of a string consort to nine parts, 3+3+3 plus continuo for harpsichord and probably some kind of bass, and there are faint signs in the make-up that at first the scoring was not for three cellos but only one. As finally realized, Nos. 3 and 6 explicitly contrast the old (rich, subtle viols in No. 6) with the new (brilliant, brash violins in No. 3), and of course do so with a tremendous sense of melody and rhythm, marvellous pieces with an uncanny grasp of truly effective string music.

Nos. 2, 4 and 5 are only in a special and newly conceived sense concerti grossi, with a quartet and two very different trios of soloists, now in combinations new to the world of Italian concertos, with a sound and *Affekt* again unique to each, and instantly recognizable. These novel scorings could well be some kind of reaction to the more uniform scoring and sounds of Corelli's concertos Op. 6 (Amsterdam, 1712), the *locus classicus* of the standard type of concerto grosso. For although Bach is not documented as knowing these works, it is hardly conceivable that Prince Johann Ernst would have brought back from Amsterdam to Weimar the parts for Vivaldi's Op. 3 but not those for Corelli's Op. 6 – twelve concertos of enormously widespread influence. Bach scholars seeking Vivaldi in the Brandenburgs might be looking for the wrong composer.

A further point concerns Brandenburg No. 5, for though now often regarded as (i) the original trailblazer for (ii) the true keyboard concerto, it is neither. It is not less or more of a solo concerto (except in having more than one movement) than some earlier pieces by Handel, such as the Sonata in *Il trionfo*, 1707 or the harpsichord obbligato aria 'Vò far guerra' in *Rinaldo*, 1710. For a soloist to have so modest a role in a concerto's slow movement as he does in the Fifth Brandenburg (partner in a trio) would have seemed as odd to Handel in his concertos for organ as to Mozart in his concertos for piano. Nevertheless, there are some striking parallels between the Fifth Brandenburg and these various isolated Handel pieces. They each have the movement-shape of a concerto with solo episodes of somewhat naive, flashy broken chord textures. These solo episodes reflect Italian habits, even rival them, and moreover can exist in more than one version, as is the case also with Vivaldi: like more than one Vivaldi concerto, the Fifth Brandenburg has a so-called cadenza in two surviving versions, probably the longer of which was specially made for the margrave's set.[7] In such ways, but also on the personal level, one could see both Handel and Bach as competing with famed virtuosi abroad, Handel with the two Scarlattis, Bach with Louis Marchand.

If by 1700 the continuo keyboardist in Italian operas, cantatas and concertos was beginning to be more conspicuous in the ensemble than written scores suggest, it becomes easier to see how a work with solo organ like Vivaldi's Concerto RV 779 (same period as Handel's *Il trionfo*) comes about.

---

[7] Note that the so-called cadenza of the Fifth Brandenburg Concerto is not a true *cadenza* (though its last thirty bars are one long preparation for the cadence) but the *final solo episode* of a ritornello movement, prompted by episodes in e.g. Vivaldi's Violin Concerto RV 208, a work already (?) arranged by Bach for organ, BWV 594.

Mattheson, who had observed Handel's playing on more than one occasion, reported later (1739, 88) how in his stage productions Handel often turned his harpsichord accompaniments into inimitable improvised solos. (Let us hope this was during episodes in arias when the soloist was not singing.) It would be nothing strange for the cosmopolitan musicians of Cöthen or Berlin-Brandenburg to know of such Italian practices, and there was even a potential link between London and Cöthen through members of the Lienicke family of musicians. Of Bach too it was later reported that he made a habit of accompanying in such a way that 'one thought it was a concerto', according to his pupil Mizler (Dok II, 321). And earlier, in playing the Fifth Brandenburg, he also 'must have captivated by the lightness and elasticity of his fingers' anyone who heard him play it, as Burney said of Handel's playing in *Rinaldo* (1789, 224). Bach being Bach, however, his concerto solos could never be criticized by Burney, as Handel's were, for containing 'not one learned or solid passage'.

There is no evidence that the Margrave of Brandenburg or his musicians used Bach's concertos, rewarded their composer or even acknowledged them, much less put him in the way of a royal appointment in Brandenburg or Berlin. This is so despite a broad hint in the dedication when Bach describes his desire to serve on occasions 'more worthy of your Highness' (*plus dignes d'Elle*: Dok I, 217). A Berlin student taken in by him in Leipzig in 1725 (Dok II, 218) is not known to have had any connection with the margrave. For Bach's later concerts in the Leipzig *Collegium*, the Brandenburgs' idiosyncratic and old-fashioned scoring are unlikely to have been of much use, except perhaps for parts of Nos. 2 and 5. No set of 'Six Concertos' is listed in the Obituary, although other sets of six pieces are, and during the whole Leipzig period Emanuel may never have known the 'Six Brandenburg Concertos' as such. One of two movements from the First Brandenburg used in a cantata of 1726 (BWV 207, 'Vereinigte Zwietracht') was fundamentally re-scored and expanded with phrases for the chorus, resulting in an ingenious and convincing metamorphosis.

SOME OTHER MUSIC AT CÖTHEN

In Cöthen, the period July 1719 to May 1720 saw considerable court expenditure on copying and binding music, commissioning and printing texts, and hiring musicians. All this was apparently for performances of music not otherwise documented or described, so one can only conjecture what works of Bach contributed to a lively musical scene beyond the performance of ten or so cantatas, or rather *serenatas* (qv), that have survived in part. Thereafter, until he leaves for Leipzig, Bach's output is uncertain, and it is possible that poor documentation reflects a dropping-off in the production of ensemble works, not unconnected with a change of priorities at court. Quite apart from the philistine wife the prince married in 1721, his uncertain finances requiring the *cappella* to be reduced by a third in 1720, and some trouble with his domains, the prince's life was also marred by bouts of sickness. Hence the visits to the Carlsbad spa waters (1718, 1720) and hence even the cantata-texts that – at some stretching of the imagination – seem to refer to illness, which was the case three or more times over these years. In general, however, the chronology makes it quite likely that over the 1720–21 period, Bach devoted a lot of creative energy to less public music, for keyboard and for strings.

A major part of the capellmeister's job was to produce works for voices and instruments marking one or other event at court, in particular the prince's birthday when a serenata text would be set to dance-like music (BWV 66a, 173a, 184a). There seems to have been a particularly active hiring of outside musicians over the turn of 1718/19 and beyond, presumably at the capellmeister's request, and many of the known cantata arias have demanding parts for wind soloists. It is possible that the three violin concertos best known today (two solo, one duo) also originated during the Cöthen years, inspired on one hand by the playing of the fine ex-Berlin violinists and on the other by the challenge of creating concertos more thoughtful and less reliant on virtuoso fireworks than Vivaldi's. (Not that Bach's are easier to play: the D minor Concerto known in the harpsichord version BWV 1052 but also probably for violin originally, taxes both harpsichordist and violinist.) All movements in these works follow Venetian models up to a point, with striking themes reflecting the natural rhetoric of string instruments, plus many details typical of Bach, in both melody and harmony.

Yet the regularity in the organization and the attention to detail especially in the inner parts all result in an idiom distant from the many conventions found in Italian concertos. The imitation, the harmonic tension, the purposeful bass-line – even the moments when the violin engages in traditional string effects are peculiar to J. S. Bach. At one point in the finale of the A minor Concerto there is a persistent, grinding open e′-string effect inherited from earlier composers (the so-called *bariolage*) but infinitely more original, almost distracting the ear from the effortless imitation below and the splendid effect of recapitulation when the soloist joins in for the theme at the end (Example 15).

In the later transcription for harpsichord, BWV 1058, this 'grinding' effect is much less conspicuous, and disappointingly so: by *c.* 1740, perhaps

15 Violin Concerto in A minor, finale

it was looking a little old-fashioned, or seemed to the composer to have
been too specific to the violin.

The formal devices in these concertos, such as the slow movements of
the two solo ones for violin when the bass-line slowly throbs and periodically returns, can be traced to Vivaldi but not the density of their detail,
their harmonic drive and the solo melody. Typical melodic details are the
soaring *cantabile* slow movements and the little dactyl patterns in the
allegro themes, and typical harmonic details are the occasional turns of
direction and the lively ritornello themes in unison. That Vivaldi's influence could just as easily have produced a much thinner kind of composition – not much counterpoint, commonplace sequences, unadventurous

harmonic rhythm – is suggested by other German concertos of the time, such as the transcription, attributed to Bach, of Telemann's G minor Concerto, BWV 985 (*c.* 1714?). The density of texture as Bach worked it in the English Suites might well be a reaction to such thinness.

On 22 January 1720, Bach also began a little album of keyboard music for Friedemann, then aged nine: the *Clavierbüchlein*, corresponding in size and format to the album of organ-chorales later called Orgelbüchlein. Few glimpses of any composer's life and fatherly affection are clearer than appear here, throughout but especially in certain little pieces of music: two allemandes, started by the father and continued by the son, who in one of them could not quite get the hang of returning to the tonic without further help, which father supplied. The Clavierbüchlein would have instructed Friedemann in rudiments, notation, clefs, figured bass, fingering, ornamentation, playing and reading in many different keys, composing in certain styles and genres, and, up to a point, in extemporization. (For some further speculations on the relationship with Friedemann and on the programme of instruction, see pp. 353f and 345.) The book also gave the child practice in a very important art: to learn to copy accurately, as when the composer writes out the first bar of the C minor Prelude WTCI and leaves the rest for the pupil to copy.

The album is the first of four important books of keyboard pieces compiled and/or given thoughtful titles during the Cöthen period, between 1720 and 1723:

Clavier-Büchlein 1720, 'Little Keyboard Album for W. F. Bach'

Das Wohltemperirte Clavier I 1722 (or 1723?), first part of 'Well-tempered Clavier'. On the possibility that the title was the result of second thoughts, see p. 337

Auffrichtige Anleitung 1723, 'Straightforward Guidance', the Two- and Three-part Inventions

Orgel-Büchlein 1722/23, 'Little Organ Album'. On this title being written in some time after the pieces, see p. 96.

In effect, all the titlepages refer to *learners*, the first to Friedemann, the others in more general terms. Although, on one reckoning, the latter three titlepages date from a period after the death of Kuhnau in June 1722, i.e. when Bach may have had eyes set on the Leipzig cantorate and its potential for teaching gifted young musicians, all four would also fit in with Friedemann's doubtlessly increasing skills. These three also have titles well in the style of contemporary publications, to be a part of which may also have been the intention. 'Album' was a common word for little books of prayers; 'well-tempered' was in circulation following Werckmeister's books;

and if 'genuine guidance' (or 'upright instruction') seems a more fanciful title, it is less fanciful than 'monthly keyboard fruits' (for Graupner's suites, 1722). It is also more explicitly didactic than 'musical church- and house-enjoyment' (for Vetter's chorales, 1713).

The Inventions' titlepage makes their intention quite clear, i.e. through them the young, inquisitive musician will learn to play neatly in two parts (*reine spielen*), then to manage three parts accurately and well (*richtig und wohl*); then to find good ideas (*inventiones*) and learn to develop them; and above all, to achieve a singing style in playing on the keyboard (*cantable*) and to acquire a taste for composition. Bach was not the person to write a practical tutor, but his titlepages, as far as they go, do lay out a programme of sorts: to learn to play without mistakes and sustain the counterpoint, to develop a good touch, and to think as a composer, i.e. find ideas and what to do with them. Except in giving models for a prospective composer, the programme rather resembles Couperin's fuller plan of instruction in his *L'Art de toucher le clavecin* 1716, for which, and especially for the word *cantable*, see also p. 304, below.

Teaching Friedemann and individual pupils cannot have been Bach's only outlet as a musician, one with an urge born of the Lutheran duty to instruct and demonstrate to others. There is a further fair-copy compilation of music made in 1720 which also has a clear double programme, in this case (a) to stretch the player and (b) to provide compositional models. This is the collection of six works for solo violin, the *Sei solo* marked 'Opus I', three sonatas and three suites. Their common name today, the 'unaccompanied violin partitas', is doubly misleading. 'Unaccompanied' would be better replaced by 'without a continuo part', because the instrument makes its own accompaniment and the composer himself describes them as *senza Basso accompagnato*; and 'partita' is neither appropriate for the three sonatas amongst the six works nor entirely so for the three suites, each of which Bach called 'partia'.

Quite apart from the overwhelming subjective impression left by these unique violin pieces, their systematic organization (Italian sonata, French suite), their carefully scanned range (three *exempla* of each genre, a variety of headings) and the very length of certain movements (the fugues, the chaconne), all suggest a maturing in the composer's idea of a coherent group. They are matched by the Six Suites for cello, apparently seen by their composer as a sequel, Opus 2 to Opus 1, called respectively *Pars 2* and *Pars 1* in Anna Magdalena's later copy of them. This numbering need not mean that the cello suites were composed second, and on the contrary, one might suppose them to have come first, not only because of details of style – these, as so often, can be used for arguments either way – but because such very formal music for cello or tenor viol without a bass part was less innovative than for violin. If the violin solos did come first, they were directly respond- ing to what could well have been a traditional interest of court musicians in 'upgrading' the fiddle music of tavern and marketplace. The notation of both sets of solo string works is also noteworthy in being less literal than most of the keyboard music: notes are often given a length not pos- sible in performance, and the score represents an ideal such as other music rarely does.[8]

Who played either set of solo string works is not known, nor how regu- larly if at all such music was heard at court, but some interest in them is likely: courts and their various *Meister* were expected to 'upgrade' anything and everything, buildings, dress, furniture, *objets d'art*, music, the decorative arts. Both of Bach's sets look like aristocratic and newly demanding versions of solo fiddling, elevated to levels of new expressiveness by carefully consid- ered harmonic movement and an intimate knowledge of Italian and, espe- cially in the cello set, French characteristics. (Telemann's published sonatas for violin of 1715, dedicated to the young Prince Johann Ernst at Weimar, had continuo and were more within convention.) The system with which Bach went about things is clear in both sets, as when the three violin fugues, in Sonatas 1, 3 and 5, demonstrate three distinct types of fugal counterpoint and three distinct ways to shape a fugue. Also, each violin suite has features or movements the others do not, such as a prelude, or a set of variants, or a chaconne, or a rondeau. Another set of conscious differences is explored in the cello suites: they contrast six different preludes, much as the later Six Partitas for Harpsichord do. They also vary in their technical requirements: No. 6 is for five strings (probably the violoncello piccolo), No. 5 for scor- datura (top string tuned down a tone). The latter recalls a viola tuning in No. 5 of Heinrich Biber's *Harmonia artificiosa-ariosa* (Nuremberg, 1712) and earlier Biber pieces circulating *via* J. J. Walther, violinist in another court at the time, Dresden. It would be odd if Biber's publication had not reached Cöthen by *c.* 1720, or if Bach knew nothing of the various violin-tunings that had been required in a work closer to home and his upbringing, Pachelbel's *Musicalische Ergötzung* of 1691/5.

The resonant sound of fiddle-strings in the dances by the Weimar com- poser Johann Paul Westhoff (Pieces or Suites, Dresden 1696) speaks for an

---

[8] But there are examples in keyboard music. Thus the big pedal-points at the ends of the A minor Fugue WTCi and the French fugue in The Art of Fugue BWV 1080.vi are 'ideal' and can not be played as notated.

16 a J. P. Westhoff, Suite No. 1, opening Allemande
   b BWV 1002, opening

approach to solo violin music inevitably influencing anyone who had ever
heard it. Perhaps many more such solo violin works originated in Central
Europe than is now documented, and the unique surviving MS of Biber's
Passacaglia of *c.* 1676, like Pisendel's solo sonata of *c.* 1716, gives only a
hint of them. The more familiar Bach was with Biber and Westhoff,
however, the more striking the tendency of his solo violin music to veer
towards melody rather than multiple-stopping chords which, though naturally often prominent, do not form the raison d'être of his music. A comparison between any two movements by Westhoff and Bach can illustrate
this, as in Example 16 (a) and (b). Harmonically, the second is also richer
despite its thinner texture, having three modulations in the first three
bars.

The unfolding logic of the harmonies of a Bach prelude for instruments – cello or violin, lute or harpsichord, organ or ensemble – is one of
his best-known hallmarks, something one sees already evolving in an early
harpsichord toccata (D minor, BWV 913) and taking many, many forms.
On one level formulaic and seemingly predictable, in practice the logic of
these harmonies produces examples for any view of music as something
that 'touches the soul' through harmony. Whether the music that results is

as natural to string instruments as Corelli's, however, is a question not often asked, although in particular the three violin sonatas' conspicuous sense of 'struggle' in the sensitive part of the aural spectrum is probably responsible for the cello suites being more popular today. For this 'struggle' and rigour can be distancing, and the sense one often has of a composer persistently challenging himself is prominent in the *Sei solo*. How well he could play them himself is an open question (see a remark on p. 303), but they have many touches of the didactic – even in such formal details as giving each of the four movements of the B minor violin suite a variation, which is essentially an 'instructive' idea, a model or demonstration.

Over this period work must have continued on movements collected in the Well-tempered Clavier Book 1, a major work which, in a manner by now characteristic of J. S. Bach, supersedes all earlier collections, such as the twenty preludes and fugues in J. K. F. Fischer's *Ariadne musica* (re-issued a few years earlier, in 1715). It does this not only in the unique accomplishment of its forty-eight pieces, each of them a complete individual far beyond putative models, but in the use they make of all twenty-four keys. Obvious though it may now seem to order a set of pieces (a) in all the keys, (b) first major then minor, and (c) rising by semitones, in fact each of these elements was distinctly unusual, even odd, at the time, and it is a measure of the Well-tempered Clavier's achievement that this no longer seems unusual, a point worth repeating (see p. 336). Rising by semitones was, of course, out of place in a single continuous piece of music, such as Marin Marais's contemporary *La Gamme* (1723), as it modulated through its twelve keys. Even to begin a set of pieces at C major was not entirely self-evident, for while this key often by then did begin collections (Kuhnau's *Clavierübung*, Fischer's *Ariadne*), and its signature begins the series with no accidentals, D minor was the longer-established first key, particularly in organ music (the French *livres*, Fischer's *Blumenstrauss* of 1732), and it too originally had no key-signature.[9]

Both WTC1's preludes in their earlier form and the Inventions as they were copied in the *Clavierbüchlein vor W. F. Bach* had diatonic not chromatic orders, as did other sets Bach worked on at some point, such as the group now called 'Five Preludes & Fugues'. The Clavierbüchlein's order for both Inventions *à 2* and *à 3* goes by step from the simple to the more complex key-signatures (C major round to C minor, as in Fischer's *Ariadne*), which does have a certain sense to it. As to using the twenty-four

---

[9] Modern editions of organ music by Bach, Buxtehude and others beginning with pieces in C major and rising by step to B minor (as in the NBA) are in this respect anachronistic.

keys: Matthesons's book of 1719 for organists included figured-bass exercises in all twenty-four, and in 1720 such interests must have been growing in Central Germany. Judging by a turgid curiosity like F. Suppig's unpublished *Labyrinthus*, Dresden, June 1722, in which a fantasia passes through all twenty-four keys, Bach was responding to this interest, even to this very MS of a work that Mattheson was referring to a few months later (Mattheson 1722, 152). Suppig's family was active in the Cöthen-Dresden region, and this was also the year in which Bach's colleague Fasch, who had some connection with Suppig, was appointed in nearby Zerbst. Contact between Fasch, Suppig and Bach is not impossible.

If Bach did know or know of the *Labyrinthus*, three important points would follow. First, WTC1 is newly 'inventing' its sequence of keys, since no more than Marais does Suppig proceed by rising semitones. Secondly, since the very titlepages of *Labyrinthus* and WTC1 have much in common (see Rash 1990, 51, 129), including the orthography of the titlepage, this makes it distinctly possible that WTC1's title and date were made (or added: see p. 337) as a conscious allusion to Suppig. What may have driven him is by no means always clear. And thirdly, WTC1 is bypassing, even rejecting, the arcana of temperament theory by means of forty-eight practical examples, not all of whose keys were usable in Suppig's tuning (explained at length) for the usual keyboard.

If WTC1 is no longer plausibly seen, or its title interpreted, as some kind of vindication of equal temperament, nor is it merely a book illustrating compositional method, though this must have been one of its aims. Its compilation was completed apparently only two or three years after the little album for Friedemann was begun, and it may have represented a further step in the boy's 'schedule of study' with his father, study both as a performer (including the mastering of rare keys) and as a young composer (including preludes built on note-patterns, and fugues on distinctive styles of counterpoint). Its title has been the cause of some misunderstanding during later periods. *Clavier* is a word already found on the titlepage of Friedemann's album and means any keyboard except, by convention, the full-sized church organ; it does not of itself mean clavichord or even, specifically, harpsichord, but its sense varies according to context. *Well-tempered* need not mean equal tempered and certainly does not definitively do so, as one might expect if the composer was making a point of it.

For young composers especially, the WTC is more a Counsel of Perfection than a practical book of instruction. Some of the preludes are imitable up to a point, i.e. in so far as the kind of note-patterns illustrated in Example 14 above, or found in other preludes such as D minor, F-sharp major or B-flat major, are not beyond an imaginative student to match. But the subsequent harmonic development in each and every case is hard to imagine possible for even the most talented student. Then the fugues: the very first is hardly a model to follow or could have been meant to be so, with its quite exceptional array of *stretti*, and few of the remaining twenty-three fugues would be of much help to any but the most advanced student – and then to analyse, not emulate. Rather, despite being so intensely practical, the book demonstrates something more intellectual: an ideal range, a potential scope, for its two quite specific kinds of music, the keyboard prelude and the keyboard fugue. It does this by creating an idiom realizable on any keyboard instrument (though only an up-to-date harpsichord suited all forty-eight pieces?) and giving the player both a world of expressiveness and a distinct tactile pleasure. Intricate workplans conjectured for it by modern commentators, such as symmetries erected on the number of bars, voices, notes or appearances of the theme in successive pairs of fugues, do not easily correspond either to any perceptual organization of the book or to one's musical experience of it.

DEATH OF WIFE MARIA BARBARA

After he had had a blissful marriage with his first wife for thirteen years, he experienced in Cöthen in 1720 the severest pain, on his return from a journey to Carlsbad with his Prince, in finding her dead and buried, despite having left her fit and well on his departure. (*Obituary*)

Emanuel was six when his mother died and, one imagines, was not unwilling to speak in the Obituary of a 'blissful marriage' to which he owed his own existence. The story of his father's shock on finding her dead and buried depends for its pathos on whether the Cöthen court payment he received on 4 July was in person or on account, for this was three days before the funeral (Dok II, 68, 76). Nevertheless, whether true or not in all respects, what Emanuel describes is a crippling experience that cannot have been unfamiliar in those days – Telemann had lost his wife after the birth of his first daughter – and one that allows a little lifting of the curtain on personal feelings. Had his father spoken to him later in these terms, and was it even a déjà vu after the experience with the twins born in 1713 (see p. 65)?

Maria Barbara, aged thirty-five, was buried with the unusual honour of the full choir of the Cöthen Latin School (Dok II, 76), on the prince's order if indeed he had returned from Carlsbad by then, but in any case as a sign of her standing in the town. Whether because of his wife's sad death, or because of typical quarrels between a community's clergy such as dogged him in several of his appointments, or for some yet other reason, a few months later in the same year Bach was looking at another job, one with some prestige, in a city with which (and with whose clergy) he was already somewhat familiar. This was at the Jacobikirche, Hamburg, for which see below. 'Some other reason' could include a desire for more pay (in Hamburg or after subsequent negotiation in Cöthen), a wish to run a major church's music, to develop widely-renowned organ recitals on its famous instrument, to join in the other musical life of a major city, to avoid any disappointments then developing in Cöthen, to give a growing family other opportunities, or to have a simple change of scene.

It is unlikely that the visit he paid to examine an organ at Gera in 1721 or the pieces he wrote for the courts at Schleiz in August 1721 and Zerbst a year later (where he had connections by then through his second wife) were made with a view to appointment, since jobs here would have represented a clearer step down. Works written for court celebrations, as at Zerbst, did not necessarily require the presence of the composer away from home. But life at Cöthen seems to have deteriorated for him when the prince married on 11 December 1721, taking as princess someone who was still being called a philistine by Bach nine years later (*eine amusa*, 'a muse-less one': Dok I, 67), and who brought a new category of expenditure for Leopold's limited resources. Whether the situation would have improved for Bach or the other musicians when the prince became a widower less than eighteen months later, in April 1723, one cannot say, for Leopold was not in the best of health himself and his finances were not flourishing.

For someone like Bach with a family, working for a church of repute offered more security and was less liable to the will or wellbeing of a prince, even if becoming an organist in a big city church was not obviously the step for a court capellmeister to take. But a major church, if still with its dangers – clergy suspicious of organists' ineradicable contumacy – provided a home and a clear contract of employment. For a composer active in music outside church, Hamburg, one of the two biggest cities in the empire, would also have offered opportunities. And if there had been pressure on Bach in Cöthen to have his children not in a Lutheran school but in a Reformed, as may have been the case (see BJ 1979, 103), then here too was a reason to move elsewhere. There is a further point. In Bach's biography a pattern emerges in which, despite initial enthusiasm, ardent creativity and his employer's active support, the chronology of his music implies a gradual dampening of spirits in each of the jobs he held. The pattern implies that he felt less and less appreciated or encouraged for the work he originally took on with such zeal, turning then to other kinds of music about which he personally was passionate and hugely productive, in this way privately satisfying his Lutheran duty to develop his God-given talent. This progression is clearest in his longest employment, Leipzig, but may be glimpsed elsewhere.

THE HAMBURG RECITAL (AUDITION?)

During this time, about 1722 [November 1720], he made a journey to Hamburg and had himself heard there for more than two hours on the beautiful organ of the Catharinenkirche [St Catharine's] before the Magistrate and other prominent people, to general wonderment. The aged organist of this church, Johann Adam Reinken, then nearly a hundred years old, heard him with special delight and made him the following compliment, particularly for the chorale 'An Wasserflüssen Babylon' which our Bach, at the desire of those present, played extempore at great length (for almost half an hour) and in a varied manner, such as the finest of the Hamburg organists had once been accustomed to do at Saturday Vespers: 'I thought this art had died, but I see it still lives in you'. This judgment of Reinken's was all the more unexpected in that many years before he had set this chorale in the above-mentioned manner, which was not unknown to our Bach, as too that Reinken had otherwise always been rather jealous. Reinken urged him thereupon to pay him a visit, and showed him much courtesy. (*Obituary*)

Amongst the many points being made in this long account was that Bach was fêted in Hamburg – significant to Obituary readers, for this was Telemann's city – and that he was praised by the then oldest living representative of the German Protestant tradition, Adam Reinken. Thus the Obituary emphasizes once more the world of traditional German church and organ music, and there is nothing here to say whether Emanuel knew that his father was in Hamburg in order to offer himself, along with seven others, for a job at the Jacobikirche. Nor, as with the earlier Hamburg visits, is anything said about whether he saw any operas there, though the season was well under way. Reasons can be conjectured for supposing either that he 'must have done' or that 'it is unlikely he did', depending not least on whether one imagines his mastery of so many musical styles coming from private study or actual experience.

How Bach got to hear of the vacancy at the Jacobikirche, even whether he left for Hamburg because of it, is another unknown, although once again active contacts between musicians can be supposed, and he would not by now travel for nothing. Perhaps when he got there he learnt that instrumental players he could call on in the great city were inferior to Cöthen's, or that Hamburg's church music was in the doldrums at this moment (at least, before the appointment of Telemann in 1721), or that his authority would be subject to the city's overall music director, which would not have suited him. Whatever the reason, he left before the full audition, saying he had to return to his prince in Cöthen. This rather resembles the *excuse* he gave at Halle seven years earlier that the duke in Weimar had not given him his release. It certainly seems that in December 1720, Hamburg had made him an offer and expected a reply (Dok I, 27).

The passage in the Obituary follows immediately on the remark that over this same period, Prince Leopold of Cöthen had the greatest satisfaction in his capellmeister's work. If Bach's interest in leaving Cöthen for Hamburg had arisen at least partly in the aftermath of his wife Maria Barbara's sudden death, one might think Emanuel would know, especially as Mattheson had drawn attention to the Hamburg job-search by gossiping in print later about the auditions for it (Dok II, 186–7). But how serious his father's interest was is not certain. Although the previous organist of the Hamburg Jacobikirche had had a salary only about half his at Cöthen, fees and payments in kind were considerable and dependable, and a Council-appointed organist's *ex officio* status in the city would be respectable. Also, the church's four-manual Schnitger organ was something to inspire any organist, as was Hamburg itself, with its cultural life and institutions – attractions for the father of a growing family. On the other hand, to exchange life in a musically active court for the church-dominated organistship in a Hanseatic city would not have been overwhelmingly tempting, especially considering how poorly equipped with singers its churches were when compared to Leipzig, Halle, Lüneburg or Dresden (Kremer 1995, 182).

The Obituary said that Bach's recital was in Reinken's church, the Catharinenkirche, but there could be some muddle here: perhaps his father played an audition recital in the Jacobi, Reinken heard him there (he was one of three judges), then invited him 'to pay a visit', in the words of the report, to the Catharinenkirche? Or it could be that the Catharinenkirche was the official trial church for organists applying to Hamburg's five main churches, being also the place where Telemann had his inaugural performance less than a year later (Mattheson 1740, 202), and therefore the audition recital was here. The remark about Reinken's jealousy rings true as something told by Bach himself, as are other phrases found in the report ('hundred years old', 'other prominent people', 'general wonderment', 'with special delight', 'urged him', etc.).

But since some details could easily have come from Emanuel's knowledge of other accounts, one wonders whether from his father Emanuel knew the Catharinenkirche organ to be unusually 'beautiful', or from a remark by Mattheson (1722, 256)? Does the whole reference – the second one to Reinken in the Obituary – have something to do with Emanuel's personal knowledge of Reinken's spectacularly long setting of 'An Wasserflüssen Babylon', still being copied in the Bach circle in 1750 or so?[10] Did the Obituary mention extemporisation because Mattheson had implied in print that Reinken was less of an improviser than a fine player of pieces he had practised? This observation of Mattheson's was made shortly after Reinken's death in 1722, and his whole account might be responsible for the story appearing in the Obituary so many years later, even for the wrong date being given there. One thing does seem likely: that Mattheson was so much in evidence at these auditions that he and Bach had some kind of contact. Of what kind can only be guessed, but nothing suggests it clearly to have been warm or productive.

The story of playing to Reinken was important to any interest the Obituary had in invoking the idea of apostolic succession. His quoted words to Bach even have something of John the Baptist about them, a form of blessing, as readers must have realized. (The remark of Reinken can hardly have been welcome to his successor at the Catharinenkirche, who had been the official substitute since 1717.) By 1720, traditional chorale-fantasias were no longer familiar even in Hamburg, and the story does rather confirm (or imply, for the sake of its readers in Saxony?) that the city's musical traditions had faded. Mattheson's warm praise in his book of 1740 for the older Hamburg composers such as Scheidemann and Weckmann, no doubt meant as a slight to those more recent, could have prompted Emanuel to relate the story and so imply where the new gravitational centre was. The whole account makes Emanuel appear, as many people still do appear, to view J. S. Bach as at heart a composer of organ and keyboard music in the North German traditions of virtuosity, rather than as a Thuringian cantor of cosmopolitan tastes.

In most contexts, the musician's phrase 'in varied ways' (*auf verschiedene Art*) referred to a set of variations, indeed one that could last half an hour, whereas Reinken's extant setting is a fantasia of the old type, its more or less separate sections showing off separate parts of the organ. Many of the 'arts of playing chorales' were being lost by the time the Obituary authors were writing, and they also knew that Leipzig had no tradition of popular organ recitals comparable to those in northern cities from Haarlem to Lübeck,

---

[10] The extant copy was made either by Bach's son-in-law Altnickol about the time the Obituary was being written, or by a pupil of his (see BJ 2002, 42). See also the Postscript.

concerts in which hymn-variations played a big part. What Bach would have played for a further ninety minutes – the two unusual references to the time taken sound like details the protagonist himself proudly recounted – is unknown but could well have followed the scheme as laid out in Clavierübung III published nineteen years later, and which formed both a coherent recital-plan and a programme of Lutheran devotional texts.

There does not seem much doubt that the Hamburg performance was an audition of sorts, 'one of the last old-style organist auditions' (Kremer 1995, 219) such as had been held in major churches. As is clear from Werckmeister's book *Orgelprobe* , organist-applicants needed to be tested in improvising a fugue on a given theme, in playing a chorale 'in various ways', in realizing figured harmony and in transposing. Playing 'before the magistrate', as the Obituary puts it, could mean either a celebrity recital at Saturday vespers or, more likely, a public trial, as of a short-listed candidate for an important municipal position. Equally uncertain is what 'playing at the desire of those present' means: that he played a recital rather than a regular adjudicated audition, to which a ranking capellmeister would not happily submit? The phrase also exonerates him from presumptuously borrowing Reinken's theme, though it seems that in Hamburg to play this particular hymn-tune 'in various ways' had long been expected of candidates, as when seventy years earlier Matthias Weckmann, another famous organist, improvised on it at his Jacobikirche audition in 1655. An important detail in the chorale 'An Wasserflüssen Babylon' is that it is one of very few hymns actually mentioning the organ, which it does in its very first verse.[11]

The Jacobikirche organist H. Friese had died two months before Bach's visit, in September 1720, and the church, its Schnitger organ, its status in the city, and the city's musical life (this last not yet obviously in total decline?) all offered good prospects, especially as the overall directorship of the city's five main churches looked to become vacant soon. Before Telemann was appointed to this directorship in 1721, perhaps he was somehow involved either in Bach's presenting himself for the Jacobikirche job, or in his not taking it if he were offered it. One notes that just as Telemann called himself 'Chori Musici Hamb. Director' on the titlepage of his book of cantatas (*Harmonisches Gottesdienst*, 1725–6), so Bach was to call himself 'Directore Chori Musici Lipsiensis' on his first publication at exactly the same period (Partita No. 1).

---

[11] For much the same reason, and despite *Orgeln* being a mistranslation of Vulgate *organa*, it is the only hymn mentioned in a text published on the dedication of the Silbermann organ at Ponitz in 1737 (near Altenburg: see Ahrens 2003, 133).

The decisive trial at the Jacobikirche took place only after, and quite possibly because, Bach had returned to Cöthen. But Mattheson, who was either involved in the adjudication or made it his business to comment on it later, also made a point of criticizing the opening of Bach's Cantata 21 for its repetitive word-setting, which rather suggests that he had heard the cantata in a service, even as part of a formal audition. Furthermore, over ten years later Mattheson was still quoting the famous subject and countersubject of the organ Fugue in G minor, BWV 542 as if he had heard them on that occasion (Dok II, 219). This fugue's subject happens to resemble an old Dutch song, and there has long been floated the idea that Bach used it as a salute to Netherlandish-Frisian connections, including Reinken himself. If (i), Louis Marchand had been cited in the Fifth Brandenburg Concerto and (ii), this had been for a public occasion, citing a Dutch song for another public occasion is certainly possible.

Whether Bach ever coupled the shattering Fantasia in G minor with this Fugue, either on paper or in performance, is not known, but it is an important work in many ways, like a massive reworking of (or model for) the prelude of the Solo Violin Sonata in G minor. As such it offers a little more insight into the composer's interests during the Cöthen years in harmonic archetypes adaptable to all kinds of instrumentation. The Fantasia allows for an organ's weightiness and majesty such as a solo violin, in the same key with rather similar harmonies moving on the same principles, can only imitate. Musically, the extraordinarily different ends to which similar means are worked in these two preludes, for organ and for violin, are difficult to match in music elsewhere, and say much about the composer's self-given task to 'research' into music by applying its language in many different ways. Pieces can be similar in theory but not in effect or *Affekt*. Somewhat comparable, but an actual transcription this time, is the opening movement of the last of the violin solos, the E major Violin Partita in its version prefacing the Leipzig Election cantata in 1731, No. 29. The cantata's new, big scoring for trumpets, drums, oboes, strings and solo organ, and its new tempo word 'Presto', amount to a noisy and boisterous re-interpretation of a work that was already as noisy and boisterous as a single violin could make it. A yet later version presumably for solo lute, or for a keyboard instrument that imitated lute (see p. 282), offers yet another interpretation of the same piece by reverting to a chamber-like delicacy.

Mattheson's criticism of repetitious word-setting in Cantata 21 is not without interest (Dok II, 153), since contemporary critiques are rare. Was his objection that repeating words and phrases is less appropriate for a Sunday cantata than an opera aria, particularly if it offends the rhetoricians'

17 Cantata 21.ii
'I had much grief in my heart'

rules to repeat only complete phrases, and these only for proper emphasis? As the criticism's context suggests, repetition is at its worst when there are gaps in-between. (See Example 17.)

Since Mattheson must have known many an Italian aria in which a few words are much repeated – more than this – was the problem here that the native language makes repetition unnecessary, even tiresome, especially when the stretto produces 'I, I, I' across the voices? In this instance, it is possible that the work originated with another text where repetition was less inappropriate, and that the new text criticized by Mattheson had some significance for him personally (see BJ 1993, 44). Also, it would not be unknown for singers to have handled it badly.

Mattheson notwithstanding, the Jacobikirche committee certainly considered Bach to be one of the eight official applicants for the job, invited him to declare his interest in accepting it, and then, on 19 December, learnt by letter that he had declined. Mattheson said later that it was because the organist who was eventually appointed, J. J. Heitmann, paid 4,000 marks for the appointment, thus demonstrating his ability at 'preluding better with dollars [*Thalern*] than with fingers' (Dok II, 187) – and prompting the main preacher (probably Erdmann Neumeister) to say that an angel coming down from heaven and playing divinely (*göttlich*) might as well fly off again if he had no money. But the church committee had minuted that such payment was not required, adding nevertheless that one could be accepted from a successful candidate as a token of his gratitude. There was some ambivalence here: Heitmann's own eventual successor was appointed on condition of a payment being made.

If Bach was the successful candidate, refused to hand over a sum and consequently left the scene, the motive need not have been entirely to his credit. In a large Hanseatic city, it was not unreasonable for a church official to pay for a stake in its business. However much Mattheson objected to it, the custom was for the successful organist to contribute, as befitted his status in a city where, after all, only certain classes or higher levels of appointment did attract such pre-payment (see Edler 1982, 107). It was actually a sign of an employee's high standing that he should be in effect 'a stakeholder' in an institution for whose 'partners' such as himself extra fees would accrue automatically, for all the weddings, baptisms and funerals in a populous parish.

SECOND MARRIAGE

He married for a second time, in Cöthen in 1721, Miss Anna Magdalena, youngest daughter of Mr Johann Caspar Wülken, Court Trumpeter to the Duke of Weissenfels. (*Obituary*)

Anna Magdalena was born in on 22 September 1701 in Zeitz, where her father J. C. Wilcke had been a court trumpeter before moving to Weissenfels in 1718: once again, then, the court of Weissenfels directly or indirectly has a role in the life and work of J. S. Bach. Evidently a precociously accomplished singer, she could well have come into contact with him before he was a widower, on some such occasion as a professional visit to one of the ducal courts in the neighbourhood, visits that both of them, as fee-paid musicians, are known to have made over the period 1720–1. Or perhaps Bach had been commissioned to search for a singer for Cöthen and found her (heard of her?) in the nearby court at Zerbst, where she had performed as a teenager with her father, and where her brother was trumpeter. Curiously, any such search would have been at much the same period that Handel too was looking for singers, though farther afield than Bach.

Fourteen months after Maria Barbara died, and quite possibly earlier, Anna Magdalena was at Cöthen and a member of the Lutheran congregation. She was appointed 'court singer' by September 1721 at the latest, when both she (just turned twenty) and Sebastian stood as godparents to the son of a colleague in Cöthen (Dok II, 82). Her court appointment was made presumably on the recommendation of Capellmeister Bach, whose predecessor's wife had held a similar appointment. She must have been already sufficiently *grata* in the community to be godparent again four days later, this time without Bach. It is a plausible guess that the new copies of soprano cantatas Bach had already worked with in Weimar, his own Cantata 199 and Francesco Conti's 'Languet anima mea', were made for Anna Magdalena to sing.

Evidently capellmeister and soprano became close enough that they were soon married, on 3 December 1721, she aged twenty, he thirty-six. The record says 'by order' of the prince (*Befehl*: Dok II, 83), indicating his permission either for an important court appointee to be married or for this to be elsewhere than in church, or for both. However conventional it was, especially for Lutherans in a Reformed town, for a widower to marry at home and to buy discounted wine for the wedding, Bach seems to have done both, and reduced his expenses accordingly. His eldest child, Catharina Dorothea, was only some seven years younger than her new step-mother but likely to have been better prepared for a fundamental change in her life than Anna Magdalena herself. Even with mutability and mortality being as they were in the eighteenth century, Anna Magdalena's fate – to have thirteen children before she was forty-one, and by her early thirties to have seen seven of them die over as many years – was hardly average.

Unfortunately, the chief biographical record of this very interesting period around Bach's second marriage, about which tempting speculation is hard to resist, concerns only formalities about money. Thus, a few weeks after the wedding, Bach's Erfurt connections, apparently including his elder sister Marie Salome, asked for a change in the legacy of their uncle Tobias Lämmerhirt's widow, originally intended for Marie's brothers as well as herself. (Perhaps she did not know they were still alive, and legal claims *in ignorantia* cannot have been rare.) Sebastian objected in writing on behalf of himself and his brother Johann Jacob, an oboist, and apparently won his case: he seems to have tried to contact him in vain (Dok II, 83), and Johann Jacob died in Stockholm six months later. In the following August Sebastian was also paid for an unidentified birthday cantata for the prince of Zerbst, in which perhaps his wife and new brother-in-law participated, and where the position of capellmeister was filled that year by J. F. Fasch. Fasch's starting pay was barely half of Bach's (and Anna Magdalena's) at Cöthen, and he was soon to apply for the Leipzig cantorate.

After his marriage Bach also continued to receive a court payment each year for holding rehearsals in his house and for maintenance of the harpsichord, which included acquiring new strings (Dok II, 70). At least financially, all this would have been a consolation for there having been no lucrative offer from Dresden, if this was something he had been seeking. Since the gifted Anna Magdalena, who was something of a local diva, was soon receiving a salary three-quarters that of her new husband, and since both were more highly paid than anyone else, the court's musical expenditure was much dominated by husband and wife, with what ill feeling amongst their colleagues no-one now knows.

It is reasonable to suppose that Anna Magdalena earned it well with performances of solo cantatas in the mould of 'Amore traditore', BWV 203. Although this one (at least, in its known form) is for bass, and is neither certainly authentic nor certainly from this period, it nevertheless conforms to Italianate chamber styles known far and wide in courtly circles – including Cöthen itself, from the time of the previous capellmeister. Perhaps the version for bass comes from early years in Leipzig, after a soprano version for Cöthen? Its Neapolitan text is known elsewhere, and BWV 203 in shape and character is the nearest thing in the Bach oeuvre to a pure Italian chamber cantata. Although some details are unusual – its ABA arias are irregular, cello seems not to be required, and the extravagant harpsichord part is exceptional – none was unique for a genre less moribund than has sometimes been assumed. The keyboard part, along with the Fifth Brandenburg's, doubtless typifies practices developing at the time. Some such busy accompaniment is illustrated in F. E. Niedt's *Musicalische Handleitung* (1721) but in BWV 203 is a good deal more musical and imaginative.

For the forces at Cöthen a suitable church cantata is No. 199, and there is the (faint) possibility that Anna Magdalena was soloist in a cantata for the prince's wedding, in the same month as her own. No doubt the cost of the prince's musical establishment was at least partly to blame for his increasing financial problems about this time, though how far the Bachs were aware of this is not recorded. Was it a reason to look elsewhere for an appointment? In the early 1720s, finalizing the WTCI would be something to monopolize the thoughts of any composer, although in 1722 the first of two albums was also begun for Anna Magdalena, comparable to Friedemann's and similarly called by her *Clavier-Büchlein* (with Friedemann's approval?). Enough of the 1722 album survives to show that it was to have a mix of keyboard pieces, acquiring over the years most of the small-scaled, captivating French Suites, with one in E flat challenging those players used only to older keys. (Was it transposed from D for this purpose?) The name 'French Suites', which appears only in posthumous references, is not certainly authentic: there is amazingly little in them that is anything like Parisian harpsichord music of *c.* 1720, nor is it certain that there was a fixed set of six as such. But they have a distinct character, elusive but unmistakable, and not hard to imagine as written specially for Anna

Magdalena, thinner in texture than the English Suites and less demanding, though still instructive.

One can hardly help seeing the two Anna Magdalena Bach Books as tokens not only of Bach's warm affection for his young wife but a continuing support for her musical advancement. Did the start of first book have anything to do with her first pregnancy in summer 1722? In important respects, its Sarabande in G major anticipates the Aria in G major written much later into the second book (this is the Aria of the Goldberg Variations), and both are unusually tender. So is the little chorale setting BWV 728 in the first book, an exquisite paraphrase of a hymn-melody and very suitable for harpsichord, even perhaps a model for Anna Magdalena's own chorale-playing. Amongst the dozen songs in the second album, begun in 1725 after the family's move to Leipzig, is an arrangement of a bass recitative and aria from Cantata 82 now rewritten for soprano, taxing and likely to be reflecting Anna Magdalena's talent. Did she choose such pieces herself, including 'Bist du bei mir', already a favourite in that city? G. H. Stölzel, who in 1718 published this as one of five arias, is also represented in Friedemann's album by a keyboard piece, though for his stepmother songs of the day were clearly of more interest even if, as in this case, the bass-line is rather different ('improved' by Sebastian?). It is puzzling that Bach seems never to have composed a complete set of songs of the same kind, though one cannot be one hundred per cent sure he did not, especially during the 1730s when other songbooks were being prepared for publication in Leipzig (see p. 234).

The second album's versions of harpsichord partitas Nos. 3 and 6 introduce a very different tone from the sweet galanterie of the songs which, in some way one can only guess, suited the young woman. Were the partitas deliberately stretching her abilities? Successfully? A 'bridal poem' written out in her hand is testimony to her happy marriage, according to Spitta (I, 759), and it is possible that the 1725 book was begun for her birthday or wedding anniversary (22 September, 3 December), with some new pieces brought from Dresden,[12] where Sebastian had been playing in September that year. Less speculative is that in the first Leipzig decade, she made copies of other important works, including the three complete sets of solo works (organ sonatas, violin sonatas, cello suites) – perhaps as gifts for Sebastian's pupils, or even for sale. The disappearance of her portrait, reliably recorded in 1790 (Dok III, 501), is doubly unfortunate, as there would be some indication of its date and possible origin.

---

[12] Including the well-known Minuets in G major and minor, by Christian Petzold, organist and Friedemann's predecessor in Dresden (BJ 1978, 54).

SOME OTHER MUSICAL ACTIVITIES

To return briefly to the cantatas written in Cöthen: before his death in 1721, the poet Christian Friedrich Hunold ('Menantes') wrote three texts used by Bach in birthday cantatas for the prince, full of the customary words of fame, praise, happiness, deference, blessings etc., and set with music to match: bright extrovert 'dance-arias' for one or two solo voices and instruments, usually (one assumes) contrasted with a more meditative aria at some point, and the whole interspersed with brusque but wordy recitatives. Final choruses are very unlike final chorales in church cantatas, always (as far as known) dance-like and more often than not in triple time, again matching the text but now more specifically: its pronounced metre which, especially the dactylic, transfers easily to music. Whether the melodic inspiration is quite on the same level as that of the Brandenburgs is arguable, but the dance-characteristics found in both, considered along with those in the keyboard suites of the same period, illustrate the composer's constant, tireless re-creation of recognizable genres. The three repertories – serenatas, concertos, suites – give the picture of a composer working a great deal with concert music for a court.

Like other librettists publishing such texts, Menantes introduced dialoguing into both recitatives and arias, neither of which Bach had much difficulty in converting from 'secular' to 'sacred', for which terms see pp. 364f. The dramatic or rhetorical principle remains versatile, so that congratulatory cantatas served a prince on his birthday (BWV 66a, 173a) or New Year (134a) just as well as the King of Heaven at Easter (BWV 66, 134) or Whitsun (BWV 173). Recitatives in particular are of so standard a kind that a text 'Heaven thinks of Anhalt's fame and happiness' in a birthday cantata for 1718 can be changed for 'the grave is demolished and with it our misery' for an Easter Cantata in 1724.

It does look as if the Bach household had a strong interest in French keyboard music around the time of the move to Leipzig in 1723. E. L. Gerber, whose father had been a student in the mid-1720s, said that Bach liked Couperin's works, recommended them and observed his 'playing styles' (*Spielmanieren*: Dok III, 471). Whether by this Gerber was referring to anything more than the ornaments is nowhere specified, but other things were surely studied in lessons – touch, fingering, phraseology. The falling-off of musical quality and originality in Couperin's later books makes it likely that it was the first two of 1713 and 1717, plus the playing tutor *L'Art de toucher* of 1716, that most influenced what Bach passed on to students. For someone who had copied Grigny's *Livre d'orgue*, the heavily detailed notation and many rubrics in Couperin's books were not a problem, nor, if Bach himself had written the Brandenburg dedication, was their language.

How big an influence Couperin was is not obvious, and even Gerber Jnr may have been merely reprocessing something written years before by J. A. Hiller, then Thomascantor, who reported that Bach held Couperin in 'great respect' (*viel Hochachtung*: Dok III, 199). And Hiller too may have been depending on a similar remark by F. W. Marpurg, published in the year of Bach's death (Dok III, 4). Any such interest Bach had in French styles had certainly been selective. Although for most of his life he regularly produced *ouvertures* and suites, he did not pursue the types of organ music he had meticulously copied from de Grigny's book. Was it too bound to an alien liturgy? Nor in his experiments with sustained form does he seem to have cared very much for French rondeaux or for the newer kind of light movement one finds increasingly in Couperin. These were all too simple and insufficiently adventurous harmonically? Rondeaux of Bach that do exist are either spacious gavottes (B minor Flute Overture, E major Violin Partia) or succinct, breathless dances, none with the gentle tenderness of so many Couperin rondeaux.

Also elusive is any sign that Bach knew or cared for certain French characteristics: the density of ornaments, the tenor tessitura, the personal and programmatic titles, the crossing of hands on two manuals (*Second livre* 1717, *Troisième* 1722). Nevertheless, in the English Suites there are many moments close to Couperin, as in other music copied, as these were, by Gerber in the 1720s, who seems also to have been familiar with Rameau's ornaments. Although the anonymous 'Les Bergeries' in the second Anna Magdalena Book is probably a work by Louis Marchand, and came from a MS version, it was published in a richer version in Couperin's *Second livre*. This is a book likely to have been known at some point in the Bach household, judging by Emanuel's later use of one of its titles, 'Les langueurs tendres', for a piece of his own.

THE FAMILY

[Anna Magdalena bore him] thirteen children, namely six sons and seven daughters. (*Obituary*)

In Spring 1723, just as Sebastian was involved in the Leipzig job-search, Anna Magdalena had her first child, a daughter who died aged three. Seven of her first ten children died young but none of the last three. The six surviving were:

Gottfried Heinrich, 27 February 1724 (disabled in some way: Emanuel
  says 'not developed', Dok I, 267)
Elisabeth Juliana Friderica, 5 April 1726 (married her father's pupil
  J. C. Altnickol, 20 January 1749)
Johann Christoph Friedrich, 21 June 1732
Johann Christian, 7 September 1735 (the 'London Bach')
Johanna Carolina, 30 October 1737
Regina Susanna, 22 February 1742

By mid-1726 Sebastian had six living children, and by 1733, when
Friedemann left Leipzig, there was a further surviving child at home. Of his
twenty children, there were never more than nine living, and early deaths in
the larger Bach clan were well known: four of his sister Marie Salome's seven
children died early, while Johann Günther, from a branch of the family in
Erfurt (see p. 2) saw ten children die under five. In recording the number
and sex of Anna Magdalena's children, so many of whom died, the Obituary
was likely to be drawing not on Emanuel's memory but again on a family
document, with entries made by the paterfamilias.

The new musical entries made from time to time in the two Anna
Magdalena Bach Books would have benefited her own children, as they were
taught by their father, their siblings, herself or father's pupils, and copyists
such as his nephew Johann Heinrich. Several of the youngest Bachs worked
on the second of the albums. The polonaise Emanuel contributed in about
1732 was one of several keyboard pieces he composed while a student in the
university, presumably living at home. Another piece was added at that
period by another student who taught the younger children in the mid-
1730s, B. D. Ludewig, again suggesting the albums were used to instruct
Anna Magdalena's children. Some further remarks are made below on what
these albums set out to teach (p. 346). Why Friedemann has no entries in
the 1725 book might be explained by the now missing pages, although in
that case one wonders why they were torn out. Altogether, these are tantalizing documents, and conjecture about the various personal relationships
involved is hard to resist.

Some indication that Sebastian was a solicitous father comes from a few
documents concerning the children's education, career or abilities, i.e. the
areas likely to leave behind written testimony. Thus he lists the handi-
capped Gottfried in the genealogical table and describes him as 'inclined to
music, especially keyboard' (Dok I, 261), and in a testimonial he praises a
student for teaching his younger children (Dok I, 141). He is clearly anxious
about his difficult son Bernhard (Dok I, 107); for Friedemann, he copies
out a grand prelude and fugue for organ, BWV 541, apparently for the

twenty-two-year-old's first major job-audition in 1733; he bequeaths keyboard instruments to his youngest son (Dok II, 504); and he visits Berlin/Potsdam at least in part for Emanuel, whose son – the first grand-son, whom Sebastian never meets – is named after him in 1748. So is his next grandson, by his daughter Elisabeth, in 1749, and reasons to keep the name-pair 'Johann Sebastian' are easy to imagine.

He also continued to work professionally with Anna Magdalena, whose singing probably continued far longer than is suggested by the scant docu-mentation, as at Cöthen in 1724, 1725 and again in 1729. A later remark by E. L. Gerber, son of the Bach pupil already mentioned, that she was never able to make use of her outstanding talent in public (Dok III, 470), is cred-ible but only up to a point. In any case, her part in teaching music to the children, likewise not 'in public' and unreported, must have been crucial.

CHAPTER 5

Leipzig, the first years

The city of Leipzig elected our Bach in 1723 as its Music Director and Cantor at the St Thomas School. He followed this call, though leaving his gracious Prince unwillingly. Providence seemed to want him away from Cöthen before the death of the prince, which occurred soon after and against all expectation, so that he was at least no longer present at this sorrowful event. Nevertheless, he had the sad pleasure of preparing in Leipzig the burial Commital music [*Leichenmusic*] for his deeply beloved prince, and to direct its performance in Cöthen in person. (*Obituary*)

These are the Obituary's only sentences to refer openly to the city and its cantorate in Leipzig – which is not so surprising, in view of the difficulties that were to come and were witnessed by Emanuel as he grew up. Yet this was the job Bach held longest and in which he produced so many mature masterpieces. The contrast with the Obituary's earlier remarks on the Cöthen appointment, where his employer was said to be 'a connoisseur and lover of music' and where Bach performed 'to his greatest satisfaction', could hardly be missed by the reader: neither is claimed for the Leipzig position.

Three other absences from the Obituary's report are striking. The former cantor Kuhnau is not mentioned, as he had been in the earlier biography of Bach (Walther 1732, 64), and as Zachow had been at Halle (see above, p. 93). Nor is mention made of the Leipzig churches: it is the 'city' who elected him, and since *cantor* and *music director* imply school and municipal duties, evidently nothing further need be said about either of them, the Thomaskirche and the Nikolaikirche. And finally, nowhere does the Obituary take the opportunity to suggest a happy, fruitful relationship between cantor, the churches and their people. Despite this, 'our town' is expressly mentioned in the valedictory poem appended at the end (Dok III, 89), and the authors, along with many of its readers, knew Bach almost exclusively from Leipzig.

In important ways, inevitably, the city and its cantorate is an unspoken focus of the Obituary, and much of what it says beyond biographical data is authoritative only for this period. Emanuel was only just nine years old when the family moved there, and one can take much of what is said about his father as performer, teacher and person to be drawn from the Leipzig period, and this alone. Little is revealed about his earlier years beyond a few details: the only Weimar works specified in the Obituary's worklist are the Orgelbüchlein and what it calls 'Six Toccatas for Harpsichord', both probably familiar to Emanuel as he grew up learning keyboard. (No set or fixed compilation of Six Toccatas survives or is now known about.) Furthermore, reticence about life and work in Leipzig means virtual silence about what now seems such a huge part of the composer's life: the colossal output of cantatas and other church works. Certain organ recitals and musical celebrations might reach the newspapers from time to time or inspire praise from listeners, but the weekly cantatas go by without comment. How were they taken by the people? Were they more than a job of work? Was the standard of performance always inadequate?

In general, there seems to have been something inappropriate in remarking on aspects of a musician's musical activities in church, judging by the other obituaries published with Bach's in 1754. Nor, naturally, does Emanuel say anything about his father being third choice for the Leipzig cantorate. If he did know about this, conceivably the reluctance claimed in the second sentence above is an indirect allusion to it, as if his father was as reluctant to take the appointment as the church was to offer it him. In a letter written to Georg Erdmann in 1730, Bach did claim that he had originally meant to stay at Cöthen for the rest of his life (Dok I, 67), and the Obituary's warm references to the appointment there doubtless relays what Emanuel had heard said. But since Cöthen was not the greatest centre for such a versatile musician, and since he could have dropped his Leipzig application at any point just as he had at Halle and apparently at Hamburg, these claims are hard to accept *simpliciter*. They rather suggest later disillusionment. So does another claim in the Erdmann letter: that for him to go from being a capellmeister to being a cantor was 'not at all fitting' (*gar nicht anständig*). Considering Leipzig's importance, that is unlikely to be true, although it could have been something he came to feel over time. How many English cathedral directors of music have found their initial enthusiasm waning?

However fine Cöthen's musical potential was once, with exceptional players and an enthusiastic prince, the position of a court-dependant without binding contract in a modest establishment would not compare favourably with a regular appointment to one of the best-known cantorates in Protestant Germany. The city itself was more than ten times bigger than Cöthen, with at least three claims to wide fame: unrivalled mercantile fairs atttracting many visitors, a renowned and large university, and an exceptional number of active publishers. Nevertheless, attractive though all this seemed from a distance, it is not surprising that after six or seven years working hard in church and school there Bach would look wistfully at a different kind of musical career elsewhere, as he does in the Erdmann letter of 1730 (see pp. 274f). There were towns and courts elsewhere, most of them needed other kinds of music than sacred choral, and some might even have been relatively free of the heavy hand of clergy in school and church.

The Obituary's second sentence implies that being 'called' to a position was not merely a conventional, quasi-self-denigrating way to refer to a successful application but signified a dutiful acceptance of divine will. That would match other pious expressions, whatever disillusion with Leipzig arose later. The third sentence is more clearly misleading, since the prince did not die until 19 November 1728, and nor was his death 'against all expectation'. Emanuel must have forgotten the prince's obsequies and the music performed on that occasion, on 23 and 24 March 1729, in which his brother and mother took part; or his father's subsequent references to the prince's death were misleading. *Leichenmusic* four months after death cannot mean ordinary funeral music, rather a committal service in which the body is re-interred in a prepared mausoleum. Since this music included eight arias and two choruses that appear in the St Matthew Passion, one of them its final chorus, it is clear that the late prince was indeed 'deeply beloved', and deeply mourned with fitting music, by his former capellmeister.

For some reason, the Obituary adds that Bach was there 'in person' to salute the late prince: was this to express further his regrets at losing this connection? How far the greater fondness for Cöthen grew from the retrospection natural to advancing years will never be known, and it is possible that by 1730 the teenage Emanuel was hearing within the family many grumbles about Leipzig. The Obituary's three fulsome sentences about Cöthen are rather out of proportion and do suggest several things: that Bach spoke often of the prince and of their relationship, that Leipzig afforded nothing comparable, that someone so respected at a prince's court as himself was not to blame for vexations at Leipzig, and that family members and intimates were only too aware of all this. The result is that at least for readers far from Leipzig, the city's and church's part in his life would appear secondary.

Bach kept the Cöthen capellmeistership as a title when he took up the cantorate and may well have returned to the prince on special occasions. He also used his court title on the first publications he ventured for himself, the harpsichord partitas Nos. 1–4, 1726–1728, and prefaced a manuscript version of the first with a poem saluting the prince's newborn son (Dok I, 223). Though not certainly Bach's own work, the poem convincingly conveys a charming mixture of respect and affection that one supposes to have been quite real, not least in referring to the baby's mother, Leopold's second wife, who perhaps was less of a philistine than her predecessor. A further sentence in the Obituary concerning 'the beloved prince' (Dok III, 84) again hints, in a way hardly to be missed by careful readers, that the late cantor had been better valued and happier in Cöthen than in Leipzig. Bach's not calling himself 'cantor' on official documents suggests that he kept some distance from the church, liable therefore to be at loggerheads with those whose outlook was limited to it. In testimonials for students written after his royal title was conferred, he signs 'court composer' and 'Capellmeister'. It is also very likely that some factions in city, church and university were closer than others to the royal court in Dresden, and wished their music director to be more of a town's capellmeister (leader of public music) than a cantor (official of church and school). Later, away from Leipzig, in a provincial town like Weissensee in 1738, he would be known by such terms as 'the famous Chapel Director' or 'the famous composer Mr Bach' (BJ 1999, 22, 26).

Titles do appear to be informative. In his first entry in the Leipzig church-books, in connection with Gottfried Heinrich's baptism on 27 February 1724, Bach wrote his own title carefully, *Director musices u. Cantor* (BJ 1979, 12), a phrase kept in the Obituary's first sentence above – 'director' in the town of Leipzig, 'cantor' in the church and its school. 'Director' implies something similar to Telemann's prestigious town directorship in Hamburg, a municipal version of capellmeister, such as another applicant for the Leipzig job, Christoph Graupner, also described himself in his *Monatliche Clavir Früchte* of 1722. Bach's title 'cantor' appeared only in documents dealing with teaching duties in the school, but like his predecessor Kuhnau (who had argued for the title *director musices*) he would be responsible for all the principal churches. Mattheson commented impertinently on the increasing tendency for organists to use the title *director* (1740, xxxiv), though for Telemann in Hamburg it was correct.

Although, being published in Leipzig, the Obituary could assume many readers were familiar with its subject and his activities there, the authors were not about to acknowledge support when he had received so little. But nor would they actually criticize the authorities in print, especially when the widow needed their help and when Emanuel was about to apply again for the cantorate, having failed once before on his father's death.

THE APPOINTMENT PROCEDURE

The many-stranded order of events around J. S. Bach's Leipzig appointment, fully documented as they would be for an important parish church with professional choir and municipal responsibilities, gives some idea of the procedure for a 'director of music'.

5.6.1722   the previous cantor, Johann Kuhnau, dies aged 62. (As early as 1703, during a period of illness, Kuhnau learnt that Telemann had been approached to succeed him.)

14.7.1722   the twelve-member Council (the *Enge Rat*) discusses J. F. Fasch (capellmeister in Zerbst), G. B. Schott (organist of the New Church, Leipzig), C. F. Rolle (cantor in Magdeburg), G. Lembke (cantor in Laucha), J. M. Steindorff (cantor in Zwickau) and Telemann (music director in Hamburg).

9.8.1722   Telemann auditions for the job, and is offered it two days later. He may also have presented the annual Leipzig Election cantata that month.

3.9.1722   Telemann seeks dismissal from the Hamburg Council.

6.11.1722   Telemann declines, despite Leipzig's offer to compromise on teaching-duties (i.e. to reduce them); obtains a salary increase in Hamburg, where the honour his fame brings to the city is recognized (Kremer 1995, 143).

21.11.1722   Council considers two new candidates: A. C. Duve (cantor in Brunswick) and G. F. Kauffmann (music director in Merseburg).

29.11.1722   Schott, Duve and Kauffmann audition on Advent Sunday; Fasch, a former pupil in the school, declines, in part because of not wishing to teach there.

21.12.1722   C. Graupner (a Leipziger, now court capellmeister in Darmstadt) and J. S. Bach apply.

15.1.1723   Graupner unanimously chosen, on condition he makes a successful audition of two cantatas the following Sunday (as later was the case for Bach). Perhaps as a precaution, Rolle and Bach were also invited to audition. At this point, the teaching component is not discussed (or not minuted).

17.1.1723   Graupner auditions with two cantatas.

2.2.1723	Schott auditions (in the Nikolaikirche), Rolle and Kauffmann having withdrawn.
7.2.1723	Bach auditions with Cantatas 22 and 23: 'much praised', according to a Hamburg newspaper (Dok II, 91).
8.2.1723	Bach receives twenty thalers for travel and subsistence.
?.3.1723	Graupner fails to obtain release from Darmstadt.
9.4.1723	Council discusses Bach, Schott and (still) Kauffmann; also an unnamed musician 'from Pirna', near Dresden.
13.4.1723	Prince Leopold writes graciously, releasing Bach from Cöthen.
19.4.1723	Bach (only now?) writes a letter of intent to take the job.
22.4.1723	Bach formally elected.
5.5.1723	Bach shows his Cöthen release and signs his written undertaking.
8.5.1723	Bach is presented to the consistory court by Superintendent Deyling, who adds a testimonial by J. Schmid, Doctor of Divinity in the university, approving the candidate after the statutory theological-confessional test.
13.5.1723	the consistory court signals acceptance.
16.5.1723	Whitsun: 'entered on his functions' in the university (Dok I, 39) – with a cantata?
30.5.1723	performs first cantata, in the Nikolaikirche
1.6.1723	new cantor formally introduced at the school (Superintendent Deyling's absence is publicly noted).

The theological-confessional test, which required detailed knowledge of the New Testament and catechism, was no mere formality: only a few months earlier, a Zwickau organist had failed the Leipzig Consistory's examination (BJ 1998, 27). On 13 May, Bach was also obliged to sign the 'Visitation Article' set out for school and church personnel in Saxony, swearing to uphold 'pure teaching', Lutheran as against Calvinist (Dok III, 630).

The earlier stages of the appointment were under the authority of the Council, which notified both the superintendent of the Thomaskirche of the choice and the church pastor as inspector of the school. The council's first choice, Telemann, withdrew partly on the question of teaching duties in the school,[1] and so officially did Graupner. Telemann and Fasch were both well remembered in Leipzig, where they had been university students

---

[1] C. P. E. Bach's candidature at St Thomas in 1755 was also rejected because of his declining to teach, despite Telemann's support for him. But some cantors, such as Sebastian's brother's colleague in Ohrdruf, Elias Herda, were as much teachers of theology, Greek, Latin etc. as they were musicians.

and manoeuvered against Cantor Kuhnau, or so he seems to have felt. At the time, all three early candidates (Fasch, Telemann, Graupner) had good jobs elsewhere and may have been doing little more than testing the water, as Bach had been at Halle and probably Hamburg.

Except for Handel, Telemann was probably the best-known German composer of the time, had been a student in Leipzig, was highly literate, knew Greek, and had founded the still functioning concert-series or *Collegium musicum*. For Graupner's candidacy, Darmstadt had bigger prestige than Bach's Cöthen and so put him on a higher level. That Bach was in touch with one or all of the three early candidates is possible, as relations between them seem to have been good enough for Graupner to support Bach in writing to the Leipzig council, describing his virtues in three areas: he was 'strong on the organ', 'experienced in church things and *Capell* pieces' (cantatas), and able to 'perform his allotted functions honestly and appropriately' (Dok II, 98). Whether Bach had solicited or knew of this testimonial is unknown but both are likely, something that would put his supposed reluctance (as reported in the Obituary) in a new light. That he remained on good relations with Graupner is likely, since in the 1730s, in Darmstadt, Graupner's son was copying various of his harpsichord works.

The Council discussions have a depressingly modern ring to them. Burgomaster Lange thought that if Bach accepted, they could forget Telemann, 'on account of his conduct' (Dok II, 94). Several Council members focused on the teaching duties attaching to the cantorate (five hours per week in the church school, plus musical instruction), some on the musical ability required; one of them wished the cantor's compositions to be 'not theatrical', others wished him to pay for his own teaching substitutes; one thought Bach a clever man, another thought the post had been vacant long enough and they should get on and vote. When by April a member speaks of having to take a 'middling' candidate because the best have withdrawn (*mittlere*: Dok II, 92), it is less clear than has often been thought whether he means someone of mediocre ability or someone of only average fame and rank – almost certainly the latter. As the third person in the school hierarchy, after rector and conrector, the cantor held a position of more than musical importance, so the question of a candidate's current status was not trifling. Eventually some councillors seem to have been swayed in Bach's favour by considering him famous enough, more so than the other candidates, and thought him certainly capable of inspiring the students (*Studiosi animiret*: Dok II, 95).

On 19 April 1723 Bach signed to be available to take up the post within four weeks, to undertake duties in the school, both regular classes and individual singing lessons (Dok I, 175), and if he needed assistance for Latin classes, to engage someone at his own expense with Council's approval. The final undertaking of 5 May 1723 was very specific and is a good example of the kind of contract the holder of an important position in Protestant Germany signed:

set (and 'bequeath to') the boys of the school the example of a discreet life
to the best of his abilities, bring the music of the two main churches to a
    good standard (? *in gutes Aufnehmen*)
show respect to the Town Council and do its bidding if it requests the presence
    of the choristers, but not to take them out of town without permission
obey the school authorities
restrict admission to boys who already have a foundation in music, or who
    show aptitude for it
teach the boys both in vocal and instrumental music
order the churches' music so that it be not too long and not operatic
    (*opernhafftig*) but conducive to devotion
provide the New Church with good scholars (*Schüler*, i.e. singers)
treat the boys carefully and friendlily; punish in moderation, or report
    delinquents
perform faithfully the teaching duties in the school
himself pay for any teaching substitute (i.e. for lessons other than in music),
    who must be competent
not to leave town without the burgomaster's permission
as far as possible, always to accompany the boys in funeral processions
to accept no duty (*officium*) in the university without the Council's
    permission. (Dok I, 177–8)

Since the same document would have been given to Telemann to sign had he accepted the appointment, Bach was not going out of his way to be complaisant or obedient. Nor in such a city was the undertaking exceptional. In fact, what he was agreeing to was, in important respects, very like the kind of requirements made of musicians at Esterhaza when Haydn joined the orchestra in 1761 (see Harich 1971, 134), requirements that had probably been made also at Weimar and elsewhere.

The church and school clergy of Leipzig, faced with a *fait accompli* by the burgomasters' council, were no doubt keen to specify in this document what in less important institutions was left implicit. Indeed, the new appointment was a good opportunity to banish any slackness that had resulted from the recent contention there had been amongst teachers in the school (see Schering 1941, 40). The *Thomasschule* or Thomas School was a boarding-school and church-music institution of high prestige, quite different in function and schedule from a regular boys' school such as that of the Nikolaikirche in the same city. It was, as the rector claimed, of benefit to the whole town (Schering 1926, 51), just as the housing within it was of benefit to the cantor.

Basically, the signed undertaking is only expanding on the two main obligations of church musicians as generally understood (see Edler 1982, p. 82): first, to perform duties obediently and willingly; and secondly, to lead a blameless life. In view of later dissension between cantor and clergy, it is interesting that nothing is said in the document about who appoints choir prefects, or chooses hymns, or arranges where the major musical event of the year, the Passion on Good Friday, is to be heard. Nor is anything said about such contractual items as the pension for the appointee's widow, somethingTelemann insisted on at Hamburg when making a deal to remain there (Kremer 1995, 335). Two other questions raised by the document are, Did Bach really ask for and obtain permission for all his trips he made from Leipzig during his tenure? And, Did funeral processions at which he accompanied the boys include walks to the scaffold for public executions? Neither is further documented, but *Yes* is likelier to both than *No*.

Bach later told his friend Erdmann that he had delayed accepting the offer for a quarter of a year (Dok I, 67), which seems to be not quite true, unless he had taken the success of his trial performance in February as an official sign of intent. The normal annual income of 700 thalers he mentioned to Erdmann would not have been a huge incentive in view of the 770 he and Anna Magdalena had jointly received at Cöthen, and it seems that Telemann and Graupner had each had 1,000 thalers or more mentioned in their respective negotiations at Leipzig (Wolff 2000, 244). But Bach's entitlement to a range of perquisites and a capacious family apartment was an attraction, and though he ranked about twelfth in the municipal pay-rates, even the city burgomaster's salary was only twice as large (Szeskus 1991, 17, 10). From the city Bach received 'money for wood and light', corn, firewood, and, from Whitsun 1723 to Whitsun 1750, wine three times per year, at Easter, Whitsun and Christmas, plus some minor legacies *ex officio*. It seems that like his predecessor, he also took a third of his statutory fee for parishioners' weddings in the form of wine (Dok III, 342).

Nevertheless, the simple perquisites might suggest if anything that as a non-graduate schoolmaster and musician his social rank in Leipzig was not very high, and was unlikely to rise much. As teacher in an important school, the cantor would generally be assumed to be a graduate, though this would not have guaranteed him due respect: Kuhnau, though a graduate of its university, had had problems in Leipzig, complaining about challenges to his authority and about musical resources at Thomaskirche, doing so as recently as 1720 (in Spitta II, 866–8). At Hamburg during the eighteenth century, the gradual lessening of expectation that a successful candidate would hand over money for his appointment (see above, p. 153) indicates in its own way a lowering of the organist's professional and hence personal status, since more important municipal appointees continued to do so for their appointments.

At the audition, Cantatas 22 and 23 must have puzzled many of those present, although the texts were similar to those set by Graupner for his audition a month earlier and had probably been sent on to Bach in Cöthen. Neither work, except for the finale of No. 22, has the immediate melody or easy approachability of the cantatas soon to be published by Telemann, or the anthems Handel wrote in 1717–18 for the Duke of Chandos. Cantatas No. 22 and 23 sound as if their composer is trying to impress with complex, refined musical detail such as could flatter a committee but leave the congregation, and perhaps the choir itself, rather at a loss. Is the cantatas' lack of secco recitative and true *da capo* in arias an anti-operatic gesture made for the sake of his potential employers?

Cantata 23, prepared in Cöthen, shows signs of being enlarged with a final chorale movement probably at the last minute, perhaps if or after Bach had witnessed Schott's audition. Both new works already raise questions some Leipzigers must have had over time about their cantor's music, leaving him in turn resentful and antagonistic. One is, was a parish-church congregation up to recognizing in Bach's cantatas and Passions the affecting meditation on Scripture that they offer? Cantata 23 reminds one of the Cöthen cantatas for special occasions, thoughtful rather than immediate, aristocratic rather than popular. A second question follows on from this: if a cantata with recitative, chorus, arias, duets and chorale was too 'operatic', rhetorical or affecting, and thus inappropriate in a parish church, was the only music considered suitable the kind with simple tunes, predictable harmony, elementary counterpoint, familiar word-painting and naive rhetoric? If so, Telemann or Graupner would have supplied it with less challenge to themselves or their listeners.

NEW LIFE IN LEIPZIG

On 22 May 1723 the family, presumably including its new infant daughter, moved from Cöthen to Leipzig. The move was announced in a Hamburg newspaper, as were the mode of transport (four wagons, two carriages) and the fact that the apartment for them in the Thomas School had been renovated (Dok II, 104). Syndicated newspaper accounts about a prime musical appointment were not rare, but since the paper that reported Bach's first Leipzig performance also gave an unusually detailed report of another of his performances decades later (the visit to Frederick the Great in 1747), perhaps there was some special correspondent. Bach himself?

The newspaper too spoke of his being 'called' to the Leipzig job. If the correspondent was Bach, it is striking that he would send reports to a Hamburg newspaper now and again in 1731 (concerning his recital in Dresden) but not a regular autobiography to a Hamburg biographer, Johann Mattheson, despite being asked to do so. His biography in the *Lexicon* of 1732 compiled by Walther is also brief, a fraction of the article on Kuhnau. It seems that he kept away from such things, but whether from modesty, immodesty, indifference, shortness of time or, in Mattheson's case, scorn, is impossible to know. One can read various things into silence: had he already met and taken against Mattheson on one of his earlier visits to Hamburg? Was Walther finalizing his book and planning its publication in Leipzig just as his relative Bach, who may have helped him in some details, was looking to leave the city?

While quoting the number of wagons seems rather excessive for a newspaper, unless exceptional in some way, a touch of pride is suggested in its remark, supported by other documentation, that the house was renovated (*renovirte*) for the family moving in. Had it been a condition for accepting the job? Bach had been offered no such thing at the Jacobikirche, Hamburg three years earlier? A renovation costing 100 thalers reflected the cantor's status, presumably, and it also implied that his rent-free housing was a benefit of great value, as indeed it was. (Other building work is recorded in 1726–7 and in 1744–5, as well as major reconstruction in 1731–2.) Thanks to traditional hierarchies and the presence of school prefects elsewhere under the same roof, it is unlikely the family was particularly inconvenienced by the choristers' dormitory and classrooms situated in the same building. The arrangement was not unusual.

But the house and its appointments can hardly have been a minor matter for Anna Magdalena, who was to have so many children there between 1723 and 1742, the first, Gottfried, almost exactly nine months after the move. The church house had three floors plus cellars, a successor to various buildings made at and along the old city wall, facing at the back into a section of the garden partly encircling the city in place of the old moats and ramparts. Whether or not from any agitation on the part of the Bachs, the substantial rebuilding of 1731–2 resulted in an imposing five-storey block with an attic of three further storeys, the whole comprising cantor's apartment, study, classrooms, choristers' dormitory etc., and the rector's house between school and church.[2] The family lived elsewhere in the town from June 1731 to April 1732, returning just two months before Christoph Friedrich was born.

Over the early period in Leipzig, Bach visited nearby Stöntzsch twice to test a small organ, and wrote a cantata for the new school-building's dedication, the lost BWV Anh. I 18, reworking it for the king's nameday the following year. Somewhere in the house, both before and after renovation, and presumably on a regular schedule, the full scores of the newly composed cantatas were used by copyists each week to extract vocal and instrumental parts in time for Sunday (or for a Saturday rehearsal?). A stock of valuable paper and other supplies had to be maintained and stave-lines had to be drawn, with sometimes less than happy results. (Only in the 1740s do printed staves appear, for the Wedding Cantata No. 195.) But the precise schedule from begininng to end can now only be conjectured. For example, the Whit Monday cantata No. 174 had its parts finished on the day before (see NBA KB I/14, 92), and, assuming these were the parts used, when or even whether it was rehearsed is unknown.

Several of the regular copyists have been identified, some of whom probably lived in the building, even *en famille*: J. A. Kuhnau (nephew of Bach's predecessor), C. G. Meissner (who also copied various organ works), J. H. Bach (son of brother J. C. from Ohrdruf), J. L. Krebs (pupil, son of Weimar pupil J. T.) and others from the school, as well as the two oldest Bach sons. Friedemann sometimes scribbled on copies being made by the others, Emanuel was modestly active from the age of fifteen. Pupils and sons maintained copying duties throughout the Leipzig period, new ones taking over as others moved on, up to the second-youngest son Johann Christoph Friedrich (aged sixteen when working on Cantata 195 in the late 1740s) and even beyond. One late copyist, C. F. Barth, was used by both Bach and his two successors. Anna Magdalena served as copyist longer than most, occasionally copying a vocal or instrumental cantata-part, or a section of it. Her copies include chamber and keyboard music, either complete sets (the violin and cello suites) or possibly once-complete (organ sonatas, WTC1), sometimes with Sebastian (WTC2) and family members (this in the two albums), and it is not difficult to imagine circumstances in which she assisted, why some copies remain incomplete, and why particularly chamber music

---

[2] The pulling down of this building in 1903 is matched by the barbarous demolitions dating from the years of East German socialism: the remains of the Leipzig Johanniskirche (for a traffic island), the Dresden Sophienkirche of Wilhelm Friedemann Bach (for a cafeteria, 1962) and the still-standing Leipzig University Church in 1968.

featured. Why however, her copying so often included only the notes of the music while Sebastian wrote in the headings, dynamics etc. is open to conjecture – was he 'supervising' her?

For the cantatas, the copying of parts belonged only to the late stage of production and is assumed to have been for particular performances. But even before the actual composing began, a set of seasonal texts had to be chosen, and one can understand how a composer might seize upon some convenient publication of them, as happened in 1726 when the initial impetus in cantata-writing appears to have subsided. Less than half the texts set in the course of the cantata-production have been identified, leaving open the question how many Bach wrote or arranged himself – whether differences between cantata-texts as printed in known books and as set in known cantatas were the result of changes made by the composer, and if they were (and in each case), why. Truly significant doctrinal differences between him and the selected authors are unlikely.

Adding to the need for efficient planning ahead was that a set of texts for several Sundays had to be approved by the clergy and given to a printer in time for the congregation to have the textbook in front of them for the relevant services. This was a custom from before Bach's time and had several functions, not least for the cantor's income: he published them and had them sold. More importantly, they helped devout and attentive listeners recognize in the music any emphases it was giving to the words. A particular musical effect in the setting of a particular word would not so much 'express' it (as this word is used today) as mark it, underline it, make it clearer, pointing up its scriptural significance. Bach's reliance on certain established effects when setting standard words and ideas to music, and his almost automatic manner of creating counterpoint, are elements of the routine inevitable in the composition of the Leipzig cantata-cycles, hinted at in the few extant sketches and drafts. Both the effects and the counterpoint were part of the craft of composition, characteristic and original while remaining in line with convention.

Anyone familiar with the running of a major church's liturgical-musical programme can imagine how often difficulties must have arisen at some point in the scheduling. It is possible to find in the series of Leipzig cantatas some not only more difficult than others but spaced out over the weeks as if deliberately, so as to allow the boys more weeks to prepare them; but this is no more than conjecture and depends on changing ideas of what is difficult or what standard was expected. On feast-days not only the cantata but Latin mass movements had to be planned, perhaps copied, presumably rehearsed, and also needing to be planned for any Sunday was the music to

be heard during Communion. This was either some organ-preludes alternating with sung chorales throughout, as Bach noted in a summarized order
of service, apparently for his first Advent Sunday, 1723; or on feast days there
was other music, a Latin movement (perhaps a Sanctus), sometimes an aria
from a cantata.

Also needing to be thought out and planned were practical matters, such
as a schedule for arranging the varying body of instrument-players. Who
prepared this, found the substitutes if necessary, checked the church instruments? In addition, until 1733 payments were made to Bach for maintaining the modest harpsichords in the large churches, the Nikolaikirche and
the Thomaskirche, used (only?) for rehearsals. This duty he could consign
to others, though little is certain about his arrangements for the tuning of
church and school-house instruments after Friedemann left in 1733. At least
the reed-stops in the west-end organ of every church must have been regularly tuned, but these were the responsibility of the successive organists, not
the cantor.

There were also students to care for, some of whom would be active
in copying other kinds of music, including keyboard. One of them,
B. C. Kayser, came from Cöthen and may have followed Bach to Leipzig,
first as some kind of secretary, then as a law-student in the university, remaining in contact with the Bach family, and continuing to copy – elegantly and
musically – important organ and harpsichord works even after appointment
to the Cöthen court in 1730 (Talle 2003). It is not clear how many students
at any one time Bach was teaching privately, whether they had group-lessons,
whether any lived in, and how much time he gave them, but it would be safe
to assume there were fewer students in 1723 than a year or two later.

The calls on the cantor's time and energy are barely imaginable, considering the other, more hidden duties that also fell to him. The moneys he was
allowed for hiring performers on such occasions as New Year, the very cash
itself, had to be managed, as did the smallest items like claiming for the cost
of candles he supplied for the choir gallery. Then a bigger and regular part
of the job as *director musices* was to approve the appointment of the municipal musicians (*Stadtpfeifer*), which extant reports suggest was something
he took seriously. As well as the annual election cantata in August, in some
years there were also special outdoor events for the king's nameday. Add to
the ceaseless activity this entailed the constant coming and going of visitors, and one sees how apt for the family home was Emanuel's word
'dovecot'.

In a later petition to the king, Bach said he took up his function at the
University of Leipzig at Whitsunday 1723, which was early that year

(16 May), but whether he performed a cantata or was merely 'on the books' from then is not documented. On 30 May 1723 he performed the cantata, No. 75, 'to good *applausu*' in Leipzig's largest town church, the Nikolaikirche, and the published report made a point of calling this 'his first Music' after appointment (Dok II, 104). Being in two parts, the cantata was heard either side of the sermon, as a Hamburg newspaper pointed out, and it is likely that the chorale heard three times in it ('What God does is well done') had special significance at that time and place. Its thirteen different movements demonstrated the new cantor's total mastery of chorus, aria, recitative (both secco and accompanied), sinfonia and ritornello chorale, with two fine solos for the town trumpeter. See also below, p. 180.

During his first August, Bach supplied and apparently directed a cantata, now lost, for the university's celebration of the birthday of Duke Friedrich II of Saxe-Gotha, a report of which event, written in Latin by a recent graduate, speaks of the music 'admired by all' and composed 'by the greatest craftsman, Bach' (*omnes admirantur, a summa artifice, Bachio*: BJ 2004, 219). Already by then, however, the university annalist was noting that Bach's responsibility in the university was limited to four special services per year, while the regular new services were in the hands of the university organist J. G. Görner (Dok II, 105): this was going to lead to trouble later and did so, from September 1723 on. Meanwhile, on 1 June the new cantor was formally introduced to the Thomas School, which occasioned a mild row concerning the respective bureaucratic authority of town council and church, and which in turn led to further written exchange: not Bach's fault but again a warning-sign. Notwithstanding, two weeks later Friedemann and Emanuel were admitted to the school, aged twelve and nine, and as the letter Bach wrote in 1730 to his old friend Erdmann said, one attraction of the university town of Leipzig had been that he had sons inclined to be studious (*studiis zu incliniren*: Dok I, 67).

Since so little detail is known of Bach's previous daily life as Cöthen capellmeister, one cannot be sure how startling he found his heavy duties as Leipzig cantor, but within a month or so of his first cantata, he had delegated school-teaching to an experienced senior boy with the superintendent's approval, as notified to the Consistory. Telemann's duties in Hamburg at that period were just as full, with directorship of the opera added to his jobs as cantor and supplier of municipal music. Furthermore, he was much more active in publishing his own music. In Bach's case, it seems that opting to write weekly cantatas – works far more detailed in every respect than Telemann's – meant that for the moment, his musical emphasis was on the sacred. Duties in connection with this included directing the performers for four churches, two major and two minor; supplying municipal music on occasion; training and auditioning the choristers; rehearsing the choir and the eight regular instrumentalists (some of whom played more than one instrument); scheduling prefects for certain music both in the Thomaskirche (the motet without instruments) and in the two minor churches (to lead the hymn-singing, etc.); teaching the ablest boys; composing and directing music for the bigger funerals and weddings (sometimes one or two for each a week); overseeing the organs and their players; taking on university students as private pupils; and arranging for some of them to take part in cantata performances, as players or singers.

Each year there was also directing music in the university church at Christmas, Easter, Whitsun and Reformation Day, i.e. at times of the year when there was already much happening. For funerals and weddings a fund of works was adaptable for those occasions that were grand enough to have more than just chorales, and such wedding cantatas as Nos. 195 and 210 had several performances. These are major works, articulating in their way the idea of marriage as no ordinary celebration of a happy event but as one of the sacraments, music full of detail and complexities of the kind that require adequate rehearsal. While they imply as much effort on the composer's part as any other kind of cantata, on other less elevated occasions there must have been a throwing together of movements to create pasticcios, or other motets and cantatas were simply re-used.

The alternating of the cantatas in the two main churches, one week the Thomaskirche, the next the Nikolaikirche, was not in itself a heavy duty, but on feast-days it was a matter of both churches (see below, p. 179). Cantatas premiered in the Thomaskirche have sometimes been described as more demanding, less traditional than those in the Nikolaikirche, but a distinction is possible (I think) only after special pleading. As any cathedral organist today knows, other cantorial duties such as the auditioning of choristers was a major task, considering everything this involves, and judging by the one report of such auditioning that survives, it was something Bach took care over (Dok I, 131–2). Where assistance was customary, as when students copied out parts or played and sang in cantatas, or when prefects monitored the choristers for funerals, weddings and street-music (musical visits to prominent burghers' houses at Christmas and New Year, etc.), someone had to be in overall charge. Even the welcome income for boys and cantor from the various extra duties had to be managed with efficiency and propriety. If prefects themselves auditioned choristers, they still had to be supervised, and distributing the boys between services in the four Leipzig churches cannot have been problem-free.

How far Bach was obliged to pay for assistants himself, and whether he did so regularly in the form of lessons, is not clearly recorded. Before him, Kuhnau had already found that adjunct salaried positions were disappearing, a sure sign that the 'authorities' interest in a well-ordered churchmusic was dwindling' (Schering 1926, 99) before Bach ever came to Leipzig. Probably, the cantor's traditional duty to check and make an annual inventory of the string and wind instruments owned by the two major churches became less pressing for much the same reason, i.e. the church took less responsibility for supplying them. It is easy to believe that Bach was a no-nonsense director of the school's and church's music, and administered the firm rules for behaviour (including fines for musical mistakes) published in the various issues of the school regulations, the *Thomana Ordnungen*, qv. He too, presumably, obeyed its rules, so that for one week each month he was responsible as cantor for leading morning and evening school prayers, and for checking the infirmary, boys returning from other duties, their general behaviour etc. As for the choristers: they certainly had calls upon their time that must inevitably have interfered with their other studies.

Without doubt, Bach could have used other composers' cantatas more than he did, just as he used other older music at other points in each service, and a big question is how far the compulsion to produce weekly cantatas was self-given. 'Largely', is probably the answer, for he could also have re-used the previous cantor's music at least some of the time. In Hamburg in the 1720s, Telemann was expected to produce two cantatas for each Sunday outside Advent and Lent, plus an annual Passion, but unless his apparently facile way of composing (as suggested in his publications) is misleading, the musical effort going into them does not compare with that required for the thirteen movements of Cantata 75. The thin scoring of Telemann's published cantatas – sometimes 'thinned down' for solo voice, solo instrument and bass line from more elaborate MS versions – can be found in more intricate form in Bach cantatas, but these almost always include other movements much bigger in all respects. Using choralemelodies to give a cantata an overall shape would not mean less work.

Whether Bach's industry in the first two years was aiming at creating new spiritual experience or merely new musical forms, both of which meant relying on himself, is not a simple either/or. A born musician would always turn a cantorate into a creative musical office whether or not he was aspiring to be a grand capellmeister elsewhere, and it seems all the more extraordinary that neither Emanual Bach nor Agricola says anything about this cantata output, except as an item in the worklist. Nor is there much clue about the way such pieces must have loomed large in the early Leipzig years day by day, when Emanuel was nine to twelve years old. Nor anything about their impact on congregations over a period of twenty-seven years. Perhaps the authors took all this activity for granted as part of the job, a regular obligation, troublesome not least because texts had to be found and approved beforehand. Perhaps Emanual had seen his father compose them quickly as a job of work, to be copied and rehearsed and then put away for later use. Or in fact he recalled very little from the early Leipzig years and was aware that cantata-production had slackened off over some twenty years. Even so, had his father, as a composer and Believer, ever conveyed a sense of thinking his work on cantatas to be paramount, one would expect this to emerge in the Obituary.

THE PLACE OF CANTATAS

The main weekly service in the Thomaskirche or Nikolaikirche was a big event. Three or four hours long and beginning with bells at 7 a.m., it proceeded with a series of musical items interspersing the prayers, readings and liturgy (hymns with prelude, a motet, other special works on some twenty feast-days), mostly in older idioms but including the modern cantata before the Creed, perhaps with a Part II or another cantata after the sermon and/or during Communion. At least a dozen cantatas in the first Leipzig cycle had a second part, or were matched by a second cantata, but how regular a practice this remained is not known: more than sources suggest?

It does seem appropriate after a long sermon to have some instrumental music without (yet more) words, and accordingly the inaugural Leipzig cantatas 75 and 76 had their Second Part begin with an instrumental sinfonia, measured and elegant. Even when there is no full instrumental movement, as with so many later cantatas, the introductory bars of an opening chorus or aria will have brought suddenly to the service a new and refined sound after all the hymn-singing and organ-playing – soft melodies from strings and woodwind, or a more vigorous ensemble sound if the words require it. These solid and substantial 'preludes', especially those introducing the chorale cantatas (see pp. 189f), gave congregations a moment when the whole character of a long church service quickly changed, and one can only imagine the effect on them of the opening bars of Cantatas 180 or 139, calculated to please. However, despite the usual working assumptions today, the more prosaic details of these services are sometimes unclear, such as the hymn-singing (were the verses accompanied?) or the chorale-preludes (what exactly are they for?). The role of the organ is especially uncertain: was there a big voluntary closing the service, and if so, did Bach himself ever play it? Although he remarked in a letter to the king in 1725 that the organist must play through to the final hymn but the cantor can leave after the cantata (Dok I, 37), he is saying nothing certain about either a final voluntary or who would play it if there were one.

There can be no doubt about the effort put into the services and their new music by the new cantor. In particular, his first Christmas season meant a massive amount of work, presumably prepared during the weeks of Advent when there was no ensemble music in services. From Christmas Day up to 9 January some seven major services in thirteen days meant nine major works for choir and instruments, including the Magnificat at Christmas vespers and the performance of other service music. Emanuel was probably too young to be fully aware of the effort involved in all this, but the Obituary's silence does leave its readers to see them as 'jobs of work', part of the normal obligations of a cantor. Only when apparently asked about these activities twenty years later does Emanuel say anything about them, and then very little, namely that he worked devoutly according to the contents of the text as a whole (see also p. 373) – nothing about the search for new expressiveness in unexplored territories of harmony and melody, nothing about the sustained work over years that this required, nothing to indicate whether these 'church things' (*Kirchenstücke*) were regarded as more than a chore.

The chief feast-days when service music in one church was heard in the other at vespers later the same day, beginning at 1:15 p.m., were Nativity, Easter, Whitsun, New Year, Epiphany, Purification, Annunciation, Ascension, Trinity, St John, Visitation, St Michael, and Reformation. Regular congregations in each of the two largest churches could have amounted to some 2,500+ people (about ten per cent of the city), amongst whom the elite classes (officials, merchants, professionals) were represented out of proportion to their number by a factor of four or more. It has been estimated that the number of Bach's church performances alone over the period 1723–50 came to about 1,500 (Wolff 2000, 251). For some in the congregation, the cantata's impact and significance probably equalled the much longer sermon's, though how many people came specially for it, were not distracted by the various othere noises in the church, attentively followed the text, or could even read it, are a few of the unknowns. But judging by the various origins of the texts used over 1723–8, so many of which are very direct (first person, present tense), Bach was constantly searching for suitable sources – yet another demand on time. As too with some of Handel's anthem texts, there is still some uncertainty about who wrote or compiled them, and in particular who felt it necessary to have new recitatives written when an earlier non-liturgical cantata came to be rewritten for church.

The first two cantatas to be performed after the new cantor's arrival raise interesting questions about the composer's expectations. Cantata 75 is a big two-part work, probably prepared over the previous weeks in Cöthen, handsomely copied, demanding of performers and listeners, variously scored, and surveying several types of melody. Since each half closes with a vigorous setting of the chorale, the librettist could have been the composer himself. The text reads like a sermon on the Rich Man and Poor Man, integrating psalm-text, chorale-text and exegesis, and could be taken as a musician's 'personal statement', one in which he was employing his skills to shape an 'address', as he moved from a massive opening chorus in the minor (a very original dance-like prelude complete with dashing fugue) to the major chorale at the end. Cantata 75 means to impress, rather as if it were a musical equivalent to the kind of verbal address – the 'cantor's inaugural speech' – given when a new appointment was publicly confirmed in contemporary Hamburg. In October 1721, Telemann had entered on his cantorate with a lecture 'on the excellence of music in church' and heard it received 'with big applause' (*mit grossem applausu*: Kremer 1995, 136), just as Bach's Cantata 75 was heard in Leipzig (*mit guten applausu*: Dok II, 104). There seems to be some intended equivalence here.

Similar points could be made about the following week's cantata, No. 76, whose extant score has many corrections, looking as if conceived at first on too large a scale, written in a great hurry and quickly completed. It too has a prominent part for trumpet, no doubt for Gottfried Reiche, the venerable town musician acquainted with Anna Magdalena's parents. There was another two-part cantata the following week, No. 21, now making use of an older Weimar work. The new Cantata 24 for the next Sunday was shorter and coupled with another one brought from Weimar, No. 185, lighter in style and scoring. (In Weimar, its opening and closing key of F minor must have been very adventurous, deliberately modern, irrespective of pitch.) Such two-part or twin cantatas appear to have dropped out later in that first year, and works become closer to Kuhnau's in performing time. It is reasonable to suppose that the singers or the instrumentalists or the composer, or indeed everyone concerned including clergy, had found the cantor's initial efforts too taxing. That he was over-taxed himself is suggested by there being four earlier non-liturgical cantatas being reworked for the Thomaskirche over the last months of the first cycle (Easter and Whitsun, 1724). In at least one case, No. 134, Bach seems to have found the re-used recitatives matching the new texts so ill that for another performance seven years later he re-composed them.

Whatever the strains of the first few weeks in Leipzig, the mass of duties barely hindered what Bach seems to have seen as his prime duty: to compose – in the first instance cantatas. There were some sixty per year, the first set straightway on taking up appointment, all of them major works. By the middle of July 1723, he is already writing an opening chorus in Cantata 136 that startles with its scoring (horn solo), form (a striking vocal fugue) and invention (e.g. an aria that seems to 'rewrite' the recent B minor Invention à 3). By the late summer, he is introducing a chorale-melody into the opening chorus of Cantata 77 with startling effects in its harmony. Choruses generally needed extensive rehearsals, especially for the boys, and the arias of the first Leipzig cantata-cycle can give the impression of a driving creative energy not always hitting a tone of natural melody and effortless construction.

If this is a fair judgment, one can imagine why: the sheer industry necessary in a short space of time, particularly if a composer resists conventionally easy solutions. The very availability in Protestant Germany of so many cantata-texts in the period after 1710 encouraged hundreds of settings that exceeded by far the number of anthems produced by Anglican composers of the time. The better courts would have a composer and poet who collaborated, as Bach had at Weimar with Franck, but how familiar he was with repertories elsewhere, such as at Schleiz or Darmstadt (some 1,400 cantatas by Christoph Graupner), is not clear. The close connection Bach's cantatas had to points in the church calendar seems not to have been the case with Handel's Chapel Royal anthems, written over much the same period. The only series of performances of other cantatas known to have been performed in those Leipzig years were the eighteen works by a distant cousin, Johann Ludwig Bach, chiefly from February to April 1726. These were some years old, courtly in style, not unlike Sebastian's in the sequence of movements, and like his polychoral motets, melodious. In all respects they are polished enough for one of them to have been formerly regarded as Sebastian's work (BWV 15), but less demanding. Perhaps the minor role played by the choir in some other cantatas of 1726 meant that by then Bach was putting his trust in solo singers, much as Telemann did.

Why exactly ten of Johann Ludwig's cantatas were used during that church year when, in addition, the Good Friday Passion was another outside work (the Anonymous St Mark), is a question not answered by known events. (That St Mark received two new chorales, one at the end of Part One, suggests special adaptation for Leipzig and its vespers.) But the lone use of a Telemann Advent cantata some years later (1734) probably because of current work on the Christmas Oratorio, may suggest an answer: in 1726, during Lent, Bach had begun working on the St Matthew Passion. Whether it incorporated earlier music or not, the Passion was a big project, growing into a huge work fully realized only over time.

The care and thought necessary for the cantatas mean that they are as free of conventional short cuts as possible. Amazingly rarely do they call on common-property formulas of harmony, counterpoint and melody such as one recognizes in Handel's Chandos and Chapel Royal Anthems, likewise written to order. When a familiar formula does appear in Bach's cantatas – a certain bit of imitation, a certain dance characteristic – it gives the impression of a deliberate citation: not a mere formula but a weighted allusion, a useful association, specifically chosen. In endlessly drawing on Italianate idioms, Handel had the advantage that they were then more or less new to English congregations, however conventional they may now seem, and his own inimitable touches only enhanced their attraction. Bach, on the other hand, was participating in a more thoughtful musical culture in which he could best make his mark by developing the work of predecessors at a more intricate level, outdoing them in complexity and critical use of convention, though fortunately leavened by his immense melodic gifts. The Bach cantata may follow in the footsteps of his immediate predecessors at Leipzig but results in a far fuller musical panoply.

The Magnificat, from the first Leipzig cycle, is a work of enormous charm and total originality, with a distinct aura to its melody, really not quite like anything else, and immediately recognizable. Yet just as Handel in his early English anthems adopts details of style from older London composers (Purcell and others), so Bach's Magnificat alludes subtly to the work of various earlier Leipzigers: Kuhnau, Melchior Hoffmann (composer of the 'Little Magnificat' Anh. I 21) and Kuhnau's predecessor Schelle, as well as the other applicants in 1723, Telemann and Graupner. A certain simplicity in the harmony, delicate instrumental colours, appealing tunes, succinct arias, moderately complex counterpoint, five-part chorus (cf. Schelle's SSATB) – all this suggests an attempt to fall in with the common pursuit of tradition. So does the inclusion in the Magnificat of four chorales dating from Schelle's time, 'cradle' songs for the children. And any tendency there had been for substantial pieces of music to refer in their final moments to their opening now reaches new heights in the Magnificat: the opening theme returns strikingly at the end with a brevity and discretion that under-lines the finality.[3]

Was Bach's first Advent in Leipzig a moment when his melodic sense began to flower? For the dedication of the church and organ in Störmthal a little earlier, 2 November 1723, Cantata 194 used revised arias from a Cöthen work and gives a more conventional impression than either the Magnificat or the St John Passion, work on which may have been about to begin. As usual with a parody work, No. 194 has its own recitatives or linking narrative, with words appropriate to the dedication of a new House of God and to its purpose, and with a chorale closing each half. (There is no reference to music or the new organ: the church itself was the centre of attention.) Stylistic conventions are far less in evidence in the Magnificat or Passions, which are so original that the musical pedigree of many a theme, scoring or a turn of phrase is elusive, even rather mysterious. Cantata 194's opening instrumental prelude and choral fugue are much closer to textbook models, in this case the characteristic themes and rhythms of *ouvertures*, with a fugue for voices such as few if any Parisian composers would have made.

If the Magnificat did originate in summer 1723 for the Feast of the Visitation (BJ 2003, 41), then a new melodic sense was already flowering – or Bach was now consciously aiming to produce charming melody, in shorter arias and richer choruses than usual, and these for the special asso-ciations of Mary's hymn. Particularly unfortunate is the lost music for the birthday of Duke Friedrich of Saxe-Gotha in August of this year, for it might have been much like, even related to, the Magnificat. A conscious aim to charm visitors at the Leipzig Michaelmas Fair late September and early October 1723 (Nos. 48 or 95) is possible but hard to demonstrate, though a clearer case might be made for some cantatas sung around the time of later fairs, such as Nos. 114, 149 or 96.

SOME OTHER MUSIC

The first half decade or so of life in Leipzig saw Bach busy also with more domestic music: finalizing the French Suites for harpsichord, a year or two later the six sonatas for violin and harpsichord, and over time the harpsi-chord partitas and the organ sonatas. All were useful not only for the music-making of a growing family but were potential publications, though only

---

[3] A typical 'mini-recapitulation' with a roughly similar feeling of finality rounds off a smaller, perhaps contemporary piece: the Aria from the Harpsichord Partita in D major, BWV 828.

the partitas achieved that. Like the cantatas, these collections never idly follow the conventions.

At times, the six violin sonatas betray a driving earnestness and artifice, producing some ungrateful moments for violin that suggest they were compiled from mixed originals. However, by the time the first harpsichord partita was published in 1726, the driving earnestness so characteristic of the early Leipzig period in general is turning into something deft, refined and new. Some partita movements composed earlier, especially in No. 6 (Gigue), have a grinding quality that is totally absent from the new No. 1: this is an original, one-off masterpiece in which suite-conventions have been totally subsumed in the interests of a new, elegant lyricism, both melody and harmony freshly re-conceived in a new way of writing for the instrument. In some respects this is a finer art than setting orthodox texts in church cantatas, since for these a fund of expressive conventions can be more readily called upon and re-interpreted. But for such harpsichord works as the two well-known fantasias in C minor and D minor ('Chromatic'), there are no established conventions or useful antecedents, and the difference between the tight sonata binary form of the first fantasia and the free, story-like expanse of the second demonstrates how limitless the composer's horizons had become.

With the announcement of 1 November 1726 in a Leipzig newspaper that the first part or *partita* of a set of suites was now available (Dok II, 160 – too late for the Michaelmas fair), Bach begins an occasional series of advertisements for music of his own and of other composers he has for sale. This is an activity far removed from church and school duties, and one notes that Kuhnau had published his sets of suites and sonatas while he was still only organist at the Thomaskirche, i.e. not yet with a cantor's responsibilities. His successor, however, was taking advantage of Leipzig as a publishing centre and responding to a general increase in engraved publications in Germany. Though hard to play, the partitas used the more modern G-clef for the right hand (like Handel's of 1720 but unlike Graupner's suites of 1722) and must have sold well enough for a complete edition of all six to be made in 1731 and running to at least two editions. In principle, the set recalls Kuhnau's, the fourth edition of whose Clavierübung II (1692) appeared only in 1726 – a goad perhaps to Bach, who took over its title. Later, having published this first set himself, he issues parts II and IV of Clavierübung through publishers elsewhere (Leipzig, Nuremberg) but part III, the organ chorales, again by himself. What the financial implications of this are, i.e. whether self-publication produced higher or lower receipts for the composer, is not recorded.

Kuhnau's two books of suites introduced many interesting details: their title, a particular key-sequence, some notational details (slurs, *piano* echoes), preludes constructed from broken chords, inverted themes in gigues, a reference to French *Art*, a final inscription (*soli deo gloria)*, and much else. But they surely did not require anything like the careful thought in Bach's Partita in B flat. Even he could not turn out six or seven such suites easily, nor assume there was a market for them – perhaps buyers preferred, as they could have more effortlessly played, Kuhnau's homely suites, domestic keyboard music of the kind that long circulated.

Bach's mature suites and cantatas have this in common, that they are likely to consist of six or seven movements organized as a sequence of contrasts. Although there is no true correlation between the genres – a final chorale will not usually have much in common with a final gigue, though it might – the principle of alternating the vigorous with the contemplative is, from a composer's point of view, similar. Performers of both kinds of work still find them taxing. Various references to the harpsichord partitas during Bach's lifetime attest to their unusual difficulty, and this must also have been so with the cantatas, hence in part Scheibe's famous criticism in 1737 (see below, pp. 310ff). As the six partitas' overtures have little in common, so any six cantata choruses will work shape and counterpoint in six different ways. Sometimes it is puzzling why one way has been chosen above another, or why a cantata has, e.g., two consecutive arias without intervening recitative or vice-versa. By no means do the texts themselves always suggest one way of setting them rather than another.

According to the extant sources, the 'final chorale' of a cantata was not as usual in Weimar as it became: in Nos. 182 and 172 (1714), for example, it is the penultimate movement. If it had ever been customary for the congregation to sing a chorale after the choir's cantata, then for the composer to choose it, even its particular verse, would be to integrate it more effectively. Likewise he may have made his own contribution to the Passion stories, for the textbook of the poet Picander used for sections of the St Matthew Passion contains no chorales and only cues for the Gospel text. Various sources for a cantata's chosen chorale were used, suggesting careful consideration. No known hymnbook was followed exclusively, nor were the newer books ignored. Although the listener can often sense a musical raison d'être for the choice, Romantic tendencies to associate a melody with a meaning are inappropriate. It can only be a guess that the melody known in English as 'O Sacred Head' appears in the Christmas Oratorio as auguring the Passion (Spitta II, 400f), since many and diverse hymn-texts were sung to this melody, as many as twenty-four, according to Mattheson (1739, 473).

Formal strategies of one kind or another have become so expected of Bach that admirers can forget how unusual this is. Already in Cantata 4 (Mühlhausen?) the seven verses of Luther's Easter hymn were planned symmetrically: chorus, duet, solo, chorus, solo, duet, chorus, prefaced by a prelude matching the final chorale. Yet musical contrast is more obvious than theoretical symmetry or even theological significances in a text. The text-plan of Part I of Cantata 75, from an opening chorus (trust in God), lyrical recitative (useless world), aria (Jesus my all), short dramatic recitative (heaven and hell), aria (I suffer willingly) and lyrical recitative (clear conscience) to a final chorus (trust in God), produces a convincing 'programme of faith'. But it also produces a strikingly varied programme of music containing seven movements, thirteen with Part II, mostly of a kind never heard previously in the Thomaskirche.

The demanding nature of the inaugural Cantata 75 does make one wonder how well it was performed and received and/or whether it served as a warning to the new cantor. By the time of the 1726/7 cantatas, the first nine works have an opening chorus but the rest are without, surely a response to practical problems with the choir.

FURTHER CANTATA CYCLES

Like the Nunc dimittis in an Anglican evensong, the cantata in Leipzig followed the Gospel and preceded the full Credo. But unlike evensong, the Lutheran service went from Credo to sermon, and thus produced a sequence of special significance for the Reformation church: a reading of the Word, then a meditation on it through music, then an affirmation of faith, then instruction based upon the Word. To a Lutheran, the beauty of specially expressive music in this sequence was God's gift to mankind, its delightful sound the most direct 'path to the soul'.

Cantatas were performed from the back gallery, 'watched' less directly by members of the congregation than was the case in an English cathedral quire, but still a means by which a composer would realize the Lutheran duty to 'God and his neighbour' (see below, pp. 262f). To recount the Gospel is duty to the first, to express it beautifully is duty to the second. Whether the congregation sang inwardly or outwardly with the final chorale, they certainly knew it and, in one or other important sense, participated. Probably, many a cantata's final chorale had already been sung in the service as a regular hymn, or was about to be. For an experienced organist-composer, these melodies, with their texts heard outwardly or inwardly, could easily be introduced into arias or even recitatives, and ideally recognized immediately by the congregation.

The cantata's movements allowed its text, full of allusions and associations for the believer, to be presented in various sounds calculated to please and alert the listener. First, a stirring chorus expressing the Gospel sentiments, then a reaction to this in a recitative and aria, a drawing of the moral in another recitative and aria (generally very different form the first in scoring and *Affekt*), and finally an epigram- or epigraph-like verse taken from a related chorale and set as an SATB hymn. All, even the final chorale, could be realized in widely different musical types, variously scored, from intense solemnity to startling ebullience, and texts however apparently 'unmusical' could be conveyed in effective music. Thus, in the first few months at Leipzig, hypocrisy itself is chastised in striking lines in Cantatas 179 and 24, despite preachy texts unlikely to inspire lyricism. The music of Example 18 is full of the gesture one might associate with an Old Testament prophet, and draws on a rhetorical motif from a much earlier work. Such resemblances, even as fleeting as this, are actually quite rare, but they do happen, and Example 18 can stand for others that attentive listeners find from time to time in the cantatas. Emanuel borrowed the opening gesture for his *La capricieuse*, H 113.

Of the first annual Leipzig cantata-cycle over a third are older works revised and re-scored: indeed, almost the whole of the known Weimar repertory, hence in part our knowledge of them. For a cantata such as No. 21 four versions can be identified from *c.* 1713 onwards, varying only in detail and perhaps reflecting performances on five different occasions in different places (Halle?, Weimar, Hamburg?, Leipzig and Zerbst). Generally, the conversion of the Weimar cantatas for performance in Leipzig meant relatively minor re-scorings to allow for a bigger choir, some different instruments and pitch, and a bigger church acoustic. The aim time and again was to compose with all possible variety, tirelessly seeking new ways to set the words. The first works of the second cycle, Nos. 20, 2, 7, 135, 10, 93, 178, have such varied ways of handling the chorale in the big opening chorus as to astonish any close observer. Moreover, they are never very like organ-chorales, showing a whole new range of ways to handle a hymn-melody; and when any are arranged for organ (see FN 4), they are far less idiomatic to the instrument than original organ-chorales. The periodic lines in the hymn-verse being used are scored simply enough to give the choir relatively little trouble in the choral movements, and in the second cycle, generally speaking the treble parts have become less demanding, a clear sign again of the practical composer. Especially the cantatas of later years (e.g. Nos. 140, 80, 97) stand out in detail and conception from choral works of any other composer of their time.

18 a Cantata 179.ii
'Alas, Christendom today is in a bad way: most
Christians in the world are lukewarm Laodocians
[neither hot nor cold: Revelation 3:16] and inflated
Pharisees, who make an outward show of piety and
bend their head to the ground like a reed'
    b Toccata, BWV 916.ii

It looks as if in his first months at Leipzig Bach had overestimated both singers and players, including the brass-players and even the brass instruments themselves. Nevertheless, much of the second cycle (June 1724 to May 1725) has every appearance of a co-ordinated musical-liturgical plan matching the cantata-cycles of Telemann and other colleagues elsewhere, though on a grander scale. The forty cantatas to March 1725, all new, keep up a strikingly high level of inspiration not least in their opening choruses, from the charming and delightful (No. 1, Annunciation) to the stirring and disturbing (No. 26, transience of life): no wonder that after the Good Friday Passion of 1725, only five days after Cantata 1, two older works were brought in for the Easter services! The series sustains a 'purely musical' interest in exploring such things as the French-Italian difference, with a stately French *ouverture* for Cantata 20 in June but a dashing Italian string sound five months later for Cantata 26. For the chorales chosen, no plan has been discovered beyond seasonal suitability – no 'compulsory' hymn-book or 'superior' melodies, though a factor may have been their familiarity to the congregation. Following usual practice, the older chorales have had their apparently irregular metres and rhythms ironed out.

From Trinity 1724, and perhaps as a further gesture towards the congregation, chorale cantatas predominate: some forty works that are in effect sophisticated variations of a strophic hymn, weaving around but preserving its words and narrative, and taking the form of a suite-like succession of movements that include recitative. Clearly, a congregation would feel more *au fait* with chorale texts than with a totally new poetic text, and earlier Thomascantors (Kuhnau, Schelle) had already introduced them. Increased emphasis on chorales, specifically big settings for chorus composed around them, may have been responsible for the opening chorus of the St John Passion being replaced in 1725 by a chorale setting. For around Lent–Easter 1725 there were at least four other such choruses: the big chorale movements opening Cantatas 1, 125, 126 (two days later!) and 127. It is striking that as far as is known, Bach virtually never re-used material from this greater series,[4] although he did return to chorale-based cantatas for another dozen or so works later, half of them with unadorned hymn-texts. In the sheer amount of music and its appeal to the congregation, one could view the series of chorale cantatas as Bach's most ambitious project ever.

The choral works of 1724–5, including pieces for occasions, constituted a huge drain on creative energies, whatever *modus operandi* Bach developed

---

[4] It is not certain that Bach himself was responsible for the six organ transcriptions known as the Schübler Chorales, which include movements from chorale-based cantatas Nos. 93 and 140.

in order to cope, and it is possible that a week's visit to Gera at the end of May 1725 served as a welcome break. The cycle's cantatas often have important flute parts, so either he had found a Leipzig flautist he could trust or perhaps had brought one back from a visit with Anna Magdalena to Cöthen a year earlier. Some such explanation is also possible for (certain) cantata arias that require the violoncello piccolo: although Leipzig had good string players and makers, Cöthen inventories also list such instruments, one of 1724 (BJ 1998, 70). Keeping up contacts outside Leipzig is quite likely: a set of parts for the 1725 Sanctus re-used in the B minor Mass was borrowed by Count von Sporck of Bohemia (Dok III, 638). In Leipzig as in Weimar, a viola d'amore player seems to have been available only for certain periods, but for trumpet-playing Bach could regularly call upon the virtuosity of Gottfried Reiche, chief of the *Stadtpfeifer* and active until October 1734. Doubtless because of Reiche's abilities Bach used the trumpet much more than before, adding parts to earlier works when appropriate and producing some extraordinarily lyrical moments (BWV 77.v), as well as using it for chorale-melodies and even watchmen's fanfares recognizable as such by any Leipziger (BWV 70, see Example 26).

The writing for flute is often gracefully rapturous, as in the aria of Cantata 114 and elsewhere at the time (1 October 1724. See Example 19). There is often a sumptuous quality in such music against which the voice sings as if no more than one amongst equals, in this case a flute soloist whose carefully articulated melody has a sustained length worthy of Rakhmaninov.

Is it really the case that the text, as for the equally luxuriant first aria of Cantata 115 (5 November 1724) quoted in see Example 8 (a), was the springboard for such extraordinary musical richness? As the composer read the text for a cantata, very distinctive musical sounds must have suggested themselves, and yet these are generally at a level of inspiration beyond mere words: for example, the pathos and languor of the flute for the words in Cantata 114 (Example 19: 'Where will the refuge for my spirit be in this vale of misery?'), or the throbbing bass, gorgeously realized harmonies and heavy siciliano rhythms for those of Cantata 115 (Example 8 (a): 'Ah, indolent soul, what? still asleep?'). While both movements are striking enough to remind one of the two Passions, the relationship between words and music is not simple, for could one not exchange these texts and match the music of each to the other's words?

It could seem that the massive, beautiful choruses opening the chorale-cantatas from Epiphany to Annunciation 1725 – especially Nos. 3, 1 and 127 – exhausted either the composer's creativity or the choir's vocal

19 Cantata 114.ii
'Where, in this vale of misery, will
there be any refuge for my spirit?'

energies, for from Trinity 1725 big choruses are fewer. Since this third cycle
also included the easier works by Johann Ludwig Bach and the Anonymous
St Mark Passion, it seems that Bach was reducing his commitment of time
and energy, having also experienced the limitations of Leipzig performers.
In 1726 four cantatas were written with big solo parts for organ (*organo
obbligato*), quite likely for Friedemann or some other reliable pupil to play
in the Thomaskirche. (The absence now of a separate organ part need not
mean that the composer himself was the soloist, playing from the full score.)
The idea of the continuo organist becoming a soloist, which for Bach had
apparently lain more or less dormant since Mühlhausen, was gradually
emerging in the work of various composers at that period, and received a
particularly splendid realization in the Election cantata of 1731, BWV 29.

Music performed in the university church in honour of the late Queen of Saxony in October 1727, Cantata 198, was richly scored and demanding. Its text, an 'Ode of Mourning', was the work of J. C. Gottsched, university professor of philosophy and later of poetics, and Bach set it despite the complaints of the university organist Görner, who was paid off. One of the several reports of this royal event unusually describes the cantata as composed in the Italian manner (*nach Italiänischer Art*: Dok II, 175), which could refer obliquely to the fact that Bach set the poem, which was printed and distributed amongst the congregation, not as a single-movement ode but as a regular cantata, even dividing it into two parts. How many of the apparent changes to Gottsched's text Bach was responsible for is not as certain as once thought, but with or without the poet's approval, the cantor was probably well paid. (In 1738, collaborating with Gottsched on another work now lost but commissioned by the university to salute royalty, he received 50 thalers, a large sum perhaps to cover fees for the string-players.) Reports were united in praising Cantata 198, as well they might be, for its level of melodic and harmonic inspiration is high, even resembling moments in the St Matthew Passion and justly being re-used in the St Mark Passion of 1731. The special mention in one report of an organ prelude and postlude in the memorial service (Dok II, 174) prompts the conjecture that as well as playing harpsichord in the cantata, Bach was the organist, writing or revising the B minor Prelude and Fugue, BWV 544 for the occasion (Wolff 2000, 317). This is a suitably elegaic and majestic preface to the cantata, which begins in B minor.

Some time after texts by Gottsched and a second Leipzig poet, Christiane Mariane von Ziegler were set, up to a dozen by the poet Picander appear in the fourth or fifth cycle 1728–9, perhaps as part of a series intended to be complete and matching others being produced by contemporaries. The texts came not necessarily from Picander's publication in 1728 but from personal collaboration between the two men. The composer's relationship with any of his authors is unclear – whether the academic poet Gottsched or the popular versifier Picander – and often the subject of speculation in the Bach literature today. He needed texts more specific to the church seasons than Gottsched's or von Ziegler's freer poetry, though whether Picander's complete cycle published in Leipzig in 1728 was actually designed for the city's use is unknown, despite the author's praise for Bach's settings (Dok II, 180). Much is uncertain about this period, but 1728 does look like a fallow year before work was begun on the Picander texts, with not much more than the wedding cantata BWV 216 (partly old material) to show for it. There could be several reasons why a certain church year of cantatas is not known to have been completed – like the church year of organ-chorales in the Orgelbüchlein – but one could be that, as Telemann's were to prove, it would be hard to avoid a mortal sameness.

Such 'fallowness' does suggest a pulling-back of some kind, but whether from disillusionment, contentment with existing repertory, diversion of creative energy, or some other personal or professional reason, is uknown. One striking novelty of the year 1729 is the Phoebus & Pan cantata, BWV 201, a work in which there is not the smallest sign of any falling-off. On the contrary, it looks as if Bach was taking on newer *galant* styles here for his own musical purposes, caricaturing them in Pan's aria 'Zu Tanze' and contrasting them in the same cantata with the traditional grace of Apollo's aria. Or for his new Collegium duties in 1729 (see pp. 206f), he was aiming to appeal with music that begins like a Brandenburg Concerto. Or for a potential job elsewhere, he was demonstrating what he could do outside church. If it is true – a big 'if' – that Friedemann went over to Halle in June 1729 to invite Handel, then visiting his mother, to visit Leipzig and meet the cantor, as Forkel reported after Friedemann's death (Dok III, 422), then a piece like BWV 201 would have been a fine example of current composition to show him.

After the initial work on Picander texts, only one new cantata is now known for the Trinity season of June–November 1729, No. 188, and this re-uses the finale of the lost Violin Concerto (D minor?) BWV 1052a as its prelude, requiring the choir only for its final chorale. Also relatively undemanding was an old collection of motets purchased for the church again in 1729, Bodenschatz's *Florilegium portense* 1618, used for funeral music or *a cappella* introits in the services of the two main churches. Did the motets without instruments increasingly replace the cantata? Generally, and in view of sparse documentation after the early 1730s, the question arises just how regularly the cantatas went on being performed. Less and less? Or every Sunday till the end of Bach's life, with parts re-used and/or re-copied, year in year out? Organized by the cantor or by his prefect? Sometimes unrevised? Discouraged by the clergy? Details of Bach's life in this connection are strangely uncertain over a long period of time, and the very uncertainty suggests a less rigorously kept programme as time went by.

THE PASSIONS

On the term 'Passion', see Glossary.

The Obituary's worklist includes 'five Passions' and 'five annual cycles of cantatas, for all Sundays and feast-days'. How Emanuel would know these details he does not say, but his father could have spoken in these terms, or his orderly arrangement of the performing parts made it easy to recognize 'annual cycles' (*Jahrgänge*) when the musical estate was distributed. Since 'five cycles' makes a *prima facie* case for there being as many as one hundred cantatas now lost, some importance attaches to a phrase that has been much discussed in the literature. In the now accepted chronology, cycles III and IV become increasingly patchy and V is largely missing, unless either the gapped series of 1725–27 represents parts of cycles III and IV, or the last cantata of the Christmas Oratorio is a remnant of a genuine fifth cycle. Either is possible, but the chances that there was ever a full fifth cycle for Leipzig are slight. The last known newly-composed cantata for a regular Sunday seems to be the chorale cantata BWV 14 of 1735. This apparent falling-off is matched in another known worklist of the time, J. F. Fasch's for the court church in Zerbst. It seems that both composers created a repertory and then relied on it.

There is another possibility: since the Obituary's worklist of instrumental music includes pre-Leipzig works, so its phrase 'five cycles' might include the Weimar cantatas, a cycle of sorts, and shelved with the Leipzig cantatas. Something similar might explain the 'five Passions', for the Obituary does not say all these were Leipzig works. Only four are documented, St John 1724, St Matthew 1727 (or possibly 1729), a lost St Mark 1731 (BWV 247, with five choruses and arias from Cantata 198), and a further pastiche or anonymous St Luke (1730?). But Emanuel also knew another work, the old Anonymous St Mark Passion, attributing it to Keiser and probably aware that it had been worked on by his father at least three times: at Weimar in 1712, at Leipzig in 1726 (with additions) and again in the late 1740s.

Whatever the truth about the 'five Passions', it is through Bach's settings of St John and St Matthew that a distinct, monumental representation of the Crucifixion story was achieved, a representation with neither true precursors nor successors, even in Hamburg. By 1718, the Hamburg composers Keiser, Telemann, Handel and Mattheson had all set a version of this central story with a libretto by B. H. Brockes, and now in Leipzig Bach draws on Brockes for eight of the thirteen non-Gospel or 'poetic' texts in his St John Passion, a work in which that he creates what is virtually a new art-form on a new scale. Brockes's 'passion oratorio' conveys the Gospel story not verbatim but in his own words, and such settings were neither quasi-liturgical events nor performed in the church. The Passion that Bach may have compiled for Gotha in 1717 would have been of this kind, perhaps bequeathing some arias to the St John Passion (1725 version) and Cantata

55 (1726). Some of the arias in the 1725 St John Passion – i.e. the non-Gospel sections – could also be considerably earlier than the version of 1724, and indeed it would be strange if all its music was new, considering how much older music was used during that first Leipzig year. But it seems to have been there that 'oratorio passions', works setting the Gospel text itself, came into their own by serving the special Good Friday vespers as these were celebrated in alternate years in the two main churches. Vespers opened and closed with a congregational chorale and included prayers, a sermon between the two parts of the Passion, and after Part II a motet. The final choruses of the two Bach Passions were not, therefore, the last music heard in the service.

Telling the story in a musical sequence of choruses, arias and recitatives is common to both kinds of Passion, with the Gospel text or a new text, but the narrative, weight, length and even special liturgical placing of Bach's pair of Gospel settings give them a unique stature. The very chorales are like a Greek chorus speaking for a congregation, even countering despair in the text, as in 'O Schmerz', St Matthew Passion. To have any of them appearing more than once, in different keys and with different texts (many of them, as with the arias, as if from the first person) is an imaginatively dramatic gesture. The two verses of a chorale sung with an aria in-between at the end of Handel's Brockes Passion (1716–17)[5] move in this direction, but the repeat is literal and the dramatic potential limited. Commentators have interpreted certain details in the St John and St Matthew Passions as suggesting that the composer consulted other texts and other settings, but a certain caution is required when assessing the jackdaw mind of J. S. Bach. The chief and foremost impulse was without doubt his own response to the terrible story told, in rather different ways, in the two Gospels.

Not long before, in 1721, Bach's predecessor Kuhnau had established a tradition for an annual Passion performed alternately in the two main churches, with the Gospel's text and narrative (including *dramatis personae* and chorus), verses of familiar hymns, and lyrical interludes with colourful instrumentation (the arias). Enough exists of Kuhnau's St Mark Passion to suggest it was dramatic in its text and perhaps in its performance too, but hardly in its musical qualities (see Schering 1926, 25–33). Nevertheless, Kuhnau's initiative gave an opportunity to his successor, and he took this up with every sign of enthusiasm during at least the first four Leipzig years. Surely aware that Kuhnau's setting of the St Mark Passion had been

---

[5] Performed on five reported occasions in Hamburg between 1719 and 1724, and partly copied by Bach nearly thirty years later, but from what exemplar is not yet known.

repeated in 1722 and again the next year, over the period of the job-search, Bach evidently accepted the task of preparing the following year's. (Perhaps he had also got to know that Handel's Brockes Passion was performed in Lüneburg in 1723.) He assumed or presumed that his new Passion of 1724 was for the Thomaskirche and so announced it, but the Council insisted he keep to the alternating plan and re-announce it for the Nikolaikirche. At this, he countered with requests for the harpsichord in the Nikolaikirche to be tuned and for more space to be made available in the choir-gallery (Dok II, 140), though how this was possible is unclear. It would not be out of character for Bach to have known all along what was expected, and to have been testing his authority as *director musices* in this way, especially for a work requiring grander than usual forces.

At some time during the first winter in Leipzig, then, the St John Passion was composed for the Good Friday vespers of 1724 and performed in the Nikolaikirche, with what impact one can only guess. No congregation had ever before experienced anything so gripping as its opening bars, and when a year later the work was revised with a different, calmer opening chorus, one can only assume the composer wished for some reason to introduce the Gospel with a traditional Passion chorale, in this instance 'O Mensch bewein'. The replacement is an imposing but much less dramatic chorus, in principle rather like a long Weimar organ-chorale, and it could well be an earlier work though used again later in the St Matthew Passion (see below, p. 200) and in principle not unlike a Leipzig chorale-cantata movement. But why replace the *tragoedia* of the original chorus with the *lyrica* of the second? Because contemplation was thought more desirable than drama to preface the Gospel, and if so by whom? One easily understands why Bach would go back to the original opening chorus in later performances, as he seems to have done.

Although the Passions may have influenced others being performed elsewhere during Bach's lifetime, as in Naumburg and Greiz, neither went on to have anything like the influence on German composers that *Israel in Egypt* or *Messiah* had on English. As with his first Leipzig cantata-cycle, Bach appears to aim at affecting a larger and more socially mixed congregation than at Weimar,[6] and as with the second cycle, he was incorporating major chorale-settings at key moments, perhaps with the same aim in mind. The level of inspiration for both Passions is unfailing: every aria melodious, all harmonic movement faultless, every word of the Gospel and

---

[6] Szeskus 1991, 53 calculates percentages of the usual congregations in Leipzig as roughly one quarter upper/professional class, one half middle class, and one quarter the remainder, including students.

every chorus set with an uncanny freedom from the ready formulas that sustained Handel's and Telemann's Passions. In the St John especially, the effect is ceaselessly dramatic through music which is, as far as it could be, astonishingly free of the conventions of the day's Italian opera.

That five major changes made for the 1725 version of St John Passion produce an appreciably different work is a good example of the re-thinking the composer consistently gave to the genres in which he worked. It not only begins with a chorale-chorus but ends with one, and, as noted already, may have included arias from a lost Weimar Passion. Amongst its changes is the passage added from St Matthew's Gospel describing the drama of Jesus's death. Then another version leaves this out while yet another (late 1730s and 1740s) returns to the first and most familiar form, harmonizes some chorales with greater richness, keeps the excerpt from St Matthew's Gospel, and apparently requires a greater number of performers. Different religious emphases can be read into the changes, as when the opening chorus of the second version now focuses on mankind's sin and thus the idea of redemption: was this Bach's idea or one of the clergy's? But there could also be unknown practical reasons for the changes, and the composer was not alone in seeing such major works not as fixed and unalterable but as needing to be rethought, to a lesser or greater degree, each time they were revived. Even the Anonymous St Mark oratorio, which circulated in several versions as well as Bach's, was revised for a performance in the 1740s, this time to include seven movements from Handel's Brockes Passion, chosen from the corresponding points in the narrative.

Three (or five) years after the St John Passion of 1724, the St Matthew Passion was to develop the concept yet further, indeed beyond any other musical work of the period. How far the sometimes sudden modulations and surprising sequence of keys reflect the work's evolution may never be quite certain, but clearer is that by 1736 and possibly earlier, the putatively original chorus had developed into a double chorus, with a large and matching *instrumentarium* that includes both organs (Dok II, 141) and more or less everything but brass and timpani. It seems that step by step Bach conceived several functions for the double chorus: the sense of action is heightened as one or other takes on a *persona*, or responds to the other, or exploits contrast and dynamic shades. However, although the Obituary refers to the Passion 'for double choir' (*zweychörig*), its Chorus I still remains dominant, and the polychoral element never became as integrated as it was in, say, the motets for double and triple choruses by Johann Ludwig Bach. In addition to its two choruses, the St Matthew Passion is characterized by wide ranges of key, scoring, genre, timbre and volume, producing an impact full of surprises for the seasoned listener. (Always startling in the opening chorus, I find, is the sudden major key emerging as the trebles sing their chorale-melody – a calm, sustained line piercing an otherwise churning minor lament.)

While Bach seems to have collected his non-Gospel texts for the St John from various sources, he relied on the local poet Picander for the St Matthew, observing his unequal division into two parts of the six main events (preparation, Gethesemane with arrest; then Caiaphas, Pilate, crucifixion, burial with farewell). Current books of published meditations on the Passion were known to both men, and they might well have discussed them together (see BJ 1979, 115). Yet one is hardly aware of essential differences between the two Passions because of different text-origins. I doubt if any baroque opera begins with such a sense of impending tragedy as the opening chorus of St John (those wailing oboes!) or leaves behind the impression of so terrible a story and cathartic exhaustion as the final movement of St Matthew. It is not easy, even in Handel's operas, to find passages as theatrical as the crowd-scenes in St John, but here the theatre is not a baroque opera-house but one's own imagination, heightened by the starkness of Good Friday, both now and for a congregation of the time who had heard so little music in church during Lent. The narrative itself provides the drama, and while strictly speaking no elaborate music is more than optional to the Passion story (the Gregorian reading of St John's narrative at the Roman Mass on Holy Saturday is a simple intonation), it is there to underline what is already written and already familiar.

One particular moment in the story, Peter weeping bitterly after the Denial, is instructive in this respect. Here, the St John is much more extravagant than St Matthew, pulling out every rhetorical stop, plaintive melismas, rising and falling chromatics, conventional musical effects for conveying distress. On the other hand, at this moment St Matthew is simple, brief, light, without old-fashioned rhetoric – and much more affecting. Perhaps it was for some such reason, and not because it is taken from Matthew's Gospel or because the clergy found it too theatrical, that Bach omitted Peter's weeping from one version of the St John. Other examples of the St Matthew Passion's drama-through-reticence are the succinct close to the aria opening Part II (it stops almost in midair) and later, the four soloists' final brief farewells, so winsome as to give an impression of being temporary or provisional. That Bach knew the power of understatement at telling moments is clear from the simple, brief but exquisite discord when the tenor asks the question, 'And for your part, what will you do?' in St John Passion, as the earth trembles at Jesus's death.

Particularly full of *Affekt*, as if in response to the sheer sadness of the story, is the way that movements might combine an old chorale and some new poetry, as in 'Mein teurer Heiland' in St John or 'O Schmerz!' in St Matthew. Whether Bach himself was responsible for this idea is uncertain. Two extant Picander cantatas of Bach, BWV 156 and 159, also combine chorale and new poetry, and if the men were close acquaintances, Picander could also have known Bach's earlier use of chorale-melodies. St John was performed four years before Picander published his first book of cantata-texts, but to use complete chorales within arias or choruses was a natural extension of using bits of them, which the composer had done ever since the early funeral Cantata 106 of *c.* 1707. 'Mein teurer Heiland', however, has a sweet, newly composed melody beyond even the most tuneful moments of Cantata 106, and although the phrases of chorale enter periodically much as in an organ chorale-prelude, they do so far more tellingly.

To respond to the trial scene in St John as Bach does, with an organized key-plan, returning choruses, and a symmetry around the pivotal chorale 'Durch dein Gefängnis' in the second part, is to be true to John's Gospel itself, where the trial is not only central but has its own kind of formal elements, such as a classical peripeteia. (This is the 'potential reversal of circumstances' or turning-point when Jesus could have responded to Pilate in a conciliatory way.) Less obviously symmetrical but as surely planned is the key-scheme of St Matthew, which wanders more than once from minor to major sharp keys and through to flat keys, moving from an elegiac E minor at the beginning down to a tragic C minor at the end. The penultimate chord of the St Matthew, a particular dissonance needing resolution and found already at a similar place in the St John, is in theory typical of French chaconnes, but the effect here is much more painful, beautiful, long and voluptuously scored. Yet however sustained the richness of the St Matthew Passion, with its long prayer-like arias and its hugely colourful layout, the St John has a touching quality of its own that hits the listener from first to last, from the dreadful opening reiterations of G minor to the final, overpowering hymn. This hymn alone, an unusually long chorale-verse, is a masterpiece of uncanny music, more than a mere hymn as it moves towards an expression of powerful, defiant hope, surely elevating the hearts of a congregation.

For many, the St Matthew Passion is a work of even more obviously passionate commitment than St John: a work unique in scope and grandeur, revised and later re-copied in a particularly careful autograph, with red ink for the Gospel texts and opening chorale-melody ('Agnus Dei'). That Bach should use movements from it for the mourning music for Prince Leopold, three weeks before the 1729 Good Friday performance, raises several interesting questions. Was it possible to salute the late prince with such special music merely because Cöthen had better instrumentalists? Or music caviar to the general in Leipzig was better appreciated in a court setting? Or the music for Passion, funeral, burial or mourning was perfectly interchangeable? (The music for Leopold also included two movements from the late Electress's so-called Mourning Ode, BWV 198.) Ten non-Gospel, contemplative movements were extracted from the Passion in memory of a beloved prince, four months after he died: months during which the Passion was either being composed for Good Friday 1729 or, had it been completed two years earlier, was now being revised. Nine arias (6, 8, 13, 20, 23, 39, 49, 57, 65) and a chorus (68) would then be mourning for both a beloved prince and a beloved Saviour, and one might speculate that the soprano arias (8, 13, 49) were for Anna Magdalena to sing at the Cöthen event. The cantata's text for the Passion arias 49 and 65 match the music so convincingly, with long notes on appropriate words etc., as to leave it far from obvious which came first.

In Leipzig in 1729, four new string instruments were made for the church, and if they were ready in time for the Passion that year (Dok II, 199) one can imagine that the accompaniments to Jesus's words – soft sustained string chords, known already in the Anonymous St Mark oratorio of 1726 – were more than usually significant. (Not the least dramatic gesture in St Matthew Passion is the silence from the strings when Jesus cries 'Eli, Eli'.) The various revisions to each Passion suggest the composer to have made a tremendous personal investment in them, part-musical, part-devotional, not rushing revisions such as those of 1725 for St John. But by March 1739, any resistance there might always have been to his grand Passion dramas, particularly amongst the clergy, seems to have come to a head, when an under-registrar of the town council (why he?) informed Bach that his piece for Good Friday vespers was not to be performed until he had obtained permission for it. This was probably the St John Passion, copying work on which abruptly stopped, it seems, to be picked up again only for a later performance in 1749 (BJ 1988, 44). Bach's reported reply was that there had always been such music, that he cared nothing about it, would get nothing out of it, and that it would only be a burden (*ein onus*: Dok II, 339). He would inform the superintendent of the ban, though if it was the text that was objected to, the authorities should (he implies) note that the setting had already been heard a few times.

All this suggests either that someone was objecting to the text, the interspersed non-Gospel sections set in emotionally charged arias, or that Bach had not submitted the text for approval, as he should have done. The latter is certainly possible, although if the objectors were clergy, then they were hiding behind the clerk. Either way, the composer's pique is as understandable as it is unmistakable. Both Passions were open to criticism by puritans and Pietists, despite the fact that no discriminating person could mistake their drama and sentiments for those of the theatre. How regular their performance was after the early 1730s is uncertain, as with cantatas, but there is likely to have been a growing indifference on the composer's part. Copies could be re-used, it is true, but there are more documentary traces left of slighter works by other composers being used than of revivals of the Passions. Assuming that with age did not come indifference or undue indolence, Bach must still have been deeply affected by whatever reception was given these works, particularly if it had deteriorated during his years as Thomascantor. History seemed to be repeating itself: Kuhnau's Passion had not been found appropriate for performance in the Thomaskirche until four years after it was done in the smaller New Church (Schering 1926, 24), and it is more than likely that not everyone cared for such presentations, at least as part of a regular liturgical event in a regular church.

Though not strictly relevant to such performance, there is a further dimension to the Passions not easily envisaged today: their story of a public execution. This, after all, was being told for a Lutheran congregation and by a group of performers who had all witnessed public executions. New city regulations in Leipzig in 1721 (Schneider 1995, 180f) specified that a procession of heavily armed soldiers was to accompany the 'poor sinner' to the place of execution outside the gates, beyond the Johanniskirche where Bach himself was to be buried nearly thirty years later, and at certain moments in the formal procedures the choristers sang *Sterbelieder* (hymns for the dying), as they had done for many years. The school rules even specified that small boys be allowed home on the days of execution to witness events with their parents (Schering 1926, 90). On one occasion during Bach's tenure, the wind-players, presumably the very same who played in the Passions, processed publicly with the workmen sent to build a new scaffold.

How far Bach, like the superintendent of the Thomaskirche, was personally involved in these events is unknown, but the procedures were public, and as *director chori musici lipsiensis* he was ultimately responsible for the music. The choristers were present at the start of the procession and perhaps beyond, and it was a contractual obligation of Bach's to accompany the boys at funerals (see above, p. 168). Although they were not frequent, recent executions had been particularly grisly: a young woman or 'child-murderess' on 3 December 1723, and a botched beheading on 13 February

1727, a few weeks before the St Matthew Passion might have been first heard. There were others in 1724, 1740 (three, as in the Gospel story) and 1739, the last on the Market Place. Such events suggest very graphically that 'Ach! Golgotha' in the St Matthew aroused more than a vicarious, expressive horror at the place of an execution long ago. Similarly, the city regulations' specification of the military's duties emphasizes the important part played by soldiers in the two Gospel accounts, ensuring judicial formality and saving Jesus from any lynch-mob, as well as (for St John) scrabbling over his vestments and thus fulfilling the scriptures. All this must have been very realistic for the Passions' listeners. An especially affecting moment occurs in the St Matthew Passion when the captain of the guard finally recognizes the Son of God – a telling gesture for those Leipzigers (including J. S. Bach) familiar with the military on these occasions.

OTHER MUSICAL ACTIVITIES

Not long after, the Duke of Weissenfels appointed him his Capellmeister. (*Obituary*)

Since this sentence follows immediately on the reference to Bach's 'funeral music for his deeply beloved prince in Cöthen' in March 1729, its phrase 'not long after' relates to this and not to the original Leipzig appointment. A new titular capellmeistership would follow only on the lapse of an old: the Duke of Weissenfels's conferred title would replace the Prince of Cöthen's.

Before the move to Leipzig, it must have been clear to Bach and his gifted wife that there were advantages in living in a city connected in various ways to the capital city of Dresden and its musicians. What it would have meant to him to be the first non-university-graduate in living memory to hold the Leipzig position is not known. As already noted, three preferred candidates, Telemann, Fasch and Graupner, had all been students in Leipzig, though not necessarily full graduates. (Their withdrawal raises the question whether they know too much of the city and its ruling elite to want the job.) In Walther's *Lexicon* Kuhnau was still being remembered for his knowledge of theology, law, oratory, algebra, maths, foreign languages, *poesi* and *re musica* (music theory), and a court appointment for Bach at the grand and important residence of Weissenfels would have enhanced his status on paper and perhaps in spirit.

After moving to Leipzig Bach kept some connection with the courts both at Cöthen, where he and Anna Magdalena received a performance fee in December 1725, and at Weissenfels. At the latter he stayed for some time in February 1729, and after appointment remained titular capellmeister there until the *cappella* was disbanded in 1736. In official documents he consistently used his successive secular court-titles first (at Cöthen, then Weissenfels, then royal Dresden), and only secondarily his assumed title *director chori musici* in Leipzig. Whether or not official and formally invested, this *directorship* brought with it a certain status, especially for musical visitors to the Leipzig Fairs. The New Year, Easter and Michaelmas Fairs also brought publishers and authors of books of music and music-theory to the city, and its cantor is as likely as any other citizen to have bene-fited from what was on sale and who came to buy. But so many books being produced might have been counter-productive: it is possible that Mattheson's mass of publications (of which there were 'as many as he had lived years', according to Burney 1785, 8) discouraged Bach further from trying his own hand.

Bach's appointment as titular court capellmeister at Weissenfels in 1729 could well have been the result of representations he made following the death of the Cöthen prince on 19 November 1728, though for two months he was still using the Cöthen title (BJ 1994, 15). Successive Dukes of Weissenfels had not been indifferent to gifted musicians, and the ducal castle was the nearest major residence to Leipzig, with a splendid chapel and organ. It had been in this castle, in February 1713, that Bach had a secular cantata performed, soon after which the Duke of Weimar raised his salary (because of this success in Weissenfels?); and it was for Duke Christian's visit to Leipzig in January 1729 that another such cantata was presented, BWV 210a. The duties of the capellmeister were informal and unsalaried, but how long the title remained valid, following its conferment some weeks later, is unclear: was the present of some venison from Weissenfels in 1741 (see below, p. 294) an annual gift of the kind generally made to an honorary appointee?

The Weissenfels connection tempts many a speculation. Here in the town lived Anna Magdalena's mother until her death in 1746: did her daughter ever sing the dazzling Cantata 51 (*c.* 1730) there? The piece certainly reflects musical tastes at courts in Weissenfels or even Dresden, where its scoring for singer and trumpet was not unusual. Was it bringing a court's brilliant, light tastes to Leipzig or was it rather something to appeal to a potential court employer? Perhaps neither, but it is always tempting to explain gaps in the Bach biography as times when he was looking for good court positions else-where, for now or later. Another uncertainty arising from his various con-tacts with the nobility is to what extent did he, in titles, letters and fulsome acknowledgments, mean to flatter, grovel before, woo or merely defer to dukes, princes and kings? Simple deference is the likeliest, for his flowery politeness was conventional and entirely unexceptional. Only anachronistically can it now be described as 'fawning'.[7]

One cantata apparently written for and performed at Weissenfels for the duke's birthday on 23 February 1725, BWV 249a, is interesting for being the first setting of a text by Picander, and also one of three forms of a work known as the Easter Oratorio. A second Picander text, likewise set to the same arias (BWV 249b), was another birthday offering, made in 1726 for Count Joachim Friedrich von Flemming, Governor of Leipzig, brother of the *Premierminister* Flemming who was acquainted with Handel and, it seems, host for the abortive Marchand-Bach 'competition' in 1717. (Of course, one wonders whether Bach knew of the Flemmings' connection with Handel. Surely he did?) As Prince Leopold of Cöthen's funeral music shared certain arias with St Matthew Passion but linked them with different recitative, so these three cantatas likewise shared arias, resulting in two secular works and one sacred. It is not clear whether in February 1725 Bach already had written the Easter Oratorio and used its arias for a birthday cantata meanwhile, but all the movements have a distinct, festive feel to them, a sound more of a concert than a liturgy, suitable for the events outside church clearly relished by their composer.

One hears something similar in cantatas written in honour of two professors in the University of Leipzig in 1725, BWV 36c and 205, the first such works of the new cantor, who evidently worked with enthusiasm and a wish to please. Both were revised later for similar occasions, BWV 205 with its brilliant choruses and arias, all of it unmistakably graphic (rushing winds, and so on) and melodically inspired, like so much in this particular Bach repertory. That barely a half of the documented so-called secular cantatas have survived so as to be performable today is a great blow to the true understanding of J. S. Bach, for he brought to such works the same restless inspiration as to the Passions. Furthermore, from such cantatas and serenades as now represent the fifty of so known to have originated for various dedicatees (royalty, nobility and academics), one can conclude that Bach was, in some degree, an active member of certain social circles in the city, not merely their paid minstrel.

Only from hints or guesses can one visualize his personal and social contacts. Thus it was probably through the lord of the manor responsible for

---

[7] As in the superficial reading of one politically committed book, E. Said's *Musical Elaborations* (New York, 1991), 64. Even the flattering acrostic written for Frederick the Great (see p. 257) was not exceptional: the poem set in the Duke of Weimar's birthday aria over thirty years earlier (BWV 1127) picked out in **bold** the letters of the duke's name, like a chronogram.

restoring the nearby church of Störmthal, and having an organ built for it, that Bach was invited to take part in the inauguration of both a few months after his move to Leipzig. Similarly from some personal connection, no doubt, he obtained the texts for nine cantatas in April and May 1725 from Mariane von Ziegler, the daughter of a burgomaster involved in Bach's original election. By the mid- and late 1720s he was well-known in certain professional circles, being 'very well received' for an organ recital in Dresden in September 1725, frequently called 'famous' (*berühmt, rühmlichst bekannt, praestantissimo, clarissimus, celeberrimus*), praised by a visitor from Brunswick above the organists in his own town, and compared favourably with Frescobaldi, a comparison that would have held great significance for any professional musician. Not all noble dedicatees were indifferent to music, on the contrary: for example, the court chamberlain for whom the Peasant Cantata was written in 1742, Carl Heinrich von Dieskau, became *Directeur des Plaisirs* (including musical administration) at the Dresden Court a few years later, and was dedicatee of some published lute-music by a Bach pupil, Rudolph Straube. In so many documents Handel might be portrayed as more of a charismatic figure, but he had the advantage of living in the royal, capital city of a strange land in which people from polite society talked and corresponded about the theatre and its musicians, and lionized its foreign geniuses.

As a sign of his activity in Leipzig, in March 1729 Bach became director of the Collegium Musicum, a concert series for polite society run by a group of musicians and students, since its foundation in 1702 by one of the students at the time, Telemann. It is not known whether Bach was freely chosen in recognition of his authority or solicited the directorship for the contact it brought with instrumentalists useful in church (Schering 1926, 344). Although the previous director G. B. Schott, with whom Bach had good professional relations, left in 1729, something a student said later implies that by 1724 Bach was already directing concerts (Dok III, 476). Hence the parts of the Overture in C, BWV 1066 being copied out around then? It is easy to believe that he began taking part in public chamber music as soon as the pressing duties of cantor permitted, either composing or re-using music from his Cöthen years. In particular, the 1730s saw chamber and keyboard music of great originality, a match for the vocal masterpieces of the first decade.

CHAPTER 6

Leipzig, the middle years

THE COLLEGIUM MUSICUM AND CHAMBER REPERTORIES

How soon after taking on increased duties with the Collegium in March
1729 Bach worked on his concertos and other music for mixed ensembles,
and then performed them in the Collegium concerts, is not clear. One imagines very soon: he certainly made copies about then of suitable pieces from
elsewhere, such as full-length instrumental *ouvertures* (suites) by Johann
Bernhard Bach of Eisenach, successor to the admired Christoph (†1703).
Just as unclear is whether there is any direct link between Collegium activities and an apparent falling-off in church cantatas. Composing up-to-date
music for outside the church need not have dampened creativity within it:
organ music (church music of a kind) was still being worked on, and to a
surprising extent the different genres remain independent of each other,
both in musical style and in the attention given them.

Whatever the Collegium commitment, particularly while Bach was
director in 1729–37 and again on and off from 1739, it must have been pressing, very willingly undertaken, no doubt, since by now the cantata repertory was rich enough to satisfy any church's requirement. The Collegium
met regularly each week, more often during the Spring and Autumn
fairs, and the programmes gave all the opportunity that was desired to try
over or repeat the various secular cantatas, especially those with big forces
like BWV 205. His sons and pupils certainly benefited from experience in
the Collegium, as several of them later attested (see Dok III, 408), especially when applying for jobs. At least one outstanding pupil, J. L. Krebs,
seems to have participated while still at school and into his twenties (Dok
III, 654).

Complaints about Bach in respect of his school duties at this period –
that he slighted, neglected or abandoned them (see Dok II, 205) –
could, assuming they were justified, reflect these other priorities. Any
disgruntlement he felt with school or church was more than likely

reciprocal, though it would not be a contradiction if he also brought into church various musical ideas from his Collegium experiences – the big collection of instruments that supported two choirs in the St Matthew Passion, for instance, or the 'orchestrated' version of the first movement of the Third Brandenburg for the Whitsun cantata of 1729, BWV 174. This last is of particular interest since the added horns and oboes reinforce the ritornello and so leave the original strings in their episodes rather like soloists. The effect is that of a novel kind of concerto, quite possibly a result of those new Collegium experiences and, for all anyone knows, one of several such 'modernizations'.

The new court title at Weissenfels used by Bach from mid-1729, the taking on of the Leipzig Collegium, and the work with new kinds of instrumental music in the later 1720s (the violin sonatas, organ sonatas, harpsichord partitas), does suggest that some years after appointment as cantor Bach was putting increasing store by his activities outside church, as would any creative composer and potential job-seeker. A variety of chamber or instrumental works, including the violin concertos and at least one of the overtures, probably dates in their known form to the years around 1730, some if not all of them new arrangements of older works. It is also reasonable to guess that some of this music was written or arranged for the two oldest Bach sons to play, such that there was a 'family element' in the Collegium at the time – although in that case, it is odd that the Obituary's worklist does not specifically include the unmatched violin concertos. (Considered more dated than the harpsichord versions?) A certain involvement in Leipzig life outside the Thomaskirche is also suggested by the secular cantata or *dramma per musica* 'Phoebus & Pan' (1729), performed – so one might guess – as a satire on pedantic Beckmessers in and out of the university (see below, pp. 292f).

The Collegium directorship going to Bach, rather than to his predecessor's assistant C. G. Gerlach (a Bach pupil), might have been due to the influence of burgomaster Lange, who was surely aware that many cities in Europe were beginning to encourage important musical societies, where well-to-do subscribers hired a professional composer-director to run regular up-to-date concerts of vocal and instrumental music. In Britain, the Music Society in Edinburgh, also dating from the 1720s, was joined by others in English cities, newly formed clubs run by a board and keeping better formal records of accounts, programmes, events and even committee meetings (in *sederunt* books) than seems to have been the case either with the Leipzig Collegium or the later series, the Grosse Concert (see p. 276). Although the Collegium depended on the good will of the performers and seems to have been informally run in a coffee-house or its garden, open to gentlemen and ladies who paid only for what they consumed, nevertheless such people were there capable of judging 'the worth of a clever musician', according to a report of 1736 (Dok II, 278). Bach's student Mizler, who wrote this report, said that 'any musician' who wanted to be heard could play there, especially students, amongst whom were potential virtuosi. What organization and paperwork all this required of Bach himself is without record.

In winter, the concerts were heard on Friday evenings from eight to ten p.m. in Zimmermann's coffee house near the city-centre, and in summer on Wednesdays from four to six p.m. in the 'coffee garden' outside the walls, on the way to the Johanniskirche. It was in the garden in June 1733 that a new *Clavicymbel* was to be first played, the like of which had not been heard before (Dok II, 238), a claim which could just be referring not to harpsichord but to one of the new fortepianos. (For a Leipziger, these could well have been associated with the royal music-making in Dresden, where one of the new Florentine pianos might have found its way.) Presumably the new instrument was paid for by Zimmermann and stood in some kind of raised, covered loggia of the kind found in London plea-sure gardens at that time, as at Vauxhall where organ concertos were played and for which the youngest Bach son was later to write several sets of songs. No single programme of the Leipzig concerts exists, nor is there much information on their nature: was anyone paid, was the director contrac-tually appointed, are we speaking of concerts as such or more convivial gatherings, etc? Chance references imply that visiting composers and touring instrumentalists participated, as no doubt they did in philhar-monic societies across Europe at the time. (At Ulm in 1725 and 1726, another Collegium series performed two concertos probably by Bach: see BJ 1974, 124.) According to a city guide of 1732 (Dok II, 235), on Thursday evenings at a similar time and in another house, a second Leipzig Collegium was held by Bach's organist at the Thomaskirche, J. G. Görner, but how truly open such events were, and whether they always admitted women, is not clear. Neither?

Suitable programme items were transcriptions, various solo and ensem-ble suites, sonatas, concertos, secular cantatas, and songs of the kind sparsely represented in the second Anna Magdalena Bach Book. The last are straightforward tuneful songs far simpler than the formal church cantata arias, a type of music all their own, perhaps reminding some of the listeners of Telemann's now lost Leipzig operas from earlier in the century. Like those elsewhere, the Collegium programmes are likely to have been dominated by Italian chamber music, concertos and cantatas, and by more local imitations of these, including works by Telemann and various Dresdners. A list of music-books left by one Leipzig merchant on his death in 1734 suggests the kind of repertory interesting to such amateurs: flute sonatas, violin sonatas and concertos, all by a range of Italian composers from Corelli to Veracini (Szeskus 1991, 60).

Pupils and sons were also involved in copying music suitable for these concerts, just as they were for the church music, and there are indications of a wide repertory. Known items include works by Handel (cantata 'Armida abbandonata', some copying done by Emanuel), Locatelli (Concerto Grosso Op. 1 no. 8, with the pastorale, *c.* 1739), Albinoni, Vivaldi, Conti, Porpora and Steffani (BJ 1981, 69). Not many composers of Corelli's generation are likely to have featured much, Vivaldi and his imitators rather more. Bach's own contributions can be guessed to include the instrumental *ouvertures* such as the well-known orchestral Overture in D major, BWV 1068 (for a special event in about 1731) or the Flute Overture in B minor, BWV 1067 (for a special visitor in about 1738). The Solo Violin Concerto in A minor and the Double in D minor, probably older works, have parts copied by the composer in about 1730, and the transcriptions of them for harpsichord would also have suited the Collegium. Whether Anna Magdalena participated in singing songs or taking the solo part in works like the 'farewell cantata' BWV 209, with its not very expert Italian text but a wonderfully polished, modern concerto movement for flute and strings, is also not recorded.

Later in the 1730s the three flute masterpieces, the Sonata in B minor, the Overture (Suite) in B minor and the now incomplete Sonata in A, were copied, but at least the first and probably all three of them had another version, even in another key and for a different instrumentation. Many a sonata, made for flute and harpsichord, or two flutes or violins or lute and flute etc., had several contemporary versions, not all of which need have been made by Bach himself. However, the more he participated in the copying of parts or scores, as in instrumental parts for the Flute Ouverture, the more he may have had the Collegium concerts in mind. Alternatively, his visits to Dresden in the 1730s were reason enough to make copies of new or redrafted works for flute, to be played by one or other of the famous court flautists, Buffardin and Quantz. Equally likely to have been composed for, arranged for or re-copied for the Collegium are the three gamba sonatas, each of which has its own history, and which may never have been collected as a set. It could be that the concertos for two or more harpsichords, all of them arrangements, belong to the earlier Collegium period rather than the later. Since sometimes the part for first harpsichord in these concertos makes bigger demands on the player than the other parts, it is reasonable to suppose them arranged for Friedemann or the composer himself to play, assisted by younger pupils or sons.

The unrivalled solo harpsichord concertos BWV 1052–1059, written out as a set by the composer in about 1738, were all probably made from earlier string or wind concertos, the earliest perhaps BWV 1052, 1053 and 1059. They often recall superficially some of the concertos by Albinoni (Op. 9, 1722). 'Unrivalled' not only in quality, these works also stand largely alone at the time in existing at all and in establishing, at least for Leipzig, a special genre: that is, the solo keyboard concerto. Examples of this were not yet being produced and published in anything like the numbers they were from the 1740s on, across Europe. The composer continued to work on their collected score, making changes in certain figuration as if he was working out for himself how to give the comparatively low-amplitude harpsichord (or fortepiano?) a solo role in the string ensemble – how to make a true keyboard concerto, in short. Such a work would be altogether 'busier' than an organ concerto, where the organ's usual textures if not thinned out would easily overpower strings and its tuning clash with theirs. If, as sources suggest, the first movement of the E major Harpsichord Concerto was being reworked a dozen years after it had appeared for organ obbligato in Cantata 169, which itself probably goes back to a movement from an earlier concerto (for oboe d'amore?), it suggests how the composer's idea of transcription developed. See Example 20, for first solo entry in the two versions.

It seems that the idea of a 'solo keyboard concerto' had been gradually maturing over time. Assuming the fifth complete bar of Example 20 (b) had not been unintentionally omitted in the cantata version – and nothing in the latter's sources suggests this – it is striking how both are possible, with or without the bar. Had its original movement been for oboe, the harpsichord's b. 5 might be leaving traces of a place to breathe, between beats 3 and 4.

Emanuel's version of the well-known Harpsichord Concerto in D minor, BWV 1052a, now dated to *c.* 1734, must be based directly or indirectly on a violin original ten or more years older, and was probably made for him to play, in which case one wonders why its impeccable ritornello structure was not something he re-created or developed further in his own works. In 1739 Friedemann came back to Leipzig for a month-long visit, with two lutenists from Dresden (one of them the renowned Sylvius Weiss: see p. 238), and it is easy to imagine family concerts with appropriate works. Or the concertos served Friedemann and Emanuel in their burgeoning

20   a   Cantata 169.i, organ obbligato part, b. 9
     b   Harpsichord Concerto, BWV 1053.i, b. 9

careers elsewhere, even their father on one particular visit he made to
Dresden in 1738. A Thomaskirche student, J. F. W. Sonnenkalb, later
reported often hearing house-concerts played by 'the whole Bach family',
including Friedemann, Emanuel, Christoph Friedrich, Johann Christian
and son-in-law Altnickol: he must be speaking of the late 1740s, when
Sebastian no longer played much outside his home and when the oldest
sons were there in Leipzig only on visits (Dok III, 148).

   The set of solo harpsichord concertos would have had to be re-copied
for the engraver, or a keyboard score made, if publication had been
intended for any of the pieces. Six were 'pure' harpsichord concertos (two
others with woodwind solos) and could have made a published set if

completed as such. It is a curious coincidence that 1738 was also the year of the first complete set of keyboard concertos to be published: Handel's Op. 4, published in London 'for organ or harpsichord' and strings, and like Bach's compiled from a variety of sources, one of them originally a concerto for quite another instrument (harp). Although there is no evidence that Bach or the Collegium musicians knew these Handel works, despite being published also in Paris at about the same time, they caught the public taste for new kinds of concerto, had a huge sale, were much imitated, and have never been out of print.

To see any of these concertos by either composer as 'anticipating the classical piano concerto' is misleading. They are conveying in their busy figuration how the keyboard, like the violin, might participate in a consort and step forward from time to time with its own solos. That is still partly true of the classical piano concerto up to Beethoven's 'Emperor', for even there the soloist plays along with the orchestra, often from a figured bass. But as there is no 'orchestra' as such for Bach's harpsichord concertos, and the soloist is instead a partner in a chamber consort, the relationships are different – too different for the later concertos to have needed the earlier as precursor. Nevertheless, as a group, but especially the concertos in D major and the D minor, Bach's transcriptions could claim to be the most developed and significant keyboard concertos before Mozart's piano concertos of 1784–6, extrovert in their outer movements, rapt in their middle. There is no unbridled virtuosity in the solo part, and in fact, the harpsichord concertos are less demanding on their soloist than the violin versions are on theirs.

In the case of the 'multiple' concertos – three for two harpsichords, two for three, one for four, all of them transcriptions, the last from Vivaldi's Op. 3 no. 10 – the sound-world they create is unique, elusive and unlike any other music, even string concertos by Bach himself or Vivaldi. One is soon aware of a special sound-world in the opening bars of the C major Triple, the dance in the middle of the D minor Triple Concerto, the bare fifth opening the A minor Quadruple, the antiphonal effects, and the harmonies produced by simultaneous harpsichord embellishments. In taking the opening tutti octaves of the D minor Triple, a traditional feature of Vivaldian ritornello themes, and giving it to three keyboards instead of violins, the effect is reinforced, and the concerto offers a fine, typical example of the way features of a style are adapted to produce a sound-world never entered by the originators of those features.

Whether the Six Sonatas for Violin and Harpsichord were suitable for performance at the Collegium is uncertain, for although called 'sonatas', and therefore, as usual when Bach used this word, Italian in conception, the virtuosity they require is for a counterpoint as carefully wrought as that of the six sonatas for organ, which at times they resemble. There is little of the flashy Italian rhetoric that was becoming popular in the 1720s, although if Friedemann could play them he was a gifted violinist. In the Collegium it would have been the *Kenner* or connoisseurs in the audience who would most like them, while the *Liebhaber* or music-lovers were drawn more to sonatas for flute or oboe, as no doubt they were also to songs and secular arias. But then, a different question arises: where are these sonatas and songs? Does the Organ Sonata in E flat disguise a no longer extant mixed trio sonata? Considering the use made of wind instruments and of course solo singers in the church music, there is a striking absence of both woodwind sonatas (or trios or concertos) and songs (strophic Lieder) amongst extant Bach works, despite the Obituary mentioning 'a crowd of instrumental things of all kinds and for all instruments' in its worklist.

The appearance of many movements in different forms means that in some cases the 'original' version is not only unknown but, as normally defined, may never have existed. A work could be as it were a matrix, a neutral open score that was open to different applications, and it is not impossible that Bach (like Handel?) kept a portfolio of such pieces. For the movements of the Concerto in A minor for flute, violin, and harpsichord, BWV 1044, all of them known in other versions, the sketchy sources – merely a set of parts from the middle of the century – inspire conjecture about who made the version (not the composer?), when (before or after 1750?) and why (for house-music, for royal concerts in Berlin?), and plausible support can be found for each of these answers. Even when the medium of a work is reliable in the extant source, as is the case with the Solo for Flute (the 'Partita' in A minor, BWV 1013), this source is likely to transmit no more than one possible and even incomplete version of a work, at one of several possible pitches, and for one of several instruments solo or otherwise. If certain harpsichord concertos, including the C minor double and D minor triple, were originally (or equally) for oboe, as some others are known to have been originally (or equally) for violin, is it only by chance that these versions are now missing? There also remains the puzzling absence of songs, considering the obvious success of those few that survive in the second Anna Magdalena Book and Schemelli Song Book (see pp. 233f). There must be losses here, resulting in no more than a partial picture of what was happening in the middle Leipzig decade.

Something to have emerged already before 1730, however, is of great interest in the wider history of musical form. In the first movement of the C minor Organ Sonata, by drawing on his past experiences in paraphrasing melodies, varying and deriving counterpoint from them, Bach introduces a long passage (almost half the movement) that takes the themes, extends them, alters them, modulates with them, varies the bass-line and moves back to the tonic in time for the return of the opening theme. In symphonies and sonatas of the classical period, this section would be called 'The Development', and it anticipates the work of symphony writers in Esterhaza and Mannheim, though unknown to them.

THE FIRST PUBLISHED SET OF PIECES

1730 began with the birth and death three days later of Anna Magdalena's seventh child, and was a year that saw less than a handful of new church cantatas but several signs of serious problems for Bach: a reprimand from the council and a long letter of complaint from him about working-conditions (see below, pp. 217f), plus at least one solicitation for a job elsewhere. Judging by Passion settings prepared around that time – St Luke (anonymous) and St Mark (lost, mostly a parody) – there was some lessening of effort on behalf of the Thomaskirche. In its musical language, the St Luke Passion is so juvenile that whoever wrote it, and however interested Bach was in preparing simple works for the Leipzigers, by no means is it certain he ever performed it. Between the letter of complaint and the job-solicitation Bach probably produced one of his most popular cantatas (BWV 51) and in addition, having published the fifth harpsichord partita that year (the last to be composed), he was now collecting all six to publish in 1731 as his first complete volume, Clavierübung I. Cantata 51, in being called *cantata* by the composer rather than the customary *concerto*, may well have originated not for the Leipzig services but for a court performance in Weissenfels, Dresden or elsewhere, for which its immense vivacity is appropriate.

Certainly the Six Partitas, discussed further on pp. 228ff, had nothing to do with the church or the school, and to publish at all was not as obvious a step to take as it was for Handel in London or Couperin in Paris, where so much music appeared in print. Unfortunately, the local copperplate engravers used by Bach for Clavierübung I were not experienced enough in music notation to produce consistently good work, or even get the order of movements always right, and particularly for Partita No. 4 there is a sad contrast between the quality of the music and the quality of the engraving.

Adding to the technical difficulty of playing many a movement was having to interpret the scrappy and cramped print, though most of the work by Balthasar Schmid in Nos. 1 and 2 (1726, 1727) is reasonable. Schmid was a pupil of Bach at the time and later, better experienced, was to produce for him the Canonic Variations, the Goldberg Variations and the titlepage of Clavierübung II. His early work in 1726 might have been in lieu of payment to Bach for lessons (Butler 1990, 33).

Rather than having them printed, an organist in Thuringia or Saxony hiring out his manuscripts or selling MS copies himself could produce a good return, as Bach's pupil J. L. Krebs implied when he reported some keyboard music of his being sold in unauthorized MS copies at a lower price than the engraving (*Andere Piece*, 1741, preface). But there were other, musical reasons to publish. It is quite possible that the partitas were consciously responding to other keyboard music of the day, works both of first rate quality (Rameau's *livres* of 1724 and *c.* 1728) and those less so (Graupner's suites 'mostly for beginners'). Partita No. 5 reminds one of the subtle, delicate harpsichord-writings in Rameau's outstanding book of *c.* 1728 – in which case Bach's response was immediate. So it would be to the models of binary structure Rameau offers. Graupner's influence appears more indirect. His twelve suites are strangely unlike earlier works of the kind and, perhaps inspired by Kuhnau's *Frische Clavier Früchte* (1696) raise the question whether there was a tendency for German composers to search for the greatest possible originality in their suites, i.e. away from the much-worked formulas of Couperin and Handel. An example of where such a search would lead Bach is Partita No. 2 in C minor, in which there seems to be no convention that is not thoroughly, even drastically re-considered: familiar *ouverture* rhythms, a characteristic Andante melody, a two-part (!) fugue, a seamless allemande and sarabande, powerful courante hemiolas, a breathless rondeau, and a totally un-capricious Capriccio. Whether, like Bach in Partita No. 5, Graupner or anyone else would conceive a suite consisting entirely of movements in four kinds of triple time, slow, medium, fast, and medium-and-fast (Minuet), is doubtful.

Altogether, the range surveyed in the partitas is important as indicating how Bach wished his first publication to represent him. No two dances are alike, and there is a clear desire to impress each conventional type with an individual manner, approaching the idea of 'character piece' (*Charakterstück*), as when an original minuet in No. 3 becomes a *burlesca* on publication and, presumably, as played. In Graupner's suites can be found many little details such as left-hand octaves that are re-worked just once and to far greater effect in the First Partita. The six sarabandes take what could be learnt from d'Anglebert's and Couperin's books but apply a more intense harmony towards six very different conceptions of what a sarabande can be. The differences between them go well beyond the variety found in French sets, and yet they do not contradict the dance's character. They are still sarabandes. Similarly, the six allemandes do not, I believe, have even a common tempo between them and yet remain undeniably allemandes. Variety has become a more than usually fine art.

The difficulty in playing the partitas was remarked on at the time, both by a professional musician (Mattheson: Dok II, 22) and an amateur (Dok II, 223), the latter the nineeen-year-old Luise Kulmus (future wife of Gottsched) who described them as 'making me seem like a beginner each time', a sentiment shared by many a player ever since. Several of the better-off university students acquired prints of the partitas, others made copies for themselves, so it is possible they were used in advanced lessons. But such students were exceptional, and other composers sometimes made a point of saying the music they were publishing was not too difficult to play. Two years after Clavierübung I appeared, Graupner, whose 1722 suites Mattheson also thought difficult, promised that his more recent *Vier Partien* contained no difficulties, just as G. A. Sorge was to do with some organ-chorales he published a few years after Bach's Clavierübung III chorales (see p. 225). Although he can not have been indifferent to a wide circulation, Bach was obviously aiming at something unusually searching and educative in his published keyboard music, as he was in a diffferent way with his early Leipzig cantatas. If the keyboard music was hardly as 'unfathomably difficult' as Luise Kulmus found some of it, it was more consistently demanding even than Rameau's and Scarlatti's.

In miniature, keyboard works suggest something about a composer's thinking that could be extrapolated to bigger works. One apparently minor but in fact significant detail is Bach's increasing use of 2/4 time for movements aiming to be up-to-date. This new metre has two strong beats, often under a syncopated melody, often stately and deliberate. Except in his transcriptions of Italian concertos, 2/4 time is absent from Bach's keyboard music until Clavierübung I, but now there are examples in three partitas. In No. 4 it appears for a certain kind of modern aria found increasingly in sacred music (Cantata 9) and secular (Cantatas 213 and 214), the last performed a few months after the 1733 visit to Dresden, seat of fashion. Telemann and others were writing attractive tunes in 2/4, but an aria like 'Kron und Preis' in Cantata 214 (to become 'Grosser Herr' in the Christmas Oratorio a year later) looks like a more tuneful version of aria-types in the Dresden operas – something like 'Se mai più sarò geloso' in J. A. Hasse's opera *Cleofide*, whose premiere in the Zwinger Palace opera house at Dresden in September 1731 Bach is conjectured to have heard.[1]

THE ROYAL TITLE AND ASSOCIATED MUSIC

In 1736 [19 November] he was named Royal Polish and Electoral Saxon Court Composer, after he had previously had himself heard several times publicly on the organ in Dresden, to great applause, before the Court and music-experts there. (*Obituary*)

The sentence follows immediately on the one naming him capellmeister in Weissenfels (above, p. 202) and bypassing the work with the Collegium, the university, the school and the city's churches.

In this latest instance, 'Court Composer' was an honorary title, probably given in recognition of significant performances offered to the elector in his kingdom's second city by its *director musices*: it did not denote a regular functionary such as capellmeister, concertmaster, *director chori musici* or even court-organist, though it would not preclude his offering and performing works there. In London, Handel's appointment as 'Composer of Music to his Majesty's Chapel Royal' in February 1723 was also less than a regular capellmeistership – the wording is not unlike Bach's – but he did produce a few pieces for the Chapel (often reconstructing earlier works), was occasionally ordered to supply a special work, and was paid well. Had knowledge of Handel's appointment penetrated to Leipzig?

Despite the frequency with which works of music or literature were offered or dedicated to kings and queens, and despite the many titles of royal appointment conferred on various kinds of *craftsman* across the kingdom of Saxony (not least in Leipzig), such a title for a composer was exceptional. It must have followed on the recommendation of significant persons, however eager for it the composer himself had been. For reasons one can imagine, a petition seeking the title had been sent in the later summer of 1736, shortly after or even during a period of contention with the Thomas School rector (see below, p. 321). If the Obituary thought that the appointment followed directly on organ recitals in Dresden and was the result of pubic acclaim – not in the new Frauenkirche in any case, since the recital there was not until 1 December – it was probably mistaken.

---

[1] Hasse uses this aria at least twice in *Cleofide*, as well as in the opera's version made for Venice in 1736, *Alessandro nell'Indie*.

It does seem, however, that one organ the Obituary had in mind was the dazzling new instrument of the dazzling new (but unfinished) Frauenkirche, an organ for whose inauguration on 25 November Friedemann wrote a poem (see Ahrens 2003, 97), perhaps as part of soliciting the appointing committee on his own behalf. If so, he was backed by his father, who was presumably there for some days in late November 1736, before playing the organ's very first full concert on 1 December, in the presence of courtiers including Baron von Keyserlingk, later associated with the Goldberg Variations. A Dresden newspaper of 1 December 1736 reported the inaugural event and referred to the same three items as the Obituary: the organ-playing in public, the 'special admiration' of the crowd of listeners (for whom 'applause' probably did mean hand-clapping) and the subsequent court appointment. Though uncommon, such praise for a performance was not entirely exceptional, appearing in the newspaper at least in part because the splendid Silbermann organ was brand new. Similarly, in 1720 the Dresden organist Christian Petzold had inaugurated the earlier Silbermann organ in the Sophienkirche with 'music worthy of astonishment' (BJ 1979, 57).

Nevertheless, the Obituary's phrase 'heard several times' might reflect its authors' knowledge of other reports such as had already appeared in Hamburg concerning the 1731 Dresden recital. Once again one is left to wonder if it was from a preserved newspaper cutting that the authors knew such details, otherwise rare for them, and that they neglected other public successes of Bach because they had no printed evidence to refer to. No wonder the selectiveness of the Obituary, which presumed on its Leipzig readers remembering their deceased cantor, led a later reader, Forkel, to ask Emanuel many questions! Neither knew that on 28 November, fresh from his royal appointment, Bach had written one of his letters of complaint about the Thomas School rector to the Leipzig Consistory but then kept it back ten weeks or so before sending. Why, is unknown but could be indicative: proud of his royal appointment, he first drafted a strongly worded letter, had it professionally copied, and signed it with his new title then or later, having meanwhile waited to see if the quarrel could be resolved.

Already on 27 July 1733, a month or so after Friedemann's appointment in Dresden and almost six months after the death of the then Elector of Saxony, Bach had sought a court title from his successor, Friedrich August II, in a petition accompanying or connected in some way to a set of twenty-one vocal and instrumental parts for a *Missa* or Kyrie and Gloria, later known as the first two movements of the Mass in B minor. The period of mourning for six months after the death of the previous elector on 1 Feburary 1733 had meant a gap in instrumental music in the kingdom's churches, affecting even the Passion on Good Friday that year. But it gave a never-resting composer chance to work on composing/arranging a big two-movement Lutheran mass and completing a score ready for part-copying, probably about the time mourning was lifted on 2 July, or in connection with the birth of a prince celebrated on 19 July. Probably, these vocal and instrumental parts of the Kyrie and Gloria , made with exceptional care by himself, Anna Magdalena, Friedemann and Emanuel, were his first setting of these words and thus particularly apt for presenting to the new monarch as a typical large-scale *Missa* suitable for Dresden. The uncommon involvement of so many family-members in the project (plus one other copyist) and the exceptional care with which the parts were copied, suggest the whole project to have been 'beyond his Leipzig obligations' and 'a private affair' of the composer (Schulze 1983, 5).

The Kyrie and Gloria for the Elector of Saxony were larger-scale than Bach's other settings, BWV 233–236. As with other two-movement masses such as J. C. Pez's, apparently performed in early summer 1724, there were occasions in Leipzig for which such works were appropriate. But some may also have been made with an eye to Dresden, and like certain movements in the Elector's Gloria were very carefully derived and selected, for their quality, from earlier cantata-movements. The new Latin texts were similarly underlaid with great care, and such music as the little opening 'prelude' on *Kyrie* is appropriately Italianate for a major Dresden work: its phrygian cadence and very brevity can be found in, e.g. the *Responsoria pro hebdomada sancta* of 1732 by J. D. Zelenka, the court's church composer. (For further remarks on the complete B minor Mass, see pp. 258ff.) Although on 20–21 April 1733 the new elector visited Leipzig, the kingdom's second city, there is no evidence that any of the *Missa* had been performed on that occasion, despite later surmises. In Dresden, the most suitable place for a performance before the Frauenkirche was complete enough for its organ to be dedicated, and long before the new Catholic Court Church was built, would have been Friedemann's Sophienkirche near the palace. Were Friedemann and the Sophienkirche, whose organ was then the best in Dresden, in the composer's mind while parts were being prepared? – to salute his new Roman Catholic king in a Protestant church, sue for his support in Leipzig, and draw attention to his gifted son (who, unlike his predecessor, held a town but not court position), all in one operation? Perhaps, but there is no record of performers being assembled for such an event, and in August 1733

Friedemann reported that the Sophienkirche organ was badly out of tune (Schulze 1983, 8).[2]

A question is why, since the Dresden court is known to have employed full-time music copyists, Bach sent a set of elegantly made parts rather than (as with another royal offering, the Brandenburg Concertos) a copy of the full score. This may have been customary with chamber works offered to a patron (e.g. the Sonata à 3 in the Musical Offering), but with such a work as the B minor Kyrie, it is hard to see how the capellmeister, on to whom presumably such things were passed, would have much idea what kind of work this was beyond its obvious complexity. But parts, carefully notated with performance details (tempi, slurs) made it easier to put on a performance? In the years around 1730, J. G. Pisendel, Dresden concertmaster and an advocate of music able to combine Italian and German styles, had been inviting new compositions from court-musicians across Germany and, acquainted with Bach since 1709, is likely to have included him, though this is not documented. Maybe Pisendel asked for parts, or Bach did send a copy of his score, later lost but originally included within the accompanying petition's reference to 'the present small work' (*gegenwärtige geringe Arbeit*: Dok I, 74).

Like the music's titlepage, the petition attached to the parts was written out neatly by a scribe in Dresden, one who also worked for Zelenka. This task needed arranging and adds to the impression that the work involved in composing, copying and dispatching the Kyrie and Gloria must represent a big investment on Bach's part, an effort that was presumably worth it if he were asking for *Protection*, as he was again in October 1737 during a further quarrel with the Leipzig rector. The 1733 dedication implies that there would be other 'slight works' he could offer, perhaps the Magnificat in D, revised and re-copied about this time in a calligraphic fair-copy on paper with the same watermark, indeed as if for a similar dedication. According to the petition for the royal title, any such acts and consequent recognition would be of help in combating the 'one or other injury' (*ein und andere Bekränckung*) Bach was experiencing in Leipzig, including a reduction in expected fees. His problems 'might disappear entirely' (*gänzlich nachbleiben möchte*) if he were granted a court title. However, Bach cannot have realistically expected that problems in Leipzig would lessen if royal favour were conspicuously shown him: town councillors and clergy were not above being resentful, covertly or otherwise.

---

[2] Or Silbermann's tuning did not suit the newer keys found in the two Kyries (B minor, F-sharp minor).

It is possible that the visit to Dresden in September 1731, and a recorded absence from Leipzig in March 1729, had already been in connection with a paid position at the elector's court, the capellmeistership – especially if it is true, as Emanuel later said, that about then his father was heard by the important Dresden court musicians J. A. Hasse, his wife (a court diva) and J. J. Quantz, and enthusiastically praised by them (Dok III, 418). The incumbent, J. D. Heinichen, died in July 1729 after a sickness, and only two years later did the young Hasse take up his position, and then without confirmation. The Bach visit to Dresden included recitals both at court and in the Sophienkirche, the Protestant church next to the elector's residence, and were no doubt visited by court musicians and other personnel. (Schütz's chapel in the palace, now well known from an early engraving, was still there in part but much altered.) Bach's petition of July 1733 to the king ends with a specific offer to supply, in return for the title, 'music for the church and orchestra' (*Kirchen Musique sowohl als zum Orchestre*). The last word almost certainly refers not to instrumental music as such, as for a modern 'symphony orchestra', but to a physical location in the royal palace, i.e. the place in the theatre in front of the stage where the instrumentalists sat ('orchestra' as defined in Walther's *Lexicon*, 1732). It seems that Bach was offering to compose theatre music, opera and ballet.

A big Latin Kyrie and Gloria for choir and instruments was certainly not inappropriate for Friedemann's Lutheran church, any more than Latin mass movements (and a Magnificat on Christmas Day) had been in other important Lutheran churches such as Lübeck's. Father-and-son collaborations cannot have been rare at the time, but whatever concrete results there were from the Dresden visit, over the following year and a half Bach wrote and performed several major cantatas in honour of the royal family (BWV Anh. I 12, 213, 214, 205a, 207a, 215). The four he performed in Leipzig for successive kings, in 1727, 1734, 1735 and 1738, must have been a highlight of such 'evening music' performed by the university's students, with a tone and text close to Dresden's formal opera – more so, perhaps, than the birthday cantatas for non-royalty (BWV 205, 207), though this should not be overstated. In particular, and to commemorate the elector's naming as 'King of Poland' in 1733, Cantata 215 was given a grand evening performance a year later on 5 October, in the open air, with a procession, torches, students, marshals etc., and found great favour with the king who, to the evident surprise of Leipzig's town chronicler (Dok II, 250), actually stayed on his balcony to listen to the music.

In the Collegium concerts too, Bach is likely to have consciously developed connections with Dresden musicians, quite probably engaging in the 'game of reciprocated invitations' still known to many an organist today: they come to Leipzig, he goes to Dresden. More importantly, perhaps, three times in 1733 and several more over the next three years Bach not only cele- brated royal birthdays, name-days and the formal coronation of the elector as King of Poland (Cantata 205a, 19 February 1734?), but is likely to have been responsible for the notices of them appearing in the Leipzig newspa- pers. The performances were in the Collegium and had nothing to do with the church, and doubtless the reports reached His Majesty in due course.

The very title *dram(m)a per musica* that Bach normally used for his various festive or homage cantatas for the royal family – some fifteen times between 1727 and 1742 – means he was aware that here he was dealing with a specific genre, not liturgical but not entirely secular either, given the divinity of monarchy. The genre was especially suitable for a great court with its own musical tastes and practices. While, as part of the awakening interest in native literature, the poet Gottsched categorized secular com- positions according to whether they had *dramatis personae* and classical storylines, to a composer musical language was not totally exclusive. With such festive works based on allegorical or mythological themes, including characters (*dramatis personae*) and a storyline of sorts, and running to more movements than church cantatas (nine to fifteen), one can see that the border into opera would have been easy enough to cross. If one is unable easily to imagine Bach working in tragic opera or *opera seria*, one certainly can in the less formal types of stage music. It takes very little to stage the Peasant and Coffee Cantatas, though neither requires it.

It is a reasonable assumption that Bach had been actively soliciting for a title or function in the capital city, although nothing came through until 19 November 1736. Was this because his title as capellmeister in Weissenfels had lapsed only in June 1736, on the death of Duke Christian? Or because the Dresden elector was absent from Saxony for almost two years over this period, 1734–6? In either case, any earlier approach to the king might have been for something more than an honorary title and the *Protection* it would bring. Questions are whether Bach's fitness for the highest musical job in the land, demonstrated in the startlingly majestic Kyrie and Gloria, was as obvious to the Dresdners as it might be now; and whether this music over- estimated local tastes and abilities much as the earliest cantatas in Leipzig had probably done. Meanwhile, however, the royal cantata-music for Leipzig was not wasted: movements were re-used for arias and choruses in the Christmas Oratorio, performed over Christmas Day to Epiphany, 1734–5.

Using his existing but re-written music in church was an important part of a composer's life and work. As is not always the case with Handel, Bach's re-use of his own material suggests he was perfectly aware of what was well-wrought and beautiful in his music – knowing (as we might say) a fine piece when he saw it. Not only do his parodies demonstrate music's ability to match a text's general *Affekt* and individual words, he makes his choice of music almost as if to demonstrate such versatility. Whatever the immediate reason for adapting an older work – unwillingness to 'waste' commissioned pieces, affection for them, sense of economy (as when instrumental pieces are also re-used), shortness of time, in some cases indisposition, even slowly diminishing energies – there was also for Bach, though less obviously for Handel, a natural urge to work further on his music. To rewrite, improve, revise, elaborate on, re-consider, learn from previous work: there are many instances of this throughout his life, whatever the circumstances, and mostly one supposes positive reasons for it rather than negative, such as shortness of time. Re-using would be part of his drive to 'return God-given talents with interest'. (See further on parodies, pp. 367f.)

From the point of view of the text, there was nothing unusual or improper in using music composed for a different set of words, and in some cases it would not have cost much more trouble to compose entirely from new – as seems to have been Telemann's policy. Bach must certainly have had an efficient filing system, in his memory or on paper, from which he could call up suitable movements to re-use, in some cases (such as in the completed B minor Mass) from many years earlier. It is possible too that in first working on the homage or congratulatory Cantatas 213, 214 and 215, he already had further use in mind for them in an appropriate sacred work, indeed a sequence of cantatas for the next or next-but-one Christmas-to-Epiphany season. Festive music was festive music, and in the days when a monarch was God's anointed, what was suitable for a new-crowned king in Dresden was suitable for the newborn king in Bethlehem. Once converted to a work for church services, these were not then re-revised for other purposes, though the 'secular' version might be (BWV 36a-c). There must be an intentional policy operating here, but quite why is not obvious. It might be misleading to assume that by nature a composer would want to bring non-church music into church *ad majorem gloriam dei* but not to take the church's music outside – misleading because his fundamental piety could just as well lead him to do the opposite.

In the nearly twenty earlier movements converted into the Christmas Oratorio, the music's motifs and the text's words were both versatile. An echo aria with pastoral overtones serves Hercules in his search for virtue in one cantata (213, itself perhaps already a parody) just as well as it does the Christian soul in its search for salvation in another. So many classical *topics* such as the pastoral appear in biblical contexts – here, salvation through the Good Shepherd – as to make transference between them plausible, even if in this instance the aria gives the impression of a naive piety that the puritan might consider out of place in a Christmas cantata. But that quality can also be there in the original aria. In any case, although the melodious style of these congratulatory cantatas was in general perfectly appropriate for Christmas, not all of it was. The gavotte-chorus originally closing BWV 213 and apparently intended to open Part V of the Christmas Oratorio was then discarded and replaced by another chorus, just as catchy but less obviously a dance-finale.

Nevertheless, the overall tone of the Christmas Oratorio is still one of immense warmth and light, meticulous in its contrapuntal detail and wide-ranging in its melodies, from a dashing violin theme that could have come straight out of Corelli or even Legrenzi (the parody aria 'Ich will nur dir zu Ehren leben') to a courtly dance very much at home in Royal Polish Dresden ('Nur ein Wink von seinen Händen'). The last follows at the point that Herod asks to be told where the Christ-child lies, and it is much like a polonaise, as is another A major aria in a birthday cantata (BWV 214.iii). Were one to look for allegory in the Christmas Oratorio aria, the unmissable graciousness and puzzling metre of the aria 'Nur ein Wink' (where is the first main beat?) seem to allude to the persona of Herod as it is drawn in the first Gospel: outwardly charming but deceitful. In general, however, polonaises are surely to be understood as dutiful allusion to the 'union' of Poland and Saxony, as when one such aria in Cantata 210a appears in five known versions, including those addressed to the Duke of Weissenfels and the Leipzig governor, Joachim von Flemming.

The idea of six separate but linked cantatas as for the Christmas Oratorio was not unique: see a note on Buxtehude's Advent concerts on p. 50. In Dresden at much the same period Georg Gebel was setting a St John Passion that was performed on six days in Holy Week a few years later, in the church at Rudolstadt. Like Bach's Passions, it uses the full Gospel text, and like the Mass in B minor introduces both old and new styles of music, both the *stile antico* and *moderno*.

ORGANS AND ORGAN MUSIC

Readers of the Obituary would probably assume that when Bach tested an organ he would play an inaugural recital, both improvising and taking one or more of his bigger organ pieces with him. It was probably for a particular occasion that the major preludes and fugues were composed or fundamentally revised, and paired in the form in which they are now known. Some must have originated precisely as the Obituary implies: to please the Weimar duke. And judging by extant copies, students worked on them just as they did on the chorales.

Some reports of Bach's playing could be speaking of organ music played for admirers after services, much as Handel is said to have played after evensong in St Paul's. What other purpose the big preludes and fugues had is less certain than their still unrivalled status in the repertory would suggest, such as whether they ever served as postludes to regular or festive services. But characteristic of them is that all are individually shaped, each freshly worked, two barely alike. Preludes might follow the concerto or ritornello plan but one will explicitly be a dialogue (BWV 538), another will give the option of dialoguing (BWV 544); one will dance like a polonaise (BWV 548), another stride heavily (BWV 546). Similarly, while several fugues have or tend towards an ABA shape, they do so differently each time. Restlessly testing what can be done with the type of music in hand is as clear in the big organ works as it is in the opening choruses of cantatas.

The likely gestation period of the unique publication Clavierübung III (1739) is close enough to the Dresden visit of 1736, and the 'several times' he played there, for one to see it as an ideal organ-recital programme for such occasions. Its plan is

a majestic prelude of large proportions, concerto-like in shape
then a set of extensive chorales interspersed with smaller settings, first of
the mass texts (Kyrie and Gloria), secondly of Luther's six catechism
hymns
then some intricate pieces demonstrating 'textbook' counterpoint
finally, a monumental three-section fugue.
In having not only a practical but in some sense a theological plan, the book is peculiarly revealing of the kind of performer J. S. Bach was, and in this respect says much about his priorities generally. Its beginning and ending in E flat major (i.e. with three flats) is often taken as some kind of allusion to the Trinity, and a simpler musical reason for the key – that it prepares for the following chorales – is no evidence to the contrary, since they could be in any key. The complexity of the greater Lord's Prayer setting is legendary, but throughout the book a level of contrapuntal imitation and inversion constantly pushes the music away from the familiar and complaisant. The greater Eucharist setting, BWV 688, is another example. Since the volume draws specifically on a corpus of strict Protestant doctrine (Luther's mass and catechism), its basis is therefore rather different from the seasonal hymnbook of the Orgelbüchlein. An important musical influence

was undoubtedly a classic long known to Bach, Frescobaldi's *Fiori musicali,*[3] better models than which no composer could have found for either the fughettas or for the use of plainsong.

Alone amongst the Clavierübung volumes, Part III was 'prepared for the lovers and particularly connoisseurs', while the other three parts were only for 'the soul's delight of music-lovers'. Whether or not Part III represents the Dresden programme, complex and unworldly like the first Leipzig cantatas, the report of 'great applause' at the 1736 recital fits in with other testimony of the time, as Bach earns the reputation of an incomparable organist and contrapuntist. Alas, there is no comparable report of the two B minor Mass movements being heard on the same occasion, though their encyclopedic range of styles is more approachable. But Clavierübung III's plan for an organ-recital seems to match what was expected in Dresden: G. A. Homilius, a Bach pupil according to Forkel, was described by several writers as attracting 'all connoisseurs and music-lovers' to his Sunday vespers recitals in the Frauenkirche, carefully preparing for them on the day before various chorale-preludes and a fugue (John 1980, 36ff). Such organ-recitals were more than concerts, for in sight and sound, the Frauenkirche organ was designed to cap a symbolic east-wall arrangement: a vertical line led up from reading-desk (the Word), font and altar (the Sacraments and Gospel), flamboyant retable (Revelation) to the organ at the apex (the people's songs of faith). While the organ played, the eye would inevitably be drawn up in contemplation, as in a more sober way it was to the altar-crucifix in the Thomaskirche during a Passion performance.

Occasionally, Bach had been examining or inaugurating other organs since becoming cantor in Leipzig, the *ex officio* status of which would alone bring him regular invitations, hence, perhaps, the clause in his contract about leaving Leipzig only with permission. The only formal organ-examination he is known to have undertaken during the previous period was of the large Leipzig Paulinerkirche organ in 1717, for which the university paid him twenty reichsthaler. At Gera in June 1725, he received thirty to test and play two smaller organs, while in September 1732 the Martinikirche in Kassel paid him fifty. Anna Magdalena accompanied him to Kassel (Dok II, 228), perhaps via Mühlhausen. Three weeks earlier they had lost their one-year-old daughter Christiana Dorothea, two months earlier still Johann Christoph Friedrich had been born.

There is no record of solo organ music in Störmthal when Bach was present for the inauguration of the church in November 1723, nor at Gera,

---

[3] 1635: exactly a hundred years old if Clavierübung III was begun in 1735, as is possible.

but on both occasions he was probably heard. Other occasions were at the Dresden Sophienkirche in September 1725 and 1731 (Silbermann organ) and probably at Weissenfels in 1725 and 1729, then Kassel Martinikirche in September 1732, perhaps Mühlhausen Marienkirche in 1735 (where he accompanied his son J. G. B. Bach on his audition), then Weissensee in 1735 (en route home from Mühlhausen) and again in 1738, Laucha in 1738, Altenburg in 1739, Naumburg in September 1746 (Hildebrandt organ) and Potsdam in 1747 (Wagner organ). Although the last three of these had a new, large and celebrated instrument, lesser organs were also involved, plus Leipzig itself and environs (Johanniskirche 1743, Stöntzsch 1731–2, Zschortau 1746), and it seems that autumn was a popular time for such visits. At the Kassel organ-examination in 1732 the newspaper referred to him as the famous Herr Bach of Leipzig (Dok II, 226), and he was handsomely paid, but the invitation to him probably came from a much earlier contact: the builder was J. N. Becker, former apprentice of the builder supplying the Mühlhausen organ in 1708.

By chance, a copy of the masterly Toccata and Fugue in D minor, BWV 538 mentions the Kassel visit, giving a hint of one reason why so many mature organ works were written by a composer who was after all not a regular Sunday organist: they were pieces for a church 'concert'. This Toccata seems to have been played before the young Prince of Hessen-Kassel and inspired an enthusiastic eye-witness account published more than ten years later (Dok II, 410). Another eye-witness account speaks of hearing Bach during the Leipzig Easter Fair, in May 1729 (Dok II, 196), and while it is not clear where and what he was playing, the visitor compares him favourably to Frescobaldi and Carissimi, presumably therefore as an organist. It is easy to believe that at least in his earlier years in Leipzig, Bach put on concerts for visitors to the fairs, and if he did, he is unlikely to have been alone in doing so. J. G. Görner, from 1716 organist at various times in all three main churches, was evidently gifted and active, and his successor at the Nikolaikirche in 1729, Johann Schneider, was highly praised by another eye-witness (Mizler III, 532). Significantly, in saying of Schneider that his 'preludes' were of such 'good taste' (*Vorspiele ... gutem Geschmack*) that one could hear nothing better in Leipzig except Bach's, Mizler could be implying that Bach played voluntaries for the regular services. A later eye-witness speaks specifically of Schneider's fugues as an opening voluntary (Schering 1941, 66), but this was his job as organist, not the cantor's.

At Naumburg, where today the recently restored organ gives the best impression of a major local instrument belonging to his later years, Bach seems to have recommended its builder Hildebrandt (Dok I, 113), former pupil of Silbermann with whom Bach tested the organ in September 1746. Since the tonal quality of surviving instruments by Hildebrandt and Wagner does not, in my view, quite compare with that of Silbermann, an interesting question is whether Bach preferred the first builder to the last and if so why – because Hildebrandt was more amenable, agreed to build in an old case, and preferred heavy bass tone? Or Bach had a sense of loyalty to him as the builder of Störmthal, as harpsichord tuner in the big Leipzig churches, and as maker of a lute-harpsichord he owned (see below, p. 282)? Or Hildebrandt had fewer contractual commitments than Silbermann, who made him sign an agreement not to encroach on his privilege in Saxony (Dähnert 1962, 33–42).

Any of these reasons is possible, and may say something about Bach's friendships. That Hildebrandt worked on new organs and repairs in and around Leipzig in the 1730s is probably a sign of the cantor's support for him, as might be the many clavichords and harpsichords of his that were also owned locally. (Thirteen out of sixteen in an inventory of 1745 were in or near Leipzig: see Dähnert 1962, 231). Equally possible is that if Hildebrandt and Silbermann were reconciled by the time of the Naumburg organ-test in 1746, Bach had helped bring it about.

HARPSICHORD MUSIC

It is hard to imagine that in Dresden in December 1736 Bach played only the new Silbermann organ in the Frauenkirche and not also harpsichords in the apartments of such courtiers as Keyserlingk who, perhaps, had been instrumental in obtaining the new honorary title. A plausible guess is that Bach brought with him his latest publication, Part II of Clavierübung, and played it in public or private, new works expressing up-to-date Dresden tastes for 'Italian vigour' and 'French suavity', though with a previously unknown attention to detail. The modest size of Part II compared to Parts I and III recalls that of another recent *Clavierübung*, Vincent Lübeck's of 1728 (containing a prelude, fugue, suite and chorale). And in its way it keeps up a Leipzig tradition established in Kuhnau's *Clavierübung* I and II (1689, 1692), where French courantes are joined by Italian jigs.

In Clavierübung II, the style-difference between French and Italian music that had inspired Bach for thirty years is now expressed with total clarity in the volume's two pieces, which take advantage of a growing interest in two-manual harpsichords amongst Dresden musicians. If the Italian Concerto was some years old before publication in 1735, perhaps it did not originally specify two manuals, any more than had the earlier transcriptions of Vivaldi's string concertos, where equally they are not absolutely necessary. Generally, keyboardists either distinguished between a concerto's solo and tutti sections by touch or they ignored them, perhaps 'imagining' them as Vivaldi himself had to do on the small instruments he knew. By 1735 Bach was surely responding to developments in two-manual harpsichords, just as in the second work, the B minor Overture, he seems at last to be imitating the French emphasis on the tenor part of the compass. (Its Courante allows for the rich, more sustained tessitura of the French harpsichord as well as any music coming out of Paris.) This work also exists in C minor, almost certainly an earlier version, more idiomatic and natural under the fingers (so many a player might feel) and resulting – to offer a personal view – in the greatest of all keyboard suites. This and the other C minor Partita (No. 2 of Clavierübung I, presumably composed earlier) are conspicuously different in intention. Curiously, the later one is more conventionally French than any of the partitas (despite the sad absence of an Allemande), and most like the orchestral Overture in C, BWV 1066. It has the rich melos, tessitura and sensuality of Couperin, now fully absorbed, and the old prosaic Reinken school of keyboard-writing is thrown off for ever.

In a comparable way, the Italian Concerto is a concentrated, clear-cut example of an idealized Italian concerto of three standard movements, with a slow harmonic rhythm that is itself Italianate, and since both works are as if solo versions of orchestral music, neither is quite like other Bach music though just as useful as a model for students. As well as in its overall form, the Concerto is full of reminiscences of the details he had learnt from transcribing Italian works twenty years before: beginning with a full chord, giving the soloist busy figuration of certain kinds, jumping from one tessitura to another, then a semi-ostinato slow movement, with a cello-like bass, followed by the breathless finale, etc. Both Prince Johann Ernst's concertos and various remnants of students' work in concertos that have survived imply that young composers did work on such concerto idioms (see below, pp. 341f), but as for the French *ouverture* conception, it is quite likely that in the new age of music societies and orchestral symphonies this was dying a natural death.

Neither work in Clavierübung II represents the most up-to-date styles in either Italy or France, for both are instead resisting the lighter styles of contemporary music in those countries, assuming it was familiar in Leipzig. In addition, the volume also provides two characteristic examples of J. S. Bach's increasing 'thoroughness', one slight, one profound. Thus the engraving of 1735, in at least one issue, has *Il fine* at the end of the Italian Concerto and

21 Keynotes of Clavierübung I and II

Fin at the end of the French Overture, just as the titlepage refers to *Gusto* (Italian, qv) and *Art* (French): little pedantries to raise a smile, perhaps, as when a quarter of a century earlier Bach had added 'tournez' for some page-turns in his copy of Grigny's *Livre d'orgue*. More significantly, Clavierübung II's pieces, in F major and B minor, are tonally as far apart as possible, major-to-minor at the distance of a tritone – hardly an accident, as the B minor suite was probably transposed down for this publication. Moreover, F major is a continuation of the key-sequence of the six partitas:

B-flat – c – a – D – G – e – F

although, strictly, F minor would be more logical. Either way, B minor (*H moll*), the eighth key, contributes the alphabet-letter completing the German names (A B C D E F G H). Note, however, that the tonal plan is not merely a paper-scheme: Clavierübung I's keynotes make a curiously melodious line, completed by the very next chord Bach published but then totally opposed by the next (B minor). See Example 21.

If Example 21 says something about a composer's manner of thinking, so does another detail. The suite halfway through Clavierübung II opens with the dotted rhythms of a French ouverture, but so do the pieces halfway through the other Clavierübung volumes. Moreover, the respective keys of these overtures produce a pair of relatives and a pair of dominants:

relatives: Clavierübung I and II (D major and B minor)
              Clavierübung III and IV (E minor and G major)
dominants: I and IV (D to G major)
              II and III (B to E minor)

A central overture is like the 'inner exordium' of a sermon, the moment when the preacher 'starts again' for rhetorical effect. But why the four keys were organized, if they were, as relatives and dominants is a mystery, especially since there is then a disturbing implication: that the Goldberg Variations (Clavierübung IV) are in G major because the middle chorale of Clavierübung III had been in its relative minor. Is it really possible that the paradigmatic bass theme for the Goldberg was chosen because its traditional key was the one needed for this overarching plan? Either that, or there is a strange set of coincidences here.

It could have been soon after the royal appointment that work went ahead on systematically planning Clavierübung III (up to 1739) and on beginning to assemble pieces for a second book of Twenty-four Preludes and Fugues in all the keys (up to 1742). This collection, now always called the 'Well-tempered Clavier Book 2' though without the composer's certain authority, is an encyclopedia or compendium not only of prelude-types and fugue-types, a few originating back in the later Weimar years, but of newer ways to write for harpsichord, applying old and new styles towards a repertory that is elevated, instructive, and appealing to connoisseurs. If the fair number of preludes in binary form was prompted by other music of the time, such as the sonatas Emanuel was composing, they could be seen as models being offered to those with ears to hear. The binary preludes in F minor, G sharp minor and B minor offer some of the most modern idioms of the book, but these are so far from the simple, rattling, repetitious keyboard music found increasingly across Europe in the 1730s and 40s as to suggest deliberate avoidance of them.

The 'Well-tempered Clavier Book 2' is a harpsichordist's *vade mecum*, surveying styles from strict counterpoint in the *stile antico* to the various *galanteries à la Dresde* that had made a strong impression on the composer. One senses in it a definite relationship to the Well-tempered Clavier Book 1, in that it is consciously 'bigger' in several ways: fuller binary preludes, an even wider array of styles old and new, generally harder to play, 'heavier' in its effect (several fugues) or simply longer than corresponding pairs in WTC1. The range is unmatched. On one hand, the E major Fugue could well be Bach's strictest-ever fugue, almost every note in it derived from the subject or countersubject; on the other, the F minor Prelude goes in an opposite direction, with modern sighing motifs, a modern key, modern time-signature, binary form, simple phraseology, and a distinctive, as one might say deliberate, prettiness. The C major Prelude's many apparently authentic versions look as if it were a 'matrix' serving Bach and his pupils over many years, the 'germ' of a standard prelude-type that could take different forms according to the player's ability or imagination. In comparison, the Preludes in B major and B flat major are striking in a quite different way: they are ideal for the fortepiano, with just the right textures and snatches of singing melody to suit the new instrument. Amongst the many felicitous moments is the F sharp major Fugue's subject beginning (exceptionally on the leading note) with the ornament that had just closed the prelude.

On the tuning for WTC1 and WTC2, and whether they are 'cycles' to be conceived as such, see below pp. 335f.

OTHER MUSICAL DEVELOPMENTS

Soon after the Dresden visit in September 1731, an older cantata, No. 70 was revived in Leipzig, hard to distinguish from the earnestness typical of the first cantata-cycle. But the following week a newly composed cantata was sung, BWV 140, with an opening chorus much easier to grasp despite its majestic detail, and a chorale-aria with one of Bach's best-known tunes ('Wachet auf'). This aria is useful in suggesting a composer re-thinking convention, for while in theory the setting is old-fashioned (a newly composed melody runs against an old hymn-tune, sung line by line), in fact the melody goes its own way, throws up a surprising number of dissonances, and becomes as independent of the hymn-tune as it was possible to be. In this respect the result is not at all like traditional counterpoint, which is created by lines highly dependent on each other while pretending not to be. Also significant are the cantata's two duet-arias, in developing the traditional dialogue of Jesus (bass) and the Soul (treble) much farther than Cantata 145, for example, developed its duet, and indeed in the barely veiled erotic language of opera. Like the Song of Solomon to which much of the text (of unknown authorship) relates, Cantata 140 seems to be challenging the believer to hear the spiritual in the amatory, as if the Higher Purposes of existence subsume the Lower.

More concretely, this and other cantatas known from the 1730s give an appearance of drawing on a vast knowledge and experience: newly conceived choral variations (Cantata 80), *galant* wind-instrument solos (Cantata 100) often with catchy syncopations, a huge fund of melody both traditional and new (2/4 metre in Cantata 97), more of the stylish appoggiaturas than formerly (Cantata 177), and so on, with touches here and there of other kinds of music such as Hasse's operas or (in Cantata 14.iv) Couperin's dances. In two otherwise unknown arias in the Christmas Oratorio, No. 31 'Schließe, mein Herze' and 51 'Ach, wenn wird die Zeit erscheinen', which were new compositions either for this work (No. 31 replacing one already begun) or for a lost cantata (text-corrections in No. 51), it is possible to hear in the solo violin melodies a new tenderness, the first in responding to Mary's 'keeping all the sayings in her heart', the second in preparing the advent of the 'Ruler of Israel'. The two arias are unusually alike, and their tenderness is new even for the composer of the chorale-cantatas: the original aria planned for No. 31 had a bright, neutral flute solo.

If after 1735 no new complete Sunday cantatas are known for sure, remnants suggest that further work on them did not cease, and two wedding cantatas, 197 and 195, are witness to continued composition and/or arrangement of music being made for particular purposes or occasions. Another work probably of the 1730s and known in a version with solo flute, the Flute Overture in B minor, BWV 1067, is shot through with freshly re-thought conventions: richly worked counterpoints in what were custom-arily quite simple dances, many traditional ideas newly presented (after the fugue, a return to the spirit but not the theme of the prelude), a *galant* quasi-melancholy in the rondeau's and minuet's melody, a dazzling but del-icately worked badinerie (this to compete with Telemann?), and through-out the work a series of unusual harmonic details (e.g. *cambiate*, qv). As with the two works in Clavierübung II, one can relate the work known as the B minor Flute Overture to conventional genres while recognizing in its beauty an original and distinctive aura. That all three of these works remained isolated is a reflection of the period's tastes: Bach was bringing care and originality to genres now becoming superseded.

The influences of Dresden can be supposed in the sound-world of the Christmas Oratorio, very striking when heard in relation to either of the Passions. The difference is not simply a matter of chronology and subject-matter but of the newer tastes transforming parish-church music, especially when as here the music originates for occasions outside church. In compar-ing the opening moments of either Passion with the Christmas Oratorio's, one hears the clearest differences of which music's rhetoric is capable within one and the same genre: differences of mode (minor, major), pulse (heavy, light), rhythm, tempo, scoring and not least word-setting; compare the 'wail' opening St Matthew Passion and the 'drumbeat' opening Christmas Oratorio. These details, with the Oratorio's more immediate melodiousness (cast in regular phrases and easily grasped), add up to differences soon felt. If today the Passions are nevertheless more popular than the Christmas Oratorio, I can only think that listeners now are, for whatever reason, likely to be more affected – or more lastingly affected – by the moving and touch-ing than by the exciting and exhilarating. What was the case in the 1730s when the Incarnation and Nativity had resonances now largely unknown, however, is another question.

G. C. Schemelli's song-book, the *Gesang-Buch* of 1736 to which Bach made a few new contributions and 'improved' others (Dok II, 266), also has a modern flavour in its devotional songs – straightforward, a total con-trast to the decade's complex choral and keyboard music. The Schemelli hymn 'Vergiss mein nicht' (see Example 22) recalls the easy melody found in the Anna Magdalena Bach Books and shows the composer more than capable of miniatures when appropriate or when requested, in this case for

22 Song, BWV 505

'Do not forget me, my dearest God. Ah, hear my beseeching, ah, let Grace come upon me whenever I am anxious and in distress. You, my assurance, do not forget me'

a local publication. The easy imitation (bb. 1–2), the marking of certain words (*Noth, Flehen, Gnade*), the final hemiola, the easy melody and modulations: these would also be characteristic not only of Telemann's songs but on a grander scale many a cantata aria of Bach, and in Example 22 they leave a touching impression. Particularly in view of Leipzig's position as a publishing centre, it is unlikely that the thought never occurred to Bach, his wife or pupils, to gather such songs together for domestic buyers, as distinct from professional organists. Seeing that Clavierübung III was Bach's next publication, quite likely being prepared over the period of the Schemelli Songbook, a conclusion seems to be that his thoughts were moving in other directions, though he may well have used such easy songs in teaching harmony and figured-bass playing (see p. 350).

23 Cantata 30.v
'Come, you afflicted sinners, hurry, run, you
children of Adam, your Saviour calls you'

Full of modern touches, but now on a big scale, is a homage cantata of the time, No. 30a (1737), one version of a work taking various forms, a *dramma per musica* with *personae dramatis*, several catchy tunes in 2/4, a startlingly suave flute aria (all in triplets?), and pretty dance-arias. An aria such as Example 23, complete with pizzicato strings and unison flute and violin, could serve many an opera text quite as well as it already served two cantatas, in the *dramma* version ('What can delight the soul') and the church-cantata version ('Come, you afflicted sinners', for John the Baptist's day). While one can conjecture how it might suit the latter text – sinners are tempted by the pretty tune to hurry to their Saviour? – so one can with many an aria that steps over the theatre-church divide. The words and manner of the aria 'So hat Gott die Welt geliebt' ('God so loved the world') in Cantata 173 are such that had its earlier version in a Birthday Serenata for Prince Leopold not survived, one would have hesitated to treat it *al tempo di minuetto*, as the original marking directs. In general, the step from any of this vocal music to opera buffa is not huge, giving admirers now, and perhaps the composer himself, many deep regrets that this was never to be.

The demise of the Leipzig opera house and its company before Bach ever came to live in the city meant that there was little to tempt him in this direction, and it is not known (as it would be?) whether he ever attempted to revive it, though visiting Italian troupes in the 1740s could have given him ideas not very removed from the Peasant Cantata. Even in the Goldberg Variations, published 1741, there is one striking detail amongst its many complexities that is as direct or 'popular' as anything in the latest opera, Singspiel or theatre song: its simple phrase-structure. The Aria and all thirty variations (with a few exceptional moments in certain canons) are made up of two-bar phrases, over and over again, cleverly integrated and moulded into an integrated whole. At times, starting with Variation 1, there is even a modern but perilous tendency towards one-bar phrases. Considering that the thirty-two movements are in two exact halves of sixteen bars each (not so common in binary movements), the two-bar phraseology would seem to be courting disaster, a symmetry too far.

One is barely any more aware of the 'one-bar peril' than of the large-scale and carefully calculated structure that in fact governs this work, for the solving of self-given problems at any level seems effortless. The Goldberg contains thirty-two movements, each of thirty-two (or sixteen) bars, taking thirty-two pages in the original print, but its movements are organized not in sets of two as might be expected but three, and include in each three a canon at ever-widening intervals. Except that the canon always comes third, the makeup of the threes is at first not quite consistent, suggesting, as does an extant putative draft for Variation 5, that this particular element in the organization only gradually evolved. Even counting the canons, the variations could be understood as thirty different but equally stylized dances, original even when archetypal, and only now and then resembling previously familiar dances, as in the *allabreve* variations. This prevailing newness of aspect is mysterious and can be explained only in part by such unusual details as that all movements begin without upbeat, except for the old tune used in Variation 30.

The Goldberg as a whole is inspired by an aria whose aim, as an affecting sarabande, is to create a new and extraordinary atmosphere that becomes clearest when compared with other (partial) workings of its traditional bass-line, such as Handel's G major Chaconne, HWV 435. In the Goldberg's Variation 25, which modern sensibilities would probably regard as the most expressive movement, this atmosphere is so strong as to disguise the artistry of what is usually the simplest element of Italian slow movements: the left-hand accompaniment. Here, in Variation 25, the accompaniment is created with extraordinary care, contributing its own subtleties of imitation, phrasing, harmony and one of music history's most beautiful paraphrases of the chromatic fourth. As for strategic shapes: neither in the Goldberg Variations nor in other works of conspicuous symmetry, such as the opening chorus of

Part VI of the Christmas Oratorio, does the structural planning interfere with the music's expressive qualities. The Goldberg's various thirty-twos do not lessen the unusually touching quality of the aria and the gentler variations; nothing in the Oratorio's joyful chorus is hindered by a symmetry of two distinct halves, and by four-bar phrases as dominant as the Goldberg's two-bar.

OTHER ACTIVITIES

A spate of gifted pupils around 1740 – including J. G. Goldberg, C. F. Abel (who later came to London) and the writers Kirnberger, Agricola and Kittel – would have encouraged Bach to work on two quite different modes of music during his later years: the *stile antico* of quasi-Renaissance counterpoint and the *style galant* of simple melody and harmony, both of which were also cultivated by the modern Dresdners. The very contrast between the two kinds, roughly demarcating sacred and secular repertories, was characteristic of Dresden's musical life, which was broader and livelier than Leipzig's. Its court composers are likely to have been visited by even more foreign musicians than J. S. Bach was in Leipzig, and their music for the Latin mass on a Sunday morning was very different from the opera's the night before. Whether it was a visitor to Dresden or Leipzig through whom three Goldberg movements reached London in time for Hawkins's *History*, later travellers from England such as Charles Burney in the 1770s or Edward Holmes in the 1820s found Dresden of far wider significance.

The interest shown by Bach in so many kinds and styles of music may never be fully documented or itemized, but it lasted his whole life and took these various practical forms:

owning collections (e.g. excerpts from Palestrina masses already at Weimar)

copying foreign music and its characteristic notation (e.g. Grigny)

reworking whole movements (Corelli) or their themes (e.g. Raison, Legrenzi)

transcribing whole works (e.g. Vivaldi, Prince Johann Ernst, Marcello)

adapting others (new Christe added to F. Durante's Kyrie, late 1720s?; movement from Caldara's Magnificat in C, *c.* 1740 with two extra voice parts; bass and instrumental additions to Palestrina's Missa Ecce sacerdos magnus à 4, *c.* 1745; a Sanctus by J. C. Kerll, *c.* 1747; Pergolesi Stabat mater rewritten with new text and added viola part, *c.* 1747)

copying (Telemann Advent cantata, 1734); overseeing and/or participating in copies of choral works by e.g. Palestrina (Missa sine nomine à 6, 1742), Handel (from a score of the Brockes Passion), G. B. Bassani (six masses, *c.* 1735), Johann Christoph Bach †1703 and Johann Ludwig Bach.

Only some of these belong to the 1730s, but those years were not exceptional in a lifetime of owning, copying, re-working, adapting or transcribing a range of works by other composers. It seems that when busy with other kinds of music in the later years, he was still making use of sacred choral works from a variety of sources. The late version of Kerll's Sanctus, complete with a newly added instruments, becomes a discrete work, BWV 241, in which Kerll's plain lines are decorated to produce a much livelier setting though, significantly, without the harmony being much changed – and without Kerll being named.

Present lists of works known to Bach are provisional, but even amongst those now certain there are cases in which Bach seems to have made additions or improvements, as to Telemann's cantata 'Der Herr ist König' (before 1725). But not always: of nine Latin mass movements he copied, by a variety of mostly minor composers, more than half were unaltered (BJ 1991, 158). In some instances a puzzle is why he took the trouble at all to make a copy, and one has to assume for the purposes of making a library. Lotti's Missa, copied between 1732 and 1735, never rises above the very ordinary, leading one to suppose some other reason for copying it, perhaps connected with the owner of the original, Zelenka, and its home in Dresden where Lotti had held a position some years earlier. From the similar dates for Palestrina's Missa sine nomine (Kyrie and Gloria with two continuo parts at different pitch) and the anonymous Kyrie and Gloria BWV Anh. 25, one could suppose copies were made with an eye to Dresden, although these and other Latin works (Sanctus settings by Kerll and others, BWV 239 and Anh. 28, the Caldara re-working BWV 1082), were not without uses in Leipzig. Nor were earlier copies such as Durante's Missa, although most of these works had a range of purposes: for performance (actual in Leipzig, hoped-for in Dresden?), for making a personal or choir library, for teaching or study (if seldom for emulation), or from mere curiosity.

That a personal connection was behind the conversion in *c.* 1739 of an earlier lute suite by the Dresden virtuoso Sylvius Weiss into a sonata *à 3* for harpsichord and violin, is likely, for in the summer of 1739 Weiss and other Dresden musicians made a visit to Leipzig, which led to some 'especially fine' music-making, according to one eye-witness (Dok II, 366). Around Weiss's simple suite Bach makes new counterpoints for harpsichord and violin, aiming to give the original a sense of drive and coherence. Since this re-composition was probably made from lute tablature and therefore created on paper, it would resemble the Vivaldi transcriptions Bach had made from instrumental parts a quarter of a century earlier. Improvising a new melodic line to another composer's trio is also what Emanuel said his father was used to doing if – so he says – the composer did not take it amiss (Dok III, 285). One striking gap in Bach's copying activities is keyboard music: over the half century or so following the 'Moonlight' episode, did he really make virtually no copies for himself of organ or harpsichord music by other German composers? If so, because of a low opinion of it?

Since Bach also acted as agent for his own and some other composer's publications, according to titlepage advertisements and similar evidence, one supposes a little stock of such items as the following for sale in the cantor's office, especially during the Easter and Michaelmas Fairs, and increasingly so during the 1730s and 1740s.

Clavierübung, four volumes
eventually the Schübler Chorales, Musical Offering and Canonic Variations
Hurlebusch, *Compositioni*, 1735 (keyboard works)
Heinichen, *General-Bass*, 1728 (a figured-bass tutor)
Walther, *Lexicon*, 1732 (dictionary of names and terms)
J. L. Krebs, *Clavier-Ubung* III, 1741 (keyboard works)
W. F. Bach, *Sonate*, 1748 (for harpsichord – or fortepiano?)

Although further volumes for sale may yet be identified, the number of Bach's own compositions is small compared to the forty-two publications Telemann had for sale during his Hamburg years, as well as the other music for which he was an agent. Leipzig cantors too are likely to have acted as agents for colleagues elsewhere during the three annual fairs,[4] and when Bach bought some major theological works at auction in 1742 (Dok I, 199), it may have been on behalf of someone else. No doubt the musicians who made a point of visiting the cantor when in Leipzig, according to Emanuel (Dok III, 255), were also sometimes hawking their own compositions.

While having works for sale need not imply enthusiasm for them, nevertheless the amount of non-keyboard music by other composers that, according to documents Bach owned or had access to, is huge. His reference in Mühlhausen to building a library there (see p. 66) implies it was not automatic and deserved credit, as perhaps it did for an organist; for a cantor, however, expectations were higher. Much of this other music one would now regard as minor, though it had uses in the way that superior music by Handel or Rameau did not. He seems not to have worked on

---

[4] For example, while he was cantor from 1657 to 1676 Sebastian Knüpfer had available the MS parts for Schütz's unpublished Christmas Oratorio (Schering 1926, 436).

any of Handel's English theatre oratorios (unknown? no obvious use in Leipzig?), and when in 1746/47 he did acquire and arrange a significant modern piece, Pergolesi's Stabat mater (BWV 1083), it was presumably in some connection, actual or hoped-for, with Dresden. For such work, sons and students did the copying of parts for performance. As a teenager, Johann Christoph Friedrich was entrusted with copying the *cembalo* continuo part of one compilation of the 1740s (the Handel/Keiser Brockes Passion), and Altnickol worked on the Pergolesi copy as a student. In both cases, however, the bass figures were contributed by the master himself.

That in the 1730s Bach appears to have been neither a contributor to nor agent for the popular songbooks published in Leipzig, the *Sperontes Singende Muse* (four parts, 1736–45), is another puzzle, since he did contribute to Schemelli's songbook in the same year, 1736. (See above, pp. 233f. Like parts 2–4 of the *Singende Muse*, this was printed by Breitkopf.) Was he asked, did he decline, did he contribute anonymously? Perhaps the devotional songs in Schemelli were more appropriate for a cantor to be involved in than Sperontes' domestic songs? Or he had some personal obligation to Schemelli, whose son had until recently been in the Thomas School? Other composers he admired had compiled or contributed to books of devotional songs, such as Georg Böhm's *Geistreiche Lieder* of 1700. The gap in style and taste between the two books published in 1736 is not huge, although the marches and minuets amongst the 200 melodies in the *Singende Muse* seemed trivial for some sensibilities, no doubt, and the texts rarely elevated. Or Bach did not relish any connection with Sperontes himself, i.e. Johann Sigismund Scholze, who from time to time collaborated with young composers in staged operettas or *Singspiele*.

Some indication that Bach became selective or unenthusiastic is given by the Hurlebusch volume, a collection of outstandingly effete quality, for although he was advertised as agent in 1735 and 1736, someone else was by 1742 (BJ 1986, 71). There is no evidence that in 1729, when Vincent Lübeck of Hamburg sold his modest and equally jejune *Clavir-Übung* at the Leipzig Fair, Bach had anything to do with it, though it quite possibly encouraged him to complete his own Clavierübung I, then or soon after. Nor does he seem to have had anything to do with an important book of the time, Mattheson's *Vollkommene Capellmeister* or 'Complete Capellmeister', an unrivalled source of information published in Hamburg in 1739 but printed in Leipzig and referring several times to Bach. Mattheson's request in the *Capellmeister* for a practical demonstration-book on fugue, and his praise for Kuhnau's variations (pp. 441, 232), might – just – have encouraged Bach to work on the Art of Fugue and the Goldberg Variations respectively, although other music is a likelier inspiration. If for the Art of Fugue, d'Anglebert's organ-book of 1689 was still relevant (see below, p. 249), so for the Goldberg were the much earlier variations in G major on a similar but shorter bass-theme by the admired Johann Christoph Bach.

Just as striking as his non-involvement in the Sperontes song-book is that Bach did not serve as agent for G. F. Kauffmann's extensive collection of organ-chorales from 1733, *Harmonische Seelenlust*, at least not according to its titlepage. Engraved in Leipzig by J. G. Krügner (who also worked for Bach), published by its composer and sold in ten issues over the very years that Clavierübung II and III were appearing, the collection's ninety-eight settings are amongst the most competent organ music by any contemporary. To one copy of it Bach's pupil J. G. Müthel appears to have added a group of Orgelbüchlein chorales, as if he found them complementary. Kauffmann had been a rival candidate for the cantorate and was a colleague of Friedemann's former violin teacher Graun, so the composers' mutual acquaintance is not in doubt. His collection gave far more information than Bach's bare volumes did, laying out the chorales as actually sung in church, and adding both organ registrations and a useful preface. To publish organ music in Leipzig without involving Bach seems to imply something, but what? That Bach again declined? If so, it can hardly have been on grounds of quality, for Hurlebusch's efforts are much feebler. Perhaps the two composers' previous rivalry had resulted in estrangement; or Kauffmann's large instrument in Merseburg, which inspired the registrations he gave in the volume, occasioned envy; or poor sale for both Kauffmann's and Walther's chorale-publications during the 1730s (Dok II, 268) persuaded Bach not to get involved beyond recommending an engraver to the latter.

A more positive reason would be that Kauffmann's first issue in 1733 encouraged Bach to go his own way and think about publishing chorales of his own for the first time: the Orgelbüchlein, perhaps, or, as eventually happened, a new set of major organ-chorales, cleverer in all respects than Kauffmann's. Some of these, the chorales in Clavierübung III, seem to share enough minor detail with some of Kauffmann's settings – a motif or two, some canonic imitation, etc. – as to suggest that Bach was consciously or otherwise improving on Kauffmann, both in the quality of the counterpoint and in the carefully reasoned plan of its twenty-seven pieces.

In 1738 he may also have made his one known subscription to a publication of music, Telemann's second set of Paris Quartets, whose musical style – particularly a simple question-and-answer way of creating and sustaining melody – does not seem so very distant in general terms from certain moments in the Peasant Cantata. The Collegium concerts were also suitable for such music. However, whether indeed it was Sebastian or one of his two eldest sons who subscribed to Telemann's Paris Quartets is not certain. The subscription list says 'M[onsieur] Bach of Leipzig', which could have been Emanuel, soon to move to Berlin and thus arguably more in need of his godfather's flute-and-violin music than either Friedemann or their father.[5] If Sebastian was the subscriber, little if any sign of its direct influence on him springs immediately to the eye, certainly if one recalls Handel's patent purloining of tunes from Telemann's *Musique de Table* after he had subscribed to it in 1733.

In the realm of church music, sparsely documented but more actively sustained was the hiring-out of cantata parts, not least to organist-relations and pupils elsewhere. By 1726–7, Bach was already loaning out parts for the Sanctus later incorporated in the B minor Mass. A letter of 20 March 1729 shows that he could not or would not always oblige when a pupil requested some parts (in this case for an unnamed Passion), also that sometimes he had to pursue debts from hirers. As is clear from another letter, to his cousin Elias in 1748, he would expect payment even when letting a relation have a copy of a published work (Dok I, 118). There was little unusual in this: J. G. Walther would charge a friend for manuscript copies he made on request and even, in 1740, for a catalogue which listed the works he had available (Beckmann 1987, 224, 252). Alas, it is not known what Bach charged either for a requested copy made from his autographs or for loaning an original to be copied by the buyer, but gratis any copy or loan was not.

Records show that between 1732 and 1744, J. W. Koch, cantor in Ronneburg and possessor of an exceptional library, regularly borrowed Bach works – at least forty-three cantatas and four motets – presumably in parts, as well as music by other composers such as the former Weimar pupils J. C. Vogler and J. T. Krebs. How good such performances as Koch's were is impossible to know, but it seems that when cantatas were borrowed the pitch might have to be changed. Those without a marked seasonal relevance were particularly useful to Koch (BJ 2003, 110) and presumably to any ex-student buying music from Bach for his future job (see BJ 2005, 102). Conversely, these documented loans make it likely that throughout the Leipzig period, Bach himself also borrowed works to perform, hence perhaps some of the copies of other composers' works he made or had

---

[5] Other local subscribers to the Paris Quartets were Fasch (Zerbst), Kirchhoff (Halle), Pisendel (Dresden) and Ziegler (Halle, a Bach pupil, for whom see p. 97).

made. At least he had little need to hire instruments. But a few receipts suggest that especially in these later years the hiring out of harpsichords was quite regular (Dok I, pp. 204–6), and at one point in 1748 he had to send an impatient, even intemperate reminder to the borrower.[6] He surely sold and rented out far more than is now known, and all this would have meant some amount of book-keeping and other paperwork, organized by himself or a secretary.

While it is impossible to imagine Handel ever selling a piano, a receipt of May 1749 suggests that Bach did exactly that – his own or, more likely, one for which he acted as agent, dispatching it to a buyer in White Russia (Dok III, 633). This receipt, significantly made soon after the opening of the Easter Fair 1749, may represent the tip of an iceberg, being also a further piece of evidence for the composer's contact with aristocrats from Slav countries. How this contact would come about is unclear – perhaps through intermediaries in Dresden (where Protestant church music was relatively undistinguished) or through visitors to the Leipzig fairs, or personal contact in Carlsbad during the Cöthen years.[7] In 1749 he still had warm relations with Count von Questenberg, a lute-player (see BJ 1981, 26). Bach's business activities and, in particular, the very possibility that he was an agent for the sale of fortepianos jars against many a Romantic picture of him.

As to musical influences over the 1730s: one problem with pieces of music in the more modern styles and sometimes attributed to Bach, is that as with his earliest works, some are undistinguishably close to the work of contemporaries. A *galant* chamber work like the Violin/Flute Sonata in G minor, BWV 1020 could just possibly be a genuine Bach work written in the unpretentious style of young and fashionable composers, or, more likely, music by young and fashionable composers familiar with genuine Bach work and able to pick up some of its characteristics. The Flute Sonata in E flat is likely to be an imitation of Quantz's sonatas of a similar kind, specifically the set of *Sei sonate*, Dresden 1734, but its (young) composer could also have been familiar with Bach's Organ Sonata in E flat. The tune of the aria 'Zu Tanze, zu Sprunge' in Phoebus & Pan, BWV 201 could be either an adapted, even misremembered, version of an aria in Montéclair's

---

[6] See Dok III, 627 for a hopeful suggestion that Bach did not look the note over, only signed it. Its threat that unless the instrument is returned, 'we will never be friends' (*werden wir nie Freunde*), does not seem out of character.

[7] In this last instance, Count Jan Klemens von Branitzky in Bialystok. Other aristocrats were Hermann Carl von Keyserlingk, Russian ambassador in Dresden; Franz Anton von Sporck in Lissa, Bohemia; and Adam von Questenberg in Jaromerice, Moravia. The last two were frequent visitors to the Carlsbad spa, which implies that Bach created contacts in places he visited.

cantata *Tircis et Climène* (1728) – not otherwise known in connection with Bach – or the accidental result of deliberately aping the more simplistic idioms of the time. Something similar could be said about resemblances to any Telemann works one might recognize, in an occasional song or harpsichord piece (Gigue of the French Suite in E flat) or even a concerto (slow movement of the F minor Concerto for Harpsichord).

Writers now find reasons for preferring one of these possibilities to the other, for as is generally the case with J. S. Bach, style-dating is hazardous, and there are many surprises for the analyst. Any idea one had that some choral and keyboard music associated with his early years could not be his work because of their 'uncharacteristic' simplicity neglects the likelihood that he found imitating run-of-the-mill styles effortless and, at times, worth doing. Any idea one has that the bright appealing style of the Gloria from the Mass in G, BWV 236, reflects court music in Dresden in the late 1730s needs amending, since the movement is reworked from a cantata of 1725. But this, Cantata 79 for Reformation Day, was sung a few weeks after another important visit to Dresden and is credibly touched by the lighter spirit of the royal city. Only up to a point, perhaps: while Bach responded in many ways to his contemporaries' music, any indubitably authentic work of his that does adopt a modern *galant* style (slow movements of the Musical Offering Sonata and the D minor Triple Concerto) have a texture still relentless in its contrapuntally conceived harmony. These works are up-to-date but could not possibly belong to anyone else.

CHAPTER 7

Leipzig, the final years

Apart from events surrounding the composer's death, the Obituary's only report on the last decade is the account of his visit to Frederick the Great in 1747 and the music it led to, an account owing a great deal to what had already been in print about the event. Emanuel, perhaps not knowing, says nothing about the various visits to Dresden while Friedemann was there (1733–46) and through whom, probably, Forkel was later to say that Bach 'often went to Dresden to hear the opera' (1802, 48). If he did, and alluded now and then to its 'secular' styles in the royal homage cantatas or the Peasant Cantata (see p. 292), all the more striking is the very different music to which he gave such priority in his last decade: the fugues, canons, antique counterpoint, etc.

Although church work continued in the 1740s, there is little clear evidence of what happened each Sunday – what was sung and how enthusiastically the cantor performed his duties – or of relations between cantor and school and clergy. The Council still required special music on each August's election, but whether an older cantata such as No. 119 was often repeated or an earlier cantata re-worded and arranged (as BWV 69 in 1748), is not recorded. Similarly unknown, when Anna Magdalena was given power of attorney as early as May 1742 (Dok I, 179), is whether such a move was as a matter of course after twenty years of marriage with a man so much older than herself, or a response to some health problem of the time, or to a planned absence from home of either one or the other.

During the 1740s students were still being taught and testimonials written for them, some organs tested, visitors and fellow musicians received. But the biggest witness to professional activities in the last decade is the appearance of four major publications of music and the careful preparation of four other large and ambitious collections, left in MS but at least in part probably intended for publication. (These are discussed further below.)

One thing reasonably clear is that the 1740s saw a series of other composers' sacred works being adapted and presumably performed, or their performance planned, in Leipzig. These include much of Handel's Brockes Passion, possibly a revival of the anonymous St Luke Passion, the Passion concocted carefully from the Anonymous St Mark and the Handel settings, another by C. H. Graun, and yet another in this late period from works of Graun, Telemann, Kuhnau and Bach, probably arranged by Altnickol and probably for performance in 1750. These arrangements are known from copies or chance reference, though whether for church services or as concerts in the Grosse Concert series (see below, p. 276) is not documented: quite possibly the latter, as most are oratorios rather than Passions, much lighter in *Affekt* and effect, and so more appropriate to a concert-room. In Protestant countries, oratorios in which the verbatim Gospel was not the ruling narrative were made generally for concert-rooms or theatres, not church, or at least not its services.

If, as seems possible, cantatas and motets from a variety of sources were being introduced in the Thomaskirche services, then a greater range of music was being heard there than in St Paul's, London or St Mark's, Venice over the same period, the 1740s. How much this turning towards other composers reflects, on Bach's part, exhaustion, indifference, a failing drive, even a more positive wish to enlarge repertory, is not at all certain. He does seem to have kept up his paid duties at the university's church, supplying service music once a quarter; and he still called himself *director musices* of the city. But the picture given of the repertory in the Thomaskirche by the extant scores, parts and other documentation is so cloudy as to encourage speculation about his reasons, especially why he chose the particular works from elsewhere that he did choose (older or newer, they were easier to perform?) and what other priorities he had. If increasingly in the last decade or so he deliberately withdrew into writing complex counterpoint of various kinds, mostly non-liturgical, it may be hasty to assume the motive was anything other than musical curiosity, the happy accepting of a challenge. After all, he did not have to continue composing at all, and to 'deliberately withdraw' need not have anything begrudging or resentful or wilful about it. But of course it might.

Professional visits of various kinds also continued, often to important places with personal connections, such as Weissenfels in 1739 with Anna Magdalena, Berlin in August 1741 where Emanuel was court harpsichordist, and Dresden in November 1741 where Friedemann was organist and Count von Keyserlingk their host, receiving Sebastian and his secretary Johann Elias with 'undeserved graciousness' (Dok II, 399). Such trips must have meant correspondence before and after, considerable foreplanning, arranging for deputies and service-plans in the interim, lengthy and expensive travelling, in some cases preparing solo works for performance, and always the risk of ill health for himself or one of the family left at home. (While away in Berlin, Bach was informed by letter of Anna Magdalena being seriously unwell, surely giving him presentiments after the experience with Maria Barbara in 1720.)[1] Such trips facilitated and created contacts with potential patrons. Perhaps also in Berlin the Wedding Cantata BWV 210 for solo soprano was sung, an older work whose arias Anna Magalena may already have sung on the visit paid to Leipzig in January 1729 by the Duke of Weissenfels. And as was the case for anyone in his position, Bach continued to receive invitations to test new or rebuilt organs, and it is unikely that all of them are now known about.

Another reason for trips was to give support to his professional sons, as at Dresden in 1733 for Friedemann, Mühlhausen in 1735 and Sangerhausen in 1737 for Johann Gottfried Bernhard, and Berlin for the sake of both elder sons. At Mühlhausen on this occasion Bach also examined the organ on request and apparently without fee, a *quid pro quo* perhaps for his son's appointment. It may not be as discreditable as it seems that in 1737, after Bernhard had given in his notice, father and son claimed expenses for Bernhard's original audition in 1735 on the grounds that he needed to be spend some time there practising for it. (The claim was fruitless but sheds a little light on auditions.) Letters to Sangerhausen concerning Bernhard's application there not only draw on past contacts but twice ask about the salary, which rather suggests that money matters arose for perfectly sensible, professional reasons.

When Bernhard, then aged twenty-three, reneges on debts, his father will not pay unless he sees a signature of liability and wants to know whether Bernhard left any belongings behind when he fled (Dok I, 108–9). There is both solicitude for this son and care over accepting responsibility for him, and he appears to be distressed when Bernhard moves on without letting him know where. (In the genealogical Table, the note that Bernhard died in 1739 was added by Emanuel.) Caring support of a similar nature for Friedemann might have been behind the trips to Dresden in 1736, 1738 and 1741 (twice?). Of particular significance is that although the sumptuous new Frauenkirche had had local musicians as organist from its initial dedication in 1736 until February 1742, Friedemann then applied for the post,

---

[1] Dok II, 391. A month later she still had to decline an invitation from the chamberlain of Weissenfels. Perhaps she was having trouble with her final pregnancy, Regina Susanna, born five months later.

no doubt with support from his father, and in person (see Dok II, 400).[2] Not Friedemann but G. A. Homilius was appointed, however, and went on to be a leading figure in Dresden's Protestant church music.

If the Goldberg Variations appeared in print just before the Dresden visit of November 1741, as is now supposed, copies were doubtless in Bach's baggage. This was very shortly after Baron von Keyserlingk received his title of 'Imperial Count', when it would have been particularly appropriate for the honorary Court Composer from Leipzig to present him with a copy of his latest work. A question much discussed ever since is whether the Variations were actually composed for Keyserlingk so that his young harpsichordist J. G. Goldberg could play to him during sleepless nights, as Forkel later said. Although Friedemann was probably Forkel's source of information, there is no record of a commission or a special dedication copy, and during the work's gestation, Goldberg would have been only twelve or thirteen years old. Publication had its own *raison d'être*, of course, but the music was particularly appropriate to Friedemann, a brilliant player in a brilliant city, and at some point young Goldberg's teacher. While a specially dedicated copy for Count Keyserlingk could certainly have been made (comparable to a copy of the Musical Offering for the King of Prussia), also possible is that Friedemann's abilities inspired the Variations and that he later wove an anecdote around them. Before he left Dresden in 1746, he would have known whether they had indeed been put to that use by Goldberg.

THE ART OF FUGUE

It is just possible that the Art of Fugue, like the late set of revised organ chorales (the so-called 'Eighteen'), had a down-to-earth origin, and was begun as a further part of the published series of *Clavierübung*, 'Keyboard Practice'. Evidently, over the years from 1742 to 1746 or 1747 twelve fugues and three canons based on a single varied theme were being fair-copied (some from working copies made earlier), and revisions and additions were being made. Work towards publication began a year or two before the composer died (Dok III, 3) and a not very coherent version finally appeared posthumously, about a year later. This publication's editors seem to have drawn on some kind of portfolio that gave no clear indications of a final order or even what the intended contents were. At least two of the sons, Emanuel and Christoph Friedrich (still a teenager), were involved in compiling it.

---

[2] Also early in 1742, a structural fault had developed affecting the Silbermann organ of the Frauenkirche (Müller 1982, 268f). Perhaps either or both Bachs were consulted.

Whether the title 'The Art of Fugue' and the name for the separate movements 'Contrapunctus'[3] came from Bach himself is not entirely certain, although when reading proofs of the engraving-in-progress he evidently accepted both. The main title was added to the MS by Bach's pupil Altnickol in *c.* 1745 with, one would assume, the composer's authority – except that its fashionable word 'art' conforms to various writings of the younger generation, including the Obituary authors who seem fond of the word. These two verbal conceits (the volume-title and the movement-titles) contribute to a sense of mystique about the work, as the editors no doubt intended.

It is also possible that in the Art of Fugue Bach was responding to earlier and less systematic collections of fugues by other composers and so aiming at a bigger, better, more 'thorough' legacy. J.-H. d'Anglebert's *Pièces de clavecin* of 1689, whose ornament table was copied by Bach (see p. 132), closes with five fugues in D minor on a single but varied theme, plus another on three subjects: a modest but marked anticipation of Bach's scheme. A positive, musical inspiration for this scheme in the period around 1742 must also have been the current and recent work on WTC2, whose huge variety of style, theme-type and of course key could alone have led to the idea of a different kind of variety, i.e. one with a single master-theme and a single key, both to be explored to hugely different ends.

An indication of the interest shown in fugal composition at the time is that WTC2 itself could be in part a response to the *L'A B C Musical. Contenant des Preludes et des Fugues de tous les Tons* [i.e. 16] *Pour l'Orgue ou le Clavecin* (published in *c.* 1734) by Gottfried Kirchhoff, Friedemann's predecessor in Halle. This book circulated well enough to supply examples for the so-called Langloz Manuscript, a book of practical instruction said to originate within the circle of Bach students over these same years (see Renwick 2001). Its short, conventional fugues were of the *partimento* type (qv) and thus as much in proportion to the colossus WTC2 as d'Anglebert's fugues were to the Art of Fugue. If in the 1730s Bach did teach semi-improvised fugue and figured bass from *partimento* work, he was doing much as Handel did over the same period, presumably drawing on similar traditions (see Mann 1978).

Only in broad terms is the Art of Fugue's intended shape indicated in the extant MS portfolio (where variants of certain movements already appear)

---

[3] 'Contrapunctus', rather than the usual *Contrapunct* (German, as in Mattheson 1739, 246) or *contrapunctum* (Latin), appeared in Buxtehude's memorial publication of 1674, *Fried- und Freudenreiche Hinfarth.*

and the posthumous engraved edition. The plan is for the music to become more complicated as the volume proceeds, and then, before the finale, introducing some examples of strict counterpoint (in this case canons, comparable to the Four Duets of Clavierübung III). Emanuel spoke of there being twenty-four pieces in the edition, counting each inverted fugue and the final chorale, and surely for him an allusive number – sufficiently so for him even to extract that number of movements from a portfolio originally bigger? Sets of six, twelve, twenty-four and forty-eight pieces, even seventy-two in Gottlieb Muffat's *Versetl* of 1726, had long been familiar. Like the Canonic Variations for Organ, the Art of Fugue may have had no single form despite so many later surmises about an 'earlier version' (the MS) or 'later version' (the posthumous print), for there seems to be an element of work-in-progress about all the late works. What looks like some kind of portfolio for the Art of Fugue included at least one version of the regular fugues, plus arrangements (two fugues rewritten for two harpsichords), revisions (with change of notation), perhaps a completed final fugue, and yet other movements. 'Later' readings are not superior to 'earlier' and on the contrary, the MS's opening set of four fugues makes for a recognizable group, with a logic lost in the printed edition's different order.

Such a portfolio suggests a composer indefatigably gathering examples, counting off the ways to treat a theme, testing ways to harmonize it, exploring music's notes as a scientist might explore the elements. 'Scientific exploration' is a not inappropriate phrase for a collection of movements not only increasing in contrapuntal complexity as it proceeds but constantly reshaping its theme, i.e. 'exploring the notes'. The result is a new and unprecedented kind of variation-form, beyond the Goldberg, the Musical Offering and the Canonic Variations. Each of these four major works solves in its own way the chief problem of ordinary sets of variations as these were understood at the time, i.e. harmonically repetitious (see above, p. 55). One interesting detail is that a fugue with jerky rhythms, headed *in Stylo francese* in the posthumous edition, comes about halfway in the first MS compilation, as a Frenchified movement does in each of the Clavierübung volumes and even in WTC 2.[4] If there was any significance in this, the Art of Fugue's editors did not see it, for they placed the *francese* fugue sixth out of twenty.

Some uncommon harmonic movement can be felt in the two harpsichord duets of the Art of Fugue, which were first conceived as a pair of three-voice fugues, the first in 'correct' form (*forma recta*), the second completely

---

[4] Prelude in F sharp major, now in 3/4 time, not 4/4.

upside down (*forma inversa*). Neither of these original forms is playable by a single instrument. Not surprisingly, the lines move in ways they would not if they did not also have to work upside down, and the ear soon recognizes something rich and strange. This is so even in the fuller versions for two harpsichords where another voice is added to 'explain' or 'justify' the harmony by filling it out a little. The ingenuity required for mirror compositions when music's asymmetrical octave makes symmetry elusive results in an idiom that could easily teeter on the edge of unintelligibility, for neither the treble nor bass can quite go where it would be natural to go. Hence one might venture the word 'transcendental' for such counterpoint (see pp. 290f). There is yet a further pair of such fugues in the volume, quite different in character, with textures otherwise rare in Bach. And these four movements are matched by another foursome: a set of canons in two voices, at the octave (common), the twelfth (less so) and the tenth (unusual), plus one whose second voice inverts and doubles the note-lengths of the first. All this ingenuity has a musical purpose, for it results in a harmony recognizable as new and 'unworldly', a music challenging the logic of conventional harmonic movement as nothing else can. It also provides models for composing music of a then-popular kind created for purposes of private study rather than public concerts.

While one might react negatively to the relentlessness of such movements as the Canon at the Tenth (see p. 291), at other moments there is in the Art of Fugue much that is both exceptionally and effortlessly beautiful, direct, almost simple, with a harmony best realized (as is the Orgelbüchlein's) on the keyboard but one in principle indifferent to tone-colour. Despite their seriousness, the opening group of four fugues in the MS version remains some of the sweetest counterpoint ever created by any composer. Similarly, although it is true that Contrapunctus 4 introduces 'a highly innovative modification of the inverted theme' (Wolff 2000, 435), its bewitching effect arises from the sheer sensuality of certain harmony, particularly the flashing dominant minor ninths. Elsewhere, in the complex play of themes or canons, one has the impression that Bach is answering the initiated listener's question, 'How is he going to solve that problem?' At the same time, the harmony of the theme is so fundamental and reliable that there is no limit to the number of good countersubjects it can prompt. Many a teacher since 1751 has found that the best-ever fugue written by a particular student was one based on a theme from the Art of Fugue.

The reverence it inspired was deepened when its editors included an incomplete fugue, copied in late 1749 (?) but left unfinished in the copy the editors had to hand – because of the composer's 'last illness', according to the Obituary. Emanuel also spoke of an even more complex missing fugue, another one invertible note for note.[5] The print's editors said that to compensate for the incomplete fugue, they were adding a chorale 'dictated in his blindness to one of his friends', the so-called 'deathbed chorale' (see p. 267) which generated for the publication a highly desirable odour of sanctity. Another personal element appears in the incomplete fugue, where a theme based on the notes B A C H matches the appearance of the same notes towards the end of the Canonic Variations (composer's MS copy[6]). These two references to B A C H could well be near-contemporary, saying something about a composer in his sixties and not always in the best of health.

There still remains a big question about the final fugue: was it finished or not? The extant manuscript's last page was unusable because of badly-ruled stave-lines, like some late pages in the MS of the Mass in B minor, so any continuation needed other sheets. That the final combination of themes was likely to have been worked out on paper first need not mean the fugue was ever completed. Is it possible that, as with another incomplete late fugue (in C minor, for organ, BWV 562), no known completion means there never was one? Despite the awesomely clever way the final fugue's three themes are treated up to the break-off, in perfect triple counterpoint, their relentless exploitation could have been as tiring to the composer as it can be to a listener.

THE VISIT TO POTSDAM

In 1747 he made a journey to Berlin and on this occasion was favoured by having himself heard at Potsdam before His Majesty, the King of Prussia. His Majesty himself played over for him a subject for a fugue, which he at once performed on the piano [*auf dem Pianoforte*], to the particular delight of the sovereign. At this, his Majesty desired to hear a fugue in six real [*obligaten*] parts, which command Bach also fulfilled immediately, on a theme chosen by himself, to the wonder of the king and the musicians present. On his return to Leipzig, he set down on paper a three-part and a six-part ricercar, so-called, with some other artful pieces [*Kunststücken*] on the very theme given him by His Majesty; and dedicated it, engraved on copper, to the king. (*Obituary*)

[5] The posthumous edition and the Obituary seem confused about what is incomplete or missing, i.e. no clear indication of the composer's plan had been found in the portfolio of movements. Note that the extant autograph MS and the print do not break off at quite the same point.
[6] I.e. not the print which gives a different order, on whose authority is not known. The bar concerned is one of the last (and best) he wrote himself in this MS, P 271.

These sentences follow straight on the reference to the Dresden appointment as 'court composer' (see p. 217), referring consecutively to Cöthen, Weissenfels, Dresden, Berlin and thus consciously or otherwise putting Leipzig in the shade.

The Obituary's reference at the end is to all or most of the Musical Offering, whose origin and purpose (if not all details of publication history) are the best documented of all J. S. Bach's works, and its title the most fanciful he himself ever published. 'Some artful pieces' must refer to the full-length Sonata as well as the ten canons, for surely Emanuel knew all the separate fascicles of the complete work, including the Sonata's? Did his duties not include playing it with the king his employer, or did Frederick make no more use of this dedicated work than his late relative apparently did the Brandenburgs? Also significant in the report is the claim that on entering the room, Bach 'at once performed' his fugue: this would impress any reader who knew the theme and recognized the difficulty of creating anything from it extempore.

The visit to Potsdam on 7–8 May 1747 might have been facilitated by Count Keyserlingk, late of Dresden and recently appointed Russian ambassador to Berlin, who would have learnt from Emanuel of Bach's visit there six years earlier. The second visit is the composer's last public appearance to be recorded in the Obituary, and is full of implications, about both the event and the purpose in reporting it. An account in the Berlin Gazette is the one and only time Bach featured on the front page of a newspaper (see Dok II, opposite p. 401), but it was common for the visits to Frederick of men renowned in the arts and philosophy to be given good publicity, and Berlin newspapers were copied and distributed around Protestant Germany – Hamburg, Frankfurt, Magdeburg, Leipzig. (Four years after Bach, Voltaire famously visited and took up residence in Potsdam, having long corresponded with the king but eventually quarrelling.) The Berlin newspaper, fresh after the event, mentions no more than a *Fuga* to be composed and sent to the king, which, a reporter's inexpertise notwithstanding, is likely to have been Bach's original idea, born of his enthusiasm for a particularly stimulating theme. If all the other pieces were added only gradually, that enthusiasm was sustained and says much about the composer's pertinacity as well as wish to impress.

No account specifies where in the palace premises in Potsdam the meetings took place, for more important to the newspapers was the picture of Frederick, ravager of Silesia, Saxony and Bohemia but so accomplished an artist that he himself composed the theme for an event he was still recounting to the Austrian ambassador nearly thirty years later (Dok III, 276). The

Obituary claims a second theme to be Bach's, but there is no second theme in the print: perhaps Emanuel, present at one or both of the events, was referring to an improvised six-part fugue different from the eventual Ricercar à 6, or was relying on the newspaper report that the bigger fugue was played later, during the next evening (Dok II, 435). He was certainly not loath to imply that his father and the king collaborated closely. It was said later, apparently by Friedemann who claimed to have been there with his father, that in effect Bach had been invited by the king to Potsdam (Forkel 1802, 9), but the reports say only that the king invited him in on learning he was in the antechamber.

Nevertheless, for Obituary readers, the significance of it all was clear: Europe's most powerful living monarch invited Europe's greatest living composer. Some idea of the composer's sense of a conferred honour, as well as of his energy, is given by the fact that the Offering was conceived, composed, gradually assembled, introduced by a careful preface, engraved, dispatched (piecemeal?) to the king and advertised to be on sale in Leipzig by the time of the Michaelmas Fair, 1747, less than five months later, despite each of these steps involving considerable trouble.

Together, the newspaper and Obituary also relay a crucial detail not found in Bach's own dedication to the Musical Offering: that the king played over his theme on his (new) pianoforte. In the dedication Bach spoke only of 'Clavier', but for the newspaper so up-to-date an instrument as the *Forte und Piano* was newsworthy, a valuable sign that the king himself was up-to-date and go-ahead. His interest in improving the flute was also no secret, and six years later, the Berlin newspaper reported another example of his interest in special musical presentations: Emanuel Bach, as Frederick's keyboardist, demonstrated to the royal family and court a newly invented or re-invented keyboard instrument, a type of Geigenwerk (BJ 1999, 171), qv.

The whole occasion in 1747, though royal and therefore grander than most, must speak for many similar events across pre-Revolutionary Europe. Here, the newspaper was establishing two patriotic things: how enlightened and accomplished a liege-lord his subjects had, and how uncommonly gifted was this particular German subject. A famous capellmeister – this is the newspapers' phrase, 'cantor' being inappropriate here – visits the most famous Protestant court, is invited to play at two of the regular evening chamber concerts in the king's salon, sits down at the keyboard and improvises at length, to the conventional astonishment of those present. Then on his return home, in further obeisance to royalty, in the hope perhaps of preferment (a title, a pension, a sinecure?) and even as a sign of his admiration for the king's theme, the composer works further on it, saluting his patron's connoisseurship by including pieces in a loyal *Offering* that were either very complex or very fashionable. The pieces make up a miscellany in varying format: two big but quite different fugues, a sonata in four movements, and ten variegated canons notated in abbreviated form. There is no indication that the whole is a single 'work' to be played in (any) order, and its publication in fascicles is also reflected in the incomplete state in which almost all copies have survived. An appearance in print, by now much less exceptional than it would have been at the time of the Brandenburg Concertos, would not absolve the donor from presenting a special and in some way unique copy to the royal patron.

The report in the newspapers was more detailed than was usual in such accounts (see BJ 2001, 95–6), making one wonder whether Bach himself instigated it and even whether he was as renowned as it implies. Another distinct possibility is that the correspondent was Gottfried Silbermann, organ-builder and maker of Frederick's fortepianos, one of which was made for the king a year before. If Silbermann was the first to use the term 'Piano et Forte' in Germany, as seems to be the case, the report from Potsdam was a fine advertisement for him.[7] And if it is true, as J. F. Agricola reported decades after his student-days in Leipzig in 1738–41, that Bach had at first – in the 1730s? – found the treble tone of Silbermann's earlier instruments too weak but then after improvement gave them his complete approval (Dok III, p. 194), perhaps this very approval was one he publicly expressed at Potsdam in May 1747. Had the king played over his theme on the piano, and Bach took it up at the same pitch, then one understands why the Ricercar à 3 begins in the upper soprano range of g′-c‴, which is uniquely high for a three-part fugue of Bach. This very part of the fortepiano compass would be what Silbermann was by now mastering, giving it that silky, pearly tone one hears also in Viennese pianos of Mozart's time and used by him for seductive melodies in his piano concertos. For the same reason the G major Fugue of WTC2 suits fortepiano, was even inspired by it perhaps, the whole producing a soft celesta-like effect through the as yet imperfect dampers.

Despite the softness of early pianos, which are always more *piano* than *forte*, dynamic contrasts were possible within certain margins, whether sudden (*forte* or *piano*) or gradual (*crescendo* or *diminuendo*). So in the

---

[7] The term is found inside Frederick's piano still at Sanssouci, Potsdam (dated 11 June 1746), in another now in Nuremberg (1749), and again in a cantata-text composed for the inauguration of a fortepiano at Marienberg, near Chemnitz, in 1744 (Ahrens 2003, 308).

Ricercar à 3, as in the more modern preludes and fugues in WTC2, there are many places at which louds and softs are feasible, so much so as to leave little doubt that the composer did give the option for *crescendi* and *diminuendi*. Furthermore, in addition to its 'pianisms', the Musical Offering is made as appropriate to the royal setting as possible with its solos for flute: just as the canons flattered Frederick's scientific musicianship, and the four-movement Sonata his up-to-date Italianate tastes, so using the flute in the difficult key of C minor was both a challenge and a recognition of the king's ability as a flute-player. Particularly since his flautist and teacher Quantz had worked with him on various improvements to the flute's construction, as Silbermann had on the piano's, it seems that the Musical Offering was as much prompted by recent technology as by Potsdam's group of gifted performers.

The 'king's theme', quite apart from its fashionably sinuous effect when played by fortepiano, violin, flute or cello, had another important attraction for the composer: he could work from it both the tight, consort-like counterpoint of the Ricercar à 6 and the flashier, looser Ricercar à 3. *Ricercar*, then an obsolete term and meaning 'to search diligently' (Walther, *Lexicon*), is less matter-of-fact than *fugue* and not otherwise used by Bach, though long known by him. It is doubly allusive: to musical tradition and to classical learning, both surely flattering the king. A pair of movements in different styles recalls the various dualities in Clavierübung II and III, and the only doubt is whether Frederick himself composed – surely not improvised – so outstanding a theme. Perhaps he played a simpler form of it, and Bach extended the chromatics and added a syncopation? Or Frederick prepared it beforehand with the help of Quantz, who sometimes composed in a superficially similar vein? How trustworthy was the king's later remark (see above) is unclear, seeing that he also spoke of fugues in four, five and eight parts, none of which is known about (Dok III, 276). The titles in the print are not unambiguous: *thema regium* (for the canons) and *soggetto reale* (for the Sonata) mean 'royal theme' or 'king's theme' – i.e., as much for as by the king. Though incorporating several common-property formulas, without being paraphrased it can not be treated in canon, which one would expect of an original Bach theme, given his interests at that period.[8]

---

[8] The canons are made less from the theme than from the new counter-melodies, although the Ricercar à 3 does create something of a thematic canon *in diminutione*.

The theme's common-property formulas are: a tonic triad plus diminished seventh, then a descending chromatic fourth, a Neapolitan sixth, and an emphatic perfect cadence.

The chromatics contribute another of those unique auras to a unique Bach genre, leaving a haunting sense of melody and harmony very different from anything in the Art of Fugue, and strangely matched by the tone of the flute and violin. Any similarities between the Sonata and *à la mode* chamber works by Zelenka in Dresden or Quantz in Potsdam only expose its imaginative turns of phrase and the carefully reasoned canons, both untypical of courtly styles. Just as revealing in their way are three hand-written Latin inscriptions in the king's copy, either made or commissioned by the composer: an acrostic on 'ricercar' (also in the public print) and laudatory tags to two canons, all signs of some intimacy with Latin. How obsequious these are is now unfathomable, but they show two things about J. S. Bach: that he liked making appropriate verbal allusion (the Sonata uses simple Italian, the canons and ricercars an epigrammatic Latin), and was willing to use music to convey a message. Thus, as one canon modulates up a whole tone on each statement, passing through an octave up from C, 'so may the king's glory rise'. A modulating canon is so unusual as to suggest that the composer planned it not only as a tour de force (like the circle of modulations in John Bull's Fantasia *Ut re mi fa sol la*) but as an allegory, one shared only with the king. Perhaps Frederick knew that six keys rising by an exact tone each time results in a pitch slightly sharper than a pure octave (see Glossary, 'ditonic comma') – but this, ironically, would only strengthen the allegory.

Unlike the newspaper, the Obituary says nothing about the following day, a Monday, when Bach played the organ in the Heiligegeistkirche, Potsdam, built for the new church in *c.* 1730 by Joachim Wagner. Such a pair of performances, at court and church, closely matches Bach's appearances at Dresden, and no doubt he played other organs in Berlin/Potsdam, including the Garrison Church. (Here, some moving statuary in the organ-case represented the Prussian eagle rising towards the sun – a plastic equivalent to the musical portrait of 'so may the king's glory rise' in Bach's canon.) What the large number of listeners heard in such recitals is not known, but a description in 1741 of Bach's playing gives a broad picture: he first begins with 'something on paper', and this something (by another composer?) is 'simpler' than his own ideas; then, from this, his 'power of imagination' is set in motion (*Einbildungskraft*: Dok II, 397), and he proceeds to improvise.

On which visit to Berlin it was that Emanuel accompanied his father to see the new opera-house on Unter den Linden is not recorded, but it led Emanuel to make a later remark on his practical understanding of acoustics: see below, p. 307. In January 1748, only a few months after the 1747 visit,

Bach appealed to the king for privileges for the organ-builder H. A. Cuncius, son of the builder whose organ in Halle he had examined over thirty years earlier (BJ 1977, 137). It seems that after his widely reported visit to Berlin, Bach's name was one to have in support, though in this instance whether he actually knew Cuncius's work for himself is uncertain.

'THE B MINOR MASS'

As described in the previous chapter, the Kyrie and Gloria for the Elector of Saxony had been presented in 1733, a few years before J. A. Scheibe published his criticisms of Bach's style of composition (on this see below, pp. 310f). But although it was only in the 1740s that other movements were added to make the complete 'Mass in B minor', as the work has been called since the early nineteenth century, it is not easy to find in it much sign that the composer came to simplify his style to appease critics.

On the contrary, given the variety of its styles, the completed work has the appearance of seamlessness, literally integrated in so far as a movement from the 1733 work ('Gratias agimus') was re-used for the finale of 1749 ('Dona nobis pacem'). Since the disagreement between Scheibe and Bach was still alive in the 1740s, the work could be viewed as setting out to uphold the standards of 'serious and profound music', in the Obituary's phrase, selecting and re-using earlier works about which there is nothing facilely modern or superficially *galant*. Critics could still have found the lovely, wandering solo Benedictus more obscure than a Handel aria of the same period. In this respect, the Italian flavour to 'Et in unum Dominum' is interesting: somewhat like Handel or Zelenka in its melody, thinner scoring, unison oboes/violins in G major, and the moments of simple imitation, is it a 'conciliatory' gesture or merely another instance of the compendious survey that is the B minor Mass?

The Mass's first two sections of 1733, a Lutheran *missa* of Kyrie and Gloria, were as apt for the court's and town's Protestant congregations in Dresden as for the city's Roman Catholic royal family, and, even without being separated by lengthy parts of the liturgy, would always have made a substantial musical item. The long masses by the court's composer Zelenka, taking in various musical styles distinct from the court's operas, gave the precedent for a full-scale setting of the Mass Ordinary, though not quite to the same extent: his *Missa gratias agimus tibi* of 1730 divides the Ordinary into seventeen movements, all relatively modest, while the *Missa circumcisionis* of 1724 has a dozen or so, less than half Bach's total of twenty-seven. This total, $3 \times 3 \times 3$, may have had specific associations in Saxony: there were not only twenty-seven sections in Zelenka's *Responsories* of 1732 but twenty-seven pieces in Bach's Clavierübung III (Luther's texts). The temptation is to see the latter as alluding to the twenty-seven books in Luther's translation of the New Testament, but that can hardly be so for Zelenka.

The grand Mass conception was achieved during Bach's final years when to the original twelve movements, he repeated one and added another fourteen, nearly half of them parodies or re-arrangements of earlier works. Four from the Gloria had already been re-used for the Christmas Day cantata BWV 191 (*c.* 1743/6) – suggesting that in the mid-1740s Bach had not decided to complete the Mass? – and its re-used movement 'Gratias agimus'/'Dona nobis pacem' was itself originally from Cantata 29, last revived in August 1749. Even when a movement appears specific to the work, such as the striking affirmation at the beginning of the Credo, it is allusive: the long-note Gregorian theme against running crotchets ('answered' before being complete) not only momentarily recalls the kind of species counterpoint (qv) in Fux's *Gradus ad parnassum* but also the early 1730s psalm-settings by Giovanni Battista Pergolesi – modern music which in turn influenced Dresden composers, including the relatively conservative Zelenka. The sheer variety of styles in the course of the Mass in B minor's movements is itself 'Pergolesian', and quite possibly a further stimulus for Bach was Zelenka's large-scale but non-completed plan for six masses for Dresden in the early 1740s, the *Missae ultimae*.

So grand and compendious a work as the Mass in B minor inevitably drew on a lifetime's knowledge. Particular details like the opening 'prelude' to the fugal Kyrie, and the apparent paraphrase of the Kyrie intonation from Luther's *Deutsche Messe*, could have been prompted by the opening Kyrie of a Mass in G minor by J. H. von Wilderer, a work copied by Bach and his assistant C. G. Meissner a few years earlier. Wilderer was court composer to the Elector Palatine, also Roman Catholic, and if the source for Bach's copy came from Dresden, it would seem likely that he consulted it (and others?) on conceiving a work of his own for the Dresden *cappella*, with a chromatic Kyrie theme very like one of Zelenka's. In its scoring, length, contrapuntal working, harmony and melody, Wilderer's and Zelenka's Kyries are of course simpler, but Bach, as earlier when he was conceiving music for royalty, appears to have taken trouble to become acquainted with local tastes.

The composition or arrangement of the remaining sections (Credo, Sanctus, Benedictus, Agnus Dei) over his last three years or so speak for the composer's tirelessness, whether or not he had any specific purpose in mind for the finished work. No such purpose emerges from documents, nor is any actual performance recorded during his lifetime, but the greater his disappointment with Leipzig, the likelier that with his mass he had an eye to Dresden, for the royal *cappella* perhaps, and in particular for its fine, new and very Italianate church then under construction, the Catholic Court Church. (This has the big Silbermann organ and choir-gallery at the west end, behind the congregation as then normal for the Roman Church's rite but unlike the Protestant Frauenkirche's.) If intended for the new Court Church, the completed 'Mass in B minor' – or 'great Catholic Mass', as Emanuel called it (Dok III, 495) – would surely have been unsolicited, for the king's capellmeister himself was responsible for dedicatory masses. But circumstances surrounding the completion of the church and the court's frequent absence from Dresden in its Polish domain leave many uncertainties about all these events, though nothing need have precluded Bach from soliciting a royal pension equal to Handel's in London.

Alas, neither of two musical masterpieces of late-baroque Saxony – Bach's Mass and Silbermann's organ (contracted for in the month Bach died) – was heard by its creator. There is an important parallel between them: just as Silbermann kept traditional organ-sounds but added a few stops required by the day's tastes, so Bach kept to traditional counterpoint ('Dona nobis pacem') but reflected more modern tastes with arias tuneful ('et in Spiritum sanctum') and *affektvoll* ('Benedictus'). Neither builder nor composer was able or willing quite to suspend his traditional working methods, follow mere fashion or discard the meticulous care he had always taken with his own way of doing things.

The pious duty to develop music beyond easy solutions is suggested by the Mass's many approaches to the business of composing and incorporating musical variety. A good example of *genre-adoption* is the 'Et resurrexit', which in its key, scoring, metre, initial upbeat, prevailing rhythms, reiterated quaver movement and overall *Affekt* has much in common with the 'Réjouissance' of the Overture or Suite in D major, BWV 1069. The rejoicing is palpable, and in being complete with orchestral episodes, the 'Et resurrexit' is a writ-large version of such movements found in suites by Telemann and others at the time. Good examples of *re-worked music* include the bars added before and after the 'Crucifixus' (whose original simple and repetitive bass is preserved) and the contrapuntal detail added to the Agnus dei. This is a movement already used twice in earlier cantatas but now contributing the Mass's most personal moment, its key the flattest in the work (lower than its earlier versions), its melody constantly flagging ('miserere'), its bass-line detached (with little silences), and an overall *Affekt* intensely supplicatory (note the final open bottom string on the unison violins). For the final chorus of the Mass, there may have been practical reasons for repeating an already re-used movement, but such parodies leave no sense of slack endeavour. Even to write out the score of the repeated movement ('Dona nobis pacem') more fully the second time, probably in the last year of his life, and despite handwriting much poorer than in 1733, implies that Bach devoted a deeply sustained energy to the whole enterprise.

Since music deals only in generalities of mood such as *lugubrious* or *exuberant*, praise or prayer, and since very different sets of words can share a topic, one can only conjecture sometimes why this or that previous music is re-used. Only in one case are adjacent movements ('Pleni sunt coeli' and 'Osanna', derived from the congratulatory Cantata 215) similar enough to be unsettling, since such similarity is unusual in a Bach work: do the many details in common imply some problem in their selection – the need for a quick decision? No obvious alternative? Either way, the same music can celebrate the blessings of the Kingdom of Saxony and serve as an Osanna in the king's chapel. The kind of ecstatic love-duet familiar in the king's operas or homage-cantatas can be elevated to express the partnership of God the Father and God the Son, doing so in the delicate, exquisite scoring and *affektvoll* beauty of 'Domine Deus' (two voices, muted strings, flute, pizzicato bass). While the very repetition of the word 'resurrexit' in the opening phrase of 'Et resurrexit' hints that this was not its first text, clearly this is the word worth repeating, its effect overwhelmingly appropriate after the 'Crucifixus'. Earlier parodies, such as the cantata movements re-used in the St Mark Passion of 1731, had evidently been much less systematic.

In the Mass's re-using and revising of so much older material the composer was carefully and systematically searching for a compendium of types and styles of music, ancient and modern, delicate and massive, from the 'Crucifixus' of 1714 or earlier to the 'Et incarnatus est' of 1749. And not only styles: the scoring too suggests careful calculation, as in giving a turn to each of the five soloists during the Gloria; or taking an instrument from each section of the orchestra for an obbligato solo. Clearly, the ageing Bach's memory was active, searching some thirty-five years of music to find a movement that would suit its new text as well as the Crucifixion does, now with a hushed end leading into the Resurrection. Some listeners are disappointed that the last movement repeats an earlier one with different words, yet for a believer, the three texts ('We thank Thee, O Lord' in the German cantata, the same in the Latin mass, and the final 'Grant us peace') are entirely compatible, even if Bach had originally intended a different finale – a possibility suggested by the paper being ruled, unusually, with more staves than became necessary.

Besides, the Mass-liturgy itself being so disparate and disjunct, to repeat a movement at the end of a musical setting does help to give a sense of organization. It is one of several symmetries operating in the work, including the rondeau-like appearances of D major choruses with trumpets and drums, or the overall planning whereby the middle aria of the complete work has the most original scoring ('Quoniam', rather polonaise-like and again reminiscent of Zelenka's music). Especially in the Sanctus and Osanna, but not only there, the D major choruses lead one to another reflection: that they are the work of a composer who had studied the Book of Revelation carefully (see Cox 1985, facsmiles 274, 275) and had his own visions of seraphim and cherubim. Overall, whether one understands the completed work as Bach's final offering to his Maker, or an unsolicited salute to his monarch on earth, it is not difficult to sense something exceptional from the first bar onwards, a something that is by no means dependent on the heavy, awe-filled performances customarily given it today. With its five- and eight-part choruses alone the listener immediately enters a sound-world entirely different from that of the Passions. To hear in it now the final, generous offering of a creative lifetime experienced in so many kinds of music is more than simple hindsight.

BLINDNESS

Having reported the Potsdam visit, the Obituary jumps three years to the final months:

His sight, rather poor by nature, and weakened even more by the unheard-of ardour in his studying, whereby especially in his youth he sat all night through, brought him, in his last years, in the way of an eye disease [*Augenkrankheit*]. Partly from the desire further to serve God and his neighbour with his remaining and still very lively powers of mind and body, partly on the recommendation of his friends, who put great store by an eye-surgeon recently arrived in Leipzig, he was willing to have this [disease] removed by an operation. But despite having to be done one more time, this turned out very badly. (*Obituary*)

In the drama of the subsequent account of blindness, medication, infection, decline, stroke and death, one could miss an important detail here: that the composer submitted to surgery in order to continue work 'for God and his neighbour', *Gott und seinem Nächsten*.

This is a formula going back to Luther's translation of Exodus 20 and Romans 13, and represents the binary focus of the Ten Commandments: behaviour to one's maker, behaviour to others. The phrase is already found not only in previous relevant publications (e.g. the titlepage of

J. P. Bendeler's book on organs, *Organopoeia, c.* 1690) but in the couplet on the Orgelbüchlein's titlepage, appropriate there both for an organist's hymn-book in church and for his duty to the community as a musician. And it appears elsewhere: in a testimonial of 1743, a student was praised for his endeavours to give service to 'God and the *res publica*' or community (Dok I, 146); about then, G. A. Sorge, in a dedication of some sonatas to Bach, praised him for 'love of his neighbour', adding that this was something 'commanded on high' but rarely found amongst conceited and self-loving virtuosi (Dok II, 413). These are remarks of eye-witnesses and are convincing. To some extent the pairing of 'God and one's neighbour' parallels 'connoisseur and amateur' found at the time, for both phrases have pious allusion and appear to express something deeper than the simple desire, stated by an earlier composer (Frescobaldi, in the preface to *Fiori musicali*), to use his talent 'to assist those studying to be musicians'.

When a work like the Goldberg Variations was prepared for 'the soul's delight of music-lovers', the term *Ergötzung* ('delight') says more than it seems to say, for it implies worthy pleasure, a spiritual re-creation, a preparation to continue God's work. The idea behind 'musical delight' of this sort was well-established in Saxony, and is found on such titlepages as Jacob Kremberg's set of songs published in Dresden in 1689, where already Italian and French styles (Kremberg says *Manier*) are also promised. Vocal, instrumental and keyboard music could all be included within this very Protestant notion, Pachelbel's acknowledgement of which has already been referred to (p. 141).

Thus it is that since cataracts normally give little actual pain or discomfort and are not life-threatening, it was felt necessary – by the Obituary writer or the composer? – to give reasons for trying to cure a condition probably brought on by untreated diabetes. (This diagnosis is conjectural.) Very likely there was also a popular belief, which modern ophthamology generally shares, that loss of vision in itself can shorten life and, conversely, that restored sight can prolong it. 'Rather poor by nature' might refer to a gradual deterioration of Bach's eyesight over the preceding decade or so due to age – discernible between the MSS of the Peasant Cantata, 1742, and the Canonic Variations, *c.* 1747 – but it is also something one can discern in the familiar Haussmann portrait. In fact, cataracts have little to do with either near-sightedness or working in poor light, though at the time, 'unheard-of ardour' for work must have seemed a likely cause. Bach wanted to be of further service as a composer, and eyesight problems were yet another vexation, another hindrance to that work. But the surgery was dangerous, as events proved, and in the end everyone, neighbour, widow, children, his Maker, was left deprived.

The modesty suggested by the Obituary's remark is of a piece not only with the brevity of Bach's entry in Walther's *Lexicon*, despite being advertised as an agent for it at one time (Dok II, 191), but with his total absence from J. H. Zedler's compendious *Universal-Lexicon*, begun in 1731. Both, as well-circulating books published in Leipzig, could have been expected to celebrate Bach, especially as they included some of his close relatives (in Zedler's, Johann Christoph of Eisenach and Johann Michael). The well-known family name of 'Bach' for musicians and the 'Bachische Collegium Musicum' in Leipzig are listed in Zedler's edition of 1739, but nothing more, and not until the 1751 edition is there a biography, drawing on Walther's of 1732. This last had probably been prepared from a CV written by the author some years earlier (BJ 1991, 188) and, in eschewing anecdotes, was shorter than later biographies that did include them. If, as is now thought likely, some of Walther's other entries benefited from information supplied by Bach, all the more striking is the brevity of his own entry.

It was probably just before the Easter Fair 1750, late March or early April, that Bach was operated on twice for cataract by the English eye-surgeon John Taylor, who travelled across Europe at the time, performing such operations as far afield as Rostock, and whose treatment eight years later of the blind Handel was also less than successful (HHB, 520). A second operation, either on the second eye or repeat surgery, was particularly liable to lead to infection, blood poisoning or even meningitis. But since post-cataract infection is usually immediate, and Bach did not die for another four months, infection may not have been the cause of death. The Obituary reported that he could not see again after the surgery, and remained 'almost always ill' (*fast immer kränklich*) for a full half year, but this is vague, unreliable hearsay of either physical or psychological distress. Also unreliable is the report that he could see quite well again ten days before he died and could tolerate light once more but then had a stroke (*Schlagfluss*), followed shortly after by acute fever (*hitziges Fieber*) from which he died. Depression can follow any surgery, especially if the cataract meant a loss of colour-vision which was not then recovered. On the other hand, if Bach did fight infections for four months, then one can easily believe that indeed he had 'lively powers of the body'.

Whether like Handel, Bach used amanuenses as distinct from copyists at any point during his last six months or so, is not known for certain, although the anecdote of a chorale 'dictated in his blindness' (see below) implies that over this period he did. In the month following surgery he took in his last residential student, J. G. Müthel, presumably hoping to remain active with his help, having still a strong constitution and perhaps some minimal sight. The last music he wrote down himself, in late 1749 or early 1750, seems to have been sections of the B minor Mass and revisions to the six sonatas for violin and harpsichord, plus (finally?) monitoring instrumental parts for J. C. Bach's motet 'Lieber Herr Gott, wecke uns auf'. This, effectively a funeral motet, might now seem particularly apt but only with hindsight: the two other very different works suggest that Bach's interest in amending or completing was still active over a range of music, and that he was neither 'giving up' nor anticipating total decline.

No doubt various pupils and children on occasion could have served in the last months as amanuenses, including Elisabeth, who married J. C. Altnickol on 20 January 1749. According to his last signed letter of 11 December 1749, Bach had also had one of his students, J. N. Bammler, direct the entire church music for him 'in his absence' (BJ 1997, 40), and it was Bammler who wrote the parts of J. C. Bach's putative funeral motet, under the cantor's direction (Wolff 2000, 452). By now, the phrase 'in his absence' is likelier to indicate indisposition than professional trips. For Bach to appoint a deputy was important in view of an event six months earlier when, on 8 June 1749, representatives of the town council auditioned Gottlob Harrer as future cantor, that is, a 'replacement, should the decease of Mr Bach come about at some point', in the words of the Minister President of Saxony (Dok II, 456).

Apparently Count Brühl, the Minister President, had visited Leipzig recently from Dresden and either learnt that Bach was already unwell or, simply in view of the cantor's age, was taking precautions to have his own capellmeister primed for a key position, one that was necessarily close to the interests of the Dresden court. How tactless, precipitous or merely sensible the town council's action was is not now clear, but it was certainly not against tradition, for Bach's predecessor Kuhnau had been treated similarly many years before (see Schering 1926, 194). Moreover, since only a day after his eventual death six applicants for the job were being discussed, they must have applied beforehand, in customary anticipation. That Harrer's original audition took place not in church but in the concert-room of the *Drei Schwanen*, 'Three Swans', could be seen as either underhand or discreet – or simply as deferring to Bach's authority over music in the town's churches, as per contract.[9] There is another possibility that ought not to be ruled out: that Bach was by now less than helpful to church, school and municipal authorities, hence perhaps a complaint received by the town council in late

---

[9] It was also in The Three Swans that a Thomaskirche student later reported hearing Friedemann play in the Grosse Concert series: Dok III, 148.

1749 that for a certain visiting musician 'no usable treble in the school' could be found (BJ 1984, 53).

Although the known order of events during the late period is sketchy, work apparently continued both on the Art of Fugue (its engraving then under way) and, just as intensively, on the B minor Mass (newer movements or arrangements being made). It is not difficult to imagine the motives prompting an ageing composer to enlarge the massive compilations of musical technique that these two unique works represent, one instrumental, the other choral, one containing new creations, the other radical revisions. However, such huge, time-consuming works, neither of which was part of a cantor's duties or entered the public domain in his lifetime, need not mean a turning-away from the Thomaskirche and its music, since Bach had long had his own reasons for making collections of music and was, it seems, not easily deterred. Also, there had been at least a few big performances in his penultimate year, judging by late signs of his handwriting in MSS: probably St John Passion on Good Friday 1749 and the Easter Oratorio two days later. One Thomaskirche student reports Emanuel performing his own Magnificat there before his father died, but it could have been shortly after rather than before (Dok III, 148).

DEATHBED AND DEATH

Despite all possible care by two of Leipzig's most skilled doctors, on July 28, 1750, after a quarter past eight in the evening, in the sixty-sixth year of his life, he passed away gently and peacefully, through the merit of his Redeemer. (*Obituary*)

Just as his own father had done three weeks before his death in 1695 (BJ 1995, 181), and at a much younger age, so Bach took communion at home on 22 July 1750, and on the day of his death presumably Anna Magdalena and the younger of his nine living children were present.

In writing that the surgery and subsequent treatment overthrew his whole system, Emanuel speaks as if an eye-witness to Bach's last six months. But there is no certain evidence for this, and the final period of discomfort was probably nearer three months. Signs of deterioration in the handwriting from Autumn 1748 on, and certainly by December 1749, have been interpreted as indicating eyesight and other problems due to advanced diabetes (BJ 1990, 53–64), chronic rather than acute, exacerbated by age, and no doubt eventually worsened by the surgery and the subsequent debility or actual infections, as a source earlier than the Obituary claims (Dok II, 470). There is room for doubt on each of these points, however.

The anecdote of the Deathbed Chorale – the blind composer dictating the chorale 'Wenn wir in höchsten Nöten sein' ('When we are in deepest distress') – is a puzzle, especially for the modern reader who wants neither to dismiss any such heart-warming anecdote nor to be misled by it if it is unreliable. The story was told in a note to the posthumous Art of Fugue engraving of *c.* 1751, a publication-project probably sustained and pressed for by the main legatees (Anna Magdalena, Friedemann, Emanuel, son-in-law Altnickol), one of whom (the first or last?) was the source for the deathbed story. But note: it does not say that the piece was dictated 'on his deathbed' but 'in his blindness', and this may have had no greater significance for either the editors or their readers than Handel's using an amanuensis when his sight failed. Virtually the same chorale was copied by someone (daughter Elisabeth?) into a late MS collection of long chorales and given there the title *Vor deinen Thron tret ich* ('Before your throne I stand'), which does indeed seem appropriate to a deathbed. But when and on whose authority it was copied, who gave it this title, who is responsible for its readings, and why this title does not appear in the Art of Fugue, is not known. It might be included in the handwritten chorale-collection with no more certain authority than, under its other title, it is in the engraved Art of Fugue.

There is another problem: since in part the chorale was more than thirty years old (it is a longer version of an Orgelbüchlein chorale), it can hardly have been dictated entirely from scratch. Nor is the counterpoint much more than humdrum. If on one hand the anecdote is true, the composer's priorities in his decline become clear, for the music is void of extravagant invention and individual hallmarks and in no way interferes with the text, which is a prayer. To be simple means to be heartfelt, and to derive the counterpoint from the hymn melody is to reiterate its words of prayer, not to display cleverness. On the other hand, if the anecdote is untrue, then there need be no certainty even that J. S. Bach composed the piece: any competent student familiar both with its earlier version in the Orgelbüchlein and with the smaller Confessional chorale published in Clavierübung III ('Out of the deep', BWV 687) could have cobbled it together. Hence the puzzle.

Death notices and other reports frequently gave the time of death, as here ('about eight o'clock': Dok II, 472–3). A London newspaper reported Handel's death as 'a little before eight o'clock' on Easter (Holy) Saturday 14 April 1759, but his doctor claimed that it was the night before, Good Friday (HHB, 529), a more significant day. Bach's death was also reported in a Berlin newspaper of 6 August 1750, which added that the loss of this uncommonly gifted man would be much regretted by all true connoisseurs of music. That may be so, but in Leipzig the poet Gottsched, voluble on other occasions and not anti-music, apparently wrote nothing, nor apparently did C. F. Gellert, another poet active in the city during the 1740s and whose *Geistliche Oden* (1757) Emanuel was to set to music. The university, used to publishing eulogies for its deceased distinguished professors, was equally silent. However, six months later in a Dresden news-journal (why not Leipzig?) Telemann published an appreciative sonnet, acknowledging the deceased's abilities as a virtuoso organist, the artistry (*Kunst*) of his compositions, and the training he gave to pupils and which they would then pass on. Apparently, to Telemann what makes Sebastian 'so especially worthy' is the work of his Berlin son, Emanuel, the author's godson (*insonderheit schätzbar*. Dok III, 7).

On 30 or 31 July, Bach was buried in an oak coffin in the Johanniskirche churchyard, located outside the city walls to its east, out through the Grimma Gate. In this church he had participated in examining the organ some six years earlier (see p. 307), and was to be buried outside to the south, apparently without a gravestone of the kind customary for Leipzig's merchant classes. No less than seven of his children had already been buried there, and his wife followed nine years later, all their graves without identifiable location, though Anna Magdalena may have been buried in her husband's. Emanuel does not mention the church by name, or show any sign of this being of interest to readers unfamiliar with Leipzig, but its churchyard was the only outside cemetery in the city until 1846. As already noted, Johann Christoph Bach's motet, 'Lieber Herr Gott, wecke uns auf', 'Lord God, awaken us', was appropriate for the burial both in its text and in the connections between the two composers. But from neither Obituary nor any other source is anything known for certain of a funeral or committal service or of what music was sung, though colleagues and the choir were present as the body was taken to the cemetery church, in a procession with sung chorales (Dok II, 474). By contrast, Handel some time before his death had requested permission to be buried in Westminster Abbey and left money for a monument, though he too desired his actual burial to be 'in a private manner' (HHB 4, 528).

Already by 1800, the Leipzig journal *Allgemeine Musikalische Zeitung* complained that the grave was not to be found (Dok III, 594). But a coffin of oak supposed to be Bach's was located and opened in 1894, placed inside the rebuilt Johanniskirche in 1900, moved to the Thomaskirche in 1949 and, in the course of further work to this church in 1962–64, re-interred in its present central position near the crossing. There can be no absolute certainty that the remains are his, for although the well-known bust made in the 1890s from a skull-impression accords with the authentic Haussmann portraits of 1746 and 1748, the latter were known to the sculptor and somewhat idealized in the bust he made. (Previously in the nineteenth century there had been a similarly imaginative reconstruction of Schiller's skull, disinterred in Weimar.)

Handel left £17,500 in annuities plus £48 in chattels (HHB, 533, 539), at a time when a new two-manual harpsichord cost about £70; Bach left some 1,122 thalers in chattels, books and instruments, including a two-manual harpsichord worth 80 (Dok II, 496). By the time of his death, Handel had also amassed over eighty paintings, including some 'very good ones' (HHB, 534). There is no comparison, therefore, between their financial positions, though in both cases the composers' manuscripts and musical scores were not counted in the estate but bequeathed separately and previously. This was done by Handel formally ('my Music Books' to J. C. Smith: HHB, 441), by Bach only reputedly (chiefly between the widow and two eldest sons). Smith was a careful curator, passing the autographs on to his son, who gave them to the King's Library which lodged them in the British Museum. Philipp Emanuel accumulated and preserved his father's MSS reasonably well but not Wilhelm Friedemann, whose materials are mostly lost or scattered, despite the reverence in which his father was held in the later eighteenth century. That reverence, expressed so often with respect to Bach's skill in writing counterpoint, seems to have been less warm for all the vocal works, chamber sonatas and instrumental concertos, which in common perception were superseded by the Italianate operas, symphonies, quartets and concertos of the next generation of composers.

CHAPTER 8

Observations, descriptions, criticisms

CIRCUMSTANCES AT THE THOMASKIRCHE

It is a pity that [especially in Leipzig?] he seldom had the luck to find only such performers of his work as would have spared him these irksome comments. (*Obituary*)

'These irksome comments' are the composer's, mentioned in the Obituary by Agricola when he claimed that Bach could discern the smallest error in an ensemble (see below, p. 297). He is contrasting his subject's abilities – unparalleled gifts of hearing, grasp of harmony and melody, seriousness of purpose, technical and creative mastery of keyboards and their music – with the mundane circumstances in which he found himself, and is probably speaking from his own observations made as a student from 1738 to 1741. Here, then, would be another hint that conditions at Leipzig had deteriorated. However, although the authors are unlikely to have known it, already at Weimar Bach's first set of cantatas on promotion in 1714 seems to make heavier musical demands than those that followed: there too he had not quite found what he wanted?

In recent times, one interpretation of a range of evidence has been that the Leipzig cantatas drew on twelve or at most sixteen singers (SATB) and some eighteen instrument-players, with a total number seldom if ever above forty performers even on special occasions, but generally a good deal fewer. Other arguments have been assembled for a choir of one to a part, making only eight singers for each Passion, most also having solos, and in numbers far surpassed by the instrumentalists. This idea usefully draws attention to the poor historical authority behind the massed choirs of more recent times and implies that after all, a chorus need not imply a crowd any more than the final *coro* in an Italian opera does. But the arguments, which are based on an essentially positivistic approach to the sources, do not always quite answer general questions such as, when is circumstantial evidence real evidence, and how is a negative proved? How can it even be

270

certain that the extant voice parts were used in actual performance – always, regularly, often, seldom? – and were not merely archive copies; that they were not shared; that there never were any others (discarded, lost); and that reinforcements were rare? Since there are a few duplicate parts for some early Leipzig cantatas (75, 76, 21, 24), does this suggest that choir-levels over twenty-seven years went down? Just as a string orchestra's music differs from a string quartet's, is there not generally a more 'choral feel' to the Leipzig cantatas than the Weimar? What was the situation before and after Bach? What are we to suppose when extant parts have uncorrected errors, especially in the case of the later cantatas or the St Matthew Passion version of 1736? That they were not the parts used?

Some picture of the Leipzig performances and the cantor's life in partic-ular is provided by two documents he wrote in 1730, a memorandum to the town council expressing grievances over present conditions (the oft-quoted *Entwurff* of 23 August), and a letter to his childhood friend Georg Erdmann in Danzig (28 October) expressing interest in a job elsewhere. The first is as much about the abilities of the present performers as about their number and does not support firm conclusions; but one interpretation of it is that there should be at least two and better three singers reinforcing chorus parts already being sung by whoever takes the arias and recitatives. Since choirs of various standards were needed for the four churches, some thirty-six singers *in toto* are required, plus eighteen or preferably twenty instrumen-talists, and on occasion twenty-four. (The reference in 1738 by ex-Rector Gesner to 'thirty or forty' performers supports these figures for special works, but its context is not specific: Dok II, 332.) There has been a serious shortfall, however: the choristers leave a lot to be desired, untalented boys are admitted to the school, and the cantor can find only seventeen usable singers and seven or eight instrumentalists, including an apprentice. Of the instrumentalists (eight of whom were on the town council's books), some are retired (*emeriti*) while others are not in practice (*in exercitio*) as they should be. Following custom, university students have been willing to help in the orchestra and choir but not if they are not paid, as is now the case.

Furthermore, because 'artistry has risen a great deal' since the time of Kuhnau (*die Kunst um sehr viel gestiegen*), musicians must now be appointed who are 'suitable for the current musical taste' (*den itzigen musicalischen gustum assequiren*: Dok I, 63) and able to do the composer's work to his satis-faction. Although this last point bears on the increased demands of both singers and instrumentalists in the full-scale cantatas and Passions, with their taxing counterpoint and arias for singers and virtuoso solos for instru-mentalists, it is also the case that Kuhnau had made a similar complaint twenty years before (Spitta II, 855). Bach's challenge is of the kind he had already given Mühlhausen over twenty years earlier: that church music is 'growing in almost all communities' and is 'often better than here' (Dok I, 19). The reference he makes in the Leipzig memorandum to the need for German musicians to be competent in the music of Italy, France, England and Poland is only marginally relevant to the Thomaskirche's repertory, though the point is valid, even if one has no idea what English or Polish music he had in mind, if any. He notes that musicians in Leipzig are not treated as well as those in Dresden, where under his Royal Majesty they are paid well, are free from *chagrin*, and need only master one instrument. The result there, he adds, 'must be something admirable and excellent to hear' (*muss was trefliches und excellentes zu hören seyn*).

In this reference to Dresden several things can be read, in particular a wish to goad the Leipzig Council, as Kuhnau in 1717 had also tried (Spitta II, 863). But there may also be a sign here of Bach's own growing interest in the capital city, and the remark about its 'admirable and excellent' music looks wistful and real, something a musician would genuinely envy and respect. For some years Bach had been getting to know the musical establishments in the capital, and even his critic Scheibe commented on the close contact he and other Leipzig musicians had with them by 1730 or so (Dok III, 241). Whether he had visited Dresden between the Marchand affair of 1717 and 1724 is not documented, but it is possible. So it is that at some point he had heard male sopranos there, and recognized the advantages given by their maturity; see p. 24 for a note on sopranos. Less speculative than this is that since in Leipzig the standard and number of the choristers were the responsibility of the cantor and would therefore reflect on him personally, as they would in an English cathedral today, Bach can have been complaining either because he was being thwarted or because he was diverting blame for the situation.

Whichever of these it was – that he was thwarted is the usual interpretation – some exasperation and, one suspects, exaggeration can be read into this document, the *Entwurff*, and it is noticeable that nothing is said there about the boys who lived not in the Thomas School but at home, some of whom would participate in at least the second and third choirs. Even the best singers are described merely as 'usable' (*brauchbar*). This is a businesslike word that need not be pejorative, it is true, but any boys able to deal with their parts in Bach cantatas were more than merely 'usable'. From the time of Arnstadt onwards, Bach is on record as finding performers he worked with *imperfectis* (Dok II, 17), and whether anything in particular at the Thomaskirche prompted his latest grievances is unclear. That he was receiving less paid help from students than before seems to have been only a recent difficulty, and in this respect things did get worse (BJ 1984, 48). Perhaps problems had been building up for some time, especially for the Good Friday and feast-day performances, such as the Passion and the Whitsun cantata in 1729, which could only have been done with extra instrumentalists.

A request for the Council Election cantata in August 1730, though not unexpected, could have been the last straw, for the very next day he wrote his complaining memorandum. How great an interest he had in the bur-gomasters' elections can only be guessed – when in August 1741 his secretary Johann Elias had to remind him of that year's Election cantata, he does so in such very deferential terms as to imply he knew the reminder would not be well received. Perhaps in June 1730 Bach had heard that when the new school-rector Gesner was elected, one of the councillors hoped 'it would go better than with the cantor' (Dok II, 203), which however probably meant only 'without having so many candidates decline, as in 1723'. Some quarter of a century later, another councillor was still referring to 'many disorders' in Bach's school-duties, giving some idea of the kind of criticism the composer met with when his own emphases as cantor were on the musical side of things (Dok III, 104).

For Bach to list his grievances to the town councillors was also to go on the offensive against earlier complaints about his teaching in the school (see below, pp. 320ff). He needed to make the point that the authorities were always stinting in their payment for instrumentalists, increasingly so, perhaps, with each new cantor. It is clear that what Bach had in view was better circumstances generally – including better appreciation? – for his music and its (and his) rôle. But circumstances in many other cities were hardly better and in many cases worse: had Bach gone to the Jacobikirche, Hamburg in 1720, he may have had no more than half a dozen adult singers and fifteen or so instrumentalists, plus trumpeters on occasion. His predecessor in Leipzig had also grumbled at the standards of performance he had been able to achieve, even in carefully prepared works, and it could be that the Thomaskirche had made special efforts over the auditions of 1722–3 in order to give a fine impression to competitors. Hence, perhaps, the demanding nature of Bach's first cantata-cycle, but the fine impression could not be sustained.

To what extent the renovations to the school building from May 1731 were one positive consequence of the grievances being aired the year before is not known, but at least relations with Rector Gesner appear to have been good. His praise of Bach as organist and ensemble-director, published in

Latin in 1738 after he had left Leipzig, is not only the most extravagant then in print but suggests the genuine admiration of someone witnessing his manner of performing both as player and conductor (see below, p. 298). Altogether, it is likely that Bach had simply overrated the potential of the Leipzig situation, that there he was not going to achieve a capellmeister's authority, and that, as his predecesssor had also implied, the city's instrumentalists and the church's choristers were never going to be able to give him what he wanted for his complex music. During the Scheibe controversy in 1739 (see pp. 310ff), it was again pointed out that he was not so lucky as to have virtuosos readily at hand (Dok II, 357).

THE LETTER TO GEORG ERDMANN, 28 OCTOBER 1730

This letter to a long-established friend then living in Danzig expresses more personal grievances: his income is not as high as he was led to believe, Leipzig is twice as expensive as elsewhere he has lived, the authorities are 'whimsical and little devoted to music' (*wunderliche und der Music wenig ergebene*), and altogether he is subjected to endless 'annoyance, envy and persecution' (*Verdruß, Neid und Verfolgung*: Dok I, 67). He had left Cöthen to become cantor there only, he implies, because the prince had become less enthusiastic about music after his marriage, and had submitted to audition in Leipzig when the cantorate was described favourably (*favorable* – did he feel it necessary to justify competing for a post?). Perhaps Erdmann would speak for him if there were a suitable position in Danzig?

This request is puzzling, for although Danzig had once had a fine musical institution at the Marienkirche, where there was a large organ, the Baltic cities seem by now to have been in musical decline, and Bach working in Danzig would be as Wagner working in Riga a century later, i.e. there because of no better offer. (Curiously, Bach alone amongst composers was praised in an article in a Danzig journal of September 1736: see BJ 1988, 182.) Perhaps Bach had learnt that the Marienkirche was likely to be appointing a new capellmeister, as indeed it was, and he had been accustomed to solicit in this way, thus giving in the surviving letter to Erdmann a glimpse of his normal practice when an important position was to be free. One need not construe this letter as a desire for a court position, to which Erdmann's high-level contacts in eastern Europe might have led, nor suppose a visit to Dresden in September the following year with the same purpose in mind. But both are possible.

The letter to Erdmann is one of the very few extant personal letters of Bach and is difficult to weigh precisely. That Leipzig was expensive is likely, particularly as it grew over the years 1700–50 from a population of 20,000 to 32,000. The 'annoyance' (*Verdruß*) he reports is also credible, something he often experienced in various connnections with church and school, or at least with their personnel. But envy and persecution? Neither is clear from given records and could indicate how Bach took resistance or discouragement from colleagues, employers and miscellaneous philistines. A feeling of envy would be aroused in colleagues if he flaunted the title of Weissenfels capellmeister, which he had been assuming since 1729. A feeling of persecution would be his own reaction when, two days after the memorandum of August 1730, the burgomaster reprimanded him for absence without leave and showing 'poor desire for work' (*schlechte lust zur arbeit*: Dok II, 206), by which was meant his school responsibilities. Just as hard to evaluate as the depth of the 'envy and persecution' are his seemingly tactless reference in the Erdmann letter to the falling number of funerals (and the fees they brought in) when the weather was good, and the description of his children as 'born musicians' (*gebohrne Musici*), able already to form a vocal and instrumental consort (*Concert*) in the family. Was the first often discussed between organists, or a sign of pettiness? Does the second show genuine fatherly pride or a desire to market the collateral assets of a job-seeker?

The appearance of gracelessness is unreliable in another personal letter, this time to a relative, concerning not music but a barrel of wine sent by his former secretary Johann Elias in late 1748. In disproportionate length, Bach takes the trouble to describe how it had been damaged, that he can not yet make an adequate return for it (a gift? a payment?), and that all the taxes and costs he has to pay on such imported liquor make it too expensive a gift (Dok I, 119). Perhaps the letter was an elaborate joke. This was to a cousin from whom he recently asked a thaler for a copy of the Musical Offering, or part of it, having just told him that he had given away gratis to good friends most of the hundred copies he had had engraved (Dok I, 117). One hopes the thaler was for postage and that 'good friends' meant potential patrons.

THE COLLEGIUM OBSOLESCENT?

Just as it ignores the production and performance of cantatas, the Obituary makes no mention of concert-life in Leipzig, with the Collegium musicum. Yet Agricola himself had participated in it (Dok III, 76), and the Obituary's list of unpublished Bach works includes 'Various concertos for one, two, three and four harpsichords' and 'a crowd of other instrumental pieces of all sorts and for all kinds of instruments', any of which might well have been performed there. Emanuel was surely familiar with the Collegium, even involved in it, when it purchased a new harpsichord in June 1733, at a time Friedemann was job-searching in Dresden and just before he, Emanuel, was doing likewise in Naumburg. If their father took little part in the concerts after about 1741 the Obituary's silence is understandable, though late copies of certain works (including the A major Harpsichord Concerto, BWV 1055 and the B minor Flute Overture, BWV 1067) suggest they did appear in concerts there or elsewhere after Zimmermann, in whose coffee-house the concerts had been held, died in May 1741. There is no reference to any of the Bachs having an interest in the occasional ballets and opera-productions put on each Spring in 1740s Leipzig, but since these very likely included modern items by composers such as Pergolesi, it is an interesting coincidence that Bach's reworking of his *Stabat mater* belongs to this period.

Probably, the Obituary's silence also reflects the fact that from 1743 a new, more professionally run concert-series in Leipzig had appeared, at least for an upper-class clientele: this is the so-called Grosse Concert, similar to patron-supported series elsewhere in Europe at the time. Sixteen persons paid a yearly sum of twenty thalers each to support sixteen performers, and a point was made of attracting only an elite audience. C. G. Gerlach, organist of the New Church who officially and finally took over the Collegium in 1746 until its demise a few years later, also became concertmaster of the Grosse Concert as it developed and reached its complement of some two dozen performers. Other Bach students were also involved in it, including in 1743 its director J. F. Doles, former university student and next-but-one cantor at the Thomaskirche. Whether the Grosse Concert's performers numbered more than the Collegium's is not documented but likely – hence the name? – and this would be reflected in the kinds of works performed, such as non-Gospel settings of the Passion story in Lent.

Bach is not documented as being a member of the Grosse Concert in any capacity, and neither was his opinion recorded of the new Italian symphonies creeping into programmes as the old concert society became eclipsed by the new. Typical of the awe surrounding him over the following centuries is Schering's suggestion that he was 'too high' in public estimation for the Grosse Concert, although if he personally did not fit in with the tastes of its 'dilettanti and young artists' (Schering 1941, 263), some of his various concertos might have done so. There is no record that he was involved in any of the Passion performances put on in the modest-sized room at the Three Swans, although in principle such works as Hasse's *I Pellegrini* (performed in March 1750, the month of the cataract surgery) had much in common with Handel's Lenten oratorios in London theatres. The labelling of the (or a) keyboard continuo part *cembalo* and not *organo* or *basso* for the Keiser/Handel Passion copied by J. C. F. Bach in the 1740s (see p. 246) makes a performance outside church plausible, but by then the officials and nobility with whom Bach had been associated in the 1720s were themselves being succeeded. For the newer Grosse Concert sponsors, his title *director chori musici lipsiensis* can not have meant much, and it rather looks as if he became (as we might now say) out of the loop.

Private or family music-making over both early and late periods also left no detailed picture, even when Forkel asked Emanuel later for information about his father's activities. Quite why Emanuel does not say more in reply to Forkel is puzzling. He was sixty years old himself by then, far from the world of 1720s Leipzig, without any urge to create a fuller biography. Yet from a few details he gives in passing, such as that his father's visitors from Dresden included the flute-vituoso P.-G. Buffardin (who reported teaching Emanuel's late uncle Jacob), or that he knew how to arrange a large orchestra in the open air and did so often (Dok III, 287–8), glimpses are given of a varied musical life beyond the confines of church and school. The Obituary's virtual silence on activities beyond what is implied by the work-list and general remarks means no clue is given as to how important to Bach was his concert life. But enough concertos and chamber sonatas exist, and in enough practical sources – though these less well organized or conserved than for church music – to suggest that concerts were for him far more than an occasional solace.

The different versions of these 'instrumental pieces of all sorts' indicate something of a fluid repertory, inexclusive, made for adaptation, versatile in purpose and potential. But their contrapuntal harmony, carefully conceived structures and individual melos, mean they remain an isolated group of works in the history of music. However highly regarded they are now and indispensable to the repertory, the various forms of neither the concertos nor the sonatas survive in sources suggesting that they were so regarded in the 1740s, or even the 1730s, outside a few circles of admirers.

ORGANS AND HARPSICHORDS

As he often maintained with regret, it never could come about that he had a really large and really fine organ available for his constant use. This still robs us of many fine and never-to-be-heard inventions [*Erfindungen*] in organ music [*Orgelspielen*], which he would otherwise have brought to paper and displayed, just as he had them in his head. (*Obituary*)

This could be another criticism of Leipzig, if Bach had been pressing for a new organ for St Thomas's. Agricola is more likely than Emanuel to have known if this was the case by 1740 or so, and shortly after the Obituary was published, radical work was undertaken on a new chair organ and new pedal. Slighter repairs, approved by the cantor and organist, were made in 1747 by the builder Johann Scheibe for two hundred thalers (Dok II, 439), a sum one hundredth the cost of the new Silbermann organ in Dresden. If Bach had been agitating in the 1740s for a new organ, it was in the knowledge that had he ever taken a job in Halle or Hamburg or Dresden, he would indeed have had a 'really large and fine organ' to work with.

But the Obituary's remark also bears on the state, size and tone of the organs at Bach's disposal when he was working on his more mature organ music, in the Weimar Chapel (two manuals, about twenty-four stops) as well as the Thomaskirche, Leipzig (three manuals, about thirty-five stops). Neither can have been a joy, and the latter especially may have little to do with the composing of important works. That both organs needed wide-ranging work on them while he was titular organist was nothing out of the ordinary, though his colleagues in Freiberg or Dresden had no such needs. The Thomaskirche organ's manuals and pedal combined the work of at least three distinct periods (1598, 1670, 1721) and was entirely discarded in the 1770s. The University Church, the Paulinerkirche, had a large three-manual organ of forty-eight stops by J. Scheibe (the organ tested by Bach in 1717), on which it is possible that Bach occasionally taught pupils, although there is no clear evidence of this. Whether with the phrase 'constant use' Agricola was obliquely referring to this organ, which is unlikely to have been at the cantor's daily disposal, is likewise unknown. One can read from Bach's examination report of 1717 either that the Paulinerorgel was a very good instrument or that it was not, and the latter is likelier, although the Leipzig organist Daniel Vetter had at the time reported Bach as 'unable to praise it enough'.[1]

Like most organists, Bach can be supposed to have had more interest in playing organs in the vicinity of towns in which he lived than ever got reported. At least half a dozen new organs in the surrounding villages of Leipzig were opened while he lived there, and there were quite as many older instruments still in action too, some played by organists claiming to have been a pupil. Two exceptionally fine instruments a few miles away at

---

[1] Dok I, 166–7. The recently built organ in St Thomas is based on this Scheibe organ.

Rötha would please any visitor (that in the Georgenkirche had been dedicated with music led by Kuhnau in 1721), and the impression given by descriptions of organs published by Mattheson (1721), Adlung (1768) and others is that organists had, as now, an enthusiastic curiosity to study stoplists. The charming little instrument of *c.* 1600 in nearby Pomssen, where some funeral music by Bach was performed in February 1727 (Cantata 157?), still has certain tonal qualities that were probably much like those of the second organ in the Thomaskirche, an older and smaller instrument. This was placed in a gallery hanging on the east wall of the nave, above or (more likely?) to the side of the tower arch, facing the performers in the west gallery across the length of the nave. It may have played in the St Matthew Passion to create a special stereophony for the chorale-melody in choruses opening and closing Part I, at least for the so-called 1736 version (see Dok II, 141), joined there in its gallery by some choristers. Worked on during Bach's earlier Leipzig years,[2] the little organ was taken down in 1740, probably because the gallery was unsafe, and with or without the cantor's approval. There is no evidence that J. S. Bach cared much about preserving old instruments, and if he was responsible for the upkeep of the little organ as he was for the big, its demolition does rather reflect on him.

In view of his declared dissatisfaction with instruments he worked with, and his reported praise for organs of the Hamburg type, one would expect Bach to have dropped any personal antagonism he had towards Gottfried Silbermann and pressed for a new organ of his for the Thomaskirche. At Zwickau in 1737, his pupil J.-L. Krebs had apparently done exactly that soon after taking up his appointment. It is true that Silbermann's tuning would not have suited all of Clavierübung III, nor was he fond of coarse sub-sub-octave bass pipes or bright mixture-stops of the older type, such as Bach asked for at Mühlhausen. On the other hand, any taste for classical French music would have been admirably served by a larger Silbermann organ. Twice in poems published on the inauguration of Silbermann organs, Bach was praised along with other composers, in 1730 at Reichenbach (along with the Weimar capellmeister Drese and the Thomaskirche organist Görner) and in 1736 at the Dresden Frauenkirche (with Handel, Telemann and various Dresden musicians: Ahrens 2003, 54, 119). It rather looks as if Bach and Silbermann, though apparently on good terms at the Naumburg organ-examination of 1746, would have had a personality-clash: Silbermann, prone

---

[2] The organ-builder Zacharias Hildebrandt, well known to Bach since the Störmthal organ inauguration if not before, had put eight stops of this little organ into playing order in 1727/28 (Dähnert 1962, 56). Was this for the Passion and Christmas/New Year performances?

to litigation, had a notion of what an organ was and did not care to change it significantly for anybody.

About other keyboard instrumemts and Bach's interest in them, the Obituary says nothing, for they and their music were much less in the public eye. Only from incidental references can one build a (faint) picture of his involvement with the day's stringed keyboards: the short four-octave harpsichord of his youth, the larger single-manual, the two-manual harpsichord increasingly popular from *c.* 1720, experimental harpsichords with sub-octave strings,[3] the clavichord, the double clavichord and/or harpsichord with independent pedals, the *Lautenwerk* (a small deep spinet, with two sets of gut strings to imitate a lute), the *Gambenwerk* (probably with a wheel 'bowing' the strings), and eventually the fortepiano. But he was a cantor with an uncommon interest in instruments, their technology and any new inventions, all of which formed a big enough part of his professional persona to be picked on (mocked at) by one of his critics: see below, p. 316.

On instrument vis-à-vis music, several points can be made. First, there are many early keyboard works such as the Sonata in D, BWV 963 and the Aria variata, BWV 989 that seem to allow options: if a pedal is available, of whatever type on whatever instrument, it can take certain bass notes; if not, the score can easily be adapted. Like organs, most Thuringian harpsichords of *c.* 1700 had a compass of only four octaves C–c''', so one is unable to distinguish between their music on grounds of compass, as some writers have tried to do. Both composers and builders looked increasingly beyond this narrow compass, however, probably the builders earlier or more adventurously than the composers who, especially if they were publishing, had no wish to deter buyers by demanding exceptional instruments. Secondly, one could view especially keyboard music during the composer's lifetime as gradually moving towards specific instrumentation, resulting in repertories that were less and less interchangeable. This is characteristic of the eighteenth century generally.

While versatility did not and could not entirely disappear, each repertory increasingly required its instrument to do things another could not. One sees this in Bach's four successive Clavierübung volumes: they first require one-manual harpsichord, then two-manual, then organ with two and (for the E flat Prelude) optionally three manuals. No music of Bach is authentically labelled 'for fortepiano', since such labelling would be more restrictive

---

[3] A guess that Hildebrandt's new harpsichord for the Collegium had sub-octave strings is unconvincing: its cost of 120 reichsthaler (Dähnert 1962, 231) was not much above average for a standard single-manual.

than was customary at the time; nor 'for one-manual organ', which would be unnecessary. The rubric *à 1 Clav.* in the Goldberg Variations is unique, and is there not only to distinguish between *à 2 Clav.* or the optional *à 1 or 2 Clav.* elsewhere in the Variations but in order for the print to be characteristically thorough: every movement was to have a rubric.

Thirdly, some keyboard instruments of the time must have been 'workhorses', substitutes for 'full-dress' instruments, with simple practical purposes. Hence the clavichord, which, despite enthusiastic claims now made for it, could be best likened to the upright piano in Victorian homes or today's school studios. (While clavichord or fortepiano or even organ serves several pieces in the WTC very well – certain preludes or fugues, but few if any pairs as such – only harpsichord seems to me to suit all 96.) When a Leipzig city clerk in November 1750, doing his best to take an inventory of the late capellmeister Bach's possessions, called one of the items '3. *Clavire* nebst *Pedal*' (an instrument that went to the youngest son, Johann Christian: Dok II, 504), he probably meant a double clavichord, i.e. two separate instruments, one placed above the other, plus or near to (*nebst*) a third bass clavichord for the pedals. This would have been rather different, one imagines, from the sweet-tongued, long-compass clavichords of the later eighteenth century that substituted for fortepianos in northerly regions of Europe and were admired by Emanuel Bach. When the instrument of *3 Clavire* went to Christian, was it because his father thought a fifteen-year-old should have a practice-instrument?

This informal legacy to his youngest son gives a glimpse of another, more domestic matter. Evidently the children from the first marriage (Friedemann, Emanuel and Catharina Dorothea) and the trustee of the youngest children objected to this gift said to have been witnessed by Anna Magdalena, her son-in-law Altnickol and a representative of her own daughter Elisabeth. Though apparently resolved, the situation does rather hint that all was not well between Anna Magdalena and her adult stepchildren. How Friedemann came to inherit – if he did – the two-manual Thuringian harpsichord of *c.* 1710, later called the 'Bach harpsichord' after deposit in the Royal Museum, Berlin in 1890, is not known, nor whether its association with his father can ever be established.

Fourthly, incidental references give important hints about the part played by various keyboard instruments. The possibility that both Cöthen and Weimar had an example of the rare *Geigenwerk* (qv) while Bach was there (see Dok III, 195) suggests that the duke and the prince bought unusual objects, whether as *objets d'art* or as *objets de musique*, as the fortepiano was to be for Frederick the Great. On the other hand, the new harpsichords for the Cöthen court and the Leipzig Collegium were likely to have been grand, fit to take regular and important roles. They were doubtless far grander than those kept in the galleries of the major Leipzig churches. These latter were maintained in good order and served many purposes but are no more likely to have been used in the service than a piano kept in an Anglican cathedral today plays in the anthems or psalms.

Another probability in this under-documented area of work is that Bach was involved in the buying of yet another kind of keyboard instrument at Weimar in 1715, the gut-strung *Lautenwerk* (qv) built by his cousin Johann Nicolaus Bach of Jena. There are reports that he also had one made in Cöthen and again in Leipzig, the last by Hildebrandt: this would means three such instruments in his three locations. Two *Lautenwerke* were listed amongst the deceased's possessions, plus a veneered harpsichord, three other harpsichords ('Clavesins'), a smaller one, eleven string instruments and a spinet (rectangular or bentside: Dok II, 492–3). Perhaps the little 'Clavesin' was a simple clavichord, while Johann Christian's '3 Clavire' had been the family's practice-instrument for organ-music. (Practising on the full-sized organ meant arranging for, and somehow paying, a bellows-blower.) Although the inventory might seem rich, it is noticeable that no house-organ is listed, nor fortepiano. The rest broadly reflects what was customary amongst German organists, who showed less interest in or knowledge of fine harpsichords than their English and French colleagues. As well as a house-organ, Handel in London possessed two fine seventeenth-century Flemish harpsichords, but no other keyboards are mentioned (HHB, 441).

Quite what the attraction of the *Lautenwerk* was other than its pretty sound and an ability to range from quite loud to very soft, is unclear. According to Agricola who saw such an instrument in 1740, i.e. the one specified by Bach and made by Hildebrandt, the sound was more like a theorbo's than a lute's (Dok III, 195), which would be expected from its bigger body and bass strings. Several thin-textured two-stave works from the late 1730s, such as the F minor Suite, BWV 823, the E flat Prelude from WTC2, and even the so-called lute works, look like music at least optionally for *Lautenwerk*. One such version of the E major Violin Partia made and copied by the composer in *c.* 1736, and keeping the *forte/piano* signs of the violin version, gives some idea of what the less common instruments played other than continuo accompaniments.

Also unrecorded is whether Bach showed any interest in some of the day's other developments, such as Silbermann's *cembalo d'amour* (1730) with its double-length strings; or the dulcimer stop imitating Hebenstreit's pantaleon, a large hammered dulcimer much admired when played by its inventor-virtuoso; or experimental composite instruments like the three-manual harpsichord-plus-piano advertised in a Leipzig newpaper in 1742–43 (BJ 1991, 170). Yet both Silbermann and Hebenstreit were in Bach's circle of acquaintance, and curiosity about their keyboard instruments is easy to suppose. Emanuel owned a Silbermann clavichord (see the Rondo Wq 66), and Friedemann's appointment at the Dresden Sophienkirche in 1733 was supported by Hebenstreit, who was responsible for the court's Protestant music. On the other hand, it is not at all unlikely that Friedemann and Emanuel became far more interested than their father in the piano, certainly before improvements to it in the 1740s. To imagine the concertos for one, two, three or four harpsichords as suiting fortepiano better than harpsichord would be to overestimate the piano's tone in the 1730s and underestimate the harpsichord's, especially when accompanied by only four or five string instruments.

Amongst the Dresden musicians with whom Bach 'and other friends of music in Leipzig' had connections was the lutenist Silvius Weiss, perhaps for whom and under whose advice the three-movement work in E flat for lute, BWV 998, was composed. Written out by the composer in the mid-1730s, this works towards an idiom appropriate to large baroque lute, with a fugue-subject that harks back to WTCI, and with textures undoubtedly much easier to play on the keyboard-lute. Various other pieces for lute are known from sources not reliable enough to indicate how well Bach himself played or how his pieces for the instrument came about, but along with recorded activities by students in his circle, they do suggest the lute was not an negligible item in domestic music-making in Leipzig. For example, J. C. Weyrauch, a Bach pupil who became notary public in the city, copied several of his teacher's works in lute tablature and seems also to have been known as a composer. About other string instruments the Obituary says nothing, but various documents testify to his warm relationship with J. C. Hoffmann, member of an old family of makers of viol, violin, viola and lute in Leipzig, and holder of a royal title (instrument maker to the Court of Saxony, conferred four years after Bach's court title). Apart from the Stainer violin in Bach's inventory, the other string instruments listed there, including violino piccolo, *bassettgen* (violoncello piccolo?), a gamba and a lute, are unattributed and may have included several Hoffmanns. In his will this maker left instruments to Bach, and they were both godparents to a son of the lute-playing lawyer Weyrauch. This too suggests a circle amongst Leipzigers who had an active interest in lutes.

The Obituary's remark about organs, whether or not point-scoring against Leipzig, is plausible enough. A fine instrument such as Emanuel and Agricola knew in Berlin, or Friedemann in Dresden and Halle, would have been likely to inspire or give the opportunity for major organ works that in the event never got written. How did the authors know he had them 'in his head'? They had heard him improvise striking gestures on Full Organ or guessed that that was how the big pieces began? – now with massive chords, now with a brilliant right-hand solo, one piece a measured jig, another a swaying polonaise. However they began, the shapes and workings-out they all restlessly explored certainly needed them to be 'brought to paper'.

'HIDDEN SECRETS OF HARMONY'

If ever any composer [*Componist*] demonstrated full-voiced harmony at its strongest, it was certainly our late Bach. If ever an artist in sound [*Tonkünstler*] put into the most artful practice the most hidden secrets of harmony, it was certainly our late Bach. No-one ever brought so many highly inventive and unfamiliar ideas to what seem otherwise dry works of artifice [*Kunststücken*] as he did. He had only to hear any main theme [*Hauptsatz*] to have in mind, as if instantaneously, almost everything artful that could be done with it. His melodies were truly singular [*sonderbar*], but always diverse, rich in invention, and like those of no other composer. (*Obituary*)

These were the opening sentences of Agricola's evaluatory part of the Obituary, and refer four times to *art*: artist, artful and artifice, key words of the period. 'Otherwise dry works of artifice' probably refers to fugues and canons, even including fugues of a kind the authors knew in the Well-tempered Clavier and Art of Fugue. By 1750, more easy-going fugues of Handel and even Scarlatti were circulating, giving other ideas on creating distinctive keyboard music. The aim of Agricola's remark seems to be to still any criticisms there may be of the late cantor's style of composition, which many would consider out of date or over-serious, as the Obituary's following sentence also implies (see next section). The phrase 'any main theme' could refer to several things: the subject of fugues, the simple chorale-melodies from which a cantata-movement is derived, or the ritornello themes of a long concerto-movement.

The Obituary's remarks signify an interesting and, for the period, an uncommon attempt to evaluate music itself. Indeed, the ideas cast in these few sentences are, as far as they go, systematically referring to three main strands that form the basis for a critical evaluation of any composer's oeuvre: texture, harmony and melody. From personal experience Agricola could well have been aware of the importance the deceased placed on a student learning full-voiced harmony; see below, p. 331, for remarks on the working of five parts. For the other basic elements in a composer's make-up – the sense of rhythm and movement – there are two further references in the Obituary, one to his tempi (it was 'very lively', *sehr lebhaft*), the other to his ability as a conductor (it was very 'precise', *accurat*). No particular music or repertory is specified, but the authors must have had in mind his big ensemble works for choir and instruments, such as they had witnessed while still students and assistants.

The three phrases Agricola employs could still be a starting-point for evaluating this music: the 'hidden secrets' of harmony, 'highly inventive' counterpoint and 'truly singular' melody. In being more than merely impressionistic-laudatory, they say much about the musical training its authors received from their teacher and the priorities in their studies. No admirer of Bach has difficulty in finding examples to show him revealing new possibilities in diatonic harmony, new and imaginative ways to create invertible counterpoint, and new and unusual qualities of tuneful melody. Nor is it possible to keep these three points separate. The paraphrase melody of the chorale 'Nun komm der heiden Heiland', BWV 659, though beautiful, also cleverly shares motifs with its own contrapuntal harmoniza-tion; the melody at the opening of Cantata 3 creates a partnership with rich harmony and a distinctive timbre unique to Bach cantatas; the dancing chorus opening Cantata 201 ('Quickly, quickly') avoids harmonic com-plexity, but so elegantly! Technically similar effects are often worked to different ends, as when in Cantatas 201 and 26 the choir sings some bare octaves without harmony, the first as the Four Winds are sent back to their cave in unison, the second to mark the very nothingness of life. Neither example has the gripping rhetoric of the octaves for 'I am God's Son' in St Matthew Passion.

This book refers to the composer's 'grasp of diatonic harmony', some-thing revealed in both simple and complex counterpoint. Even recitative, a negligible musical means in the hands of poorer composers, is also 'truly singular', a blending of harmony and melody that results in an extraordi-nary expressiveness in the Passions, Christmas Oratorio and elsewhere. A ruling factor in this must be a diatonic harmony that is logical but novel, that delights with new turns of phrase, and is instinct with melody whether towards a story of death or of birth. The arresting entry of the Evangelist in St Matthew Passion, where the words beginning Chapter 26 of the Gospel are in fact shortened and made more urgent, is an instance of sen-sitivity to tonal harmony. For after the opening monumental Tragedy Chorus in the minor, suddenly there are simple major harmonies and lyrical lines for the tenor soloist as narrator. One knows immediately that

(a)

(b)

24 Cantata 60.v
'It is enough; Lord, when it pleases you . . .'
'my great misery is left behind'

the tenor's opening words, 'When Jesus had finished these sayings', can not be referring to the preceding movement, the opening chorus, but are plunging into an unfolding story.

The attraction of Bach's imitative counterpoint for many in the following generations could overshadow his achievements in harmonic thinking: the surefootedness that allows the solo works for violin or cello to follow, often by hints alone, the logic of good harmony while surprising and even momentarily puzzling the listener. Works of clever counterpoint could allow one to miss how naturally contrapuntal are the textures in, say, the tuneful late Cantatas 195 and 209. Other examples of harmonic surefootedness are themes so complete in themselves that it comes as a shock to find that they are only accompaniments to another theme, as is the case in the Finale of the Musical Offering Sonata, or the Contrapunctus IX of the Art of Fugue. In simpler music, such as the four-part chorales (see below, pp. 349f), there is a total, one might say revolutionary, development in harmonic thinking beyond the basic triads of earlier German music. Thus the celebrated chorale closing Cantata 60 has accented passing-notes (alto b1, bass b3, Example 24 (a)) and consecutive sevenths (Example 24 (b)) owed to an imaginative reworking of standard diatonic harmony. The plain rhythm of the sevenths in Example 24 (b) is calculated to leave them undisguised, while the alto and tenor quavers (a unique form of decorated suspension) have, briefly, a sweet consonance marking the words as misery is left behind. One can never over-scrutinize such passages.

Fine examples of both harmonic appoggiature and sevenths will be found in some Italian music (e.g. Scarlatti's Sonata Kk 144), for neither is unique to Bach. But it is difficult to explain why the alto f♯ of Example 24(b) is both startling and perfectly consonant in its dissonance, or why thousands of other chords are beautiful and surprising. Higher flights of fancy in chromatic lines, both those that embellish simple progressions and those more substantive in moving the music in new directions, are developed with total control. The opening prelude of the WTC is a good example of a compelling harmonic progression, and one sees why this piece attracted so many later arrangers. From its known versions, it seems to be the result of second or third thoughts, first of twenty-four bars but then expanded to thirty-five, with further logical steps in the progressions (Example 29 (b)). Very beautiful preludes produced by some earlier composers (Frescobaldi, Louis Couperin, Froberger) proceed by unexpected changes of direction, but Bach preludes, as in those for the Cello Suites, have a strangely inexorable feel to their slowly shifting harmonies.

Agricola clearly recognized some special melodic qualities, since there would be no point in a melody being singular (*sonderbar*) if it was odd or unsettling or gauche. Its very singularity is responsible for the beauty, which so naturally inclines towards the sad that the lively or noisy or exciting melody that opens many works is a relief, whether a concerto Allegro (Third Brandenburg) or a cantata chorus ('Zerreisset, zersprenget', BWV 205). In the St Matthew Passion's aria 'Erbarme dich', the special pathos in the Gospel at this point called on a certain tempo, key, harmonic rhythm, melody, scoring and manner of performance (pizzicato bass etc.), all of which accord with conventions but are re-thought in a *singular* way, like the slow movements of the violin concertos. If music is necessarily transient, and its natural gesture is towards yearning, then the result could be labelled 'sad', and the better done with pleasing melody and masterly harmony, the sadder it will be. But only minor changes in the performance alters an *Affekt*, and what exactly in many cases the composer's intention was is less certain than often assumed.

'SERIOUS AND PROFOUND MUSIC'

Following on the point about 'dry' or 'artful' music, the Obituary continues:

His serious temperament drew him predominantly to hard-working, serious and profound music [*arbeitsamen, ernsthaften, und tiefsinnigen*]; but he could also, if it seemed necessary, particularly when playing, make himself comfortable with a light and playful manner of thinking. (*Obituary*)

This remark can be seen in the same light as the previous: Agricola, and Emanuel with him, are responding to actual or anticipated criticisms. It is one of their key observations, and can be considered in its two parts which together are clearly meant to draw a rounded picture.

The first part suggests that the aura of the serious was already attaching itself to the image of J. S. Bach in his Leipzig years, which is not hard to believe, given the kind of music he was writing over the years in which Italian symphonies were coming to dominate the new world of public concerts. Even the extant portraits of him, actual images that remain to this day in the minds of modern listeners unused to conventions in formal portraits, have this serious aura. But so do other portraits by their painter E. G. Haussmann (a Leipziger appointed Dresden court portrait-artist in 1723), though in Bach's case Haussmann seems also to be representing the subject's imperfect eyesight. In general, 'seriousness of purpose' would be exactly what German authors found missing in so much modern Italian and French music, and not unjustifiably. Yet the seriousness of purpose one constantly senses in the music of Bach is only occasionally laborious: mostly, the composer's hard work in creating a Brandenburg Concerto, or the way its counterpoint can appear to be 'working hard', leads to nothing gloomy, studious, humourless. On the contrary.

Seriousness of purpose was a natural product of the kind of piety with which a Lutheran child was inculcated: the grateful reverence that could lead him in both youth and maturity to write *J. J.* (*Jesu juva*, 'Jesus help') on any sort of music – an early cantata (No. 71, 1708), thirty years later a set of harpsichord concertos for the concert-room, later still a set of chorale-preludes for church. (The autograph manuscripts for the concerto BWV 1052 and the chorale BWV 651, have *J. J.* for the first of their set.) There is no reason to think it an empty incantation, or the *I N I* in Friedemann's Clavierbüchlein a meaningless invocation (? *in nomine Jesu*, 'in the name of Jesus'). As one of God's creatures who had been taught the Gospel's parable of the talents, Bach was endowed with a gift, something to be returned with interest daily to his Maker. This meant self-application and commitment to bring the fruits of his labour, whether simple or complex music, beautiful melody or rich harmony, exciting rhythms or calm counterpoint, appropriate word-setting sacred or secular, biblical allusion or dance-music, fugues or songs, exercises for himself or others – everything. Reasoning in this way, one can believe that Bach was at his most devout not when his sacred music moved or delighted his neighbour but when it was so complex that only he and his Maker understood it. He could repay his talents with a higher interest the farther he developed it, that was his duty, as it was to do it joyfully (with 'delight in Thy statutes', Ps. 119).

Against such a background, musical obscurity or complexity would not be a virtue in itself, for the result could become turgid, over-rhetorical, even tiresome, in one way or another the consequence of vainglory. But for the God-given talent to be developed, stretched as far as its owner could stretch it, it would be necessary to explore contrapuntal intricacy and orderly system. From what was likely to have been his first illustrated hymnbook when a child in Eisenach (see BJ 1985, 31), he will have associated pious devotion with music. All is devotional for the devout man, and 'with a music that is devotional, God is always present in his grace', as Bach wrote in the margin of a house Bible at 2 Chronicles 5:13 (Cox 1985, facsimile 112). These verses in Chronicles are describing how voices and instruments are used to praise the Lord, and the margin-note, written some time after the volume was acquired in 1733, is the classic response by a Lutheran (or Anglican) of the time, who found nothing but poor theology in the Calvinist (or Presbyterian) argument against music, especially that in church. The remark would have suited very well a sermon read when an organ was inaugurated or a cantor installed.

Such an interpretation of devout Lutheranism could alone explain why at first in Leipzig Bach made a point of supplying a new cantata each week. Although court composers might please their employers in this way, a cantor was not specifically contracted to write so much, and at other moments in the service there was (as already noted) much older music being heard: the quasi-plainsong intonations, old motets, and the classic Protestant chorales already two centuries old. In drawing at first on works written at Weimar – though not as persistently as Handel drew on previous music in his anthems and canticles – Bach's Leipzig cantatas were maintaining the high, one might say aristocratic, tone and adapting it somewhat to the new conditions, bringing to a parish congregation a means of raising their sensibilities to the Word made sound, flattering them, even. If the previous repertory (Kuhnau's) was discarded, this was not simply to bring things up to date or to avoid music which Bach himself found uninteresting, if he did: rather, there was a drive to create a distinct, independent, consistent and new body of sacred music.

The supererogatory complexity of Bach's audition cantatas of 1723 already foretold a unique repertory, unmatched at the time but scarcely modern in any superficial or popular sense. If the wish had been simply to be modern, an easier solution would have been to take Telemann's new, complete church years of cantatas (soon to be published), which were simple, tuneful and practical works, at their best up-to-date and approachable. Bach's known acquaintance with certain works originating in Hamburg (Keiser, Telemann, Handel, the Anonymous St Mark) makes it clear enough that he by no means neglected or ignored other conceptions of sacred music, even occasionally made use of them instead of his own. On the other hand, it is striking how little he imitated such music, instead improving on their harmonic flaccidity and thus conveying more imaginatively than they the *Affekt* of the various texts. Seldom if ever would one mistake a Leipzig cantata movement for the work of a Graupner or Telemann, though one might occasionally for the work of another member of the Bach clan.

It looks as if especially in his last fifteen years or so, when composing in some particular genre, Bach had in mind a carefully made list of the ways in which he could reveal to the player or listener the scope of God's gift of music in a way appropriate to the genre, whatever that was. In Clavierübung III, a modern trio sonata (as if for flute, violin and continuo) is heard in two pieces but set against old Lutheran chorale-melodies played in canon; both speaking a remote musical dialect, for the Lord's Prayer and for the Ten Commandments. In the reworked Cantata 80 a contrapuntal motet for voices is developed against a cantus firmus canon for instruments, now on a monumental scale. A series of canons in the Goldberg Variations is set within the almost intolerably narrow confines of a few common-property harmonies and hovers in a world of sound unfamiliar and unrepeatable. The B minor Mass surveys a compendious musical universe stretching from a Gregorian intonation to one of the biggest scores of the time. A series of fugues and canons in the Art of Fugue, derived from a quasi-antique theme, demonstrates ways in which theme and structure can be new each time. All these works are supplying *exempla* of *teoria*, but in the process create an otherwise unknown world of beautiful sound, thus practice as well as theory.

In the complexity of their conception, and sometimes their bar-by-bar intricacy, the late works of Bach imply that beyond the high, middle and low styles recognized in Germany at the time by both composers and poets, he was creating a fourth category: the transcendental, a style beyond mere sense experience or musical grammar and logic. Although in each of its idioms the Art of Fugue is rooted in previous Bach fugues, this discrete fourth style shows itself in several ways: it transcends the keyboard in being unlike contemporary harpsichord and organ music, and in being adaptable to other instruments; it transcends mere grammatical complexity by focusing on the most basic musical relationship, tonic-to-dominant; and though instructive on several fronts, it also transcends (is more than) simple didacticism. The result is that it seems to transcend (exist beyond) the conventional range of musical *Affekte* of the day. What it is expressing, if anything, is so elusive that many have thought of it as 'abstract music', but this phrase only indicates the difficulty in finding words for musical experience of so unusual a kind.

For the 'hardworking, serious and profound music' of which the Obituary speaks, the authors may have had the Art of Fugue on their mind as they were writing. F. W. Marpurg, about to publish the first part of his treatise on fugue (*Abhandlung von der Fuge*, 1753), wrote a laudatory preface to the Art of Fugue's second edition of 1752, making one wonder whether the visit he said he had paid Bach some years earlier had acquainted him with the work-in-progress and led him to want to write a theory book to match it. Marpurg was not deaf to the work's 'most hidden beauties' (*verborgensten Schönheiten*: Dok III, 14) and thought it far from the world of 'dry and wooden' fugues (Dok III, 144), as indeed it is. On the other hand, while the Canon at the Tenth's world of sound might well be new and unworldly, the result is barely more than a pedagogical demonstration. When, as Tovey observed, a 'very fine' effect could be achieved if from a certain point on this canon's voices were doubled in thirds (1931, 39), is one to suppose that Bach must have seen this but found it irrelevant to what he was demonstrating?

Respectful admiration for Bach's counterpoint can easily divert attention away from the simple beauty of the very fugue-themes he is so often working with. The early Albinoni fugue, the G minor organ fugue, the Musical Offering theme, the Chromatic Fantasia's fugue, the Art of Fugue, the Kyrie and Cum sancto spiritu from the B minor Mass: outstanding fugue-subjects! – singable, full of wonderful potential and inspired detail. What a marvellous subject, the Chromatic fugue's! – long, original, inwardly melodious as no theme by one of Bach's contemporaries is likely to be, however experimental. A particularly happy touch is that its final statement is complete to the closing bar, despite the twists and turns of the penultimate bar. And how inspired it was to begin the theme of 'Et in terra pax' in the B minor Mass with a syncopation! – striking not only musically but textually, since it emphasizes the 'and' ('and peace on earth to men of goodwill'), not for the only time in this Mass.

'A LIGHT AND PLAYFUL MANNER OF THINKING'

This, the second part of the Obituary's comment (*zu einer leichten und schertzhaften Denkart*), sounds yet again like a defence against known accusations: nobody would have accused Handel or Telemann of undue seriousness. It needed saying, however, to those who had heard Bach playing only majestic organ works, or to those for whom he was the hero of difficult counterpoint rather than the master of dance-music and tuneful miniatures, as he also was.

While the anecdotes and other details given by the Obituary authors do give a varied picture of the virtuoso performer and respected figure, they could certainly have given a fuller picture of him as a lively, deft composer by recalling such masterpieces as the Peasant Cantata (1742), which Emanuel certainly knew and perhaps Agricola too – fuller, that is, than merely referring in general to 'some comic vocal pieces', as they do (*einige komische Singstücke*: Dok III, 86). If Bach slighted such pieces himself, in his own mind or in speaking about them, there is no sign of this in the music itself, and on the contrary, the Peasant Cantata, and to a lesser extent the Coffee and Phoebus & Pan Cantatas, tempt speculation on the success he could have achieved with comic operas or intermezzi, had the opportunity arisen. As it is, the comedy and ambiguities in such works as the Peasant and Coffee cantatas are not so far from those in Pergolesi's *La Serva padrona* (1733, performed in Dresden in February 1740), or various *intermezzi* of Hasse, for music such as this suits picaresque dramas whose very nature exudes the racy and the suggestive. The world they inhabit is not far even from Pepusch's *Beggar's Opera* (1729).

It is certainly possible that Bach avoided, even expressed distaste for, the theatre music and presentations that by the 1740s were reaching Leipzig from time to time. But for both Bach and Picander, librettist of the Peasant and Coffee cantatas (first eight verses) as well as St Matthew and St Mark Passions, there was no puritan need to evade the racy in either music or text if the occasion or location was not improper. In calling his collection of texts 'serious, playful and satirical verses' (*Ernst-Schertzhaffte und Satyrischer Gedichte*), Picander was naming three literary categories of a kind then popularly made, and perhaps they were still in the mind of the Obituary authors when they used two of the same words for the composer (*ernst, schertzhaft*). The higher, middle and lower styles recognized by poets and composers had each a place and were each worthy of professional attention. Nevertheless, only an astonishingly versatile composer could have been writing both the Peasant Cantata and, apparently over the same period, much of the Art of Fugue; and neither of these long after the Goldberg Variations. A breathtaking trio of masterworks, and none of them for church!

Style varies according to context, and for a skilful poet or composer there is no problem in having a character in the Peasant Cantata sing 'how nice it is to cuddle a bit' (*wie schön ein bisschen Dahlen schmeckt*) and following it with a saucy snatch of familiar melody. There must also have been some tittering at that point in the work, since according to the recitative the new landlord knew as much 'and probably more' about such things as the village girls and boys. But the jokes are always to be heard in the music itself: when the characters finally go off to the tavern, trailing the dudelsack like a pied piper, they sing a bourrée that apes a cantata's final chorale, or would if sung at half the speed and harmonized appropriately. Part of the point of the Peasant Cantata, from its astonishing potpourri overture (scored for a barn-dance trio) onwards, is to contrast the courtly with the peasanty, much as the Phoebus & Pan cantata constrasts the merely literate artist with the truly imaginative. Probably not all of its street-songs have yet been recognized and identified, but they include polonaises in the overture and first arias, also *Les Folies d'Espagne*, plus a minuet published in an old dance-manual (Nuremberg, 1716), a hunting song (with horn) and very elegant, extended, courtly ABA arias. The quoting of *Les Folies d'Espagne*, an old and well-known eight-bar theme, raises an intriguing question: since it has the same key as it does in Couperin's *Troisième Livre* (1722), and not the usual D minor found from at least Corelli 1700 to C. P. E. Bach 1778, was the composer privately alluding tongue-in-cheek to the piece's title in Couperin's book, 'La Virginité'?

In satirically contrasting current types of music, the Coffee and Peasant Cantatas are Bach's version of the running jokes, often about music and musicians, found in many another German source, such as Kuhnau's tales about 'beer-fiddlers' (*Musicus curiousus*, 1691) and incompetents pretending to be Italian virtuosi (*Der musicalische Quack-Salber*, 1700), or Niedt's about German organists incapable of playing figured bass (*Musicalische Handleitung* I, 1700). In the Phoebus & Pan cantata, the ass's ears pictured in music for Midas, a critic, were not the work of a composer thinking only of duty, death and invertible counterpoint, as some later admirers have implied he was. It is difficult to say what is the funniest thing in Example 25: the violin braying, the repetitive bass, the text (why *both* ears?) or what seems to be a non-sequitur.

The tone of the Peasant Cantata is clearly of a piece with the many, barely veiled sexual *doubles entendres* in the Wedding Quodlibet, BWV 524 (1707). Anna Magdalena Bach's wedding verses in her album of 1725 are milder but still with *double entendre* as well as *amour tendre*. Similarly, it would not be out of character for Bach to have been responsible for producing a particularly banal song in Sperontes's songbook of 1736 mocking the two Leipzig poetesses Mariane von Ziegler and Luise Gottsched, and – if he

25 Cantata 201.xi, b. 135
'For according to both of my ears he
is singing incomparably beautifully'

did – replacing it in the revised edition, on second thoughts (see NBA III/3 KB, 106ff). Not that one has to be prurient to tease or joke, as can be seen in the tongue-in-cheek formal phraseology, already mentioned, with which in 1741 Bach acknowledges the gift of some venison from a family friend at the court of Weissenfels, proof of 'Your Honour's invaluable favour' of which 'I never entertained the faintest doubt', and which has been meanwhile 'eaten by us to the health of Your Honour' (Dok I, 110). There is also something witty in quoting one of Luther's sayings – 'its key will be seen at the end' – in connection with a certain canon (Dok I, 222),[4] for the *end* Luther had in mind was not the final cadence of a clever canon.

Also, in using formal language inappropriately music can soon be funny, as in the Coffee Cantata's aria 'Mädchen, die von harten Sinnen. . .' ('Obstinate girls are not to be won over easily'). This has a paraphrased chromatic ostinato bass typical of a church cantata whose text suggests something far more fearful or shaming than the girl's father-defying passion for coffee. Since the late seventeenth century, coffee-houses, already criticized by Bach's predecessor in 1709 (see Schering 1926, 196), always had the

---

[4] The quotation was not unique: G. F. Kauffmann uses it too in his *Harmonische Seelenlust*, 1733, 7, for a chorale that ends on an imperfect cadence.

potential of being disreputable in any country at any time, at least if young women somehow came into the picture. The extant autograph of the Coffee Cantata, mid-1734 and called by Emanuel himself 'a comic cantata' on its cover, dates from a few months after one A.W. Platz, professor of botany in the university, had been promoted with a dissertation on the dangers of too much coffee-drinking. But by then the cantata's poet Picander had already published his text, making a link between a girl's disobedience to her father and her search for a husband, leaving us to suspect that in her elegant three-bar melody, the soprano is sighing over the sweetness of something more than coffee. Such *doubles-entendres* are not isolated.[5]

The Obituary said that it was 'particularly when playing' that Bach was 'comfortable with a light and jocular manner of thinking'. Is this its warning against taking his late learned publications as representing the whole man? Was it Agricola's eye-witness report of what and how he played in less formal settings, such as brilliant harpsichord music in the Collegium or at home? Does 'playing' (*Spielen*) mean only keyboard music, and this only around the years 1740, as Agricola would know? *Schertzhaft* ('jocular') could be a synonym for *allegro*, 'light, cheerful, bright', so implying that Bach's playing was effortless, bright, uplifting, the opposite of stodgy. The final variations of the Goldberg are easy to understand as light and jocular, but at other moments in this work (such as the three variations in the minor), and also here and there in WTC2 (the preludes in F sharp minor and G minor), a performance in the spirit of the music surely results in something not at all jocular but closer to a meditative chorale prelude for organ.

In Agricola's original remark, 'serious' need not mean 'grave', nor 'jocular' mean 'frivolous'. When familiar everyday sounds are incorporated in various pieces, such as the posthorn in the early Capriccio in B flat, the hunting horn in Cantata 208, or the trumpet-signals in Cantatas No. 214 (birthday music) and 127 (Day of Judgment), the result is neither grave nor frivolous, more a matter of having fun with old formulas. The various horn and trumpet calls associated with hunts, watchmen, proclamations, royalty etc., appear with both dexterity and greater variety than one would think possible with such basic musical *topics*. Example 26 has two totally different ways to use an everyday motif: the first is a call to prepare for Advent (a motif heard fourteen times in the cantata movement), the second is coun-terpoint to a gavotte for wind-trio (heard four times).

---

[5] At much the same period, in correspondence between Jonathan Swift and his friend Vanessa, coffee served as a code for their encounters, in a 'special sexually-charged sense of intimacy' (D. Nokes, *Jonathan Swift. A hypocrite reversed*, London, 1985, 258).

26 a Cantata 70.i, trumpet bb. 1–2
'Wake! Pray! Be always prepared!'
b Overture, BWV 1055, Gavotte II

Two points about the dozen or so different times this motif occurs in the Bach oeuvre are first, that it is re-thought each time and in a spirit the opposite of grave; and secondly, if today the composer's allusion is sometimes puzzling (why is it there in in Example 26 (b)?), it may not have been so to citizens of the time, who associated trumpet-calls, in the street and elsewhere, with many things – including, very likely, noises off when they were trying to rehearse.[6]

The Obituary's remark was to counter any reputation Bach's serious music had amongst everyday musicians, especially those engaged in the musical confections being marketed in the 1740s and 50s. But it brings us very little nearer envisaging his own approaches to performance, above all in the mature works where the intended *Affekt* is by no means always obvious or exclusive. The Aria of the Goldberg Variations is a good example: if it was meant to sound, as usual today, *andante, dolce, piano, affettuoso, cantabile e tenero*, it seems odd that none of these words (the first five of which were all used elsewhere by Bach) appears in the score. Furthermore, if the Aria were

---

[6] An eye-witness in 1728 speaks of a trumpet-chorale played three times a day in Leipzig (Schering 1941, 27). Similar triadic fanfares herald the processions in *Die Meistersinger*, as Wagner might have remembered from his early years in Leipzig.

affettuoso, so would be its 'prototype', the G major sarabande in the French Suites. So used now are listeners to being transported by the Aria's opening bars to a unique contemplative world, especially by modern pianists, that envisaging anything different, anything more 'light and playful', is difficult. But not impossible. Playful, even racy, elements in Bach's personality have been discerned by many an admirer, but playful elements in the music tend to be lost in the awful respect for his skill.

THE SCORE-READER

Constant practice in elaborating full-voiced musical works had brought him in the way of such a quick visual grasp that in the most detailed full scores [*Partituren*] he could, at a glance, take in all the voices sounding together. His hearing was so fine that in the fullest-voiced cantatas [*Musiken*], he was able to discern the smallest error. (*Obituary*)

As with the remark on Bach's ability to spot errors in performance, here Agricola seems to imply that such skills were not universal. Curiously, Walther's explanation of *Partitura* in the *Lexicon* of 1732 also says that scores were 'in order to avoid errors and correct the performers, should they make mistakes'.

By the 'voices sounding together' taken in by Bach, Agricola means instrumental plus vocal parts, a full mixed ensemble in something like the 17-stave score of the Sanctus of the B minor Mass (five voice parts, twelve instrumental) or the 24-stave St Matthew Passion (eight vocal, sixteen instrumental). *Musiken* must refer to actual performance of ensemble works, and it was following this remark that the Obituary comments on the limitations of Bach's performers (see above, p. 270). Commenting on a composer's skill in preparing a big score was not unknown: Agricola could almost be anticipating Mainwaring's remark on Handel, that 'no man ever introduced such a number of instruments' as he, a number amongst which 'not one is found idle or insignificant' (1760, 202).

There are several implications in the Obituary's remarks, none of them easily supported by other evidence. Three are, that Bach had more practice than many other musicians in composing big scores, that he somehow made use of the score in performance, and that his ability to recognize the smallest mistakes in the performance was unusual. The two sentences taken together seem at first glance to be saying that he directed, conducted, played from or at least followed the music from the full score, and that he could see from it if anyone went wrong. That may have been the case, but the separate points are rather different and say rather that (i), with his eyes he could instantly grasp a score, and (ii), with his ears he could instantly hear a mistake. These remarks contribute to the picture of a musician with practical as well as creative skills. It would be strange if he could identify a mistake only when directing from the score, especially since a fully figured bass part would have done almost as well; and almost as strange if Agricola is speaking of performances and not rehearsals.

A reader now might be merely projecting back from later practices to suppose that Agricola is describing Johann Sebastian Bach standing formally before a big ensemble and directing it from a full score, turning the pages every few seconds with one hand and conducting with the other. That is quite unlikely. Similarly, when in 1738 the former rector J. M. Gesner described him giving the beat to thirty or forty performers, with a nod to one, a foot-tap to another and a warning finger to a third, singing and playing his own part (Dok II, 332), the picture is less clear than first appears, especially when Gesner adds that all this was 'while he is performing the most difficult parts [*partibus*] of all'. What parts? – helping out during rehearsals, singing and reinforcing the bass line, playing a second continuo part, marking the beat, all with a score in his hand? During the service? Presumably, the arias and recitatives were left to the solo performers and organist.

It might seem that Agricola and Gesner had not otherwise witnessed much directing of large forces. Gesner, not a musician, mentions the possibility that there may be others as skilful as Bach (*illi similis forte*), and yet he was not alone in drawing the picture of something exceptional. One sees comparable points made by the next generation of admirers, plausible in broad outline but less reliable in detail. When Gesner speaks of Bach 'taking in all these harmonies with his sharp ear' (*harmonias unum omnes arguta aure metientem*), he seems to be anticipating points made in the Obituary: did its authors, despite having themselves witnessed Bach many a time, again make use of something they knew already in print (the dossier of press-cuttings again) and therefore more authoritative than their own anecdotal evidence?

Since big scores are only seldom to be found in Telemann or Graupner or Handel, a key phrase in Agricola's remarks is 'constant practice': his teacher learnt by experience and frequent self-application, having to find for himself a way to lay out a full score. This is plausible, and there is some variety in the layout of bigger ensembles. In its vertical order of staves, the First Brandenburg's score is much like the early Viennese symphonies of a later period, i.e. reading up:

continuo – strings – solo violin – woodwind – horns

But the early Cantata 71 has:

> continuo, chorus (BTAS), Vc, Recorder 2, Recorder 1, Bn, Ob2, Ob1,
> Violone, three 'Violae' (= Vla, Vn2, Vn1), Timp, Tr3, Tr2, Tr1

while seventeen years later, the Birthday Cantata 205 has:

> continuo, BTAS, Vla, Hn2, Hn1, Timp, Tr3, Tr2, Tr1, Fl2, Fl1, Ob2, Ob1,
> Vn2, Vnl

This last layout was misunderstood by a later copyist, either because it had originally been made *ad hoc* or conventions were by then different. Partly because of the variety of layout and partly because of the page's general appearance – equidistant staves without collective brackets, confusing to the eye (how many actual lines of music? is there one choir or two?) – pupils and assistants might well have been amazed at the composer's grasp of big scores.

The usually clear fair-copy scores of revised or newly compiled works, such as both Passions or the Brandenburgs, are of a kind not found in the earlier Leipzig period when shortage of time often meant hastily-written scores, as in the case of Cantata 105. Hand-ruling the staves could lead to a congested appearance or to other problems (as in the Art of Fugue's 'final' movement), and so could drawing in the bar-lines before the notes were written (some pages of the Brandenburgs' fair-copy score). One question might strike anyone viewing the first page of the Brandenburgs: is it making fun of the horns, with their scrappy and out-of-phase contributions looking like second thoughts, optional extras, something odd going on above everybody else's regular music? One curiosity, of Handel's scores as well, is that so little is ever abbreviated: repeated figuration and shared lines are generally written out complete, presumably to avoid misleading copyists. In an individual part, however, a patttern once spelt out may well be abbreviated if it continues further with only changed harmony (C major Prelude in the Clavierbüchlein, solo part of the Violin Concerto in A minor). The pattern's continuation is sometimes indicated or implied by the word *arpeggio* (D minor Chaconne, the recitative for gamba in St Matthew Passion). Quite why Bach did not regularly write the name of the soloists in to his scores when Handel did is also not obvious: differences in habits (Handel followed opera convention?) or circumstances (his copyists supplied the hired soloists with their copies?) or social context (his London soloists were theatre celebrities?).

Some of Bach's published pieces are quite incomplete. By not writing out complex canons but supplying rubrics for their solution (as in the Canonic Variations, the Musical Offering and the Art of Fugue), he is compelling performers to work further on what is printed in front of them, either by completing it on paper or risking problems in performance. 'Improvising' canonic answers is already difficult and risky, but in the Canonic Variations, without warning an accidental may need to be added. In the Musical Offering, for the answer to two canons the rubric says 'seek and ye shall find' (*quaerendo invenietis*). The buyers are being challenged or taught, and in the process amused on a level appreciated by connoisseurs. Perhaps some of them also noticed a particular detail in Clavierübung III: the older cantus firmi were so notated in the print that they needed no accidentals.

It would not be surprising if, like many a composer, Bach also had a more general interest in musical notation and score-layout. Very striking in his early manuscript copy of de Grigny's *Livre d'Orgue* is its fidelity to the original notation: three-stave keyboard score with French variety of clefs, intricate and voluminous ornamentation, and a wandering pedal part. His known exemplars of the prints of Frescobaldi's *Fiori musicali* and Ammerbach's *Tablaturbuch* would also have given him samples of keyboard notations conspicuously different from those that he mostly used: in Frescobaldi, four staves in open score with various C-clefs; in Ammerbach, an early form of letter tablature allowing the organist to 'score up' as he liked. Bach's publications have an unusually varied notation, with regular two-stave scores (Clavierübung I, II, IV and III partially), three-stave for organ with cantus firmus (some Clavierübung III, Schübler Chorales), four-stave organ score (Canonic Variations), no score but only parts (Sonata in Musical Offering), old-fashioned open score (Ricercar à 6, fugues in the Art of Fugue), and a mixture of score, parts and unrealized canons (Musical Offering). Such variety was archaic by the mid-eighteenth century and a further sign of consciously appealing to connoisseurs.

How frequently in his youth Bach used keyboard tablatures is not known, for in the nature of things, copies so notated would be superseded and discarded, but it can be safely assumed to have been far more than is known. See the Postscript for his early copies. (Walther's copies of earlier North German organ works, prepared for use in Weimar, always used regular keyboard score for music that had doubtless originated in tablature.) The fair copy Bach made of the little Fantasia in C minor, BWV 1121 shows complete familiarity with the organ tablature of Buxtehude's time, and certain 'South German' elements now recognized in it imply that it was *via* his brother Christoph, and thus indirectly Christoph's teacher Pachelbel, that he became familiar with this method. Since BWV 1121 might be only an exercise, a better indication of familiarity with tablature is his turning naturally to it in the margin of the first page of the Orgelbüchlein, and not rarely elsewhere when he runs out of space in stave-score.

Some notational details suggest an awareness of modern trends. An example is the treble clef for Partita No. 1 (1726, print) after the soprano clef of WTC1 (*c.* 1722, MS).[7] Another example is the increase in articulation signs and precisely marked rhythmic differences in music of a *galant* turn: slurs, *détaché* dots, snapped or plain rhythms, and triplets, here and there in MSS of vocal works (some instrumental parts of the B minor Mass) and more systematically in a few engraved publications (greater Lord's Prayer setting, BWV 682). A further example of 'modernity' is the regular use now of full key-signatures for minor keys: while Friedemann's Clavierbüchlein still has one flat for G minor, soon two is normal. Couperin was still using one or two old key-signatures in his *Quatrième livre* of 1730, but more consciously Bach re-introduced some in Clavierübung III in recognition of the old chorales, causing one pupil to speak of modes rather than keys (Kirnberger, Dok III, 301). In WTC1 all twenty-four keys have their modern key-signatures, except that where appropriate each space and line in the stave has its accidental, as indeed is more logical than today's practice. Full key-signatures were rare in 1722, although in that year Suppig's Fantasia passing through all the keys (see p. 144) also had them – a sign of some common interest at the time?

In organ music, Bach followed tradition in keeping to two staves unless the two hands and the feet played three independently registered lines, for which there were three staves as in French music. The anonymous essay of 1788 comparing Handel and Bach (see p. 314) reports with some pride that the latter had important pedal parts and used three staves 'always for music with two manuals and pedal', with which Handel's organ music could not compare (Dok III, 441–2).[8]

THE KEYBOARD PLAYER

As long as one can oppose us with nothing more than the mere possibility that there are better organists and keyboardists, we cannot be thought ill if we are bold enough to continue maintaining that our Bach was the greatest [*stärkste*] organist and keyboard-player there has ever been . . . How singular [*fremd*], how new, how expressive, how beautiful were the ideas that occurred to him when improvising! How consummately he brought them to fruition! With him, all fingers were

---

[7] Anna Magdalena's album-copy *c.* 1741 of the Goldberg Aria with soprano clef (when the print has treble clef) is puzzling. Was she practising clef-change, making a gesture of some kind, teaching the children, copying an unknown original? Soprano clef remained quite common for German organ music throughout the century.

[8] But Handel used three staves for a section in the Organ Concerto Op VII, No. 1, and even gave it the traditional German rubric he would have learnt as a child, *a 2 clav et ped.*

equally exercised; all had equal aptitude for the finest accuracy [*Reinigkeit*] in performance. He had worked out for himself such a comfortable fingering that it was not hard for him to perform the greatest difficulties with the most fluent ease. Before him the best-known keyboard-players in Germany and other countries had made little use of the thumb. (*Obituary*)

As with the remarks on harmony and melody, Agricola gives the appearance of having to find new, appropriate terms for describing his hero's gifts. As the first sentence suggests, the claim that he was uniquely gifted was being made with great care, and again the emphasis is on him as a player.

In constantly underlining Bach's abilities as an organist, keyboardist and composer of keyboard music, rather than a master of choral and instrumental music, the younger generation were not necessarily assuming that his creative work had become outmoded. To want to call him the 'greatest' performer suited the newer biographies of the day that evaluated a composer's practical abilities. So too when Mattheson described Handel as 'strong on the organ, stronger than Kuhnau in fugues and counterpoint, especially ex tempore' (1740, p. 93). To mention Kuhnau rather than Handel's teacher Zachow could have been a slip on Mattheson's part, prompting the Obituary to praise Kuhnau's successor for similar gifts. Scheibe, a critic discussed below, had also implied in print that Bach's only rival 'as an extraordinary artist on harpsichord and organ' was Handel (Dok II, 286, 300), and so left it necessary for Bach-devotees to make several counter-claims after his death. During the Leipzig years there had been in print already praise for Bach as a player, as director of the Collegium, as a clever composer and one admired as such in Italy itself. The last, not readily substantiated, was claimed by Padre Martini, who knew a few of the engraved works (Dok II, 469), perhaps *via* the steady flow of Italian musicians to the richer German courts such as Dresden.

Contemporary testimony to the composer's skill as a player refers both to organ and harpsichord. Of the organ-playing, in 1727 G. H. L. Schwanberg said, 'I have never heard anything like it' (Dok II, 179); of the harpsichord-playing, Jacob Adlung in 1758 praised his playing of Marchand suites as 'very fleeting and artistic' (*sehr flüchtig und künstlich*: Dok III, 125). Presumably the latter was alluding to the rubato, sostenuto and sensitive touch characteristic of the French manner. The Obituary contributes with its own stories of Marchand, Reinken and the appreciative listeners of Dresden but says nothing about any ability with other instruments, a versatility for which Bach praised his own students in testimonials. Later, his violin-playing, which he kept up until the approach of old age, was described by Emanuel as 'pure and penetrating' (*rein u. durchdringend*: Dok

III, 285), which looks less than complimentary, except that it meant he could hold an orchestra together better with violin than with keyboard, which is not difficult to believe. Demands on his time must alone have prevented Bach from becoming a violin virtuoso, but even before the solo violin works, his intimate grasp of violin-playing is clear from the *violino piccolo* part in the First Brandenburg, especially its third movement, difficult but practical and full of fine fiddle gestures.

Emanuel also said his father had a particular preference for playing viola, 'with appropriate louds and softs', i.e. more musically than the usual humble viola-player sawing away at inner parts by custom tedious and expressionless. Was Emanuel half-remembering performances of the Sixth Brandenburg? Or the weekly cantata choruses? Or he knew of chamber trios that exist now only in versions without viola? If his father really did prefer viola, perhaps this can be stretched to include the large viola or violoncello piccolo, required in some Weimar and Leipzig cantatas and much better known in mid-century Saxony than often now recognized. The *Bassettgen* amongst the late cantor's possessions was probably one such instrument, listed after the three violas and making, with them, a bigger group than the violins (Dok II, 493). To possess three violas suggests a keen player.

'Penetrating' was also how Emanuel described his father's singing voice, with a wide compass and good technique (*gute Singart*: Dok III, 285), qualities which he clearly found it reasonable to require of his singers. Of his imaginative realizations as a continuo-player various accounts were given by pupils, who like students today would have been receptive to a brilliant teacher. One of them, Mizler in 1738, reported that he was able to 'accompany every solo so that one thinks it an ensemble piece', with a new melody as if pre-composed, and Emanuel said he could improvise a fourth part to a trio if its composer did not mind (Dok II, 321; III, 285). Quite likely Mizler and Emanuel Bach were so used to uninteresting continuo-playing that neither of them asked whether this picture is entirely to the composer's credit, but I doubt that it is – any more than was his egregious figuring of a bass by Antonio Biffi many years before (see BJ 1997, 11–12), unless this had been with a view to analysing harmony. If Bach did insist that his pupils' continuo harmony be as complete and thoughtfully detailed as written-out harmony, one soon sees how they would produce the literal, unidiomatic and otiose realization published later by J. P. Kirnberger for the Musical Offering (see Dok III, 347–8).

A teacher's emphasis on careful harmonization could lead young continuo-players less gifted than himself to a pedantic kind of accompaniment. Were they aware, for instance, that if he or they were figuring the bass part of a cantata by running their eyes down the full score, some figures need only be cautionary and were not necessarily played ? (For example, a 4 under the bass line means 'don't play a 3 here'.) How far the four-part realizations attributed to Bach in the MS *Vorschriften* of 1738 (see Poulin 1994) represent the way people actually played continuo is a big and unsolved question, even more than is the MS's authenticity. When the teenage Emanuel wrote out a bass part which he or his father then figured, did he play the harmonies as sensitively as his own book of 1753/62 constantly recommends? Or was this very sensitivity something new in *c.* 1750, the reaction of a court musician to the dull, literal realizations of bass-lines he had long heard from church organists?

For the Obituary's final sentences above, there is a context. Already in his vastly informative and widely selling book of 1752, Emanuel's colleague in Berlin, J. J. Quantz, had spoken not only in general terms of the 'perfection' to which Bach had brought organ-playing – presumably he had heard him play, at Potsdam in 1747 and even at Dresden in 1731 (Dok III, 441), if not earlier – but also of his keyboard-technique in general. According to Quantz, each of J. S. Bach's fingers was curled and its tip drawn in to glide off the keys, producing running passages at their clearest, especially scales (*stufenweis*: 1752, 232, 329). Yet how far such touch and articulation were characteristic of Bach's earlier playing, especially before the partitas of the late 1720s, is quite uncertain, and Quantz might just as well have had at the back of his mind points he could have seen covered in François Couperin's tutor, *L'Art de toucher* and other French instruction books. For Bach's own fingering, a particular question arises for the remoter keys in Book I of the WTC: were these alone a stimulus for fully worked-out flexible fingering-system or were they left for a pupil to cope with as best he could?

Without doubt, counterpoint as it had developed in the WTC and Inventions does require a particularly careful, cohesive fingering. Hence it is that the Inventions' titlepage of 1723 speaks of players learning from them above all how 'to achieve a singing style in the playing' (*am allermeisten aber eine **cantable** Art im Spielen zu erlangen*). This *cantable* is not Chopin's but Couperin's, indicating the smooth harpsichord line already implied in *L'Art de toucher*, characteristic of French preludes and vital too to fugal counterpoint. (Scarlatti uses the word *cantabile*, for sonatas with *affettuoso-legato* right-hand solos above simple accompaniment.) That Bach also wanted variety of touch is suggested by adjacent Inventions: the fully slurred D major (or F minor) Invention supposes a quite different playing-style from the slurless D minor (or F major) Invention next to it. Such variety had to be learnt, and Bach's early playing-style must have differed from his later, for in such respects the early A minor Variations, BWV 989 are quite unlike the Goldberg Variations nearly forty years later. The instrument's sound-production and the very keyboard itself had evolved towards making greater smoothness and suavity possible, and so must have its playing.

Already in his book of 1753, the *Versuch*, Emanuel implied that his father had gradually developed a way of making the thumb and all fingers versatile, having heard in his youth great men who used the thumb only for wide stretches (Dok III, 23), i.e. not for scales or remoter keys. 'Great men' brings Reinken and Buxtehude to mind, which in turn recalls Quantz's reference to 'the Netherlanders' of former times. Both he and Emanuel are referring to composers whose fingering was doubtless less versatile and did not need to be otherwise, since their organ-tuning allowed fewer keys, their harmony had fewer sevenths and modulations, and their keyboard's sharps and naturals were shorter. Quantz may also have had in mind Mattheson's recent praise for the long dead but still admired Amsterdam organist Sweelinck, and his 'pleasant and decorous' way of playing the keyboard (*angenehm und ehrbar*: 1740, under 'Jacob Praetorius'). Certainly by *c.* 1750, anyone could see that versatile fingers were necessary for playing in all twenty-four keys.

In the same book of 1753, Emanuel claims to be using this 'new fingering' for his own Method, which was for players of a music very different from his father's. But a much earlier book, very likely known to Emanuel, had already advised that

pour continuer un roulement plus Ètendu que celui de la Leçon, il n'y a qu'à s'accoutumer à passer le I. par-dessous tel autre doigt que l'on veut, & à passer l'un de ces autres doigts par-dessus le I.

To produce a fast run more extended than that in the lesson [= the given musical example], it is only a matter of becoming accustomed to pass the thumb under whatever finger one wishes, and to pass one of the other fingers over the thumb.

Although this book of Rameau's, *Pièces de clavecin avec une méthode sur la mécanique des doigts* (Paris, 1724), is not known to have been owned by any of the Bachs, one might guess that it was and, in its subtlety and modernity, had had a crucial influence on the harpsichord partitas soon after, more so than had Handel's suites of 1720. Rameau required flexible fingers and hands, including left hand over – was this the inspiration for the extraordinary Gigue of Partita No. 1 (1726), one oddity of which is that its notation as engraved implies right hand over? Bach's skill in hand-crossing and wide leaps, without much bodily movement, was praised by his critic Johann Scheibe who had certainly witnessed it (Dok II, 286), possibly when the composer was playing Partitas Nos. 1 and 5 in the 1720s. Hand-crossing was certainly a skill of great interest, especially after the publication in 1738 of Scarlatti's book of *Essercizi*.

While Emanuel's and Rameau's treatments of fingering do not entirely coincide – Emanuel uses the little finger 5 more, on sharps and flats – nevertheless to read especially paragraphs 7, 11, 18, 22, 25–27, 33 and 61 in the first chapter of Emanuel's book alongside Rameau's of 1724 is to be struck by similarities. It looks very much as if, in inheriting a love of system from his father, Emanuel is aiming for the coherence and comprehensiveness lacking in Rameau's book, an author whom Emanuel's *Versuch* mentions only once, and then to criticize. In his preface Rameau had promised to treat matters at greater length but failed to deliver on it, and in effect this is what Emanuel's *Versuch* is now doing. In that case, if there were this connection between them, the Obituary's phrase 'keyboard-players [*Clavieristen*] of other countries' could be an attempt to demote French publications by claiming precedence.

As for the thumb: when Bach's pupil J. C. Vogler fingered a copy of the C major Prelude WTC2, he actually made more use of the thumb than one would today. Because he had a small hand? Because that was the way to phrase counterpoint? The unanswered questions about this, and indeed about all extant examples of written-in fingering before Mozart's period, mean that any uncritical use of them today is potentially misleading, merely a construct based on a positivistic reading of a few written sources. The music itself implies a great deal: using the thumbs on any sharp and changing fingers on any note are both important to the Art of Fugue if the integrity of its counterpoint is to be observed, and Bach would not need to have read Couperin's *L'Art de toucher* to learn about finger-changing. It is not easy to believe that the scales in the Chromatic Fantasia and the arpeggios in the C minor Fantasia, BWV 906 were fingered in anything but a modern way. But if they were, they go beyond those pieces by Rameau in which hand-shifting is still inevitable and pronounced, and the modernity of what Bach was achieving with such pieces needs to be recognized.

With respect to his father's playing, one can take Emanuel's remarks as relevant at best only to the mature Leipzig works. Many things had changed since J. S. Bach's earlier years: pitch had become generally lower, temperament less unequal, keyboards now had longer keys and compass, counterpoint was (with him) better wrought and sustained, and instruments' sound-production itself was less immediate.[9] As repertory had changed, so

---

[9] This, a noticeable but less easily quantified development, could be illustrated by comparing a violin or harpsichord or organ of *c.* 1650 with one of *c.* 1775, or a harpsichord with a fortepiano, a baroque oboe with a clarinet, etc.

had playing, even in details such as ornamentation and the fingering of scales and arpeggios. The ornament-table in Friedemann's Clavierbüchlein of 1720 can say little for the Musical Offering of 1747. Nevertheless, it is striking that the manner of Bach's playing as summarized in Chapter 3 of Forkel's book of 1802 – his body remained immobile, hands were close to the keys, fingers seemed hardly to move – are central to French style as outlined many years before by Saint-Lambert (1702), Couperin (1716) and Rameau (1724).

THE ORGAN EXPERT

He understood not only the art of playing organs, of uniting together their stops in the most skilful way and of letting each stop be heard according to its true character, all to the greatest perfection; but he also had thorough knowledge of how organs were constructed. [One organ he examined was at the Johanniskirche, Leipzig] in the church near to where his bones now rest. The maker of this organ was a man in the final years of his old age, and the examination was perhaps one of the severest that had ever taken place. Consequently, the full approval that our Bach publicly conferred on the organ directed no little honour as much to the organ builder as also, on account of certain circumstances, to Bach himself. No-one was better able than he to specify the stoplist for new organs and to form judgments [*beurtheilen*]. (*Obituary*)

Neither builder nor church is named by the Obituary, despite Bach's by then being buried in the same church's cemetery. Perhaps Agricola, who wrote these sentences, did not know, not having been there himself. Nevertheless, though misleading in another respect (the builder Johann Scheibe lived for nearly five more years after the examination in December 1743), the reference contains several important motifs which, considering how many organs Bach was involved in, were probably the reason for picking on this particular incident to tell at length.

First, the claims that Bach had a deep technical knowledge of organs, both as to how they could be made to sound well and how they were constructed: neither is difficult to believe in general terms, but how much farther one can take them is another question. Such claims are of a piece with Emanuel's image of his father as one who understood the physical layout of orchestras as well as organs, even orchestras placed in the open air. By some natural gift of perception he also recognized how a certain building (the banqueting hall of the new Berlin opera house) could produce an unintended and so far unnoticed whispering-gallery effect. All such grasp of practicalities he achieved from experience and 'natural' knowledge, not from a 'systematic study of acoustics' (Dok III, 285, 288) or, one infers, any other taught theory. Hard though it is to believe that a whispering-gallery effect would have gone unnoticed in a building by then several years old, Emanuel found it important to claim that nature and practice, not theory or system, were behind his father's observation. A not dissimilar point was made elsewhere about another Bach, Johann Nicolaus, the 'Jena Bach', when it was said that an organ stop he tuned by ear was superior to one tuned by the monochord (Adlung 1768, II 54ff).

On the registration of organ-stops: this point may be significant, for many organists reading the Obituary must have been familiar with the full registrations given in G. F. Kauffmann's books of chorales (Leipzig, from 1733) and were therefore puzzled why Bach's publications had nothing of this kind. Clavierübung III, the Canonic Variations and the Schübler Chorales, all appearing between 1739 and *c.* 1748, indicate nothing in the music beyond the manuals and octave-pitch, and then not completely. The late MS compilation of some longer, earlier chorales, 'The Eighteen', did not even go so far. Kauffmann was not alone in indicating the stops, and indeed, not to do so at all was somewhat old-fashioned, more typical of a time when music had circulated in manuscript and when each region's organs varied amongst themselves only in size.

Of course, to publish complex music without indicating how it might best be played drew attention to the counterpoint *per se*, and this could well have been Bach's intention. But since the day's buyers would wonder about the absence of performing directions, Agricola covered the registration issue by claiming Bach's unrivalled mastery of it. Quite where the mastery lay or could lie is not obvious, for even if it were something Agricola had seen for himself, is one to think that many other organists did not understand the nature of organ-stops and their combinations?

For other remarks on Bach's reportedly intimate understanding of organ-building, see above, pp. 60f. The reports written by his predecessor Johann Kuhnau, as at Freiberg in 1714 (Müller 1982, 420–3), imply as much expertise as Bach's if not more. Did the Obituary authors make their claim because by then this was exceptional? Or not being experts themselves, they overstated his expertise? The anecdote about the whispering-gallery effect in Berlin reminds one that evidence is seldom straightforward, for this report bears a curious resemblance to a story circulating about an 'echo tower' many years earlier in Weimar (see Wolff 2000, 506), which somebody – father? son? – could have known. In the case of the rebuilding-scheme for the organ at Mühlhausen nearly fifty years before the Obituary, one notes that not only did it have much in common with Werckmeister's book but so it did with Johann Christoph Bach's plan of 1696 for the organ in the Georgenkirche, Eisenach. At the examination at Halle in 1716, the report was written out by Kuhnau, again drawing on Werckmeister.[10] Presumably Bach concurred with the report when he signed it, and took note of its reference to a wind-gauge – Kuhnau the Leipziger was showing himself aware of this device, first described by Christian Förner in a book published in Leipzig in 1684.

Although examination of new organs that Bach is known to have made, with other musicians in the case of large instruments, supports the Obituary's last point, one might expect him to have been called upon as examiner or adviser more often than he is known to have been. It could be that once a capellmeister or cantor had ceased to be a titular organist such jobs were less appropriate; but even so, to have been so little involved officially in the organs of Dresden and of Saxony generally, is striking. (Was Silbermann, Saxony's privileged organ-builder, against Bach's partic- ipation, and were Bach's collegial relations with Hildebrandt a consequence of this?) On the other hand, it is likely that he had helped draw up speci- fications for organs he did examine or inaugurate, although only at Mühlhausen is this fully documented, perhaps because he was employed there at the time. It was after making its claims for technical expertise that the Obituary remarks on the composer never having a large and fine instru- ment of his own, 'despite all this knowledge of organs' (see above, pp. 277f).

A further detail in the Obituary's remarks was Capellmeister Bach's gen- erosity to craftsmen, a detail developed by Emanuel in later remarks to Forkel. This may have been partly to counteract a harsh point made by the organ-builder's son, already published by Mattheson, which accused an unnamed 'great man' of contributing to his father's failures (see below, p. 311). The Town Council itself recognized that the builder Scheibe was 'a poor man' (Dok II, 408) and had probably been willing to help him. The strictness of this particular examination of the Johanniskirche organ was mentioned again later by Agricola (Dok III, 192), presumably drawing on the Obituary, but considering how relatively modest an instrument of two manuals and twenty-two stops is, a long and rigorous examination proba- bly indicates problems with it. According to an account published in 1757, it had some device to make (sudden) *piano* and *forte*, which was probably a new and troublesome mechanism to couple the manuals or add/subtract stops (Henkel 1986, 47). But if Emanuel, Agricola or Forkel thought it was

---

[10] Noted above, p. 60; see also Dok I, 157ff. At the report's request, the builder, Christoph Cuncius, promised to give the organ *Cammer Thon* (Dok II, 61), i.e. lower pitch than usual. But how could he do that in a finished organ? (See also p. 334.)

unusual for examiners to ask for supplementary payments to an organ-builder they can not have read Werckmeister's *Orgelprobe* very carefully, for there he recommends it.

At least local readers of the Obituary realised that in the coy little phrase 'on account of certain circumstances', the authors were without doubt referring to remarks about Bach made in print by none other than the organ-builder's son, J. A. Scheibe, specifically the notorious criticism he had published in 1737 and again in 1745, in Leipzig this time. Scheibe had been a student there from 1725 and touchingly dedicated the first instalment of his periodical *Der critische Musikus* to his father. Scheibe Senior, Leipzig university organ-builder, was sixty-five in 1743 when the examination at the Johanniskirche was made, and his son's critique of Bach was probably still fresh in many a memory. If Bach was fair to the father, irrespective of his son's notorious criticism, does this suggest that from experience of him Agricola expected otherwise? Or merely wished to counter Scheibe's criticism?

A striking point about the reference is that it is the only one in the whole Obituary that even hints at Bach's various vexations, and some attention can now be given to the most public of these.

SCHEIBE'S CRITICISM

It was in Hamburg in May 1737, in the journal *Der critische Musikus*, that J. A. Scheibe, a former student of Leipzig University and a quite prominent musician there in the 1720s, accused Bach of the following (Dok II, 286f):

havinginsufficient 'agreeableness' (*Annehmlichkeit*) in his *Stücken* ('pieces', i.e. cantatas) discarding nature (*das Natürliche entzöge*) by means of a turgid and confused manner (*schwülstiges, verworrenes Wesen*)

obscuring beauty by too much art (*allzu grosse Kunst*)

requiring singers and instrumentalists to do what he alone can do on the keyboard

writing out every little embellishment, depriving his pieces of the beauty of harmony and leaving the melody indistinct

making the voice parts equally difficult (i.e. contrapuntal, none of them a soloist or 'chief voice' with a melody accompanied by the others)

all achieved with heavy labour (*beschwerliche Arbeit*).

The first accusation is ambiguous: 'the great man would be the admiration of whole nations if he had more agreeableness' sounds personal but was taken by his defender Birnbaum to refer to the music (see below), only which would be the concern of 'whole nations'.

The music journal in which the remarks appeared included correspondence and discussion, and it is possible that Scheibe, like Mattheson in his journals, was trying to provoke some response from Bach himself. If so, he did not understand the cantor. Scheibe had been one of six unsuccessful candidates at the Nikolaikirche in 1729 when Bach had been an examiner for the position vacated by J. G. Görner, who was joining him at the Thomaskirche. Johann Schneider who got the job was another Bach student. Eighteen months later, Bach wrote for Scheibe a warm enough but careful testimonial for the vacancy at Freiberg Cathedral, but again he did not succeed. That the Nikolaikirche episode left him with resentments is clear from other references both to this (Dok II, 365) and to Bach's allegedly treacherous treatment of his father, the builder of his own university's organ (Mattheson 1740, 'Scheibe').[11] He also described Görner as 'a wretched composer' (*ein elender Componist*: Scheibe 1745, index). But when in December 1739 Scheibe praised Bach's Italian Concerto in F major, it is possible that he had met with Bach again in connection with the new organ at Altenburg in September 1739, and they had been reconciled (see Dok II, 372, 373). That in the general tenor of his criticism Scheibe was revealing Hamburg's current musical tastes is clear from a claim already made in 1731 by Mattheson himself, that everyone knew Bach's music to be artful but unmelodic (*künstlich, unmelodisch*: BJ 1987, 24).

Nevertheless, what Scheibe had to say in 1737 amounts to the most significant critique of J. S. Bach, the most carefully reasoned evaluation of his music, that appeared in print during his lifetime. It seems to have rankled. For presumably it was Bach himself who got J. A. Birnbaum, a Leipzig teacher of rhetoric, to defend him several times at length and in detail against his absent critic. Having someone else to reply when he had been challenged may have been habitual: it seems to be the case also at Naumburg in 1746, when the organist questioned Bach's and Silbermann's positive report on the new organ, and only the latter is known to have responded (see also p. 61). And in 1749, when the rector of Freiberg published a somewhat anti-music document, Bach asked C. G. Schröter, a much-respected organist and one of his defenders against Scheibe, to respond. On this occasion Bach's opinion, probably prompted by experiences with his own school rector, was more intolerantly and rudely expressed than Schröter wanted to be associated with, and it gave Mattheson, who got to know about it, a chance to poke his nose in and offer gratuitous comment after Bach's death (Dok II, 462).

---

[11] Scheibe Snr was a far less distinguished builder than Hildebrandt, who was apparently favoured by Bach and had (accordingly?) moved to Leipzig by 1734.

Bach, who does not come out of the incident with Schröter well, must have supplied some of Birnbaum's arguments against Scheibe. It was his secretary J. E. Bach who dealt with the printer of Birnbaum's essay, asking for two hundred copies of it in time for the Easter Fair 1739, no doubt for distribution. The arguments on behalf of Bach, made rather long-windedly, include the following, here paraphrased (Dok II, 296ff):

> He deserves to be called more than *Musicant* or *Künstler* (musician, artist), since these imply mere practitioners or craftsmen.
>
> If Handel is the 'great master in a foreign country' able to dispute the palm with Bach, others think him no equal.
>
> Scheibe misunderstands *Annehmlichkeit*: music is more than merely agreeable sounds, as pointed out in an essay in the London *Spectator*. (A nine-volume translation of Joseph Addison's *Spectator* was made in Leipzig by Gottsched's wife Luise and published in 1739–43.)
>
> *Schwülstiges* is an indiscriminate charge: Bach's decorations are appropriate to the genre in hand.
>
> *Verworrenes* is precisely what his counterpoint is not, though Scheibe might have heard confused performances (of Leipzig cantatas?).
>
> *Allzu grosse Kunst* does not destroy nature or obscure beauty. By definition, any difficulty in playing is surmountable: as the Dresden orchestra shows, accuracy of ensemble is perfectly possible. (A further hint that Bach liked comparing Dresden and Leipzig to the latter's disadvantage?)
>
> Much other music prescribes ornamentation: see the organ works of Grigny and Du Mage. To specify them is to convey sensibly the composer's intentions.
>
> To have no 'solo line' is not a fault: Palestrina and Lotti did not either.
>
> Aware that he was not able always to call on virtuoso performers, Bach was able to adapt his music accordingly.

These points led to a few more replies and counter-replies, and yet several of Scheibe's original criticisms were not very well answered. Invoking Palestrina or Grigny does not really bear on his points, which were less against either counterpoint or ornament-signs as such than against superfluous complexity distracting from the melody. Scheibe was thinking of music that lacks Handel's simple melodiousness, or of melodies so cluttered with busy figuration that soloists were deprived of their freedoms and expressive *belcanto*. As to the 'beauty of harmony' being impaired: this need not mean that Scheibe recognized only the relatively simple harmony of a Handel or Telemann.

There is already more than a hint that the Thomaskirche choir and musicians found the music too difficult, which Scheibe would know from

personal experience in the 1720s. In fact, several of his points convey
less any deeply philosophical differences in taste (such as have often pre-
occupied later musicologists scrutinizing the rhetoric) than his own practical experience of problems with Bach's vocal and instrumental writing,
specifically church cantatas. He would know, as would anyone present
especially at rehearsals, that an alto soloist singing Cantata 170 or 35 is going
to find that his instrument-like lines give little chance to rest or even
breathe. Bach himself was perfectly aware of the 'incomparably difficult
and intricate' nature of his sacred music, as he called it himself in 1736 (*ohn-
gleich schwerer und intricater*: Dok I, 88). In this connection, it is interesting that when another student, Mizler, defended Bach by pointing to his
grasp of 'modern taste' (Dok II, 336), it is a non-church cantata he has in
mind, a work of homage to the king at the Easter Fair, 1738.

In 1739, again in Hamburg, Scheibe took the matter further by publishing a satirical pseudonymous letter coming as if from Bach himself, whose
idiosyncrasies of expression were familiar enough to Scheibe that he could
imitate them (Dok II, 361–2). Though cutting, it does carry conviction in
its report of a certain cantor who supposedly says

he does not concern himself with learned matters and has read no writings on music

a musician has enough to do with his art (*Kunst*) and is better engaged
in devising a musical instrument or a composition

he has never had time to learn to write rambling letters, and leaves it to
a friend on his behalf

but he can certainly write great quantities of musical notes and produce
artful (*künstlich*) scores

he is convinced he is the greatest artist (*Künstler*), and is most happy
when introducing contrapuntal artifices (*Kunstwerke*) into his music

he wonders what good are 'bald songs' (*die kahlen Lieder*) that are immediately intelligible and memorable?

if the recipient continues to be critical, he and his followers will be
severely persecuted (*auf das heftigste verfolgen*)

Only an acquaintance, and one with a grudge, could list such points – which
are not worthless even if they were not his own, as one defender suspected
was the case generally with Scheibe's writing (Dok II, 433). The points are
those of a Hamburg musician not only at home with music of Telemann and
Handel but who had good reason to imagine being 'persecuted' by the
cantor. The whole is very revealing.

Indeed, much of what Scheibe says in the original essay rings true. The
most ardent of Bach devotees can have occasionally suspected there was 'too

much art': the teeth-gritting dogma of the Four Duets of Clavierübung III and the Augmentation Canon in the Art of Fugue, the earnest calculation in early Leipzig cantata choruses and arias, the hard work represented by collections whose very comprehensiveness is distancing. Even the Well-tempered Clavier would not be free of criticism: the two volumes have become so entrenched in the repertory that one easily forgets how strange the whole idea is, how nearly alienating is the sheer thoroughness of collecting preludes and fugues in every major and minor key. And to do it twice! All too understandably Scheibe found Bach's music often the product of heavy labour, less 'natural' than Handel's.

The spoken and unspoken rivalry with Handel in the minds of the Obituary authors reached its apogee in the long *Comparison of Bach and Handel* of 1788, now attributed to C. P. E. Bach (Dok III, 437–45) and combining hard criticism with a kind of anonymous politeness. Its agenda includes referring to Bach's abortive attempts to meet Handel in person – whose supposed departure from Halle before meetings could ever take place would doubtless remind readers of Marchand's departure from Dresden. (How true it is that such meetings had been proposed is uncertain: perhaps Emanuel and others remembered Telemann's 'frequent meetings' with Handel being reported in Mattheson 1740, 358ff.) But for Scheibe, appreciation of Handel had not meant demeaning the whole of Bach. Two anonymous writings of the 1740s in favour of Bach are probably Scheibe's work (see Köpp 2003) and show his taste to be discriminating, insofar as the anti-Italian points he is making are against the modern, frothier *galant* music coming out of Italy, not against earlier Italians.

In the same way, Scheibe's warm praise for the Italian Concerto in F major recognizes it as the perfect model of a well-organized concerto for one player, as indeed it is, in its intimate awareness of what such pieces could be (Dok II, 373). Scheibe was right, even if his motive was to defend German music against Italian. The Concerto has many if not all of the light touches typical of Venetian concertos, being much more carefully thought-out than its putative models; it is planned so systematically and precisely that the three movements even have a common pulse through their proportional time-signatures (2/4 crotchet = 3/4 quaver = 2/2 minim). Such a calculated detail would not have endeared itself to Scheibe had he been aware of it, nor would the Concerto's other characteristics: it has an affecting slow movement full of written-out ornamentation of the kind Scheibe criticized; it is technically demanding, as if the composer expected other players to be able 'to do what he alone can do'; and it is throughout far less 'natural' in its melodies than most music of the time. Nevertheless, Scheibe found it agreeable.

It is possible that the original criticisms not only expressed a general idea of 'nature' then fashionable – a buzzword of the Enlightenment Period and of Leipzig poets such as Gottsched, Scheibe's teacher – but also reflected the same poet's displeasure some years previously at finding his notions mocked, or so it has since been thought, in Bach's marvellously inspired cantata *Phoebus & Pan*, 1729.[12] By its very effectiveness this rich, opera-like work, full of irresistible tunes and rhythms, could have been found offensive – if one suspects oneself included amongst those 'who judge carelessly', in the words of a text printed in hundreds. Gottsched was on record as being vehemently anti-opera. On the whole, however, there is little need to invoke a high-falutin philosophy of the Natural in Music when considering Scheibe's criticisms: if one compares Handel's 'My heart is inditing' for the coronation of George II in October 1727 with Bach's Cantata 198 of the same month on the death of the Electress of Saxony, one can see what Scheibe meant and how he would feel his opinions to be totally justified. For how ever richly beautiful to the connoisseur much of Cantata 198 is, Handel's 'My heart is inditing' (likewise composed for a queen consort) is more immediately winsome and, to more people, natural. When it came to writing an Obituary for Bach, its authors were well aware how often Scheibe and Mizler had praised Handel in various publications of the 1730s and 1740s.

Though finding fault with Bach's music rather goes against the grain of the last two and a half centuries, a rounded picture of it emerges only from taking into account its less appealing moments. To take one example: had Scheibe ever worked on the Prelude and Fugue in A minor, BWV 894, he could well have considered its 250 bars a sign of misspent energy. As a draft concerto-movement, or even an early essay in sustained writing, the Prelude and its unrelenting Fugue might have had an educative purpose in the composer's workroom – not every work of a composer was intended or fit for public listening. When, as can happen, there is little interest in the melody or harmony of a work, there is also no compensating whimsy or charm such as redeems many a careless French ballet or Italian concerto. The motivic persistence in the A minor Prelude is clever but not ingratiating;

---

[12] But in 1732 Gottsched had sent his wife-to-be the Six Partitas (see p. 216) and in 1738 Bach was to use one of his libretti for a Collegium performance (Cantata BWV Anh. I 13). Picander too had been implicated in Gottsched's criticisms of cantata-text poets (BJ 1991, 21), but quarrels and quasi-reconciliations are not unknown in university communities.

In part, Gottsched's attempts to purify German as a literary language led Goethe, a Leipzig student after Bach's death, to mock the city and its pretensions in the Auerbach's Cellar scene of *Faust*: 'it is a little Paris, and cultivates its people' (*es ist ein klein Paris, und bildet seine Leute*).

equally clever modulations in the Fugue do not relieve its obsessive beat. Length was clearly of interest to Bach, who made conscious efforts to create sustained movements, usually in some version of ritornello form, but clearly, the longer a dull, motoric piece, the less likely it will please the listener.

One of Scheibe's remarks in the letter purporting to come from Bach might be a specific jab: that he thinks himself better employed in 'devising an instrument' sounds like a reference to the cantor's interest in such fringe instruments as lute-harpsichords or the small, five-string cellos of the *viola da spalla* ('shoulder viola') or 'viola pomposa' kind. Familiarity in the Bach family with instruments never found in the regular symphony orchestra may have been behind Emanuel's mention, in the opening lines of the Obituary, of instrument-makers amongst the greater Bach family. The 'viola pomposa' was said in 1766 to have been invented by his father (*erfunden*: Dok III, 186), although it is not a term he is known ever to have used for an instrument-type that in any case existed before he was born. The reference might be to a kind of violoncello piccolo, an instrument used in some cantatas over the years 1724 and 1725, the year Scheibe entered the University of Leipzig (see above, p. 190). His remark looks like that of an eye-witness to Bach's easily imagined enthusiasms, something any self-appointed aesthetician and university-educated critic such as himself might look down on.

Broadly considered, the quarrels with Scheibe and Ernesti (see below) could well reflect in their different ways a general lowering of expectation for church music and its position in Leipzig and elsewhere. It is significant, for example, that after 1739 fewer payments than previously seem to have been made for special soloists to be brought in for the New Year music (Dok II, 135–6). Congregation numbers too were not what they had been earlier in the century. Consequently, that there were apparently no complaints against Bach in his last decade could mean simply that he and the authorities had settled to a *modus vivendi* of lower expectations generally, that he was free to use music from elsewhere and so to escape into his own interests. These he certainly had: the intense study of canon, fugue and counterpoint, the work on revising and compiling Passions including St John, further work on organ music associated with Advent and Christmas (Seven Fughettas, Canonic Variations, Schübler Chorales) and the final grandiose compilation for the Roman mass. Scheibe probably knew little of Bach's later music, either the popular or the didactic – either that which pointed in the new directions of secular music (concertos, sonatas, burlescas) or that soon to govern higher music-study (counterpoint, fugue, four-part harmonization). He would not guess that contrapuntal studies would bring Bach to the forefront of music study over the next two and a half centuries.

From the 1730s, the reduced significance of sacred music generally in Protestant countries reflected or was affected by the cultural changes now variously labelled Rationalism, Secularism or the Enlightenment, leaving music to blossom gradually in other realms. Even Telemann had the intention, in the 1740s, of giving up composing and devoting his energies to writing treatises on music theory, according to his autobiography in Mattheson 1740. (A copy of one of Telemann's treatises was politely acknowledged by Handel in 1752: HHB, 445.) Bach's intense work in counterpoint was reflecting a view of music as a technical study, and for all we know was expressing his dislike both of newer musical styles and changes in the church's priorities. Irrespective of its potential as both a personal statement and as practical teaching material, however, much of this music was also a typical sign of any mature composer's tendency towards the abstract, the transcendental, and the economy of means whereby what is merely entertaining is stripped away.

CHARACTER, QUARRELS

Of his moral character those might speak who have enjoyed dealings and friendship with him and are witnesses to his honesty [*Redlichkeit*] towards God and his neighbour. (*Obituary*)

Significantly, this sentence, originally the last in the Obituary, refers to 'God and one's neighbour'. It seems from the annotations Bach made to the law book of the Old Testament, *Leviticus*, in his copy of the Calov Bible (see Dok III, 637), that he had a particular interest in scriptural rules and regulations, i.e. in the furtherance of religious practice and custom. While his regular twice-yearly taking of communion after confession, as recorded in the communicants' lists from 1723 to 1749 (Dok II, 124–6), says nothing certain about his personal piety, it would still suggest he observed customs and fulfilled expectations, especially, one might suppose, with advancing age. Belonging to the early 1740s are a remark of admiration for Luther's writings (Dok I, 199) and perhaps the Calov Bible annotations.

Much could be inferred about Bach's understanding of music as a God-given art shared 'with one's neighbour' if the significance of a jotting he made on the titlepage to the first Anna Magdalena Book in 1722 were clear. For in listing the titles of three books by a late Leipzig theologian – 'Against Calvinism', 'School for Christians' and 'Against Melancholy' (*Ante [anti] Calvinismus und Christen Schule item Anti Melancholicum*: Dok I, 268) – he is citing three phrases with particular resonance in the Reformation's general debate about music. To accept music as a God-given art (i.e. music other than the psalm-singing authorized in both Testaments) is Lutheran, not Calvinist; music is an art that contributes to teaching Christian belief and practice; and music has a more general use as 'cure for melancholy'. If this is the significance of the jotting in his young wife's book, the pieces it contains become more than idle music-making: they were to have a confessional legitimacy, be a means of instruction, and offer an occasional consolation.

Even the few letters as they exist hint in various ways at a caring and fond *paterfamilias* and a man with some long-lasting friendships and loyalties. Two extant letters he wrote to Georg Erdmann, his Lüneburg companion and apparently later visitor to the Bachs in Weimar (Dok I, 68), imply something of this kind, and the *Menuet fair par Mons. Böhm* in the Anna Magdalena Book of 1725 might, one would like to think, be another sign of sustained friendship with an early acquaintance, and one connected with Thuringia. Likewise, he seems to have been loyal to certain organ-builders, to other instrument-makers and to several relations with whom he must have corresponded. On the other hand, it is unlikely either that he remained close to his brothers and sister, or that it was unusual for a teacher to be closer to pupils than relations. When a (live-in?) student like Georg Schwanberg stood in at the hasty baptism of Regina Johanna in 1728 with two of Bach's sisters-in-law, and also wrote the titlepage to Anna Magdalena's copy of the solo violin and cello suites, one might guess that he was more than a mere pupil. Other relations of Anna Magdalena who were visiting, playing or studying in Leipzig, including her nephew, brother-in-law, father's half sister and uncle's grandson, were no doubt some of those flitting in and out of the cantor's 'dovecot'. Although godparenting did not in itself indicate close friendship as much as it often did later, nevertheless Anna Magdalena's frequent taking on of this office (including her first 'step granddaughter' in 1747) and her diligent finding of godparents for her own children, suggest a good circle of acquaintances.

In the case of Bach's own family, no-one can have much idea how he took the deaths of so many children, including his first child with Anna Magdalena, who was then twenty-four years old. Others of her children died very soon, at the ages of a few days, or at one, three, and four years, but how unexpectedly no-one knows. Three months after Sebastian's own death, she petitioned on behalf of five of her children as having no guardian, changing this a few days later to four (Dok II, 488–9), probably because Gottfried, then twenty-six years old and with longstanding problems, had gone to his sister Elisabeth in Naumburg. Anna Magdalena herself was to die aged fifty-eight, Maria Barbara had died at thirty-five.

References to his two grandsons and to the marriage of his daughter (Dok I, 118–9) – strangely, the only wedding of a child ever celebrated in his home – are matched by known personal contacts from Ohrdruf, Mülhausen, Weimar, Weissenfels, Cöthen and elsewhere kept up in Leipzig. Even if colleagues acting as agent for two of the harpsichord partitas in Dresden, Halle, Lüneburg, Wolfenbüttel, Nuremberg and Augsburg[13] were doing it for a commission, the arrangement could only have been made with their approval, through personal contact (they had been visitors to the Leipzig Fair?) or correspondence (evidence that Bach wrote or dictated more letters than Emanuel knew about?). Contact was similarly maintained with J. G. Walther who, apparently seeking support from Bach for his *Lexicon* and for a publication of chorales in 1737, also continued to copy his organ music well after the years they were colleagues of a sort in Weimar. How warm Bach's relations were with individual colleagues in the Thomas School at Leipzig is unknown, but he did set a text by one of them, J. H. Winckler, when the renovated building was dedicated on 5 June 1732.

As for traditional family duties, standing godfather to his daughter Elisabeth's first-born in October 1749 is only one instance, and it might have seemed as odd to him as to us that he had so few grandchildren when he died: only Emanuel's three children. (Elisabeth's son Johann Sebastian had died at two weeks.) Amongst the many unknowns are how Bach would take the suicide of the school's assistant principal (conrector) in January 1742, or how the Prussian invasion of Leipzig and the major destruction at Dresden in 1745 affected him, as at least the first of these seems to have done (Dok I, 118). How his daily life was with respect to so many children is another huge area tempting any parent's speculations. Capellmeister G. H. Stölzel, speaking in 1739 of his own family of ten children, said that it was easy to imagine how much time their upbringing and general care cost him (1740, 346–7). In general, the romantic picture of Bach as a hard-working, demanding, solicitous but urbane family man who enjoyed his family, boisterous gatherings, with music, tomfoolery and drink, might not be far from the truth.

If Bach's un-docile responses to criticism and to the machinations of those around him now appear aggressive, truculent or at the very least self-protective, a positive interpretation would be that however naturally

---

[13] C. Petzold, J. G. Ziegler, Georg Böhm, Georg Schwanenberger, Gabriel Fischer and J. M. Roth respectively.

irascible or simply impatient he was, any problem he perceived got in the way of his musical priorities. Whatever hindered his creative duty would not be tolerated. Any apparent territoriality and any questionable behaviour around job-applications or money-matters were not at all outside conventional practice, though no doubt they are revealing. For a young musician simple ambition, as when he left Mühlhausen after only a year and before seeing through the organ-project, was not unreasonable, and to counter the usual adulation of J. S. Bach today by accusing him of an 'unmistakable harsh edge ... famously confrontational ... a pervasive sense of persecution and an attitude of spiteful defiance' (Marshall 2000, 502), would be an exaggeration in the other direction. Rather, he could simply have found that, unlike the Weimar duke or the Cöthen prince, his church and school superiors in Leipzig stood in the way of his work as a creative musician. Hence Emanuel describing (hearing him say?) how well his art had been appreciated in different ways in those two previous appointments.

Six particular moments of contention during his Leipzig years, known from documents and quite possibly indicative of others not documented, deserve attention. Some were more serious than others:

September 1723 and later: he already claims from the university the right, as Thomascantor, to direct music at a certain number of traditional services each year, for a fee. On being allowed only half fee, because the university had instituted newer services and appointed its own director, Bach appealed to the elector (king) in Dresden three times in late 1725, the third time on 31 December in the longest letter he is known ever to have written. Only in January 1726 did he have a ruling in his favour and only as regards the fee, not authority over the university's newer services.

Good Friday 1724: seeming (disingenuously?) to be unaware that it was the turn of the Nicholaikirche to have the great Passion performance (St John) this year, his first in Leipzig, Bach had a notice printed advertising the Thomaskirche. On being compelled to re-advertise, insisted that the gallery and harpsichord of the Nikolaikirche be improved. Next year, revived the work for Thomaskirche.

October 1727: against the objections of the then university organist, a paid commission to Bach went ahead for supplying and performing the Funeral Ode for the late Electress Christiane Eberhardine, text by the university professor Gottsched (Cantata 198). The composer directed the performance from the harpsichord, on 17 October. (In the Roman Catholic court of Saxony, the Electress had remained Lutheran.)

September 1728: complained that the Nikolaikirche subdeacon (a) chose hymns for vespers (a right of the cantor), and that (b) the hymns were not according to traditional practice but a novelty (*Neuerung*: Dok I, 55) and too long. Outcome unclear; probably against the subdeacon ultimately.

August 1730: reproached by the main town council (under the two consuls and burgomaster) for dismissing a chorister, being absent without leave, failing to teach (i.e. in some or all of the seven hours musical instruction scheduled per week) or supervise his substitute (all this without offering an explanation), failing to take a singing class, showing little pleasure in work, and generally being *incorrigibel* (Dok II, 205–6). Some payment to be withheld. A few weeks later, but before writing to Erdmann (see above, p. 274), he was denied additional payment for temporary extra duties but applied again the following year or so, despite having had no known extra duties (Dok II, 207, 222).

November 1734, criticized again for not teaching.

August 1736: a long, bitter quarrel began with the new rector, J. A. Ernesti, over who had the right to appoint the choir prefect. Documents show Bach appealing in turn to the rector, the council, the consistory and the king, none with clear success; they also suggest that since his authority had been questioned in this way, he had found difficulty with discipline in the school and the choir. The king may have ruled in his favour: he named him Court composer three months later and was greeted with a cantata on a visit to Leipzig in April 1738 (the lost BWV Anh.I 13, for which, as on similar occasions, Bach was paid handsomely).

The very length of the letter of 31 December 1725 is witness to strong feelings and a willingness, even a compulsion, to divert his creative drive into making a case for himself. The points are detailed, especially concerning small amounts of money that were surely of marginal interest to the king's ministers. But note: although all these arguments were largely about territory, which affected both the cantor's status and his income, and although they do say something about his personal relationships in church and school, none was about avoiding work as a composer – on the contrary.

Just as there may have been inter-clergy quarrels in Mühlhausen that would affect a young organist, so the seasoned cantor in Leipzig would not be helped in his work by the various tense and documented relations between superintendent, rector and town council over authority in the school and church. Any resistance to but also support for him amongst the various men in authority were as much due to pre-existing tensions in their respective spheres of influence – i.e. who expected what of their municipal *director musices* – as to any behaviour of his own. Nevertheless, it seems unlikely that Bach patiently suffered anything much, and his treatment by the university seems to have left him particularly aggrieved. So it did Kuhnau in 1710, though he at least did not have to appeal to the municipality for equipment (more instruments) as Kuhnau did in 1704 and 1709, since presumably players now largely used their own.

Several details in the first of the arguments listed above do seem to say something about Bach as cantor and his energy in pursuing something he regarded as unjust. First, to support his claim, he approached (or had someone approach) the surviving widows of his two predecessors, Schelle and Kuhnau, and obtained from them statements in support of his claim that the university service was something traditionally within the cantor's purview. (Anna Magdalena invoked the same predecessors in 1750 when asking for the widow's allowance of six months' salary.) Presumably he knew that Kuhnau had tried without much success to prevent the university, of which he was a graduate, from having its own music director, and it rather looks as if the university took the opportunity of Kuhnau's death to do what it had long intended. Bach used the two widows' testimony on his third approach to the king, which was more detailed in support of the claim, and copied out by someone else above his signature (at least for the letter now in the Leipzig University Archive: Dok I, 34–41). He also visited Dresden in September 1725 a few days after writing one of the letters to the king, and on the new Silbermann organ in the Sophienkirche (next to the royal palace) played a recital which got reported in the syndicated newspapers. Both the recital and its laudatory report – he was 'well-received by the court and town virtuosi' (Dok II, 150) – were surely part of the project to seek royal atttention, even favour.

That Bach's fee-claim was not directed personally against the university's organist J. G. Görner, whose payment might have been reduced accordingly, is clear from continuing good relations between them over the whole Leipzig period, not only professional (Görner became Thomaskirche organist in 1729) but personal, perhaps even close (he became 'trustee of the paternal estate' for the four youngest children in 1750: Dok II, 497). If the cantor's income was lower than he had been led to believe, it was not because of Görner's hardly coincidental appointment as *director musices* to the university just before Bach took up office. The situation is easy to understand. On the one hand, the university had a history of manoeuvering its church music away from the municipal cantor, who had traditionally appointed its precentor, and of turning to clever young people (J. F. Fasch in Kuhnau's time). On the other, since the university, the largest in Germany, had every right to provide more church services for its community if they were called for, and was in any case not always in agreement with the town councils, it was reasonable for it to look for someone with fewer commitments than the Thomascantor's.

Future research may show how far this series of quarrels exceeds others of the time involving senior cantors. Such criticism as there was of Telemann in Hamburg concerns his neglect not only of teaching in the Johanneum school but of the choral music at Saturday vespers (Kremer 1995, 296), and the latter complaint is not one found in Leipzig, so far as is known. At least in Bach's case, some exceptionally beautiful music resulted in the cantata of 1727 for the late queen: a work for an especially grand event, approved by the king and one in which, for once, the cantor and all the authorities of town, university and church participated. In view of the two celebratory *dramme per musica* for two university professors, BWV 205 (August 1725) and 207 (December 1726), there does seem to have been an attempt over this period to provide quite splendid music for extra-liturgical events involving university people, and all three cantatas, especially with the rattling opening to No. 205 and the First Brandenburg's opening of No. 207, gave listeners very new musical experiences. They had heard nothing like them before. In another respect too the memorial music for the queen is notable: it is the only cantata of which the dates of composition are known more or less exactly, from about the 2nd of October (Dok II, 170) to the 15th.

The contention in 1728 over choosing hymns is significant: although the subdeacon's reasons are not given, organists today trying to maintain artistic standards against obstreperous or trendy clergy can guess what was involved, given Bach's obvious devotion all his life to Luther's texts and the classical hymn-repertory of the pristine Reformation. The very orthodoxy of the texts of chorales used in so many cantatas and selected for organ-preludes in Clavierübung III begins to look like a deliberate gesture, for the composer surely knew that the Thomaskirche was originally a church of the Augustinian order to which Luther had belonged and where he had famously preached. Augustine and Luther: Fathers of the pristine and reformed Church respectively.

With respect to the school-board's complaint, quarrels between a school-rector and the cantor must have been common enough for one cantor at the time to publish a book in 1706 dealing with the lines of demarcation and potential problems arising. This is the *Directorium musicum* of J. P. Bendeler in Quedlinburg, author also of a book on organs. In Leipzig, Bach had had sufficiently collegial relations with the former rector to join with him in 1733 in appealing to the consistory court about a parishioner obliged to pay both of them fees for his recent marriage outside Leipzig (Dok I, 75–6). But the new rector, Ernesti, was twenty-two years younger than Bach, so a question is whether the quarrel arose because of a young man standing on his dignity and authority or because an older was resistant to change in his habits. Both, perhaps. Bach had already been criticized for lapses in school duties during the process to appoint Ernesti in 1734, and the new rector was soon complaining that Bach did not rehearse the boys enough (Dok II, 252, 265). This might suggest that he was expected to rehearse the treble parts of the forthcoming cantatas during school singing-classes, also that the school rector monitored standards in the service.

The Ernesti situation was especially bad, carried on through the ruling town council, dragging on for months and still being reported on forty years later (Dok III, 314). Both contestants made clear that there was a total breakdown of personal relations, especially the young rector, who devoted a great deal of (school) time, energy and rhetorical literacy to put his case that:

Bach failed to defer to him over appointing prefects, as regulations say he must.
He twice caused commotion in church by chasing away the prefect he had not wanted.
He is insubordinate.
He thinks it beneath his dignity to direct wedding-music if this consists only of hymns.

Bach answers the various points more succinctly and straighforwardly:

The cantor has always chosen the prefects, since they must be competent in their musical duties.
The rector refuses to back down despite the cantor's 'amicable representation' (*gütliche Vorstellung*).
Resolution is needed for the sake of future cantors and peace in the school.

The unembellished directness of Bach's answer could alone have irritated the young rector, for again he indulged again in lengthy, elegant, quasi-objective prose to complain that:

Bach's account is neither complete nor truthful (*wahrhaftig*: Dok II, 274ff).
He had intended and wished (*intention gehabt und gewünschet*) the replacement prefect to make a mistake.

So Bach is stubborn, insubordinate, devious, untruthful, vindictive and malicious. His defence, in the course of four letters that must have occupied much of his time during August 1736, is to ask the consistory court for protection so that he can get on with his duties.

Whether it was for royal support in the quarrel that Bach was drawn to Dresden in the autumn of 1736, or for a superior job at court itself, or because he admired Dresden's immeasurably higher musical and cultural importance, is not known. Nor is the degree to which Ernesti's complaints were prompted by petty resentment at a subordinate who had friends in high places and was insufficiently deferential to a younger, recently promoted superior, one who had been a student not long before and was still not yet thirty. If the quarrel gradually subsided, we can be sure it was not forgotten. How soon their relations had deteriorated after 1734 when Ernesti had replaced Rector Gesner – the Gesner who had published such praises of Bach – is not clear: neither the performance of a cantata to welcome the new apppointee in 1734 nor his standing godfather to Johann Christian Bach in September 1735 need indicate much. Besides, the questions of who the prefect was, and how musically able he was, mattered to a cantor who had to use the prefect for duties in the lesser churches, and who during the 1720s had had a series of gifted young musicians to call on.

The situation is not difficult to imagine: school, church and town authorities could not act as despotically as a prince but could take other steps to make life hard for an insufficiently humble composer who wanted to be left alone to do his job. Besides, the various authorities had their own little internecine tensions over spheres of influence in such things as the formal installation of school officers. For Bach, one response would be to tend to neglect official duties, and there are hints of this ever after the Ernesti quarrel, as indeed earlier. Today, a Master of Cathedral Music, sooner or later vexed by clergy or choir-school heads, might well react by becoming even more devoted to his art and its higher calling. Although one can easily believe that in Leipzig the fault was not all on one side, it may say something about Bach that no details of any big quarrel between himself as cantor and his assisting organists have emerged, i.e. a quarrel of the kind that did sometimes occur in the bigger German churches (see Edler 1982, 98ff).

It must have been an aggravation for Bach that during the late 1730s he was also criticized as a composer (the Scheibe review) and met with objections against his perhaps proudest creations, the big Passion performances (see above, p. 200). His clear irritation at the latter could alone account for any declining productivity in his last decade as cantor, just as the temporary giving up of the Collegium concerts in the spring or summer of 1737 may have been in the aftermath of the Ernesti quarrel. Depression, tension, strain? Working on the Goldberg Variations and WTC2 in the years around 1740, and through them concentrating his thoughts on complex counterpoint for keyboard and on virtuoso music-making, none of which had much to do with the church and its activities, does look like a deliberate turn in other directions. It matched the respect in which he was held by professional musicians, including those 'of the first rank' and those who would call on him and 'let themselves be heard by him' when travelling through Leipzig, according to Emanuel (Dok III, 255).

Over these years, the occasional use in the Thomaskirche of music by Handel and Frederick the Great's capellmeister C. H. Graun could be seen as another way to give people what they want. How deeply Bach actually admired their music is impossible to say. It is true that Emanuel told Forkel of his father's admiration for composers of his own generation, Fux, Caldara, Handel, Keiser, Hasse, J. G. and C. H. Graun, Telemann, Zelenka, Benda 'and generally everything that was especially valued in Berlin and Dresden' (Dok III, 289), but all these names were commonly mentioned in German writings, and there are many others not mentioned whose music was copied by Bach and his assistants. Though today Emanuel's list is often repeated *tout court*, it smacks of the names that his correspondent Forkel, a music historian, would have regarded as most prominent in the 1730s and 40s, composers that would naturally have been admired by his discerning hero J. S. Bach. The Obituary itself prefers to say more about Buxtehude and Reinken, the classics of his youth as an organist, and only twenty years after the Obituary does Emanuel propose his more up-to-date list and so pointedly refer to the two German centres of fashion in instrumental and vocal music, Berlin and Dresden. Certainly any generous composer would find qualities to admire in those named, but little useful can be built on Emanuel's remark, who may not even have known about his father's work on Palestrina and other composers of non-German vocal music.

In saying so little about Leipzig, the Obituary does give the impression of a falling-off in the composer's commitment to the job, and this is borne out by there being so little known of new cantatas over the last fifteen years or so. A sign of his being aware of the kind of music people wanted are the various copies of music by other composers (see p. 237), and in this connection, it is an interesting that his copy of a trio by J. G. Graun (BJ 1988, 48) might have been made for the same occasion as the Peasant Cantata in 1742, i.e. an occasion requiring light, bright music for a public out of church. Yet performances of both Passions were also probably prepared again in his final years. One easily imagines that his creative energy *ad gloriam dei* was irrepressible, despite the many vexations with which he was incapable of dealing supinely.

In general, how sociable Bach was, even how warm his professional contacts were, cannot be established from hard evidence. The marked similarity between his musical handwriting and that of almost all the copyists who worked for him (including Anna Magdalena) must indicate strength of personality, but of what kind? – inspiring anxious respect or warm loyalty? Both? On his death, wife, son-in-law, four sons and possibly student-helpers rallied round to preserve the fund of cantatas, and there was certainly a sense of extended family around him, though only a chance reference or two is witness to the various visitors to the home, as when Anna Magdalena's aunt stayed with them in 1742 (BJ 1987, 171). As for friendly acquaintances the Bachs had: only from occasional documents can it be guessed what these were – documents such as a surviving book-inscription of *c.* 1742 implying that Anna Magdalena was close to the daughter of well-to-do neighbours in the Thomaskirche courtyard (BJ 1997, 152), a friend who had been godmother to two of her children. Class distinctions being what they were, it is unsurprising that there is little record of any of the Bachs being closely acquainted with amateur musicians in the university's professorial circles – musicians such as Luise Gottsched, poet, keen lutenist and harpsichordist. But one can not be sure.

In the letter Johann Elias Bach wrote to Sebastian on taking up a teaching position elsewhere in 1742 one can read considerable warmth, as when he promises not to forget 'the many blessings' he had enjoyed while being a member of the household and in-house teacher for the youngest children (Dok II, 403). J. P. Kirnberger was later quoted as witnessing Bach's great encouragement of gifted students (Dok III, p. 524), some of whom certainly stayed in contact with him. J. G. Ziegler, who came to Bach in Weimar already after studying elsewhere, not only had some of his teacher's later harpsichord partitas for sale but was himself probably the engraver of Nos. 3–6. Other ex-pupils of the Thomas School seem to have continued to work as copyists for Bach, such as S. G. Heder for the 1736 revival of the St Matthew Passion. That the loyalty of students can also be inspired by a teacher's exceptional talents is clear from various reports of his playing, including one about his skill in playing full-voiced continuo published as late as 1808 by J. C. Kittel, who must have been speaking of the late 1740s.

Loyalty can also be inspired by sheer, boisterous personality, and there are hints that Sebastian was not above earthy and even coarse behaviour throughout his life. Perhaps that is why Emanuel did not care for anecdotes of the *Zippelfagottist* kind at Arnstadt, for example, or the reputed remark about Emanuel's own music, 'it's Prussian blue, it fades' (*verschiesst*: Dok III, 518). Not to his credit is the outrageous pun *Dreckohr*, 'shit ear', reportedly for the anti-musical *Rector* of Freiberg in late 1749, nor his interference in the Schröter review, nor his denial of this only two months before his death (Dok I, 122, 124), events which had involved two or three other reputable people. His calling the big organ in Görlitz a 'horse-organ, because it needs the effort of a steed to play it', according to the organ-builder J. A. Silbermann in *c.* 1741 (*PferdsOrgel, rossmässige Arbeit*: Dok II, 389) was probably less offensive: 'horse-work' was not a rare term and had been used by Mattheson to describe the job of playing the big string bass during a long opera (1713, 286). Whether Bach had actually travelled to Görlitz and played the unique organ there is undocumented, but such opinions about this organ as there were at the time (see Flade 1926, 10) gained authority by being attributed to the Leipzig cantor. The Görlitz organist, D. Nikolai, was another former student, and if Bach did visit the town, which is some distance from Leipzig, so he might have travelled around Saxony and Thuringia more than is now recorded.

Given how much detail of his father's activities Emanuel could have given to fill out the picture of a self-dependent composer, his silences may have another reason: Bach had latterly become a lone master. Special musical challenges, such as not only creating the counterpoint of the Art of Fugue but making sure it remained playable by two hands on a keyboard, must have taken even Johann Sebastian Bach a great deal of time, with meticulous work, bar by bar, piece by piece, with no short cuts. The gestation of the two big works of the final decade, the Art of Fugue and the B minor Mass, took time not least because there were no antecedents the composer could draw on for models. The seclusion necessary for such work was not only physical but spiritual, for this musical world had not been penetrated before, unlike Handel's more or less static fund of regurgitated musical ideas. The recherché nature of much of what Bach wrote in his later years is easy to imagine as the work of a recluse, actual or, at the very least, potential.

'THEORETICAL SPECULATIONS'

Indeed, our late Bach did not involve himself in deep, theoretical speculations [*Betrachtungen*] of music but was all the stronger in the doing of it. (*Obituary*)

Although Emanuel later said this remark had been added by the Obituary's publisher Lorenz Mizler and is 'not worth much', he too observed elsewhere that his father was 'no lover of dry, mathematical rubbish' (*Zeuge*: Dok III,

288). This rather goes with other signs of reticence on the composer's part, as in supplying no biography when asked, or publishing collections of music without the kind of preface familiar in recent volumes like Kauffmann's chorales, 1733 or Maichelbeck's sonatas, 1736. Such reticence could be a form of pride, and his extant letters, more than faintly macaronic and less oily than Rector Ernesti's, seem to betray something else – diffidence, a lack of fluency, a limited practice in writing. Or, such verbose writing (mostly in Latin and Hebrew) as Kuhnau's preface to a book of cantata-texts in 1709–10 was not something he admired.

In 1738 Mizler, a former pupil, founded a Corresponding Society of Musical Sciences (*Societät der musikalischen Wissenschaften*), a scattered group of musicians corresponding or exchanging letters on matters of theory or 'musical science', and this society Bach eventually joined in 1747 as fourteenth member. The 'deep theoretical speculations' of which Mizler was speaking concerned music as part of philosophical learning, the subject of his own graduate dissertation first published in Leipzig in 1734, predictably dedicated to Mattheson as well as to Bach, and apparently not faultless in its Latin. Mizler knew that Bach's predecessor Kuhnau had written Latin treatises, unpublished, on the difference between ancient and modern music, and made a point of praising other members of his society for their contributions of this kind (in Mizler 1745). His remark, at the end of the Obituary he was publishing and had probably invited, reads like an apology to the society's members for Bach not having contributed learned essays for their perusal. Yet Mizler's notion of 'philosophy' and his preoccupation with the 'mathematical grounds for composition' had aroused even Mattheson's scepticism (see Dok II, 380), and it is highly unlikely that other invited members, such as Handel and C. H. Graun, spent any more time on Pythagoras and Ptolemy than did J. S. Bach.

On the other hand, open letters on musical arcana apparently written by Handel, Krieger and many others had been regularly published by Mattheson in his earlier *Critica musica*, a music journal of sorts which likewise never numbered J. S. Bach amongst its contributors. Emanuel's description of his father as being 'too busy for the most necessary correspondence' (Dok III, 290) could be an oblique reference not to ordinary letters but specifically to this kind of *Correspondenz* in the musical periodicals published by Mattheson and Mizler. Ordinary business letters must have got written as well as dictated, and many an event in his life and many a personal contact could only have been arranged by mail, even though he could not, as Emanuel goes on to say, engage in lengthy written discussion.

Mizler had already mentioned in print Handel's refusal of an honorary doctorate at Oxford (HHB, 396, 376), an honour unknown in Germany, and had done so when Handel was named honorary member of his corresponding society in 1745. Can this have been an incentive for Bach to join when his former pupil approached him, or re-approached him, in 1747? Or perhaps he had delayed because of having a quite different idea of 'deep theoretical speculation'. For clearly, deep contemplation is necessary for the fugues, canons, complex harmonies and meticulous style-allusion in Bach's music, from his first works to his last. But – to take a particular example – he could well have openly shunned textbook calculations of interval ratios and the like while at the same time contemplating for himself the nature of music's notes and how they can be made to behave. The Art of Fugue and the Goldberg Variations are a 'theoretical speculation' quite as much as they are a 'doing of music', to use Mizler's words, and served to inspire admirers such as Marpurg, Kirnberger and Kittel to write their own theory-books later. Hence, perhaps, Emanuel's criticism of Mizler's remark.

It is possible that Bach consciously gave an impression of being unlearned before a certain kind of pedant. This is something that crops up elsewhere in the history of music, as when in 1638 the philologist G. B. Doni remarked that Frescobaldi did not know a major from a minor semitone (Gallico 1986, 187–8) or that Monteverdi showed 'little understanding' when he, Doni, tried to arouse his interest in micro-tunings (Palisca 1994, 487). For Monteverdi, Frescobaldi and J. S. Bach all to be judged guilty, there must be something wrong with the judges. Mizler could well have been one of those not ungifted people, still to be met with, who dabble in several disciplines – in his case, music, music theory, theology, philosophy, medicine, law, rhetoric, physics, mathematics, even translating and publishing – but somehow never quite achieve a genuine, mainline musicianship. When Bach did join Mizler's society, his contribution – part of the annual offering each member was supposed to make – was not learned essays but music of a flatteringly 'scientific' character: the Canonic Variations (probably first published in late 1747, before a MS score was sent to Mizler), also the six-part Canon BWV 1076 (one of those added by hand to the composer's own copy of the Goldbergs). Perhaps the Art of Fugue canons would also have been submitted in yearly instalments had he remained a member for longer, or indeed the whole work as and when it was finished.

If Bach was aware of his Leipzig predecessor's writings in Mattheson's *Critica musica* two or three decades earlier, his own inactivity could be explained in various ways: he had no literary pretensions or time or confidence to participate, or (a strong possibility) that he did not care for such things. Emanuel claimed that his father found only 'a dry kind of counter-point' (Dok III, 289) in such books as Fux's *Gradus ad parnassum*, of which he owned a copy and may even have had bound to conserve it (see Dok I, 270). Presumably it was 'dry' in its step-by-step demonstration of how to combine notes and treat intervals, all in the language of a much earlier gen-eration. If Bach said so openly, it would explain why Mizler did not dedi-cate his translation of Fux's celebrated book to him when he published it in Leipzig in 1742. Otherwise, such a dedication would be expected, con-sidering not only Bach's position as *director musices lipsiensis* but his inter-est at that time, some of it published, in the very counterpoint in *stile antico* that Fux was laying down.

That Bach was not acknowledged in three important and relevant musical publications produced in Leipzig, by Kauffmann, Sperontes and Mizler, does make one wonder why. There is also the question why he made no use of Fux (if that is what Emanuel means) with his own students, when later on Haydn, Mozart and Beethoven did: because in being closer in date and musical language to composers of 1740, Fuxian counterpoint seemed more restrictive than it was to do half a century later?

1738 to 1742 was the period both when Mizler gave lectures on Fux's trea-tise in the university and when Bach, whom one does not easily imagine attending lectures, took on two other productive students, J. F. Agricola and J. P. Kirnberger. All three became noted for writing books, mostly after 1750, and all three might just be relaying what they had been taught. Two books, Agricola's own copy of the Fux and Kirnberger's treatise *Die Kunst des reinen Satzes* (1771), include some identical realizations of chord-progressions in five parts – showing how to avoid doubled dissonances when one increases the number of parts above four – and which Kirnberger attributes to Bach (KB VIII/3). The likelier that these do represent Bach's teaching, the clearer it is that he was concerned with practical problems of everyday composition and harmonization. Certainly Kirnberger's methods for harmonizing chorales, creating organ-settings (including canons) and composing chromatic fugues could have come straight from his own expe-riences as a student in Leipzig. These are all relatively lively arts: if Bach did also at some point make a copy of Angelo Berardi's three-part treatise *Documenti armonici* (Bologna, 1687), as later claimed (see Beisswenger 1992, 341), its treatment of the rules must have seemed by comparison to produce only the old 'dry kind of counterpoint'.

Though not strictly speculative theory, the many instances that can be found of numbers 14 (= Bach), 41 (= J. S. Bach) and 158 (= Johann Sebastian Bach) – the number of bars in a section or piece, or its number of notes, or even its number of movements – have suggested to some that Bach had an interest in such things, knowing them from writings of Werckmeister and others (see Power 2001). In the preface to his *Muscalische Vorstellung* or 'Biblical Stories' of 1700, Kuhnau referred to 'a certain author' not by name but by an 'algebraic problem', i.e. a simple code in which the letter A in his name was 1, B was 2, and so on. How many such instances now discovered in the music of Bach are likely to be conscious, where and for what reason, are all open questions and just now and then important. For instance, the Fourteen Canons attached to the Goldberg Variations could be a self-reference, one not inappropriate to an arcane genre like monothematic canons. Other number-references can be found, such as ten entries for the melody of the Ten Commandments chorale in Cantata 77 or the many threes in Clavierübung III, and references to the notes B A C H (qv) have been heard in more than the late Canonic Variations and Art of Fugue. Supposed examples of Divine Proportion or Golden Section (qv) in cantata movements are matched by supposed gematria (qv) in the works for solo violin and a good deal else. Just occasionally there appears an incontrovertible Divine Proportion, as in the three sections of the E flat Fugue for organ; there, the bar-numbers 36:45:36 can reveal various arithmetical patterns, including the ratio 72:45 (1.61:1, the Golden Section). But if deliberate, this would only resemble the proportions between the three movements of the Italian Concerto (see p. 314), a musical matter, a practical organization unnecessarily associated with deep symbols of any kind.

In general, several points need to be borne in mind when considering arcane elements and allusive structures. First, the desire to prove that they are not imaginary or accidental will lead inevitably to further conjecture about their supposed purpose. The problem with this is that there is no verifiable limit to such conjecture, only common sense. Secondly, hypotheses ought also to account for both the negative (are Golden Sections discernible in other music of Bach? if not, why not?) and the comparative (what music by other composers can be interpreted in the same way? What other numbers are operating?). Without such backing, a hypothesis stands on a single shaky leg. Thirdly, most numbers involve simple musical events and are merely reminders of words or images already present, and in effect merely point to some particular detail. Such verifiable number-references as *ten* in Cantata 77 are simple allusions, not subtle tokens of confessional hermeticism or personal psychology – or even 'word-painting', since none of the ten entries pictures the corresponding commandment. Rather than a sign of 'deep, theoretical speculation', they are the work of a composer 'all the stronger in the doing of' music itself, as the Obituary said.

There is an irony in Mizler's remark heading this section: although it is a gratuitous addition and was not thought much of by Emanuel, without Bach's membership of this society there might not have been an Obituary.

TUNING AND TEMPERAMENT

He knew how to give harpsichords so pure and correct a temperament in their tuning that all keys sounded beautiful and pleasing. (*Obituary*)

When it comes to the technical matter of temperaments, the Obituary makes no claim that Bach engaged in 'theoretical speculation' about it, as it surely would have done if he had, but to its practice. He tuned harpsichords to sound pleasing. Despite a variety of opinions confidently expressed over the centuries, there remains nothing quite certain about what exactly the temperament was the Obituary was referring to, how long Bach had desired or practised any particular form of it, and how it changed (as it surely had) during his lifetime. What is more certain is that the Obituary authors, his pupils, were dominated – even misled – by what was to be music's great manual of instruction, The Well-tempered Clavier.

Frequently referred to in performance-practice studies today, the Obituary's remark matches a little too closely the tastes of the later eighteenth century to be taken at face value. The earlier situation is more elusive, since the WTC is so exceptional: after all, roughly contemporary with the original Book 1 had been sets of Inventions that still did not use all twenty-four keys, only fifteen. (Significantly, perhaps, the piece associated with Friedemann's audition in the Sophienkirche is in G major, a good key on a Silbermann organ.) Musicians after 1750, despite what was in some ways their more limited harmonic range, wanted to be able to play in any key at any time especially on the new pianos, whose tone-production, being less immediate than the harpsichord's and less sustained than the organ's, made equal temperament less and less objectionable. G. A. Sorge's report that Bach did not like the 'four bad triads' of earlier temperaments dates from 1748 (major triads of F sharp, A flat, B and C sharp: see Dok II, 450) and says nothing about his earlier practice, though it does suggest they had discussed it. Sorge was an early example of the tuning enthusiast who likes to involve Bach in his own theories.

With the word 'harpsichords', *Clavicymbale*, the Obituary seems to be visualizing the composer tuning the instruments in everyday use, for practising, composing, teaching, playing. Not only were the big church organs more the concern of professional builders, and much less often tuned, but they retained older temperaments for much longer and, requiring far fewer than twenty-four keys, had no need to be up-to-date. For playing continuo with only a soft stop or two, organists must long have tolerated awkward keys or learnt to cope with them by avoiding the well-known unpleasant intervals they would otherwise have found in Cantatas 106 and 71. It is striking how many moments in the newer keys of E flat, A flat, F minor, C minor and B minor there are in these early works. Even in 1739, a sign of the modern aspirations of the organ-volume Clavierübung III was that it began and ended in E flat major, a 'beautiful, majestic key' not in the 'head and fingers' of most organists, according to Mattheson (speaking of Hamburg? – 1731, 244). Clavierübung III also contained chorale-settings in F sharp minor and F minor, but they did not absolutely require organ (they have no pedal part) and suit the harpsichord well. Hence, indeed, their use of these keys?

It is possible, on the other hand, that a rank or two of pipes in the Thomaskirche organ, such as the Stopped Diapason or *Gedackt* in the chair organ, were tuned close to equal temperament for the remote keys the organist needed when accompanying cantatas from a transposed part. At least since Kuhnau's time, the organ-part had had to be written out a tone lower than the other parts, to make up for its high pitch. But because this means that it had to accompany in D flat a cantata movement notated in E flat, either standards of performance made it a moot point or the tuning allowed for it, i.e. a stop or two could have been appropriately tuned. Larger organs often included a stop at lower pitch,[14] and to include one instead in equal or near-equal temperament was just as feasible, in fact more so.

The unequal temperament of most organs, impossible to miss because of the sustained tone, was not necessarily a disadvantage. On the contrary, it gave piquancy to an early chorale in F minor in the Orgelbüchlein, *c.* 1714 ('Ich ruf zu dir', significantly with the thinnest texture in the book), as it also brought a sense of excitement to modulations in the bigger preludes. Nor should it be forgotten that the traditional associations of a key, reflected in the usual old tunings, gave even the Art of Fugue an important allusion: its D minor recalls the 'first key' of so many collections of seventeenth-century keyboard pieces (*tonus primus, le premier ton*) and should have a relaxed character, distinct from the keys either side of it used over the next centuries for very different music, in C minor ('pathetic, tragic') or E minor ('elegaic, wistful').

---

[14] This may have been what the examiners had requested at Halle (see p. 309). When the builder promised to introduce chamber pitch, he can only have intended this for a stop or two, for purposes of continuo.

If one assumes tunings of the day allowed keys to keep characteristics, certain distinctions become clearer in other respects too. The familiar modern key of G major with strong dominants is found in the harpsichord toccatas, suites, and Goldberg Variations; but the older key of G mixolydian, which tends towards the subdominant (fewer F-sharps), is found in many an organ chorale. When appropriate, these distinctions were observed between different musical genres. For example, it is quite in the nature of Bach's conception of chorale-settings to distinguish between the chorale for Trinity, 'Allein Gott' BWV 676 (clear diatonic G major) and that for Ten Commandments, 'Dies sind' BWV 678 (modal G of the original chorale).

Other keys have certain characteristics of a technical kind rather than aesthetic. Thus E minor often gives the impression of avoiding or being discreet about its its dominant B major,with a sharp third and flat fifth. Movements in A minor modulating to the dominant E, do so *via* an aeolian cadence F–E not *via* B major, and movements in E minor always end with a major chord even as Picardy thirds were declining.[15] F major has certain modal characteristics mentioned below (p. 363). In the mid-1730s, the composer seems to have been fond of *affektvoll* B minor arias in 2/4 time. In full ensemble music, instruments and therefore the voices will naturally observe sufficient differences between keys as to impart a distinct character to each. It is surely so that the St Matthew Passion does not travel through its array of keys – major, minor, sharp, flat (G sharp minor when Jesus is betrayed) – only to have them sound all exactly the same only a little higher or lower.

Several questions are raised by the Well-tempered Clavier, in particular Book 1. Three common views are, or have been, that Bach intended equal temperament; that he did not intend it; and that whichever this was, he wrote the WTC as vindication of it. Although in German theory 'well-tempered' was not identical to 'equal tempered', by the 1720s it could have implied this in the context of a set of pieces in all the keys, assuming that 100% equality is practical. On the other hand, well-tempered could mean a tuning system in which keys are all tolerable, but different and distinctive. Many writers since have reproduced such systems, arguing that in an unequal temperament Bach allows for the less sweet keys by tactfully underplaying any awkward harmonies. But since (i) some pieces were transposed for the collection and (ii) notation does not necessarily indicate how sustained the harmonies are, neither argument is reliable.

---

[15] If E minor is the original key of Cantata 4, keyboardists today playing a minor final chord for the continuo aria (BWV 4.vi) are contradicting this tradition.

Behind many arguments is a ruling assumption: that a single tuning was intended and that each book is a set or cycle of pieces to be played as such in the given order, and that its very title is evidence for this. Recognizing the oddity of pieces rising by semitones, some interpreters change to a more reasoned order, for instance by dominants. But today's habit of playing 'complete works' in concerts is not relevant to a group of pieces assembled for reasons best known to an habitual collector – reasons including the teaching of young players and composers in all the keys. For all one knows to the contrary, the intention in the Well-tempered Clavier could have been for the player to tune for each key as it was studied, something not requiring great skill. That no individual piece in WTC modulates very far means that no key needs to be tuned except for the piece concerned, even if theorists, who have no thought of playing all twenty-four in sequence, do not say so. The very order – major, minor, then up by a semitone – is not musically logical, nor does it make a true cycle, more a filling-in of the partial orders already familiar to composers, whose sets of pieces likewise were not cycles.

There is also some difficulty in believing that temperament was of vital importance to J. S. Bach, for is it not probable that like any composer he was more interested in the differences between major and minor? The titlepage of Book 1 carefully specifies that all the major and minor keys are present, i.e. all the keys 'both with respect to the major third or C-D-E and as concerns the minor third or D-E-F' (*so wohl* **tertiam majorem** *oder* **Ut Re Mi** *anlangend, als auch* **tertiam minorem** *oder* **Re Mi Fa** *betreffend*). Thus what it says – twice, in words and note-names – is that all the majors and all minors are to be found in the book, not that the semitones are equal or unequal. (The note-names are traditional and might be referring to the title of a local treatise by J. H. Buttstedt, of 1716; see p. 385.) Indeed, one has only to think of the totally different effect and *Affekt* of the two opening preludes – a gentle C major arpeggio with double thirds (two E's), bright and open, then a rushing sound of C minor, darker, sombre, agitated – to suppose that it was the promise of major/minor contrast that was important, not whether C sharp major was much like C major up a semitone.

A recent theory on behalf of WTC1 as a tuning-demonstration is that it indicates the temperament not in its title but in a decorative line at the top of the autograph titlepage (Lehman 2005), i.e. a continuous row of varied curlicues expresses graphically the fifths: three pure, five slightly narrow, and three less narrow. Points in favour of this hypothesis are:

the line, unique on a Bach titlepage, is otherwise puzzling
the size of each curlicue varies as tempered intervals do

dividing the ditonic comma (qv) this way was familiar from Werckmeister's *Orgelprobe* of 1698 and particularly *via* a treatise of 1724, *Sectio*, by J. G. Neidhardt (an acquaintance of J. N. Bach in Jena) instrument-makers relied on wordless lines and yardsticks; why not a composer?

Points against the hypothesis are:

five slighter curlicues appear as letter-ornaments on the titlepage of the first Anna Magdalena Book, also dated 1722, and almost certainly in her hand. (In fact, did she, not the composer, add the curlicues to the WTCI?)

a line of similar curlicues appears on each titlepage of F. Suppig's treatises *Labyrinthus musicus* and *Calculus musicus* of 1722 (see Rasch 1990), with no apparent significance beyond (possibly) expressing the circularity of keys

the WTCI line has to be viewed upside down, but the user is not told this

if a small curving line looking like 'C' does indicate where the note C falls in the series of curlicues,[16] it has to be read the right way up

no other instance is known in copies of WTCI. One early copy (B. C. Kayser, a pupil) has a tuning with fewer curlicues, i. e. Kayser was not alerted to any significance

whether this temperament is implied is hypothetical; others can be inferred

The line might, after all, be a decoration, matching the flourish at the bottom of the page, even a suggestion for an engraver. A related question is whether the book received its title only later as the composer worked further on it. Since both the curlicues and the four words *Das Wohltemperirte Clavier oder* look like additions made after the full titlepage[17] was written, the line, the words and the date might all result from afterthought. The titlepage's 'P' for 'Praeludia und Fugen . . .' is written with a flourish, as if it was the first word of the title, making it possible that just as the Orgelbüchlein's title need say nothing about original intentions, nor need WTCI's.

To return to the Obituary: note that the authors do not mention equal temperament and nor, with their words 'pure and correct' (*rein und richtig*), do they betray any expert grasp of the niceties of tuning, since too much

---

[16] But it could be a flourish on the letter 'C' of 'Clavier' immediately below, like 'C' of 'Concerto' heading the First Brandenburg Concerto in the autograph fair-copy score.

[17] At least, down to the words 'Johann Sebastian Bach' and the flourish. The remaining lines, including the changed date of 1722, look later, such that 'p. t.' represents the composer's Cöthen title 'at the time' the MS was compiled. '1732' added at the end of the MS records some revisions?

hangs on such words. (In post-Renaissance music a 'pure' interval would not be 'correct'.) *Rein* was also Emanuel's description of his father's violin-playing but is equally vague and relates only to tone; presumably his violin fifths were purer than his harpsichord fifths. Kirnberger, another pupil, is also less than fully reliable when he wrote in 1769 that no work of Bach can be put into another key without 'deforming' it (*verunstalten*: Dok III, 201). Did he not know the composer did exactly that with several pieces, both in WTC and elsewhere, and occasionally more than once? More plausible is Emanuel's remark that his father did his own harpsichord tuning and quilling, and did not thank others for doing it (Dok III, 285. Was 'others' Emanuel himself?). Clearly, remarks of this kind aim to fill out the picture of a composer capable and knowledgable in practical matters, as no doubt he was. But it is a picture drawn by a younger generation of composers of whom few, I imagine, could re-leather a piano hammer or would expect to be called upon to do so.

THE TEACHER

In the multiplicity of his song [*mit mannigfaltigem Gesang*], he delighted, taught and moved [*rührte*] young people, women, men, princes, kings and all true con-noisseurs. (*Obituary*)

These words are from the cantata-text at the end of the Obituary by Georg Venzky, another member of Mizler's Society but not a Leipziger. They give its only reference to Bach's teaching, except for the mention of 'not a few fine organists' at Weimar and for Mizler's claim (self-serving?) to have been his pupil in keyboard and composition.

It may be that by 'the multiplicity of his song' Venzky meant more than the multiplicity of sound in his big ensemble works and something closer to 'the sheer scope and variety in the music he composed'. For this scope must have been remarkable to anyone who knew him, and something that could have been said about very few composers. 'Delighted, taught and moved' are thoughtful words: by being delightful and moving, his music instructed listeners in the truths of Scripture and was not meant merely to please their sense of hearing. Venzky, doctor of divinity and school rector in Prenzlau, far from Leipzig, was unlikely to be referring to the teaching of counterpoint or even the playing of organs, though he might have heard Bach at Halle in the 1720s. While such laudatory cantata-texts, like those attached to the other obituaries in Mizler's journal, were by nature vague on the details of their subject's life and work, the generous eulogy-sonnet for Bach written and published six months after he died by fellow musician Telemann already spoke of his students and even of their students (Dok III, 6).

Some of Bach's pupils over the years were probably live-in apprentices, formal or informal, others came as students in various capacities, especially in a university town known for music-making amongst students, whatever their faculty. Actual details of the learning arrangements are rarely clear, though for a prospective cantor being trained in theology at the university, music in some form would be relevant to his studies. Kuhnau had already remarked on how much keyboard and organ-playing there was amongst the professors themselves (Schering 1926, 330). It is equally clear from Bach's many extant testimonials for students, the first only six months after becoming cantor, that he warmly supported their studies and helped conscientiously in their job-applications, rather more than many a teacher does today. The thirty-plus extant testimonials and letters of recommendation are by no means unthinkingly repetitive but tailor-made for the candidate, in this way giving a glimpse of the teacher and his expectations. No doubt more testimonials were written than survive, either in the composer's own hand or merely signed by him.

The Municipal Archive of Plauen, a town some distance from Leipzig, preserves four careful and time-consuming letters written by Bach in 1726 when he was asked to advise on the vacant cantorate. (A much earlier Leipzig predecessor, Johann Schelle, had also once been consulted there.) As he pointed out himself, Bach took some trouble to find a candidate experienced in the humanities and especially in music (*in humanioribus*: Dok I, 48), and wrote on behalf of G. G. Wagner, recommending him as skilled in composition, organ, keyboard, violin, cello 'and other instruments', such versatility being desirable for the service cantatas. Wagner had played violin under Bach and, probably, took some trouble to have a supply of his teacher's music with him in Plauen (BJ 2005, 99). After his appointment, however, the superintendent thought Wagner's Latin 'and other things' were such that 'what Mr Bach reported about him *in humanioribus* was by no means borne out' (Dok I, 52). But the wish to help Wagner is understandable, since he had recently applied unsuccessfully for a position in Leipzig, although Bach does also warn that his bass voice is, if agreeable, 'not too strong'. Damned by faint praise is how one might characterize certain other testimonials that commend, as does one of 1734, a student's 'industry and desire to learn' but not much else (BJ 1978, 73).

Two letters sent to Dresden in 1733 in connection with the vacant position in the Sophienkirche and signed by Friedemann were in fact written by his father, one formal and one more personal, the latter addressed to the

Chief Counsel to the Consistory. Finding the most influential person in a given appointment process, on this and similar occasions, must itself have given some trouble. In much the same way, he wrote more than one letter for his son Johann Gottfried Bernhard, for his application at Mühlhausen Marienkirche in 1735 and again at Sangerhausen a year later. His last known recommendation was written in December 1749, for the application of his son Johann Christoph Friedrich, then seventeen, to the court of Bückeburg. The letter was written probably from dictation, though he had written one himself for Altnickol the year before. (Presumably in connection with Christoph Friedrich's expected departure, a Luther Bible was presented to him and signed on Christmas Day 1749 by his mother, 'for her dear son': Dok I, 124.)

Earlier that year, January 1749, Bach became father-in-law to his former pupil Altnickol, whom he previously seems to have encouraged to apply at the Wenzelskirche, Naumburg (Dok I, 116), a more important church for Altnickol than his present position in Silesia, with a large new organ, and in a town much closer to Leipzig. Again, Bach wrote both to the council and personally to the burgomaster; and just as the letter for Christoph Friedrich probably drew on a past connection with the local court-ruler, so the Naumburg letter to the council referred to his previous work there as organ-examiner (see pp. 227f). He draws attention to this connection, then begs to apply on behalf of Altnickol in his absence, recommending him as follows:

Altnickol has already had charge of an organ for a considerable time

he has the knowledge to play it well

he especially understands how to look after an organ and maintain perfectly all that belongs to it – qualities absolutely necessary for a good organist. (This skill of *conserviren* was passed on by Altnickol to a later pupil: see Dok III, 207.)

he is able to direct (*dirigiren*, i.e. put on mixed choral and instrumental performances)

he has a special gift in composing, singing and violin-playing. (Thus he could lead a band for a variety of purposes. It seems he also worked with his teacher on composing organ-chorales: see Dok III, 503.)

The letter adds that the council will never have cause to regret honouring the candidate with its choice and that he, Bach, will consider it a personal favour if he is appointed (Dok I, 113).

Of course, one wonders whether Bach was looking for a particularly good position not too far away for his son-in-law-to-be. Similarly, when Altnickol came later to have the Orgelbüchlein in his possession, as he seems to have done (BJ 2001, 67), one wonders if his then father-in-law had given it him. From his earliest days with Bach Altnickol seems to have been entrusted with important jobs: copying WTC2 soon after coming to Leipzig in 1744, then the vocal parts and new bass-line of Palestrina's mass *Ecce sacerdos magnus*. (The latter work, incomplete, was probably from a score in Bach's possession ever since the Weimar years. Copying out the parts suggests an intended performance, perhaps in Dresden, where a lower pitch would make them more practicable.) That Altnickol could be entrusted to keep the fine new organ in the town church in good repair would also be important to the authorities.

Bach's shorter testimonials are necessarily more formulaic, but they summarize much the same points as the fuller recommendations, including the necessary testimony to the subject's good behaviour. With a younger student such as a schoolboy chorister, it is frankly noted whether he is only 'moderately proficient' or 'little proficient but with time will be useful, so long as he is industrious in his private practice' (Dok I, 134–5). For older students, the information is quite specific as to whether they compose and/or accompany, sing and/or play, whether in the church or the Collegium, etc. Often a personal touch is revealed, as in 1737 when testimonials for Bernhard Dietrich Ludewig note twice that he had been entrusted, probably as a live-in student, with teaching Bach's younger family (*meine kleine Familie*: Dok I, 141). The reference there was presumably to Gottfried Heinrich and Elisabeth Juliana Friderica, the daughter to marry Altnickol.

WHAT WAS TAUGHT

Some conjectures have already been made on what or how Bach taught in Weimar (pp. 114f), and practices can not have changed much during his lifetime. The transcription of a concerto by the teenage Prince Johann Ernst BWV 982 suggests that if Bach had anything to do with his music studies, which is likely, he worked with him on composition, including elementary ritornello form, simple imitation, modulations, episodes, and phraseology. A gifted student, evidently – though another of his concertos, transcribed as BWV 987, suggests that he too learnt direct from studying Vivaldi, specifically melodies in 2/4 time.[18]

---

[18] These were two of the concertos published by Telemann after the prince's death: *Six concerts*, Op. 1 (Leipzig & Halle, 1718). The MS copy of BWV 982 and other transcriptions was made by Bernhard Bach (1676–1749), successor in Eisenach to Christoph Bach and evidently in contact with Sebastian during the Weimar period (cf. Dok II, 58).

At least some of the copies of the keyboard works made by pupils must have been part of their studies with their teacher, as exercises in playing or in composing, perhaps both. In the case of WTC1, it seems the composer's extant fair copy was the one pupils were allowed to copy (see NBA V/6.1 KB, 142). When in *c.* 1732 the eighteen-year-old Emanuel made a copy of the C sharp major Prelude WTC1 one might guess that it served primarily as a playing exercise, but it would also have accustomed him to its rare key and the fingering it required, to the key's appearance on the page, to the arts of composing from note-patterns and modulating, and to shaping a coherent prelude. Perhaps it was also an exercise in learning to find an acceptable tuning in such a key, for Bach must have taught his pupils how to tune and find temperaments. The Prelude becomes therefore a model in the several areas an apprentice musician needed to master.

An old idea that some of the less firmly established parts of the Bach oeuvre – the dubious or spurious works, pieces incomplete or in mixed styles – were remnants of his teaching, often receives support from the sources. Chamber trios such as BWV 1021 and 1038 might transmit in part a Bach work, in part a student's working of a given bass. The Pedal Exercise, BWV 598, that breaks off but indicates further harmonies, might be Emanuel's unaided work or an exercise begun by or for his father. Some very early organ-chorales might convey signs of the composer's own learning as a student, perhaps his re-working of material by someone else. Perhaps the much later treatise on four-part continuo harmony attributed to Bach by a student, C. A. Thieme (the *Vorschriften* of 1738), does indeed speak for his use in lessons of older material by predecessors, in this case F. E. Niedt's *Musicalische Handleitung* of 1700. For a teacher can hardly be expected to create all his own materials, and Niedt's exercises are suitably systematic, clear and useful.

A culture based on the apprentice-master relationship leaves many blurred lines between performer and composer, as also between learner and teacher, both as to who composed what and how it is actually to be played. As to composing: some of the versions of harmonized chorales and Schemelli songs copied by various pupils, and now published in NBA III/3, may well represent the kind of harmony assignment for students such as J. L. Krebs. As to the playing: typical of fair-copy MSS, even when they contain such instructive music as the Inventions or Organ Sonatas, is that they seldom indicate anything about performance, even such basics as how to divide awkward three-part counterpoint between the hands or awkward pedal-lines between the feet. There are various possible reasons for this. Fair copies remained more or less pristine and 'neutral', for reference purposes;

or in their own copies and their notation the pupils had their own way of showing what the hands or feet played; or such music specifically taught them to look ahead and anticipate, without needing to mark the score; or their teacher did mark up secondary copies as a modern teacher might; or they left it all to chance. It is unlikely that even painstaking work today on student copies as they still exist will make it quite clear what happened, and one has to suppose that 'leaving it to chance' was not out of the question before the music-conservatory of the nineteenth century led to the memorized public recital.

A further unknown is how Bach taught his early pupils before he had available the Inventions, French Suites, WTCI and, for figured-bass work, the books of J. D. Heinichen (1711) and F. E. Niedt (1700, 1721). His own study as a child was probably conventional, with regular or irregular instruction from family members, musical odd jobs, occasional participation in making music or preparing works, and personal observation as keen as his exceptional abilities and self-motivation allowed. In the sense that he had 'studied' with Buxtehude, so also pupils continued to study with him from his twenties onwards, more formally than he had taught himself, at least as this was later described by Emanuel. Except from anecdotes, Emanuel would have known little of how the Buxtehudes, Böhms and Bachs of the day had learnt or taught, and he himself soon broke out into other directions without, as far as one knows, discouragement from his father. From the time he entered the university in 1731 as a seventeen-year old and presumably still living at home, Emanuel concentrated on harpsichord sonatas, chamber trios, concertos, woodwind solos, chiefly in proto-*galant* idioms very different from the music in which cantors had once been schooled. He admitted later, it seems, that he could not play pedals (Dok III, 440), which must be either an exaggeration or a sign that his father did not force a child to learn.

Judging by those of Bach's early chorale-harmonizations in which the organist ran his fingers over scales and flourishes between the lines of the hymn, it was from handling chorales in church that a young musician might learn both the arts of service-playing and the first steps in composition. The two rather went together, and this would be so especially at a period when most hymnbooks did not contain even melodies, much less harmonizations, and when boys received their first training in choirs singing such hymns. A chorister-organist-cantor such as Bach must have sung, played and heard the Gloria hymn 'Allein Gott in der Höh' hundreds of times in his lifetime, and in his mind have gone over many, many ways to harmonize it. Extant settings of chorales suggest that players were taught particular techniques such as variation or paraphrase or canon or double pedal-parts by trying them out on suitable hymn-melodies, and these techniques are represented in various 'spurious works of Bach', composed by pupils and others.

From various kinds of evidence it is clear that organists needed to be able to play the hymns in various keys, to learn to transpose at sight, and to improvise preludes that began in one key and ended in another – presumably to lead from one chorale to the next. (This last skill evidently became useful in the mid-eighteenth century.) In a publication of 1756, one of Bach's students, F. W. Sonnenkalb, insisted that the preludes prefacing chorales and cantatas should prepare listeners for the 'sentiment' (*Empfindung*) of what follows, a view much like that of another Bach pupil, Ziegler. This idea need not be implying a very subtle or expressive type of mood-painting, although anything it reflected of what they learnt in their lessons with Bach would become increasingly urgent as organ music followed musical fashions of Haydn's period. As for other kinds of music far from the organ-gallery: musical youth wishing to learn the arts of composing concertos, chamber music and above all opera, would not be studying with J. S. Bach in Weimar or Leipzig but would be off to Hamburg or Venice.

As the idea of Bach The Universal Instructor developed, disciples spread what they understood of his Gospel in their various appointments across North-central Germany, and sometimes commented in print about his teaching. In 1782 J. P. Kirnberger, writing his own book, claimed to follow his teacher's method in composition by going by step from the easiest to the most difficult, taking fugue-writing in one's stride – a step no bigger than any other (Dok III, 362). H. N. Gerber was said much later by his son to have studied the playing of Inventions, suites and then fugues, going on eventually to figured-bass work based on good part-writing ('in the singing of the voices together': Dok III, 476). None of this is unexpected or startling, and in particular Gerber's copy of some of the Inventions, like J. C. Vogler's copy of the first two pieces found in WTC2, gives the impression of students working with Bach on details of the kind found in Couperin's keyboard tutor, i.e. how to apply plausible ornaments *à la française* (Gerber) and where to use the thumb (Vogler).

Adding French ornaments and fingerings to 'pure' German keyboard counterpoint is indeed the kind of assignment one might expect Bach to have given his brighter students, including Wilhelm Friedemann. Thus one can imagine Gerber's French rubrics in the English Suites as coming from his lessons with their composer, and perhaps he learnt more than mere rubrics: there still remains a big question about how well Bach understood or taught the French *manière*. If the ornaments and rubrics in certain copies came from Parisian publications, were he and his pupils also fully aware of such practices as *notes inégales* and where to apply them? Did they recognize how appropriate these were to certain music, such as the courantes of the English Suites? This is possible but not recorded. There are also many possible reasons for Johann Christian Bach's pointed rhythms in the Prelude of the First Partita when he published a version of it in 1773 (*Six Sonates* Op. X, No. 1); but that as a boy he had played it with *notes inégales* seems unlikely.

In replying in 1775 to Forkel's questions about who influenced his father, and how or what his pupils were taught, Emanuel fails to give due attention to his lifelong French interests. Nor is Forkel, then enthusiastically establishing a German tradition for musical instruction, likely to have had much interest either in old, forgotten French keyboard music or in the ornamental style more appropriate to harpsichord than piano. Of overriding importance to both authors was Bach's emphasis (as they describe it) on four-part harmony, which included harmonizing chorales and realizing figured bass. If a young pupil, including Bach's own sons, did not show any gift of 'invention', he was not taken on (*Erfindung*: Dok III, 289) – 'invention' as a performer as well as composer, for ideally the two were not separate. (Scheibe, the critic, gives some insight into this when with evident bitterness he recalls his unsuccessful application at the Nikolaikirche and implies that Bach gave him no encouragement to continue. See above, p. 311). Generally, however, reports of Bach the Teacher that focus on the 'solid' sides of learning, do not give the whole picture of a musician intimate with a much, much wider range of music.

A sign that Bach's emphases were not so far from, say, François Couperin's in *L'Art de toucher* (1716) is that the Clavierbüchlein W. F. Bach (1720) explains and illustrates certain basics:

notes and clefs
a table of ornaments in the French style (called *Explication*)
fingering, with a model piece (called *Application*)
some preludes, starting in C major (playing exercises?)
two chorales (demonstrations of ornamental paraphrase?)
model allemandes (composition exercises, to complete?)

The Clavierbüchlein is very like Couperin's *L'Art de toucher* in including both a model allemande and a group of varied preludes not only in different keys and starting in C major but requiring distinctly different touch from one to another. But if Bach did know *L'Art de toucher*, the differences between it and the Clavierbüchlein would be significant, for Couperin expressly holds back on teaching even note-names to children (*L'Art*, 12–13) and, of course, has no chorale settings. These were crucial for any learning musician in Protestant Germany, and suggest that Friedemann's understanding was already developed. As anyone knows who has taught ten-year-olds, the incipits his father gives for two allemandes would be of little use to a pupil not given further attention by the teacher.

Also very like practice in Parisian publications are the Clavierbüchlein's ornament-table and fingerings, and of course *application* and *explication* are French terms. As was customary, Bach's ornament-table does not exactly follow any other, although he seems to draw on d'Anglebert's (see above, p. 132) and perhaps Dieupart's – or an unchecked memory of them. He also takes the conventional reference point for writing out realizations of the ornaments, i.e. at treble C. Ornaments had begun playing an important part in earlier keyboard albums of Protestant Germany, such as Eckelt's tablature book (see above, p. 20) and the notebook Gerber made as a teenager even before his lessons with Bach (see BJ 1978, 8), where he includes not only the signs but an important and typically German item not found in French instruction books: a group of little note-patterns of the kind one can use for creating preludes. Nevertheless, in principle the notion of an ornament-table was French. Musicians in France formalized ornaments much as the Académie Française formalized the French language, i.e. with diacritical marks or accents in order to standardize spelling and pronunciation.

Whether a Fantasia for organ in the first Anna Magdalena Bach Book was left incomplete to encourage not only her pedal-playing but her composing and improvising – any or all three – is unknown. But the second Book includes more obviously instructive material: two incomplete sets of 'Rules for General Bass', one by Anna Magdalena from the 1720s, the other by the youngest-but-one son Johann Christoph Friedrich in the 1740s. Both provide brief notes on the major and minor scale, the triads, sevenths and chord-figures, all as a book might that was in continuous use for teaching successive children. As for the various remaining rules (*Cautelen*, 'precautions'), these are, so the book says, better told by word of mouth than in writing – quoting Papa?

Two instructional MSS dating probably to the early 1740s suggest that Bach trained at least some pupils in strict counterpoint (see Werbeck 2003). The first is a two-sided page with suspensions illustrated at a basic level, as an instruction sheet or a plan or draft for a non-professional student. The second is longer, taken from a section in the Latin version of Zarlino's

Istitutioni of 1558, copied probably not direct but from the work of a previous Leipzig cantor, Seth Calvisius's *Melopoeia* (1592 and re-issues). The
section includes a short canon *per augmentationem* amongst an array of
other short canons which, though not offering much for so inveterate a
composer of canons as Bach, has an appearance on the page matching two
of his sets: the Fourteen Canons appended to his copy of the Goldberg
Variations and the engraved sheet of canons in the Musical Offering. All
were works of the 1740s and useful for the more experienced students.

From extant minuets by Friedemann and Emanuel written in canon or
partial canon, it seems likely that they learnt this particular way of composing minuets – something to survive into Haydn's period and beyond –
with their father. Two later students from Breslau studying in Leipzig in the
mid-1740s had canons dedicated to them by Bach (BWV 1077 and 1078);
a third Breslauer was Altnickol, future son-in-law. It is not too much to
imagine musical evenings with such young people in the Bach home, fea-
turing songs, canons and perhaps keyboard pieces, including those from
another album mentioned by Altnickol (see Wiermann 2003), which contained works by father and sons, perhaps intended as a Clavierbüchlein for
the youngest, Johann Christian. Much of all this activity must be typical of
widespread musical gatherings of that time and place, and indeed later, for
the Classical Viennese composers' interest in canons and quodlibets is part
of similar domestic traditions.

So far, the number of one-on-one pupils Bach seems to have had has not
been matched by any other composer of the time, and whether or not they
looked for church work as professionals, neither he nor they neglected the
discipline of fugue-writing. Nevertheless, it was in the nature of new
musical taste that counterpoint would gradually be relegated to a mere discipline, and there is little evidence that any pupil, his sons or otherwise,
emulated the musical reality of the Bach fugue in its various forms. This is
so even when pupils remained closely associated with him, such as Johann
Schneider whose few known works include some inspired by the Toccata
in D minor, BWV 538 and the opening prelude of Clavierübung III. Of the
other pupils, Johann Ludwig Krebs (in Leipzig, 1726–37) was able to
imitate certain techniques in chorale-settings, and one of his best pieces
shows him very familiar with his teacher's Toccata in C, BWV 564. Krebs
was an intelligent, gifted learner, but his music rarely if ever has his teacher's
harmonic tension. Similarly, although J. A. Scheibe studied concerto form
and copied out one of the transcriptions, BWV 972, going promisingly
through the motions of theme and binary form in his own attempts (see
Wollny 2002, 138–9), he fails in a similar way. So does H. N. Gerber in his

imitations of the Two-part Inventions and in an extant concerto also going through the motions (see Butler 2003, 226).

It could well be that although writers after Bach's death admired and concentrated on his counterpoint as teaching-material, in fact he himself also used concertos as a model for sustained thematic composition. The two very different transcriptions of what seems to be a concerto by the young Prince Johann Ernst of Weimar, BWV 595 for organ (first movement) and BWV 984 for harpsichord, lead to an interesting question: is the latter version the prince's original essay and the former the result of a reworking by Bach in order to demonstrate the potential of ritornello form? The organ version is not only longer and more varied but includes a very striking modulation and various other 'improvements' to produce something with much more character. In the case of compositions by a later pupil, Emanuel Bach, a fine opening gesture and some shifting tonalities are unlikely to disguise the paucity of harmonic or melodic development and absence of intricate form. The sources of the sonata BWV 1036, once attributed to Sebastian, suggest Emanuel to have tried successfully to imitate the fugal counterpoint he could have found in the D minor Organ Sonata, though without much harmonic development. As a generalization, pupils would probably do better when they worked in *stile antico* counterpoint and simply followed the rules, as Altnickol seems to have done in an extant Fantasia.

No doubt some part of his pupils' apparent shortcomings results from changing tastes or criteria, as for example when Krebs's F minor Praeludium makes use of the B minor Praeludium, BWV 544 but dilutes its harmonic intensity, as if aiming to appeal to a modern taste for pleasant, less demanding music. But one can only guess whether it was that Krebs did not care for his teacher's harmonic drive, was unable to match it , or was never taught it – like other pupils, he was permitted to make copies of major works always beyond the reach of the neophyte composer. The big organ preludes must have been difficult to conquer even for gifted players such as J. G. Vogler, who said as much (Dok III, 331), and pupils picked up only the basics for the skills they listed in job-applications, such as improvising or composing preludes, fugues, variations, chorales and continuo-accompaniment (Dok II, 209). Some lessons, judging from Gerber's notebook, were taken up with the grammar of imitative and invertible counterpoint and with shaping simple movements, including dances. The Allemande in the Clavierbüchlein W. F. Bach suggests at least that some pupils were taught how to construct binary movements with good phraseology and modulations.

Not even Friedemann Bach, however, could do much more than develop in his own different way, leaving the major compilations of his father's last decade as unscalable peaks protruding above the effete novelties of the 1740s and 50s. A simple principle of organization like key-sequence might be occasionally imitated by a pupil (e.g. Friedemann's Twelve Polonaises, *c.* 1765), though even this is absent from Emanuel's various sets of keyboard sonatas. Nor did copyists consistently preserve – or even notice? – the original order of pieces in many of the collections, whatever its original significance. (On whether this suggests that Bach controlled his pupils' copies, see p. 18.)

A teacher's Counsel of Perfection is useful only to a certain point, and the sheer difficulty in playing or using as models any of Bach's collections, printed or manuscript, is obvious, as therefore is their resulting isolation. In the case of WTC2 one Bach admirer, F. W. Marpurg, was led by his knowledge of it to write a new book on fugal theory (*Abhandlung von der Fuge*), but he must have been aware that except in certain organist circles, the imaginative treatment of fugue-subjects found in WTC2 was not ever going to be matched by students. In the case of the Clavierübung's settings of chorales, another admirer G. A. Sorge published his own set of simpler settings the year Bach died, using the same engraver in Nuremberg and pointing out that Bach's were 'almost unusable' by the young and unskilled (*fast unbrauchbar*: preface to *Vorspiele*). He could have been referring not only to the music's complexity but to the engraving's notation and the actual layout, difficult to grasp by all but the most accomplished musicians. A glance at the advice and instruction published by later musicians in the Bach circle – Adlung, Agricola, Sonnenkalb, Petri, Kittel – leaves the impression of organists and teachers as belonging to a somewhat low-achieving profession for which the conceptual and practical difficulties of Bach's keyboard music were a mystery.

A NOTE ON THE FOUR-PART CHORALES

From a biographical point of view, many questions remain about the four-part chorales: the harmonized Lutheran hymns, of which some 350 or so are listed, over half not known from surviving cantatas and Passions. Whether the composer set out to collect them and if so why, is not documented. Emanuel told Forkel that his father first taught composition students to realize a figured bass in four parts, probably meaning on paper; then moved on to hymn-melodies by writing alto and tenor to their teacher's bass line; then learnt to create the bass for themselves (Dok III, 289). Harmony teachers know this to be a sound procedure, although many would prefer students to learn to write the bass to a melody first.

Either way, in being practical models of four-part harmony, chorales are useful in any classroom, teaching students how to hear harmony, understand cadences and modulations, fill in good inner parts, write good bass lines, handle unaccented and especially accented passing notes, *échappées* and *appoggiature*, all so as to create smoothly shaped, on-driving music. Such were basic skills not only serving the would-be composer of all and any kind of music, on all and any scale, but are able to create a genuine music that is pleasing in itself. In such chorales, there are many touches of the unexpected, even whimsical, which students all too easily overdo as they attempt to absorb the style. Chorales, particularly those of the two Passions, offer models of telling moderation, mostly with one decoration at a time (passing note, suspension etc), with less or more chromaticism (depending on the text) and many a surprising touch.

Four-part chorales published during Bach's Leipzig years by other composers such as Telemann and Kauffmann, plus hints of his own work with young musicians in Weimar contained in the sources of organ chorales, are signs of how useful they were generally seen at the time. A collection of chorales and devotional songs not in four parts but only bass and treble, like those in Schemelli's *Gesangbuch* of 1736 (see above, pp. 233f), could be reductions from four-part settings already made, or they could be skeletal settings to be filled in by continuo-players and harmony-students. Learning polished four-part chorale-harmony had more uses than for playing hymns for church services, and the pedagogical focus around J. S. Bach both during and after his lifetime would itself have led to a continuing interest in them. From Hamburg and other centres a few sources have also survived to suggest a similar picture there, although it could be that Emanuel described the teaching of chorales to Forkel in 1774 because by then the tradition had begun to weaken, and they both wished to maintain it.

In any case, whether through pupils' loyalty, his own particular emphases, or both, Bach has bequeathed a bigger corpus of this kind of music than anyone else. A collection of 150 four-part chorales, made already by J. L. Dietel during or soon after student-years in the Thomas School 1727–35, is drawn mostly from known cantatas and could be one of several prepared for publication, roughly comparable to the same Schemelli Songbook. C. F. Penzel, a student in Leipzig after Bach's death, left a collection of 126 chorales, probably part of a bigger MS and including a dozen filled-in settings from Schemelli's songbook. But Emanuel's focus on his father as teacher hides another, perhaps main and earlier purpose of chorale-collections: to supplement the usual text-only hymnbooks of the day for the sake of organists. Gradual publication both of hymnbooks with harmonized tunes and of collections of organ-chorales would reduce the organist's need for such collections, which instead became indispensable as teaching aids for countless music students everywhere over the following two and a half centuries.

From the posthumous publications of four-part chorales, particularly the biggest of them (by C. P. E. Bach and J. P. Kirnberger, 1784–87), one could with caution make a case that those which have apparently been taken from or were used in the cantatas after 1724 tend to have a simpler harmonization than those that had other origins. It has often been noticed that over the first Leipzig cycle, from August 1723 to early 1724, Bach seems to have taken particular trouble over harmonising the chorales, which would also fit in with the imaginative use made of them in the St John Passion at that period. Another possibility is that elaborate settings such as BWV 277 and 278 ('Christ lag in Todesbanden') had an origin in the classroom, whereas the simpler setting of the same chorale in Cantata 4 had been made earlier for a church choir. The latter would have led to the former. While there is seldom a clear distinction between simple and complex, and general uncertainty about which chorales belonged to which lost cantatas, it rather looks as if the treatment in Examples 27 (a) and (b) demonstrate to students the ways of handling passing notes, suspensions, decorations, different kinds of sevenths, amd interesting vocal lines but – and this is most important – without over-doing any of them. Experienced students would probably recognize two further characteristics in such music: its lines are also very singable, if sometimes difficult; and there is often an element of caprice transcending textbook rules.

Given the complete grounding his students had in harmony – writing four-part chorales, playing figured bass in four parts, semi-improvising fugues above a bass in the *partimento* tradition, as well as practice in *stile antico* counterpoint – one might well wonder what Bach's attitude was to their very different young men's tastes when they wrote their own kinds of music. In particular, how did he react to the slack harmonic tension, the constant appoggiature enlivening thin and moribund harmony, the repeated phrases, the predictable modulations, the superficial chromaticisms, the rhetoric of louds-and-softs replacing real substance as he knew it? Charles Burney's enthusiasm for the keyboard works of 'Bach's last student', J. G. Müthel (1756), suggests that as with Emanuel's and Friedemann's publications, discerning as well as amateur musicians were to find praiseworthy qualities in those very characteristics. One could

27 a Chorale, BWV 278
    b Chorale, BWV 277
       'Christ lay in the bonds of death'

suppose that Bach simply accepted light *galant* idioms as appropriate to the style and function of music different from his own, idioms as much at home in the new sonatas, concertos, symphonies, songs and arias as careful and intricate counterpoint had been in the Art of Fugue and the Mass in B minor.

One could suppose he accepted the distinctions between genres in this way if it were not that his own music makes such little concession to light *galant* idioms, and indeed less so in the later 1740s than in some previous years. To the extent that the music of his last twenty years shows a clearer line of development than the comparable oeuvre of Handel or Vivaldi or Rameau, it was towards affirming the traditional truths of harmony (counterpoint, modulation, organization), not towards the idioms becoming widespread in the 1750s. Any sustained interest he had in four-part chorales as teaching-material for learners was a sign either that he wanted young musicians to master harmonic grammar first or that he was fighting a rearguard action – or, as so often with questions about Bach, both.

A SPECULATION CONCERNING W. F. BACH

While documents do no more than hint at Bach's personal relationships, it is difficult to imagine that he always separated the personal from the professional. Music for his young wife could both give pleasure and improve her skills; instruction of his children was followed by solicitous, personal support for their adult careers. Ironically, despite so few recorded personal details of the Bach family, nevertheless in the whole history of music the Clavierbüchlein W. F. Bach remains an unrivalled testimony to a father-and-son relationship. Something faintly resembles it in the Anna Magdalena Book of 1725, where both parents seem to be helping the disabled son Gottfried Heinrich in working on a song, BWV 515 (see NBA V/4 KB, 124).

Though probably being compiled while Wilhelm Friedemann was in Berlin, delivering their youngest brother Christian into Emanuel's family (and handing over a file of press cuttings?), the Obituary gives no hint of any favouritism for him. Yet circumstantially – certainly in respect to Friedemann's studies and career – some closeness between father and son is implied by the worklist:

Clavierbüchlein (1720)
> Album for Friedemann, begun when he was nine; re-bound in Halle after 1750; later also re-copied, probably in Halle. At least one other such family notebook came to exist, as already noted (Dok III, 491).

Two-part and Three-part Inventions (fair copy 1723).

Well-tempered Clavier, Book 1 (1722/3).

Orgelbüchlein (title 1723?): an older collection, but with new title. Signs in the MS that Friedemann used it (BJ 2001, 67).

Six Partitas for harpsichord, from *c.* 1724.
> Nos. 3, 6 for Anna Magdalena, but Nos. 1, 2, 4, 5 for Friedemann?

Six Sonatas for organ, compiled *c.* 1729.
> Said by Forkel 1802 to be for Friedemann, who may have told him so. Perhaps intended for publication to match the harpsichord partitas (published complete in 1731).

Two letters for Friedemann's application at Sophienkirche, Dresden, 1733
> Written by Sebastian, signed by Friedemann.

Praeludium in G major for organ, a newly made autograph
> For Friedemann's successful audition at the Sophienkirche?

(Friedemann's participation in preparing parts for the Kyrie and Gloria presented to the Elector of Saxony, about the time of his move to Dresden in June 1733.)

Magnificat, BWV 243, D major version, *c.* 1733?
> So revised partly in connection with Friedemann in Dresden?

Clavierübung II, published 1735
> For Friedemann in Dresden? – where two-manual harpsichords were by now familiar (extant examples by Gräbner, 1722 and 1739).

Lutheran masses, BWV 233–236, later 1730s
> Parody works, drawn from earlier cantatas: just possibly for Friedemann's wished-for appointment at the Frauenkirche, Dresden?

Contrapuntal exercises in the hand of father and son, 1736/8? (Wollny 2002)
> The Art of Fugue subject-head appears in this MS, which supports Emanuel's description of his father starting off fugue-study in two parts.[19]

Harpsichord concertos, BWV 1052–1059, compiled as a set *c.* 1738
> Perhaps for Friedemann in Dresden, or on his returns to Leipzig.

Clavierübung III, published 1739
> *ditto*, for public organ recitals?

Goldberg Variations, published 1741
> For Friedemann to play in Dresden, where he had connections with J. G. Goldberg and his patron, Count von Keyserlingk?

Copy by J. S. of Friedemann's Concerto for two harpsichords, Fk 10
> Only known complete copy by J. S. of a son's work.

Copy by J. S. of Cantata 34, *c.* 1746
> Prepared for Friedemann's first Whit Sunday in Halle?

J. S.'s visit to the court in Potsdam, May 1747
> Accompanied by Friedemann (who was looking for a position there?).

The six Schübler Chorales, published *c.* 1748
> Transcribed for (perhaps by) Friedemann? Sold by him in Halle.

Whatever other purposes any of these works had, including the use made of them by the younger sons in their turn, the question is still whether they had any special association with Friedemann and his career. The Orgelbüchlein, for instance, has a titlepage focusing on the instruction it offers 'the young organist', both in composing chorales and in playing the pedal; and one young organist was Friedemann. But this ignores the collection's more obvious if never realized purpose: to supply chorales for the whole church

---

[19] This much-quoted reference to Bach's teaching methods (Dok III, 289) says less than it appears to say, for how could one begin a study of fugue except by composing a second part? Is Emanuel implying that his father did not hold with mere passive analysis of the kind known to students today?

year, something to which its intended title, had it ever got written, would probably have referred, comparable to collections by Pachelbel (attributed, 1704) and Vetter (1713). In the case of WTC2, Friedemann's later ownership of the (or an) autograph MS, as well as an important copy of it, raises the question whether the collection was assembled, insofar as it was, partly with him in mind – music full of up-to-date challenges for keyboard players, including those playing the new fortepianos. Of course, how well any of the Bach sons mastered the musical demands placed on them is a further unknown: a twelve or thirteen-year-old will not easily conquer either the Orgelbüchlein or WTC1. But the sheer technical difficulty of Friedemann's harpsichord music from the 1730s and 40s may have been prompted by his father's collections, including the partitas. One or two of the six Partitas faintly recall details in the sonatas of Friedemann's violin teacher Graun, as if the father was responding to the son's studies.

It would be especially helpful to know how common it was for Friedemann to return to the family home, bringing distinguished Dresden musicians with him (one documented visit, August 1739), and whose idea it was for him to use some of his father's cantatas in Halle, adding his own recitatives to Cantata 130 in a very good style-match (see BJ 2003, 233). It was his father, no doubt, through whom Friedemann took as private pupil one of St Thomas's choristers (Dok III, 106). But the documentation is altogether too ambiguous on incidents that might be very significant. Anecdotes told after both their deaths report Sebastian as satisfied only with Friedemann amongst his sons (Dok III, 518), but this is merely hinted at in documents, as when son joined father in visits to Dresden (already in the late 1720s?) or apparently shared enthusiasms for keyboard-playing and working counterpoint on paper. Was Friedemann's absence without leave from Halle for several months after his father's death (Dok II, 513) purely to oversee probate and organize the family, or was he, at the age of nearly forty, too affected even to request formal leave of absence from his church? It is also tempting to speculate on the elder brothers' relationship with their stepmother: did Emanuel's application at Naumburg in August 1733 have anything to do with Friedemann's leaving home two months earlier? Or a year later, Emanuel's surprising move away from Leipzig to continue studies in Frankfurt-an-der-Oder?

Several sons, perhaps all of them, told anecdotes of their father, and of a kind familiar in many a musical family. Emanuel said his father would nudge him during a fugue when something he predicted would happen did so (Dok III, 285); Friedemann, that he joked with him about going to hear the 'nice little Dresden songs' in the court opera (Forkel 1802, 49);

Christian, that he once jumped out of bed to resolve a 6/4 chord (see p. 42). More importantly, without Forkel's note that the six sonatas for organ were compiled for Friedemann one could only guess that they were, based on their date and Friedemann's own copy of them. Taking speculation further, one could also guess that just as the organ sonatas were for him, perhaps connected with his unsuccessful application at Halle in March 1731, so were other works – for example, the sonatas for violin and harpsichord (compiled about the time he was studying violin with Graun in Merseburg *c.* 1726),[20] or the first two movements of the B minor Mass (sent to the elector in Dresden shortly after he moved there). If this were so, it would imply a father's optimism about a son's gifts. Friedemann is unlikely to have played the violin sonatas well at the age of fifteen or sixteen, or directed the Kyrie and Gloria authoritatively when he was twenty-two or three.

When eventually appointed at Halle in 1746, Friedemann evidently made special efforts with his first cantata, as his father did at Leipzig in 1723, the two being of similar age at similar career-points. Becoming more of an organist than Emanuel, at least by profession, he owned both early and late autographs of his father's organ music, including very early examples of his handwriting in the chorale-fantasias BWV 739 and 764, kept perhaps as mementos. And another 'perhaps': when he claimed much later to have written one of Sebastian's manuscripts himself, the Organ Concerto, BWV 596, did he simply mistake the handwriting for his own as a boy? He is known to have sold off various of his father's manuscripts later, but this need not imply any disrespect or compelling indigence. There are many reasons for disposing of a heritage, including persistent sadness.

A temptation is to seek in all this an explanation for Friedemann's relative failure in life after 1750, despite Emanuel's reported view that 'he could replace our father better than the rest of us together' (Dok III, 276, 613), and despite the high (if fruitless) regard in which the King of Prussia held him. In a comparable way, one can speculate that their younger brother Bernhard's problems – debts as a young organist, precipitate abandonment of a good job, moving to another city where a distant relative lived – was somehow to do with their father: Bernhard was avoiding Leipzig, or his stepmother, or a demanding father? It is certainly believable that the sons were over-encouraged, over-dependent, over-burdened by living up to expectations, and in Friedemann's case over-afflicted by his father's death.

---

[20] Graun was later concertmaster to Frederick II in Potsdam, where Friedemann's pupil Nichelmann was the second harpsichordist: another reason for Friedemann to accompany his father on the visit of 1747?

He saw his younger brother become more obviously successful even as an author on a topic (keyboard-playing) in which he, Friedemann, was regarded by many as the true apostolic successor. Had there been a special love for the first son, recognition of his unusual talent, a keen desire to discern one? Anxiety to compensate him for early loss of his mother, doubt that he was robust or had the stamina or killer instinct required for great success? Inadvertent domination, making such success impossible?

Epilogue

CONCERNING THE LIFE

One oddity of the Obituary, especially when compared to Mainwaring's biography of Handel, is how rarely it refers to other people, particularly musicians. While contributing to the picture of a self-reliant musician, this has a distancing effect, leaving much out of focus. Other documentation does go some way to improve this focus, but there being such limits to the documentary evidence, Bach's admirers have long had scope for all kinds of speculation, and this book can not be free of it.

Except for the young orphan's anguish at losing his manuscript and the mature composer's regrets at losing his beloved ex-employer, the only fully personal remark in the Obituary occurs when Emanuel speaks of his father's 'blissful marriage' to Maria Barbara and the 'severest pain' at her death. But, in picking on this, is he expressing his own feelings as her son, glossing his memory as a six-year-old, perhaps Friedemann's as a nine-year-old? Or quoting his father from later years, putting words into his mouth, desiring to speak well of both parents? Or he is speaking the simple truth? There are difficulties in accepting the last because the remark involves Emanuel himself, but it then leads to a further and intriguing question: in keeping alive, in an obituary, the memory of the composer's first wife and family, is he hinting something about the second?

From the two kinds of evidence left by the extant music and documentation, much can be divined about more personal aspects, and will continue to be divined in the future. On Bach's memory, for instance: when the letter of 28 October 1730 to his childhood friend Erdmann refers to 'nearly four years elapsing' since Erdmann replied to his last letter (Dok I, 67), and this turns out to be accurate to a few days, one concludes either that he had a very sharp memory or that he kept copies of all correspondence in a letterbook: perhaps the latter (Wolff 2000, 392), or perhaps both. Either way, there was some orderliness here. So there must have been in the

358

very making of cantata-parodies, for whatever the reasons for re-using older material, and however much labour was involved in the process, the material had to be retrieved, in both senses: from his memory and from his library, both neatly ordered, no doubt. Not all parodied works had been recently composed – a cantata movement almost a quarter of a century old was re-used for the Agnus dei of the Mass – and one can only assume that some of his own works made such a deep impression on him that he remained mindful of their quality, their associations and their suitability.

As one scrutinizes the documentation to answer such questions as 'What kind of person, husband, father, teacher, colleague was J. S. Bach?' or, 'What did he like and dislike?', speculation is inevitable. One can only begin to answer 'What were his preferences as a composer?' from works as they exist, but there is no total certainty what exactly these do represent, except that in going time and again far beyond requirements he showed himself conscientious, ambitious and (so is my impression) fascinated by music's language and what can be done with it. When he was absent from his post in order to make particular journeys – at least sixty in his lifetime, near and far, all very troublesome (at an average coach-speed of 3 m.p.h.) – was it only for the sake of personal ambition or was there not always a lively musical curiosity as well? When he wrote no title on important manuscript collections (and some works only after they were performed), was it through modesty, uncertainty or simply waiting until there was a chance for publication? Or when, in the case of the B minor Mass and the Christmas Oratorio, he seems never to have written an overall titlepage or indeed title? When he chose the anonymous-sounding title 'Keyboard Practice' for four quite extraordinary collections of music, was he objecting to the day's many fanciful titles or was he following his predecessor Kuhnau, who coined the phrase? And if the latter, was he keenly aware of how far his suites surpassed Kuhnau's? Was the intention to surpass? If so, to the Greater Glory of God or through pride, curiosity, a spirit of exploration, a self-given challenge, a delight in his natural skill – or all of these?

One thing seems clear. More so than is often appreciated, much of Bach's output can be seen as consciously affected in some way by other music, even if it is not yet fully understood how much he did know, particularly of foreign instrumental music. Since his ambition in so active a musical culture is likely to have brought a huge amount of music to his attention, he must often have reacted to it, if not under the *anxiety of influence*, then with the *pleasure of surpassing*. However disappointed he was to find his published music too thoughtful and difficult for the tastes of the 1730s and 1740s, he did not respond with 'popular' publications but on the contrary, worked towards further collections of difficult music, preludes and fugues, chorale-settings, canons, harder and on a bigger scale than anything before. Likewise, to whatever extent his cantata work did decline, the music by other composers he made use of during his last decade and more was traditional or old, even archaic.

A big question still remains why J. S. Bach influenced important contemporaries as little as he appears to have done. Handel, it seems, never drew on any of his music, though he did on work by Kerll, Krieger, C. H. Graun, Telemann and very likely others within their common German musical culture. While it is possible to find details in chorale-settings by Georg Böhm (†1733) that might suggest the younger man influencing the elder as much as vice-versa, Bach's sustained interest in the work of various French and Italian composers was never reciprocated. Although obviously the genres themselves (cantatas, fugue-collections, chorale-settings) did not travel to Roman Catholic countries, why the music for concert societies (sonatas, solo concertos, ensemble suites) did not is more puzzling. Nor did Bach's advanced keyboard volumes travel abroad much either, being (and even looking) difficult to play, and the crossed-hand music in Couperin's *Quatrième Livre* of 1730 is as if the Partita in B flat had never been written.

Any privileged attention this book appears to give keyboard music not only reflects the approach of the Obituary authors but stresses how sharp a focus it kept for Bach, from his earliest years to his last. Keyboard music shows clearly how certain 'intellectual' interests matured, as for instance the emergence of clear plans of organization for the major collections. Works like the French Suites show the composer working in miniature with formal details that would benefit any vocal and instrumental music, such as the principle of mini-recapitulation, modified returns of the opening melody already there in Couperin's *Premier Livre* 1713. On the other hand, the unusual, even strange, fugue-subjects in WTC2 suggest a composer alert to a very different tradition, i.e. the German organist's search for novel themes. As the years pass, the keyboard music seems to have fewer, not more, antecedents: the Goldberg has more levels of organization than any previous variations, Bach's own or anyone else's, and has far less in common with other sets of its time than had been the case some forty years earlier for the A minor Variations, BWV 989. It is also keyboard music that served the newly complex counterpoint so clearly and acclimatized the teacher and pupil to the fashionable new keys, leaving the choral music in these respects less 'advanced'.

A focus on the composer as keyboardist was already there in the Obituary, from its very heading ('The right noble Johann Sebastian Bach, world-famous in organ-playing') to reports of his public successes, these always as a performer. Its authors, like keyboard players ever since, can not have been insensitive to the specially palpable, tactile quality experienced when playing even the most intricate Bach counterpoint. The anecdotes involve keyboard music, from the first story (the 'moonlight episode') to the last (the 'deathbed chorale'), and reports of his playing prowess in Dresden, Hamburg and Berlin are not matched by praise of his achievements in other kinds of music. Yet if Reinken in Hamburg praised him as organist, is it so unlikely that Zelenka in Dresden praised him as composer? The weight of evidence points to his renown as partial and quite unrepresentative: how seldom, relative to its bulk, is his non-keyboard music known to have been performed elsewhere, except a few churches where the personnel had a connection with him!

More than any other major German composer of the time Bach gave an emphasis to keyboard music, and it remained virtually the only music he ever published himself. He must have had enormous facility as a player. His work with it was continuous, more even than with choral music, and it says much for the music-market of the time that so little of it was published, despite its variety – harpsichord music for the home, fugues for the study, chorales for the service, organ *praeludia* for recitals, concertos for the concert-room. To some degree, players of the keyboard music can experience feelings of physical sympathy with him, even though they cannot be exactly sure how he played, how much he hand-shifted like violinists or used his thumbs like later pianists, or in what details he changed over the years in the way he phrased and articulated. (One thing is certain: he had a strong fourth finger in both hands.) Right up to the Art of Fugue there is every sign that his playing-style or touch could vary from piece to piece and that, in such music, his hands were totally in control of the independently shaped contrapuntal lines – even that he had conceived them with this skill in mind.

CONCERNING THE MUSIC

While there are many pitfalls in trying to divine the person in the music, some revealing details do emerge. One is that there are far fewer ambiguities in Bach's scores than in those of so many by his contemporaries, where often several readings of a crux are equally plausible. Another is that he does appear to like clearcut formal structures: ritornello movements have clear division between main themes and episodes derived from them, mature fugues usually distinguish clearly between complete and partial statements of the theme, both are spacious and 'thorough'. It is hardly credible that the orderliness of mind all this suggests showed itself only in the realm of music.

One question concerns certain works not known to have been completed, arias such as the original movement No. 31 in the Christmas Oratorio (Part 3) or fugues such as the C minor, BWV 562. Amongst possible explanations is that he recognized the music was becoming congested (aria No. 31) or not escaping an unprepossessing ingenuity (BWV 562), and in both cases because 'the melos was not coming right'. In the family albums, an incomplete Fantasia might mean that he expected the pupil to finish it (Anna Magdalena's book of 1722), as too when elsewhere he wrote incipits only (allemandes in Friedemann's book of 1720). The reason for whole collections being left incomplete or unfinalized (Art of Fugue, the 'Eighteen Chorales') probably lies less in declining powers than in his being uncertain what their contents should be, for he was certain enough of the Mass Ordinary to complete his large-scale setting of it, right at the end of his active life. For the Orgelbüchlein's remaining little more than a quarter complete, various reasons are possible: the original purpose was lost (for a job not taken), he ceased to be a 'Sunday organist' needing it, and for both teaching purposes and general publication it was complete enough already. Yet one wonders whether the thought of writing as many as 164 hymn-settings, how ever short and economical, was found too daunting even by J. S. Bach as time passed, despite a frankly staggering optimism on beginning the album. Possibly, since Vetter's big publication had treated the chorales in an unvaried and simple way (see p. 48), Bach intended originally to do much the same but found it impossible not to search restlessly for variety and individuality.

One does not think of him as easily daunted, and on the contrary, music that he never completed serves only to arouse wonder that other, hugely and variously intricate works were. In the Art of Fugue, for instance, there are already two exhaustive fugues of nearly 200 bars each, BWV 1080.viii and 1080.xi. Their several subjects are worked not only to satisfy any theoretical study of permutation (qv) but to create a genuine musical shape: only gradually do the subjects declare themselves, the length is sustained by clear formal 'signposts', and there is increasing tension in both pieces. Also, when the themes do eventually combine, the final closing statement is succinct and needing no slow, drawn-out cadence popular with Italian fugue-composers of the time, including Handel. Succinct closes are characteristic of Bach fugues throughout his life, a sign that he did not take up everything in the foreign music he knew.

As well as cadences, even more basic elements of music suggest a tireless professional's keen interest in the phonemes of musical language, namely the notes and keys. Habits arose with particular keys, as with the two kinds of G major already mentioned (p. 335) or when fugue-subjects in minor keys (C, D, E, F) incorporate chromatic fourths. One peculiarity is that very often in F major, in all manner of pieces, the first accidental met with is not (as one might expect) B-natural but E-flat. This can happen in the first few bars of even of up-to-date music (the Italian Concerto for Harpsichord), and may be a 'purely musical' habit, as if for him flat keys tend towards flatter keys. Another purely musical detail can be seen in the opening fugue-subjects of Books 1 and 2 of the Well-tempered Clavier which are both, surprisingly, constructed entirely from the following notes, no more and no less:

c′ d′ e′ f′ g′ a′

These are the six notes of the theorists' venerable *hexachordum naturalis* ('natural six-note scale') and were especially appropriate for the first fugue of a collection, whether paraphrased *andante cantabile* as in WTC1 or embroidered *allegro giocoso* as in WTC2. This contrast between WTC1 and WTC2 is itself revealing. With its simpler hexachordal theme, the opening fugue of WTC1 creates many stretti as if it were deliberately saluting tradition, as it surely was,[1] while the opening fugue of WTC2 produces a more modern theme in a modern metre. Also, WTC1's fugue closes with an unusual high chord to which the same six notes have risen – an exceptional gesture for a fugue, tempting admirers to speak of 'ascending to heaven' – while WTC2's first fugue closes like a *badinerie*, down to earth and as different as could be.

Perhaps not quite so positive is the composer's liking for certain other technical devices such as inverted themes (Example 28).

Inversus is a time-honoured device, especially in the context of canons and fugues, yet in Example 28 (three quite typical cases) there is a touch of pedantry, a less than welcome cogitation behind the artifice looming larger the more one plays them. Judging by late work in the Musical Offering, Canonic Variations and Art of Fugue, this kind of artifice aimed at appealing to connoisseurs, more perhaps on the study-table than the music-desk, and not to the kind of buyer who would have preferred a few *galanteries* or a set of songs in the manner of Example 22. In cantatas, the artifice behind

---

[1] Froberger's Fantasia No. 1 has a theme C D E F G A, employs many stretti, is itself a salute to tradition, and was in print since 1650, the only such piece to be so.

28 a Prelude in A minor, WTC2
    b Duetto, BWV 803
    c Fugue, BWV 547.ii

inversions or diminution of themes was better justified by the nature of word-setting, for if the altos sing an inverted, diminished version of a chorale-melody which the trebles are singing straightforwardly, a result is that the all-important words get repeated. In Cantata 26, it is as if the people were clamouring or murmuring 'Ah, *how fleeting, how fleeting, how fleeting* is our life'.

Observations often made today – that a certain little canon 'reflects a metaphysical dimension to Bach's musical thought' or that any fondness he may have had for death-texts 'reveals an orphan's subconscious' – give an impression more of awed respect than critical evaluation, and remain unconfirmable. Searching for texts dealing with death or repentance or salvation may be fruitful, and lead to guesses about the composer's (or even his wife's) preoccupations, but guesses they will remain now that simple pious observance is so unfamiliar. Awed respect, in its way Romantic, is also behind unquestioning claims that in his music Bach was somehow influenced by powerful writers outside music, such as Pythagoras (ratios expressed in the Art of Fugue), Quintilian (rules for rhetoric in the Musical Offering), Kepler (the cosmos *passim*), Leibniz (the calculus as symbol of rationality), or a host of Lutheran theologians. Never, I think it fair to say, are such claims as these actually demonstrable.

In practice, they may actually distract attention. The first fugue of the Art of Fugue is striking from a musician's point of view not for arithmetic but for its imaginative countersubjects, here a series of freely invented,

model counter-melodies. Clever thematic integration in the E major Fugue
WTC2 or in the chorus closing Part I of St Matthew Passion – pieces
derived so comprehensively from their themes – is easier to analyse than
the warm richness in both pieces of the harmonies of E major. Even the
familiar key-plans might be distracting. In noticing that the tonics of the
Four Duets, E F G A, are the very notes of the 'highest tetrachord' in Greek
theory described a few years earlier by Walther in his *Lexicon* (1732, 601),
one might miss a more down-to-earth detail: that like so many of Bach's set
of pieces, the Four Duets are less uniform than they first seem. Sets often
do contain a work that is different in principle from the others, something
the composer must have intended, and in most cases a fruitful discussion
can be had about which work in the set *is* the exceptional one, and why.
Sometimes, arguments can be made for seeing each one as the exception.

As well as the discoveries of notes B A C H and of simple numbers in
the music (see above, pp. 331f), much is sometimes made of the so-called
'cross motif' (qv), a simple pattern of notes that in practice is hard to avoid.
This would be the case too with the notes B A C H in music in certain keys
such as C and F major, where these notes C, B♭ and B♮ easily occur in proximity. The question in both cases is, Given that four notes arranged as B A
C H or as a cross can occur 'naturally', are there moments when their
appearance is intentional? Since 'Yes' is the answer for B A C H, so it might
be for the cross motif, as at certain moments in the Passions, but the crucial
phrase would still be 'certain moments'. It is striking that in 'Komm, süsses
Kreuz' in St Matthew Passion, for example, there is no such clear allusion,
rather the motif's gesture is one of *dragging*. Much simpler is the Aria BWV
1127, for the 52nd birthday of the Duke of Weimar, since this has a recurring bass-theme of 52 notes (followed by a rest) that introduces the
soprano's song. Note, however, that in this instance, 52 alludes directly to
52 and is not a symbol, metaphor or gematria of 52 or of the duke.

Harmonic tension, mentioned in this book as a hallmark of the composer, is easy to sense but difficult to define, clearer perhaps if one compares
the harmony of two preludes which, when described theoretically, are
not very different: the C major WTC1 and an earlier work of Kuhnau
(Example 29).

Though by no means feeble or illiterate, Kuhnau's harmonies rest on
their intrinsic pleasantness, revealing nothing new and returning too soon
to the tonic, whereas not only does WTC1 avoid this but its sequence of
harmonies is so fresh and logical as to draw out a song in the mind of the
listener. Much the same emerges from comparing Bach's sets of variations
with Walther's or Handel's, which do little more than reiterate harmonies

29 a Sonata No. 5 from Kuhnau's *Musicalische*
        Vorstellung (1700), prelude
    b Prelude in C, WTC1 (see also Example 14)

and superficially embellish them. But for Bach too, true harmonic 'drive'
had to evolve: it is there in the final chorale of St John Passion but not in
the earliest organ-chorales, where mere chromaticism replaces true harmonic tension. Even the C major Prelude in Example 29 had to evolve,
so the sources suggest, and what now seems natural and inevitable in its
harmonies was the result of cogitation and playings-over.

   An evolution of Bach's melody from short phrases to longer lines is suggested by comparing the short ritornelli in the early cantatas, No. 150 with
Nos. 131 and 4, although tracing how he progressed from one to the other
is largely conjectural in the absence of sketchbooks and the loss of an
unknown number of completed works. Similarly, one has to guess how the

conventional, drawn-out, understated melody implicit in allemandes and courantes of the seventeenth century developed into the sustained melos they have in Bach's works for solo violin, cello or lute, produced there naturally by good harmony. Related to this is an experience some listeners have in those grander fugues in which they imagine hearing the subject although it is not there in the notes. Something similar occurs where note-patterns could appear more often than they actually do – in the 'Domine Deus' in the B minor Mass, for example, one can go on inwardly singing the opening flute motif throughout most of the piece.

Implicit melody is typical of another, different musical form: the recitative, where flashes of tunefulness draw in the listener, however familiar the narrative or text already is. If in the earlier Leipzig recitative the sense or sentiment is so meticulously declaimed in the melody as to leave the impression rather of 'a job of work well done', one can recognize by the time of the Passions and later (Cantata 14, 1735) an extraordinarily expressive range. The earlier recitative lines are true to genre in the rhetorical phrasing, rising or falling, pressing on or drawing out, exploring the diatonic or the chromatic; but gradually whether *secco* or *accompagnato* they become more charming, with a new relaxed melody, effortlessly touching by the time of the Christmas Oratorio. Although original hymn-lines can be set syllabically in the recitative of chorale-cantatas without losing any of the rhythmic freedoms, the cleverness behind this pales in comparison with the melodic inspiration of the best recitative, more affecting than the conventional apparatus of rhetoric could make it.

TEXTS, 'APPROPRIATE' MUSIC, ORDER-PLANS, PARODIES

In practice, theological consideration of cantata-texts today runs the risk of neglecting two points on which the composer must have concentrated: the down-to-earth challenge in setting any words (awkward vowels, inconvenient consonants, mis-emphases, etc.) and at the same time the creative challenge in making new melody. To these, good biblical knowledge, subtle allusion, pious sentiment, sincere faith and other abstractions could seem secondary.

Not every religious text suits music, but especially at the begining of an aria, the meaning and scansion of its text can give the composer his 'prompt': the melody arises – in his mind, on a keyboard – as a way of saying the words. A conventional musical vocabulary then conveys the various impressions and moods, and the instruments have their own version of the word-prompted melody, a version which in some cases must have been devised first. Many an aria-melody in the earlier Leipzig years gives the impression of being word-prompted rather than melos-prompted, however, i.e. they are not amongst the most natural and sweetly tuneful of Bach melodies. For standard topics such as *the pastoral* or *the regal* it was obligatory for him to draw on the day's conventions but with some new and original detail, as when an otherwise conventional trumpet line for 'Grosser Herr' in the Christmas Oratorio is transformed by unusual syncopations. Words of pathos or of rejoicing will often be set in drawn-out notes or melismas; words of doctrinal significance will often be set, understandably, in fugal counterpoint. Melisma and fugue are musical devices without associations but can easily acquire them in order to underline the text and its significances.

The composer looks for appropriate music, but *appropriate* might mean 'neutral', not necessarily 'the most affecting'. The large-scale chorus closing Part I of St Matthew Passion (the one originally from St John Passion) is a useful reminder that a composer can achieve his ends not only with the most expressive or affecting sounds of the day but with economical, traditional means. If this chorus is analysed bar-by-bar, all of its lines, both vocal and instrumental, will be found to be constantly and almost without break founded upon the last four notes of the chorale-melody, plain or paraphrased, rising or falling. Such a rich tissue of thematic allusion requires cool calculation and is more in style with earlier music, particularly organchorales: an old-fashioned, 'neutral' technique. The four notes concerned are sung in the original hymn to the words *Kreuze lange* ('long on the cross'), and it is to this that Bach's lines are alluding: not expressing, not symbolizing, not emoting, but reiterating and underlining. To claim more is to degenerate into programmaticism, searching for ideas or pictures 'expressed' by the music.

An *ouverture* appearing halfway in each Clavierübung volume (see p. 230) raises a question about how such an idea evolved. Did it occur to Bach only with experience of Part I, after which he actually directed the engravers to count the pages? In the Goldberg Variations, if he conceived the grouping into threes only after he began, was it a problem to fit everything into thirty-two pages? A canon at every third movement is not obvious to the listener, for some non-canonic variations sound teasingly very like canons, and vice-versa. In the final set of organ-chorales and in the Art of Fugue, any clearer grouping or shaping of the whole, had work proceeded further, is likely to have been seen rather than heard: conceptual than perceptual. The Goldberg Variations, however, seem to have both shapes: conceptual (on paper, a symmetry of Aria-variations-overture-variations-Aria) and perceptual (as normally played, a gradual 'crescendo' into the final movements). This distinction is important since many compilations were not necessarily to be performed from start to finish. Even the Passions and the Mass were not performed without break, and some symmetries in them are more to be conceived than perceived.

In the St John Passion, the simple or modified returns of choruses (easily recognized) and the symmetrical progression through flat to sharp keys and back (less so) are there for drama not theology, underlining the text not symbolizing it. Underlining a text can occur with the simplest musical device, as when the St Matthew Passion begins with a melisma for the voices, while the Christmas Oratorio begins with an emphatic *détaché*: a simple difference speaking, at a stroke, for the two totally different events, bringing Birth and Death to our attention by means of music's simplest, elementary gestures. In the same way but at a less immediate level, there need be no implication that a deep symbolism is operating if the key-plan in a cantata moves from flats to sharps, merely a natural progression from negative to positive, despair to hope. Equally elementary are such details as the soft string-accompaniment for Jesus or the canons setting texts referring to 'following' the Saviour, neither of which originated with Bach. Simple stretto is useful both for picturing the pressing, impatient crowds in St John Passion and for conveying the subtler image of 'one Lord Jesus Christ' in the Mass (*et in unum Dominum*). This last example demonstrates music's refusal to be tied to one single verbal conceit, for its theme apparently originated elsewhere, a text speaking of a quite different oneness, 'I am yours and you are mine' (see Marshall 1989, 183). A different ability of music – to change in aspect while remaining the same in essence – might seem to inspire the subject of Clavierübung III's final fugue, whose three 'aspects' are able to 'illustrate' the three-in-one doctrine of the Trinity as little else can. Curiously, however, the three aspects of the subject are not combined as they could have been if the intention had been to illustrate the Trinity.

In differing from the kinds of self-borrowing in Handel, the parodies of Bach also differ in purpose. He might either search existing compositions to find one suitable for adaptation or look for a suitable text for a movement he wishes to re-use, and it is by no means always clear which of these was the case. Nor is the old distinction between *sacred* and *secular* straightforward, and better terms need to be found. If an existing work is re-used, the new words create a new cantata that is sacred in so far as it becomes part of a regular service, thus 'ecclesiastical' (part of the church calendar) and 'liturgical' (part of the church service). But the pre-existing piece might be sacred while not part of a regular service: memorial music for the Queen of

Saxony (re-used for the St Mark Passion, BWV 247) is sacred, in no sense 'secular' or 'worldly'. If the memorial music for Prince Leopold used movements already composed for the St Matthew Passion rather than vice-versa, this would be the one major example of the reverse process from 'liturgical' to 'occasional'. But it would hardly be a move from sacred to secular, a distinction generally less than reliable or useful in an age of absolute monarchs.

Nevertheless, the fact remains that define as one might such words as sacred, secular, liturgical, ecclesiastical, occasional, devotional or confessional, Bach's re-workings are known to go in one direction only: towards use in a regular church service. Why would that be? Pious regard for the church service and its supremacy? A simple accident of sources, i.e. the church works are better and more systematically preserved? Any church cantata, whether totally new or a parody, would be sung more than once, regularly re-scheduled, not 'wasted' as a birthday cantata would be? Whatever the answers, the question amounts to this: Was there a religious or a practical reason for Bach's one-way parody procedures? Or was it sheer convention? The move from secular to sacred, and not vice versa, was also taken for granted in a discussion of parody by Kuhnau's former pupil G. E. Scheibel, in his *Zufällige Gedancken von der Kirchen-Music* (Frankfurt & Leipzig, 1721). Not for the first time, all these reasons are possible and by no means contradictory, if only because the genres do not always differ so much, and many a regular church-service cantata could have been performed, as it is, on an irregular occasion. Besides, the tone is by no means always distinctive. With a work like Cantata 210, known in two non-regular versions (a homage cantata for the Duke of Weissenfels and a wedding cantata for a later occasion), there are moments in the arias and even recitatives when one could think one is hearing music of the Passion, the most 'sacred' of all. On the other hand, there are moments in, for example, Cantata 70 when the pre-Advent call to 'Wake! Pray!' is set in a dramatic manner hard to distinguish from an opera's.

Handel's practice was rather different, for while he drew profusely on his oratorios from *Il Trionfo* (1707) onwards for music in operas, theatre oratorios, chamber sonatas, concertos and church anthems, he also re-used his relatively few church anthems in theatre oratorios – i.e. they went from ecclesiastical to non-ecclesastical, in some cases definitely secular. In addition, many of Handel's self-borrowings take the form not of re-used movements or even exact themes but of music that merely resembles an earlier piece, as if he were relying on memory or using sketches from a portfolio of ideas-for-future-use. Perhaps he was. In Bach, less often does one hear a passage that is merely *very like* another in this way. Yet it can happen, and does between certain pieces in the same key (D major) or in the same style (*allabreve* counterpoint), and such similarities are not limited to particular periods in his life.

If Bach's practices in re-using material suggest something about his sense of what is appropriate and what is not, another question is, Why does he not repeat himself more often than he does? The fine point between self-repetition and simple similarity between pieces (as, for example, between his many and various gavottes) is quite clear. Generally, the potential of a genre is surveyed with such extraordinary thoroughness that it is not easy to find anything much in common even between works that may be similar on paper. This is the case with the nine successive and radically different canons within the thirty Goldberg Variations. In the solo violin suites, by no means can one always anticipate what direction the music will take: one senses harmonic ellipses (as if a step in the argument was omitted) or can wait a long time for a simple sequence. In avoiding easy options, the composer is again combining his duties as true artist and true Lutheran, and neither can be shown to be dominant. Perhaps works that do have much in common, such as the final choruses of the two Passions or the overtures of three orchestral suites, are similar because they are more 'public': they are meeting the need a public audience has for recognisable convention.

Especially in Germany, much has been written about Bach the selector and setter of sacred texts, a topic not only difficult for non-native speakers but one that pushes discussion in certain directions, and the ensuing reverence, even vicarious piety, can disguise his musical priorities. His re-working of the standard conventions in setting cantata-texts, and the questions arising – did he prefer texts with simple *Affekte* easily expressed in music, was he indifferent to new poetry and to the poor quality of some texts, was his deep biblical knowledge so exceptional? – have sometimes led authors to soar high. The changes to texts he may have been responsible for making would support the idea that he was involved, professionally or confessionally, in them. But sincerity of belief, knowledge of theology, and the desire to convey either, can not be more than secondary for a composer.

A BRIEF NOTE ON AESTHETICS

Judging by moment after moment in the Passions and cantatas, the common idea that music expresses emotions or articulates feelings is one that J. S. Bach either shared, increasingly so as he matured, or acquiesced in as a composer who was willing to serve his neighbours in ways familiar to them. This he would do by consciously applying musical conventions

30 Cantata 202, opening
'Only disperse, troubled shadows,
frost, winds, go to your rest!'

they would recognize and be affected by. It may be that it requires an ide-
alist philosophy unknown to Bach to question whether music is 'sad' or
'happy' in any practical or everyday sense, and whether in such phrases as
a sad aria, a sad person, a sad experience or a sad emotion, 'sad' carries the
same meanings . But some of his late music seems to acknowledge that the
sense of hearing, more effectively than the other senses, admits us to a
world of imagination in which words like 'sad', 'happy', 'despair' or 'hope'
are inadequate and not quite relevant. Hence a need for the word 'transcendental'.

Exquisite slow movements such as the Air from the D major Overture
('on the G string'), the Largo of the F minor Concerto, or the Passion aria
'Erbarme dich', can arouse a feeling which listeners might well label as 'sad',
for they are touched by the beauty and transience of such harmony and
melody when performed sympathetically, and their imagination is aroused.
But the manner has to be sympathetic, and manner is not substance. If to
modern ears the soft, slow, rising string chords of the Wedding Cantata
convey something sad (see Example 30), it would come from the unhur-
ried tempo, the gentle manner in which the sweet chords were played, plus
such details as chromatic touches introduced in a major key. The same
chords played boisterously and loud evoke something quite different, and

this too would hang on conventions associated with the boisterous and loud. Music's immediate beauty having opened up listeners' receptiveness, particular impressions are then given by the text or by conventional associations, and in any case by the rhetoric of performance. To some listeners, one Passion's Jesus can easily seem *triumphant* and the other's *suffering*, but the Gospel itself can be narrated neutrally, conveying neither; any impressions given by the spoken or the sung word will derive from the existential experience of it, the *Affekt* of how it is set and actually performed. Furthermore, however well Bach is thought to convey triumph or suffering, neither need result from his personal experiences. Music is not 'painful' as some quotidian experience might be, nor need the composer have experienced pain himself, and nor need his music be expressive if he has. To assume otherwise can lead admirers to seek and find meaning in music that has no text: in the slow movement of a Bach concerto they can feel the 'expression of deep emotion' and even, depending on changing fashions amongst admirers, his 'political individualism'.

Nearly fifty years after Mattheson published his criticism of word-setting in Cantata 21 (see p. 152), and conceivably in tardy response to it, Emanuel wrote to Forkel that his father worked devoutly in his church cantatas, composing them according to the text's general sense and not individual words, which latter technique can be comical in effect though admired by some (Dok III, 284). This is convincing if 'to express' (*ausdrücken*) has no deep philosophical significance. Minor composers might well draw on conventional effects to 'express' or picture isolated words such as weeping, laughing, rising, falling, heaven, hell, etc., but so in many earlier organ-chorales did J. S. Bach. His routine in composing the cantatas is that of a master who knows the conventions and taps into them effortlessly, to 'express' words acording to expectations. But at a deeper level than this the word 'express' is problematic and begs too many questions, being one verb of many summoned in the thankless task of saying what it is that music is doing, or is said to be.

In maturer works of Bach, it seems appropriate to find another verb than 'express': the music is not expressing a particular word or idea but marking or underlining it, a kind of audible form of *nota bene!* An example would be at *sepultus est*, 'was buried', in the B minor Mass: the change of mode at this point draws attention to the words and what is to follow, but in no clear way does it *express* grief, awe, subdued terror, despair or anything else at the idea of either burial or Resurrection. Rather, it creates an air of expectancy by musical means (sudden change of key, hushed dynamic), and everyone including the performers knows what is to come. The drama is undeniable but is not so much expressed by the music as contributed by it: in a plain, recited Creed the words themselves are not dramatic. Elsewhere, Bach could be more obscurely signifying his interpretation of a text, as in employing details of Italian and French styles for two settings of the German-Latin Creed in Clavierübung III, so marking its catholicity. In this way, using music's notes to allude to ideas from outside it goes beyond contemporary practice.

The metaphors involved when describing music's effect are illustrated in Example 30, for the rising string chords correspond to a text speaking of 'troubled clouds yielding' to the sunny happiness of the wedding day. But since, strictly, notes do not rise and clouds do not yield, the matching of musical sound to verbal picture is a double metaphor, both of which depend on convention. Of course, such conventions allow words to be written with a view to how musicians would set them, and puzzling moments (i.e. if the word-setting does not obviously suit the sentiment) might need to be explained away. If the middle movement of Cantata 102 seems too carefree and vigorously jolly for a text that speaks of God's anger, there has either to be a hidden and ingenious programme ('Man is too busy to be always thinking of God's anger', etc.) or a mismatch (this, a conclusion of last resort). The first kind of explanation has become more popular than the second, but interpreters of Bach's music and its significances are often reduced to guesses, clung to with such conviction that sceptical response risks appearing soulless.

In such respects as these, the creations of J. S. Bach take one into the heart of the conundrum of music, What is it, and what exactly does it do? But just as puzzling in its way, draw as one might on his known background, is how he came to be so productive, persistently alert, have such energies, and acquire such a grasp of harmony. It is inconceivable that anyone would call him 'too idle' or 'lazy' to revise his music, as *Messiah's* librettist called Handel (HHB 357, 361). Rather, his exceptional physical and mental strengths served as counterweight to more negative trends in his family's make-up, recorded only fitfully no doubt, such as certain mental problems (an aunt and a son), an especially high mortality rate (his own children and those in other Bach families), a propensity for twins (his grandparents', his brother's, his own), and perhaps more diabetes than we know about. That he came from a musical family on both his father's and mother's side must be part of the picture, but how this would give him a rhythmic and melodic sense that has bewitched so many different kinds of musician ever since, or a mastery of harmony that established nothing less than a norm in western culture, is a mystery.

Postscript

On 31 August 2006, an article in the newspaper *Die Zeit* described the discovery by researchers from the Bach-Archiv, Leipzig, of some large manuscript leaves (34 × 34cm) in the Anna-Amalia-Library, Weimar, containing previously unknown keyboard tablature in the hand of J. S. Bach. Some key facts are:

two important chorale fantasias, Buxtehude's 'Nun freut euch liebe Christen g'mein' and Reinken's 'An Wasserflüssen Babylon' were copied, major new sources for the music they contain.

an inscription under the latter, *Il Fine à Dom. Georg: Böhme descriptum ao. 1700 Lunaburgi,* the earliest known Bach autograph, was evidently made at the 'apprentice age' of fifteen (see above, p. 22).

Bach was using tablature in his mid-teens, probably earlier (see p. 300). Pending fuller analysis elsewhere, the discovery already raises such questions as these:

whether the Buxtehude copy was made earlier, at age '12 or 13', as has been claimed; this would be while Bach was still in Ohrdruf.

since it seems that Bach did work with Georg Böhm, either as soon as he moved to Lüneburg or in/from the summer of 1700 as his voice broke (see above, pp. 20ff), was this his main reason for moving to Lüneburg at the age of fifteen?

whether *à Dom.* indicates *domus* ('house') or, more likely, *Dominus* ('master'), is uncertain, but only the former need imply a live-in pupil.

if he was encouraged by Böhm to visit Reinken (see pp. 25ff) as well as, perhaps, the Duke of Celle's band (p. 29), did his return to Thuringia in 1702 result from receiving no firm offer in Lüneburg or Hamburg? Or could he not afford to pay Böhm (cf. p. 18), and so later denied being his student (see p. 27)?

the two high-quality pieces suggest a sound value-judgement and perhaps a focus on the 'northern repertory', though whether on Bach's part or Böhm's is unclear. (Any interest in French music they shared at the time would not be represented by German organ tablature.)

if the copies were made from Böhm's own MSS, with permission, were they an inspiration for the visits to Hamburg (p. 26) and later to Lübeck (p. 46)?

some corrections in the MS might be a sign that the music was performed. Did the later meeting with Reinken (see p. 148) somehow draw on some memory from twenty years earlier?

do his early keyboard-scores a few years later (BWV 739, 764, see p. 356), also apparently carefully preserved, mark a turning away from both tablature and the long 'northern' fantasia?

in view of Christoph Bach's voluminous MSS (see p. 24), perhaps at this time the brothers were sharing sources of music.

are the leaves in the Weimar library because for some reason they were deposited there? What reason? Because such music and/or copies had dropped out of use?

While there is little support here for *Die Zeit*'s view that the discovery suggests J. S. Bach to have been a *Wunderkind* comparable to Mozart, it does underline the way any new piece of evidence can throw a quite different light on the biography as previously understood.

Glossary

à 2, à 3 etc.: old convention denoting the music's number of voices (as in a keyboard fugue) or instruments (as in chamber music). The WTC carefully labels each fugue accordingly; in general, *à 3* implies a more expansive (and difficult) fugue than *à 4*. Elsewhere, *à 2 Clav* indicates how many manuals are required for optimum effect.

ABA: 'ternary form', a movement whose (long) opening section returns complete after a contrasting section B. The B can be quite short and totally new, or longer than A, perhaps developing ideas found there. In later arias, A2 tends to be shortened to its opening paragraph.

Abendmusik: 'evening music', period term for the mixed sacred concerts given in Lübeck Marienkirche from *c.* 1650 to *c.* 1800, on five Sundays in autumn and winter (last two of Trinity, plus Advent II, III and IV), beginning at 4:00 pm. On oratorio-like works in five acts (one in each concert), see p. 50.

a cappella: an ill-founded term for choral performance especially of polyphonic music before 1700, either from which instruments are absent (thus 'unaccompanied music for choir') or in which they double or occasionally replace voices.

aeolian cadence: term commonly denoting the cadence whose bass-line moves down a semitone, originally F-natural to E. Often as a 'half close' prefacing a lively movement (in this case, in A minor or C major).

Affekt: the mood of a piece of music as felt by its listener, invoked particularly by conventionalized details of style, key, tempo, volume and *figurae* (qv).

allabreve: here, a characteristic Italianate counterpoint with a moderate beat, its part-writing incorporating particular rhythms such as dactyls and suspensions (qv).

appoggiatura: a leaning note (*appoggiarsi*, 'to lean'), dissonant, on the beat, approached by a leap and resolving up or down to the consonance on a weaker beat. Though in theory ornamental, in practice crucial to developed harmony.

arioso: 'like an aria', e.g. a section of recitative with (often suddenly) a regular beat, a moving bass-line and a *cantabile* melody (this often with repeated words).

B A C H: in German B♭, A C B♮, constituting a recognized motif or theme, *melodisch* according to Walther (1732, 'J. S. Bach'). C. P. E. Bach noted its appearance in the autograph of the incomplete fugue of the Art of Fugue and worked the motif himself in a variety of ways.

badinerie: one of several terms in Germany *c.* 1730 for bright, novel character-pieces (cf. Clavierübung I's terms 'Scherzo', 'Capriccio', 'Burlesca'). The Finale of the B minor Flute Overture, BWV 1067 and the badinerie-like first fugue of WTC2 may be contemporary.

bariolage: a 'variegated' sound, specifically the rapid alternating of open and stopped strings on a violin, producing a lively, scrabbling, quasi-obsessive effect.

belcanto: a later term useful for the lyrical, non-declamatory 'beautiful singing' of arias, thus distinguishing them from e.g. the narrative style of recitative.

bicinium: a piece for two voices or parts, by *c.* 1700 a melody accompanied by a lively, melodic bass with typical rhythmic patterns and recurring phrases.

binary: a movement in binary form has two sections, of the same length (e.g. eight bars) or, usually, with the second longer, each normally or optionally repeated.

brisé: in keyboard music, the 'breaking' of chords so that the harmony is expressed more continuously and smoothly.

Brustwerk: the small organ chest (usually with its own manual) above the keyboards, 'in the breast' of the organ and near the performers, often used for continuo, qv.

cadenza: 'cadence', used in this sense in The Art of Fugue to indicate where a canon can end; only later, the virtuoso passage for a concerto soloist before the final *tutti* rounding-off. But see also p. 135.

cambiata: a little note usually in the melody and momentarily 'changing' the harmony with a discord that in effect anticipates the next concord.

canon in diminutione/augmentatione: a canon in which the theme is answered not straightforwardly (as in a round) but in note-values smaller/larger than the theme's, usually at half/double length.

cantata: term used for non-liturgical vocal works, sometimes patently Italianate (see also *serenata*); or for church cantatas with solo voice (Nos. 54, 56, 82, 84, 170, 199). Other works now called cantatas were generally called *Musik* or *Concerto* or *Stück*, conventionally implying full ensemble works.

cantor: in Lutheran Germany, the director of a church's music and musicians, also teaching in its school (not only music) and responsible for performances on municipal occasions.

cantus firmus: here, the 'fixed melody' of a chorale sounding out in longer notes in a cantata or organ-chorale, usually a line at a time, against busier voices. Sometimes, a Latin mass-chant (taken from Lutheran hymnbooks) lies behind the counterpoint (early Kyrie, BWV 233a; opening bars of the B minor Mass) without being a true cantus firmus.

capellmeister: musician in charge of a court's *cappella* (qv), its personnel and its performances, both sacred (chapel cantatas) and secular (chamber music, opera, etc.).

cappella: the company of singers and instrumentalists performing a range of musical duties for their employer (church, court).

Chair Organ: the little organ behind the organist's back, usually in the gallery-front, played by the lowest keyboard and physically near the congregation below.

chorale cantata: a cantata-type attributed to Bach (from second half of 1724), in which some or all of a hymn's verses are set either verbatim (e.g. opening chorus and final chorale) or paraphrased (e.g. arias), and using a variety of musical forms.

chromatic fourth: a passage of six successive semitones, descending (e.g. D C♯ C♮ B B♭ A) or ascending. A phrase useful and easy to combine with melodies as countersubject, and able, when desired, to convey one or other negative *Affekt*.

Clavier: 'keyboard' instrument, of whatever kind was appropriate or conventional in the (written) context.

compass: the extent from bottom to top of a keyboard, where c′ = middle C, c an octave below, C two octaves below, c″ an octave above, c‴ two octaves above. Usually called 'range' in the USA.

concertino: see concerto grosso

concertmaster: in *c.* 1715, a recent term for the leading instrumentalist (first violinist, perhaps the continuo-player) organizing, rehearsing and conducting the band.

concerto grosso: 'large consort', a term used in *c.* 1700 occasionally, but today regularly, for an ensemble containing a small group of soloists ('concertino') within the larger group ('ripieno') and contrasting with it. Also, a type of music therefor.

consistory court: a board of clerical and other officials, with legal status, either at national/provincial or local level, and supervising the affairs of a church.

consort: old English term for an ensemble of instruments, either of one family (e.g. 'viol consort') or of mixed strings and wind ('broken consort').

continuo: accompaniment played from a bass line, most often by a bass instrument and a keyboard on which are realized the chords indicated or implied by figures.

cross motif: group of four notes whose first and last are close in pitch, the second higher, the third lower (or vice-versa), so that two lines connecting notes 1 with 4 and 2 with 3 cross each other, as in the motif B A C H, qv. The motif is conjectured to allude to the Cross and/or to the X of *Christos*.

da capo: 'from the beginning', a direction to go back and repeat the music up till *fine* or the double bar-lines. 'Da capo form' or a 'da capo aria' has the shape ABA, qv.

détaché: a bowing term for notes bowed separately – but not necessarily very short, as with *staccato* (theoretically the Italian equivalent).

diatonic: as used of this period, diatonic denotes music written in an unambiguous major or minor key, as distinct from the modes of an earlier period or the shifting tonalities of a later. (The American term 'tonal' for diatonic is more ambiguous.)

diminished seventh: interval produced by three superimposed minor thirds, thus in D minor (mode I) from C♯ up to B♭, in C minor (a modern key) from B♮ to A♭. Also, the chord made from such thirds (so C♯ E G B♭), with marked *Affekt* – anxious, wistful, dramatic etc. The chord's alternate notes form tritones, qv.

ditonic (or Pythagorean) comma: small but perceptible difference between a pure octave (doubled frequency) and one reached by six pure tones (C D E F♯ G♯ A♯ B♯), which is sharper.

échappée: a short note off the beat that leaps in the opposite direction to where it was going; as if an unaccented passing-note (qv) that does not pass.

elector: one of the nine German princes entitled to elect the (Holy Roman) Emperor. In this book, 'king' and 'queen' are sometimes used for the Elector and Electress of Saxony, since from 1697 to 1763 electors were also called (not always by the Poles) King of Poland.

figura: a 'figure' or small, distinctive note-pattern in one of many shapes, catalogued by such contemporary theorists as J. G. Walther.

galant: eighteenth-century term now applied to light, elegant music from *c*. 1730, mostly not for church. In 1726, 'Galanterien' (modern dances) are referred to both on the titlepage of Partita No. 1 and in the preface of Gottlieb Muffat's *72 Versetl.*

Geigenwerk ('violin-work'): a keyboard instrument in which rotating wheels 'bow' any gut or metal string brought into contact with them by special mechanism connected to the keys.

gematria ('geometry'): term for the method of finding significances in Hebrew scripture by replacing a word with another of the same number when calcuated on a basis of letter A = 1, B = 2, etc. Giving note-names their number equivalents can appear to reveal musical patterns or intentions.

'Germany': the Peace of Westphalia (1648) gave the individual dukedoms, kingdoms etc. the power to form their own alliances, making them practically independent states. The formal unity of 'one Germany' was achieved only in 1871.

Golden Section: point at which a smaller of two parts is in the same proportion to the greater as the greater is to the whole. Both this proportion (1:1.62) and the square root of five (1:2.236) seem to govern the physical measurements of an extant Leipzig clavichord of *c*. 1750. At a point in music just before two thirds of the way through, corresponding to this ratio, something conspicuous is often heard.

gusto: see below, *manière*.

Hanseatic: a city, usually of some importance, with prominent merchant class and municipal institutions, and belonging to the *Hanse*, a German commercial league. See maps.

harmonic rhythm: a not very felicitous phrase denoting how frequently a piece of music's harmony changes. A single chord for the first four bars of the Sixth Brandenburg Concerto is a 'slow harmonic rhythm'. Large-scale slow harmonic rhythm, as in the opening and 'Lightning and Thunder' choruses of the St Matthew Passion, was surely sketched out on paper first.

hemiola: here, bars of six beats alternating (or simultaneously employing) two groups of three and three groups of two, producing a pleasing ambiguity.

imitation: contrapuntal device in which a voice imitates the previous motif or theme, at the same or different pitch, sometimes overlapping it ('stretto', qv).

imperfect cadence: one ending (most often temporarily) on the dominant, unlike the perfect cadence (qv). The aeolian cadence (qv) is also 'imperfect'.

invertible counterpoint: in which each line can serve equally as the bass, whether in two, three ('triple invertible'), four ('quadruple') or more parts. Hard to do well.

Lautenwerk, Lautenclavicymbel ('lute work'): a keyboard instrument of short scale and gut strings, producing *forte, piano und pianissimo* by touch (Adlung II, 138).

leading note: the seventh note of the scale, rising melodically to the tonic (so B in C major or minor).

manière: the specific 'style of composing, writing, singing' French music (Brossard 1705, 277), with characteristic rhythms, ornaments, strong-weak gestures etc. *Goût* or *gusto* (Clavierübung II) denotes 'style' rather than 'taste': Couperin's directive to play with *le bon goût* implies 'in the appropriate style'.

melismatic: melody in which one syllable is sung to several notes, perhaps many; or a smooth instrumental line imitating this.

melos: here, the quality or state of being melodious; the general melodic character of particular music.

Neapolitan sixth: a chord associated with Neapolitan cantatas of *c*1675, the 'flattened supertonic, first inversion' (in C minor, a chord F A♭, D♭) before a dominant (G major). For Bach, an italianate allusion whether traditional (Toccata, BWV 564 *Adagio*) or modern (both 'Kyrie' subjects of the B minor Mass).

notes inégales: 'unequal notes', specifically running quavers played unequally (long-short) in certain French dances with a crotchet beat; for a lilting, mannered effect.

obbligato: instrumental part (for violin, organ, oboe etc.) not dispensable or replaceable by others in an ensemble, but necessary for a solo line.

ordre: F. Couperin's categorical term for a collection of dances: an 'order' of pieces within the same 'class' (key), and thus not a fixed 'set' (suite) to be played as such.

organ-chorale: Lutheran hymn-melody re-worked for organ. Often called 'chorale-prelude' but not necessarily a prelude to anything. Generally longer and more intricate than the sung verse of a hymn.

ostinato: an 'obstinate' phrase repeated (sometimes paraphased) throughout a piece or a section, generally in the bass, creating continuity and length.

ouverture: a specific French genre, with a stately, rhythmically marked prelude and then a lighter, imitative section (seldom a true fugue, unlike Bach's and Handel's). As in certain Dieupart suites (copied at Weimar), sometimes the opening section then returns. A series of dances can follow, making a 'suite', sometimes long.

paraphrase: here, treatment of an existing melody so that while all its notes are there (usually on the beats), others weave around them so as to create a new melody. The descending chromatic fourth qv is paraphrased in the opening soprano theme of the St Matthew Passion.

parody: a vocal work in which a new sacred text replaces the original text, here without mimicry or the ridicule associated with the word in other connections.

partimento: figured-bass exercises teaching players how to 'improvise' fugues by indicating where e.g. a theme may enter above the bass. A term not obviously appropriate if it means 'division', more so if it means 'a point of departure'.

partita: (i) the 'division' of a piece, e.g. a variation, or (ii) 'part' of a set of pieces, e.g. a single suite. Bach used it for the suites in Clavierübung I, but not certainly for the hymn-variations now known as 'chorale partitas'. (*Partita* appears in the Italian title of Krieger's *Sei partite* of 1697, where the German title had *Partien*.)

passing note: a small but important dissonant note passing by step between two consonant notes a third apart, either on the beat ('accented') or off ('unaccented').

Passion: as in the *Book of Common Prayer*, 1549, 'Passion' is the vernacular of *passio*, 'suffering'. Bach's title *Passio Domini nostri J. C. secundum Evangelistam Matthaeum* indicates 'The suffering of our Lord Jesus Christ according to the Evangelist Matthew'; thus in musical settings since at least the eleventh century.

pasticcio: 'pie, pasty, mishmash', a work assembled from (not basely imitating) other works, particularly by other composers of the genre concerned, e.g. operas or Passions.

pedalpoint: a note held or much-repeated through changing harmonies, usually but not necessarily in the bass; in organ music, generally played by the pedals.

perfect cadence: a conclusive close made by two chords, dominant followed by tonic (so G major rising/falling to C major or minor).

permutation: a contrapuntal technique, particularly in fugues, in which the several themes can appear in any – but carefully varied – vertical order.

Picardy third: the major final chord of a piece in the minor (*une tierce picarde*, 'a sharp third'), still so usual that before *c.* 1730 a minor final, if intended, is striking.

Pietism: a religious and pastoral practice so called from P. J. Spener's *Pia desideria* (Frankfurt/M, 1675), and becoming a personalized, introspective form of belief emphasizing a crushing contrition that assured the believer of grace through works. Banned from Saxony in 1691, then established in Halle and its new university, founded in 1694.

polychoral: modern term for a composition for two or more choirs (vocal and/or instrumental), so made for purposes of contrast, drama, alternation, conjunction etc.

praeludium: here, specifically a 'prelude' of large proportions for organ, in several sections or movements, thus rather corresponding to the violin's sectional sonata.

'princely': though a word often used to translate *fürstlich*, English usage has no such equivalent of 'ducal' or 'royal', leaving 'capellmeister to a prince' less ambiguous than 'princely capellmeister'.

privilege: the authorized right of a craftsman such as an organ-builder to accept (be the first choice for) as many contracts in a specified territory as he wishes.

quodlibet: 'what you please', music using several themes successively or simultaneously; for humour in Variation 30 of the Goldberg Variations but not when four hymn-lines appear together in the Canonic Variations, BWV 769.v.

range: in the USA, the usual term for compass (qv) but strictly only a part of it.

real answer: see tonal answer.

recitativo secco: later term for the 'dry recitation' when a solo singer, accompanied only by continuo, takes the narrative further, as freely as speech, and before or after more meditative music. Recitativo accompagnato has instrumental accompaniment and is therefore more measured and regular.

rector: headmaster of a school, normally, as then in England, an ordained clergyman living on the school premises. Conrector, 'assistant headmaster'.

reeds: organ-pipes with a reed (like a clarinet), creating power and variety. A 32′ reed is a rare, loud stop two octaves below the written note.

ricercar: name for the two fugues of The Musical Offering, 'seeking out' complex ways to develop fugal counterpoint (Bach's only known use, perhaps from Krieger's *Clavier-Übung*, 1699 or, better, Frescobaldi's *Fiori musicali*, 1635).

ripieno: see 'concerto grosso'.

ritornello: 'little return', a passage returning complete or in part, in the same or another key. (Used by Bach for the recurring passage for strings in the aria BWV 1127, 1713.) 'Ritornello form': a movement so constructed, with its interspersing episodes usually for fewer instruments. 'Ritornello chorale': a chorale-setting with the melody's lines separated by ritornelli, resulting in a fuller movement.

rondeau: a dance or dance-like movement in which the opening theme, regular in length and ending in the tonic, returns unaltered after each of a number of episodes.

rubato: a later term denoting flexibility of the beat, done for expressive purposes.

secco: see recitativo secco.

sequence: a phrase of melody and/or harmony restated with a difference, up or down a note or more. Continuing a sequence beyond a certain point is a risk not always avoided by Vivaldi.

serenata: non-church cantata for a special occasion such as a public figure's birthday, performed in the evening (*séra*) out of doors, and keeping loosely to a plot, often mythological. Bach's non-church cantatas employed varous terms – *cantata, dram[m]a per musica*, even *cantata gratulatoria* (BWV 215).

sevenths: triads (qv) to which a seventh note above the root is added, thus C E G with B or B-flat, discords needing resolution. Those notes can appear in any order (E G B C, G B C E etc.) and are still 'sevenths'.

siciliano: a term used in the period, though seldom by Neapolitan composers, to denote a gentle, tuneful movement with dotted rhythms like a gigue but much slower.

sinfonia: usually, a fully developed movement for instruments only, prefacing the first or second part of a cantata.

Singspiel: a species of German opera, with spoken dialogue between songs and choruses, often of a popular, even picaresque nature, both in text and music.

six-four chord: see triad.

sostenuto: in harpsichord music *c*. 1720, a manner of playing by holding the notes as long as appropriate or practical.

species: as formulated by J. J. Fux (1725), five ways in which a simple line of semibreves can be countered by another, increasingly complex, line while observing old grammatical rules. As such, 'species counterpoint' teaches students to handle intervals and can in itself lead to reasonable music.

Stadtpfeifer: 'Town pipers' (English waits), municipal employees playing on certain public occasions. Traditionally, Leipzig had four wind- and three string-players. Of two applicants in 1748, Bach preferred the one who played the oboe 'more purely and better-toned' and the violin 'with greater dexterity', i.e. instruments useful in church (Dok II, 452).

stile antico: a term from the period (Mattheson's *stylus antiquus*) denoting the 'old style' of vocal counterpoint of Palestrina etc., often taught (after

1725) *via* Fux's species, qv. Today, *stile moderno* is sometimes used antithetically.

stoplist: the contracted-for number and types of stops in a given organ, the more the bigger the instrument.

stretto: 'narrow' imitation in which a theme is imitated before it finishes, a procedure often requiring some harmonic ingenuity.

suboctave: sound an 'octave below' notated pitch, produced by certain sets of harpsichord-strings, organ-pipes, or many a large string bass (violone, etc.).

suspension: a crucial harmonic progression in which a note held over the following strong beat creates a discord requiring resolution (down, occasionally up) on the weaker beat, producing continuity and variety.

tablature: for German keyboardists, musical notation not with notes on a staff but with pitch-letters and rhythmic signs, running from left to right in lines corresponding to the part-writing.

temperament: a tuning in which notes are not pure (which would make sharp octaves) but are 'tempered' or modified. The greater the number of notes modified, the greater the number of acceptable triads (qv).

tessitura ('texture'): the part of the compass qv in which the music is predominantly lying, thus 'high' or 'low'.

tetrachord: in Greek theory, four adjacent notes in a model scale illustrating possible divisions of that fourth (e.g. where the semitone can lie).

tonal answer: the fugue-subject as 'answered' in the dominant but with notes that might emphasize the dominant's dominant being lowered a tone. A 'real answer' is the subject transposed in the dominant without such alteration.

triad: here, the common chord of three notes (e.g. major C E G, minor C E♭ G). In a six-four chord, the notes have a different vertical order (G C E), producing an 'unstable chord' requiring resolution.

tritone: the interval produced by notes three whole tones apart, e.g. C-F♯, successive or simultaneous. (Strictly, C-G♭ is a 'diminished fifth' not a tritone.)

vespers: for Lutherans, an afternoon or evening service with New Testament canticles; shorter and lighter than the 'Main Service' but often with important music, including organ solos and special choral items. Something of a 'church concert'.

References

Jacob Adlung, *Musica mechanica organoedi*, with additions by Johann Friedrich Agricola, ed. Johann Lorenz Albrecht, 2 vols. (Berlin, 1768).

Johann Friedrich Agricola: see Adlung, and Obituary.

Christian Ahrens & Klaus Langrock (eds.), *Geprießener Silbermann! Gereimtes und ungereimtes zur Einweihung von Orgeln Gottfried Silbermanns* (Altenburg, 2003).

Andreas Bach Book = Leipziger Städtische Bibliotheken, Musikbibliothek, MS III.8.4.

Carl Philipp Emanuel Bach, *Versuch über die wahre Art das Clavier zu spielen*, 2 vols (Berlin, 1753, 1762).

[*Selbstbiographie*] in Carl Burney, *Tagebuch seiner musikalischen Reisen*, Bd. 3 (Hamburg, 1773), pp. 199–209.

Klaus Beckmann, and Hans-Joachim Schulze (eds), *Johann Gottfried Walther. Briefe* (Leipzig, 1987).

BJ = *Bach-Jahrbuch*.

Kirsten Beißwenger, *Johann Sebastian Bachs Notenbibliothek* (Kassel, 1992).

Johann Philipp Bendeler, *Organopoeia oder Unterweisung wie eine Orgel . . . zuerbauen* (Quedlinburg, c. 1690).

Heinrich Besseler, 'Markgraf Christian Ludwig von Brandenburg', BJ 43 (1956), pp. 18–35.

Erdmann Werner Böhme, *Die frühdeutsche Oper in Thüringen* (Stadtroda, 1931).

Sébastien de Brossard, *Dictionaire de musique* (Paris, 2/1705).

Georg Heinrich Bümler obituary: see Mizler.

Charles Burney, *An account of the . . . commemoration of Handel* (London, 1785). *A general history of music*, vol. 4 (London, 1789).

Gregory Butler, *Bach's Clavierübung III. The making of a print* (Durham NC, 1990).

Johann Heinrich Buttstedt, *Ut, mi, sol, re, fa, la, tota musica et harmonia aeterna* (Erfurt, 1716).

Joachimus Camerarius, *De Philippi Melanchthonis ortu* (Leipzig, 1566).

Clavier-Büchlein für Wilhelm Friedemann Bach = Yale University, Irving S. Gilmore Music Library, MS Music Deposit 31.

Howard H. Cox (ed.), *The Calov Bible of J. S. Bach* (Ann Arbor, MI, 1985).

Gregory Butler, 'Toward an aesthetic and pedagogical context for J. S. Bach's *Italian Concerto* BWV 971', in ed. Martin Geck, *Bachs Musik für Tasteninstrumente* (Dortmund, 2003), pp. 223–230.

Ulrich Dähnert, *Der Orgel- und Instrumentenbauer Zacharias Hildebrandt* (Leipzig, 1962).

Dok I, II, III, IV = *Bach-Dokumente*, I ed. Werner Neumann and Hans-Joachim Schulze (Kassel etc., 1963), II ed. Werner Neumann and Hans-Joachim Schulze (Kassel etc, 1969), III ed. Hans-Joachim Schulze (Kassel etc, 1972), IV ed. Werner Neumann (Leipzig, 1979).

DDT = *Denkmäler der deutschen Tonkunst*.

DTÖ = *Denkmäler der Tonkunst in Österreich*.

Arnfried Edler, *Der nordelbische Organist* (Kassel, 1982).

Fk = Martin Falck, *Wilhelm Friedemann Bach. Sein Leben und seine Werke* (Lindau, 2/1956).

Ernst Flade, *Der Orgelbauer Gottfried Silbermann* (Leipzig, 1926).

Johann Nicolaus Forkel, *Ueber Johann Sebastian Bachs Leben, Kunst und Kunstwerke* (Leipzig, 1802).

Christian Förner, *Vollkommener Bericht, wie eine Orgel . . . soll . . . gebauet werden* (Leipzig, 1684).

Claudio Gallico, *Girolamo Frescobaldi. L'affetto, l'ordito, le metamorfosi* (Florence, 1986).

Karl Geiringer, *The Bach family* (London, 1954).

Genealogical Table = Dok I, pp. 255–67.

Andreas Glöckner, 'Gründe für Johann Sebastian Bachs Weggang von Weimar', in Hoffmann 1988, pp. 137–43.

'"Na, die hätten Sie aber auch nur hören sollen!" Über die Unzulänglichkeiten bei Bachs Leipziger Figuralaufführungen', in Leisinger 2002, pp. 387–401.

'Bachs Es-Dur Magnificat BWV 243a – eine genuine Weihnachtsmusik?', BJ 89 (2003), pp. 37–45.

Janos Harich, 'Haydn Documenta', *Haydn Yearbook* 7 (1971), pp. 70–163.

Johann David Heinichen, *Neu erfundene und gründliche Anweisung zu vollkommener Erlernung des General-Basses* (Hamburg, 1711).

HHB = Berndt Baselt *et al.* (eds.), *Händel-Handbuch Band 4: Dokumente zu Leben und Schaffen* (Kassel/Leipzig, 1984).

Hubert Henkel, 'Zur Geschichte der Scheibe-Orgel in der Leipziger Johannis-kirche', in Reinhard Szeskus (ed.), *Johann Sebastian Bachs Traditionsraum = Bach-Studien* 9 (Leipzig, 1986), pp. 45–50.

Winfried Hoffmann & Armin Schneiderheinze (eds.), *Bericht über die wissen-schaftliche Konferenz zum V. Internationalen Bachfest der DDR 1985* (Leipzig, 1988).

Johann Hübner, *Genealogische Tabellen*, 4 vols. (Leipzig, 1727–37).

Reinhold Jauernig, 'Johann Sebastian Bach in Weimar', in Heinrich Besseler & Günther Kraft (eds.), *Bach in Thüringen* (Weimar, 1950), pp. 49–105.

Hans John, *Der Dresdner Kreuzkantor und Bach-Schüler August Homilius. Ein Beitrag zur Musikgeschichte Dresdens im 18. Jahrhundert* (Tutzing, 1980).

KB, see NBA KB

Johann Peter Kellner, *Lebenslauf,* in Friedrich Wilhelm Marpurg, *Historisch-kritische Beiträge zur Aufnahme der Musik,* Bd 1, St. 5 (Berlin, 1755), pp. 439–45.

Johann Philipp Kirnberger, *Grundsätze des Generalbasses* (Berlin, 1781).

Johann Christian Kittel, *Der angehende praktische Organist,* vol. 3 (Erfurt, 1808), esp. p. 33.

Kai Köpp, 'Johann Adolph Scheibe als Verfasser zweier anonymer Bach-Dokumente', BJ 89 (2003), pp. 173–96.

Joachim Kremer, *Das norddeutsche Kantorat im 18. Jahrhundert* (Kassel, 1995).

Konrad Küster, *Der junge Bach* (Stuttgart, 1996).

Bradley Lehman, 'Bach's extraordinary temperament: our Rosetta Stone, 1', *Early Music* 33 (2005), 3–23.

Ulrich Leisinger (ed.), *Bach in Leizpig – Bach und Leipzig. Konferenzbericht Leipzig 2000* (Hildesheim, 2002).

[John Mainwaring], *Memoirs of the life of the late George Frederic Handel* (London, 1760).

Alfred Mann, *Georg Friedrich Händel. Aufzeichnungen zu Kompositionslehre / Composition lessons* = HHA Supp. I (Kassel, 1978).

Hans Schmidt-Mannheim, 'Die Peter-Heroldt-Orgel in Buttstädt', *Acta organologica* 28 (2004), pp. 155–88.

Friedrich Wilhelm Marpurg, *Abhandlung von der Fuge nach den Grundsätzen und Exempeln der besten deutschen und ausländischen Meister* (Berlin, 1753).

Robert L. Marshall, *The music of Johann Sebastian Bach. The sources, the style, the significance* (New York, 1989).

'Toward a twenty-first-century Bach biography', *The Musical Quarterly* 84 (Fall 2000), pp. 497–525.

Johann Mattheson, *Das neu-eröffnete Orchestre* (Hamburg, 1713).

Exemplarische Organisten-Probe (Hamburg, 1719).

Critica musica, 2 vols. (Hamburg, 1722, 1725).

Der musicalische Patriot (Hamburg, 1728).

Der vollkommene Capellmeister (Hamburg, 1739).

Grundlage einer Ehren-Pforte (Hamburg, 1740).

Lorenz Christoph Mizler, *Musicalische Bibliothek* III (Leipzig, 1752).

Musicalische Bibliothek IV/1(Leipzig, 1754), pp. 135–142 (G.H. Bümler obituary), pp. 143–157 (G. H. Stölzel obituary), pp. 158–176 (J. S. Bach obituary).

Möller MS = Staatsbibliothek zu Berlin, Preussischer Kulturbesitz, Musikabteilung, MS 40644.

Werner Müller, *Gottfried Silbermann. Persönlichkeit und Werk* (Leipzig, 1982).

NBA KB = *Neue Bach-Ausgabe, Kritischer Bericht [Critical Commentary].*

NBR = Hans T. David & Arthur Mendel (eds.), *The new Bach reader,* revised and enlarged by Christoph Wolff (New York, 1998).

Johann Georg Neidhardt, *Sectio canonis harmonici* (Königsberg, 1724).

Werner Neumann, *Sämtliche von Johann Sebastian Bach vertonte Texte* (Leipzig, 1974).

Friderich Erhard Niedt, *Musicalische Handleitung*, Part II edited and enlarged by J. Mattheson (Hamburg, 1721).

Obituary = Dok III, pp. 80–93 (see also Mizler 1754).

Claude V. Palisca, *Studies in the history of Italian music and music theory* (Oxford, 1994).

Samuel Petri Quantz, *Anleitung zur praktischen Musik* (Lauban, 1767; Leipzig, 2/1782).

Martin Petzoldt, *Bachstätten. Ein Reiseführer zu Johann Sebastian Bach* (Frankfurt am Main, 2000).

André Pirro, *L'Esthétique de J. S. Bach* (Paris, 1907).

Pamela L. Poulin, *J. S. Bach's Precepts and Principles for Playing the Thorough-Bass or Accompanying in Four Parts. Leipzig, 1738* (Oxford, 1994).

Tushaar Power, 'J. S. Bach and the divine proportion' (PhD dissertation, Duke University, 2001).

Johann Joachim Quantz, *Versuch einer Anweisung die Flöte traversiere zu spielen* (Berlin, 1752).

    Lebenslauf, in Friedrich Wilhelm Marpurg, *Historisch-kritische Beiträge zur Aufnahme der Musik*, Bd 1, St. 5 (Berlin, 1755), pp. 197–250.

Jean-Philippe Rameau, *Traité de l'harmonie reduite à ses principes naturels* (Paris, 1722).

    Nouveau système de musique théorique (Paris, 1726).

Rudolf Rasch, *Friedrich Suppig. Labyrinthus musicus. Calculus musicus. Facsimile of the manuscripts* [with introduction] (Utrecht, 1990).

William Renwick, *The Langloz Manuscript. Fugal improvisation through figured bass* (Oxford, 2001).

Johann Adolph Scheibe, *Der critische Musikus* (Leipzig, 2/1745).

Arnold Schering, *Musikgeschichte Leipzigs in drei Bänden*, II *von 1650 bis 1723*, III *von 1725 bis 1800* (Leipzig, 1926, 1941).

Markus Schiffner, 'Das Musikleben in Arnstadt um 1700 von der Standort Johann Sebastian Bachs', in Hoffmann 1988, pp. 85–91.

Wolfgang Schneider, *Leipzig. Streifzüge durch die Kulturgeschichte* (Leipzig, 2nd edn, 1995).

Winfried Schrammek, 'Orgel, Positiv, Clavicymbel und Glocke der Schlosskirche zu Weimar 1658 bis 1774', in Hoffmann 1988, pp. 99–111.

Hans-Joachim Schulze, ed., *Johann Sebastian Bach. Missa H-moll BWV 232¹, Faksimile nach dem Originalstimmensatz* (Stuttgart, 1983).

    ed., *Die Thomasschule zur Zeit Johann Sebastian Bachs: Ordnungen und Gesetze, 1634, 1723, 1733* (Leipzig, 1985).

Walter Serauky, *Musikgeschichte der Stadt Halle*, II/i (Halle & Berlin, 1939).

Friedrich Wilhelm Sonnenkalb, *Kurtze Entscheidung der Frage: wie sollen die Praeludia eines Organisten bey dem Gottesdienste beschaffen seyn?* (Torgau, 1756).

Philipp Spitta, *Johann Sebastian Bach*, 2 vols. (Leipzig, 1873, 1880).

Gottfried Heinrich Stölzel obituary: see Mizler.

    [*Selbstbiographie*] in Johann Mattheson, *Ehrenpforte*, pp. 343–7.

Wolfram Syré, *Vincent Lübeck. Leben und Werk* (Frankfurt, 2000).

Reinhard Szeskus, *Johann Sebasian Bachs historischer Ort = Bach-Studien* 10 (Leipzig, 1991).

Table, see Genealogical Table.

Andrew Talle, 'Nürnberg, Darmstadt, Köthen – Neuerkenntnisse zur Bach-Überlieferung in der ersten Hälfte des 18. Jahrhunderts', BJ 89 (2003), pp. 143–72.

Georg Philipp Telemann, [*Selbstbiographie*] in Mattheson, *Ehrenpforte*, pp. 355–69.

    Lebenslauf [1718] in Johann Mattheson, *Grosse General-Bass-Schule* (Hamburg, 2/1731), pp. 160–71.

Charles Sanford Terry, *Bach: a biography* (Oxford, 1928).

Thomana Ordnungen, see Schulze 1985.

Evard Titon du Tillet, *Le parnasse françois* (Paris, 1732).

Donald Francis Tovey, *A companion to the Art of Fugue* (London, 1931).

Richard Wagner, *Gesammelte Schriften und Dichtungen*, 10 vols. (Leipzig, 4/1907).

Johann Gottfried Walther, *Musicalisches Lexicon* (Leipzig, 1732).

    Praecepta der musicalischen Composition [1708], ed. Peter Benary (Leipzig, 1955).

Walter Werbeck, 'Bach und der Kontrapunkt. Neue Manuskript-Funde', BJ 89 (2003), pp. 67–95.

Andreas Werckmeister, *Erweiterte und verbesserte Orgelprobe* (2nd enlarged edn., Quedlinburg, 1698).

    Organum gruningense redivivum (Quedlinburg & Aschersleben, 1705).

Barbara Wiermann, 'Altnickol, Faber, Fulde – drei Breslauer Choralisten im Umfeld Johann Sebastian Bachs', BJ 89 (2003), pp. 259–65.

Christoph Wolff, 'Johann Valentin Eckelts Tabulaturbuch von 1692', in *Festschrift Martin Ruhnke*, ed. Klaus-Jürgen Sachs (Neuhausen-Stuttgart, 1986), pp. 374–86.

    Johann Sebastian Bach. The learned musician (Oxford etc., 2000).

Peter Wollny, 'On miscellaneous American Bach sources', in ed. Gregory Butler, *Bach perspectives* 5 (2002), pp. 131–50.

    'Ein Quellenfund in Kiew. Unbekannte Kontrapunktstudien von Johann Sebastian und Wilhelm Friedemann Bach', in Leisinger 2002, pp. 275–87.

WTC1, WTC2 = *The well-tempered Clavier*, Books 1 and 2.

Index of works (BWV)

The text may refer to a work either by title or by BWV number.

Index of names

'Pupil' includes those known to have taken instruction either privately or as a boy of St Thomas School, and those having some close contact with J. S. Bach in various locations.
'Appts': musical and other appointments

Abel, C. F., 1682–1761, from 1714 gamba player in Cöthen, 127

Abel, C. F., 1723–87, son of preceding, from 1759 in London, 127, 237

Addison, Joseph, 312

Adlung, J., 1699–1762, from 1728 organist at Erfurt Predigerkirche, 9, 279, 302, 349, 382

Agricola, J. F., 1720–74, pupil of J. S. Bach 1738–41, from 1751 court composer at Berlin, 5, 237, 255, 275, 282, 284f., 331, 349

as Obituary author, 80, 177, 270, 288, 292, 295, 297f., 302, 307ff., 310

Ahle, J. G., 1651–1706, from 1673 organist in Mühlhausen, 56, 60

Ahle, J. R., 1625–73, organist at Divi Blasii, Mühlhausen, 56–7

Ahrens, C., author, 150, 255, 279

Alberti, J. F., 1641–1710, organist at Merseburg Cathedral, 17

Albinoni, T., 1671–1750, Venetian composer, 19, 45, 53, 82, 83, 89f., 209f., 291

Altni(c)kol, J. C., 1719–59, pupil (from 1744) and son-in-law (from 1749) of J. S. Bach, 265, 267

as pupil/copyist, 133, 149, 240, 246, 249, 340f., 347

Altnickol, Johann Sebastian, 1749, grandson of J. S., 2, 160, 211, 319

Ammerbach, E. N., c. 1530–97, organist from 1561 at the Thomaskirche, 84, 300

d'Anglebert, J. H., 1635?–91, Parisian composer, 44, 90, 132, 249, 344

Arnold, J. H., cantor in Ohrdruf until 1697, 16

Augustine of Hippo, Saint, 323

Baal, J., 1656–1701, German composer (?), 107

Bach, Anna Carolina, 1747–1804, daughter of C. P. E. Bach, 318

Bach, Anna Magdalena (née Wilcke), 1701–60, second wife of J. S. (1721), 91, 140, 153–6, 171, 172f., 190, 219, 226, 245, 246f., 266ff., 281, 293, 301, 318f., 322, 327, 337, 346, 353

as singer, 5, 154, 169, 200, 202, 203, 209

Bach, Barbara Catharina, 1679–?, elder sister of Maria Barbara Bach, 42

Bach, Carl Philipp Emanuel, 1714–88, fifth child of J. S., 1740 musician to Frederick II at Potsdam, 1767 succeeded Telemann at Hamburg Johanneum, 6, 7, 13, 42, 73, 85, 112, 136, 165f., 175, 194, 246, 257, 267ff., 281, 350f., 355

as author and composer, 5, 45, 113, 179, 239, 252, 254, 266, 277, 283, 293, 302f., 305f., 328, 348, 351, 378

as Obituary author, 1, 14, 26ff., 30, 38f., 40, 44, 62f., 65, 70, 117, 120, 122, 145, 148–9, 193–4, 292, 307ff., 320, 326 et passim

as son, pupil, copyist, 4, 21, 64, 96, 101, 128, 160, 163, 209, 210, 248, 342

Bach, Catharina Dorothea, 1708–74, daughter of J. S., 5, 64, 65, 72, 154, 281

Bach, Christiana Dorothea, 1731–2, daughter of J. S., 226

Bach, Elisabeth (née Lammerhirt), 1644–94, mother of J. S., 2, 5, 8f., 12, 374

Bach, Elisabeth Juliana Friderica, 1726–81, daughter of J. S., in 1749 married J. C. Altnickol, 13, 159, 160, 265, 319, 341

Bach, Friedelena Margaretha, 1675–1729, sister-in-law of J. S., 64, 72